Economic Change and Political Liberalization in Sub-Saharan Africa

ECONOMIC CHANGE AND

POLITICAL LIBERALIZATION

IN SUB-SAHARAN AFRICA

EDITED BY JENNIFER A. WIDNER

THE JOHNS HOPKINS UNIVERSITY PRESS / Baltimore and London

© 1994 The Johns Hopkins University Press
All rights reserved
Printed in the United States of America on acid-free paper
05 04 03 02 01 00 99 98 97 96   6 5 4 3 2

The Johns Hopkins University Press
2715 North Charles Street, Baltimore, Maryland 21218-4319
The Johns Hopkins Press Ltd., London

Library of Congress Cataloging in Publication Data will
be found at the end of this book.

A catalog record for this book is available from
the British Library.

Contents

Preface and Acknowledgments

The chapters of this volume were originally discussion papers written for a colloquium on the economics of political liberalization in Africa. The meeting took place at Harvard University on March 6–7, 1992, under the auspices of the Center for International Affairs. The editor wishes to thank the Ford Foundation for its support of the African participants and for underwriting the costs of reproducing the papers. She owes a special debt of gratitude to Michael Chege, of the Ford Harare regional office, for taking a special interest in the project, and to John Gerhart. Other major sponsors include the Huntington Fund of the Center for International Affairs, without whose support the project could not have proceeded, the Hugh K. Foster Junior Professorship in African Studies, the Harvard Committee on African Studies, and the Du Bois Institute of Harvard University.

The authors are indebted as well to a number of conscientious discussants, many of whom provided careful written comments on the chapters included here. They wish to thank, in particular, Samuel Huntington (Harvard University), Thomas Callaghy (University of Pennsylvania), Thandika Mkandawire (CODESRIA), Peter Anyang' Nyong'o (Forum for the Restoration of Democracy, Kenya), Makau wa Mutua (Harvard Law School), Jorge Dominguez (Harvard University), William Foltz (Yale University), Martin Kilson (Harvard University), Kenneth Shepsle (Harvard University), Sam Nolutshungu (University of Rochester), Amii Omara-Otunnu (University of Connecticut), Douglass North (University of Washington), Stephen Haggard (University of California at San Diego), Michael Roemer (Harvard

University), Pauline Peters (Harvard University), Colin Leys (Queens University), Ruth Morgenthau (Brandeis University), and Kinuthia Macharia (Harvard University).

Finally, the editor wishes to thank the students who worked hard to make the conference from which the book derives a success. Siddhartha Mitter, Mary Hilderbrand, and Alissa Lee helped draft a data book, detailing the sequence of political change in each country, and provided general research assistance; Beth Hastie provided editorial assistance; and Chris Briggs-Hale offered invaluable logistical support.

Economic Change and Political Liberalization in Sub-Saharan Africa

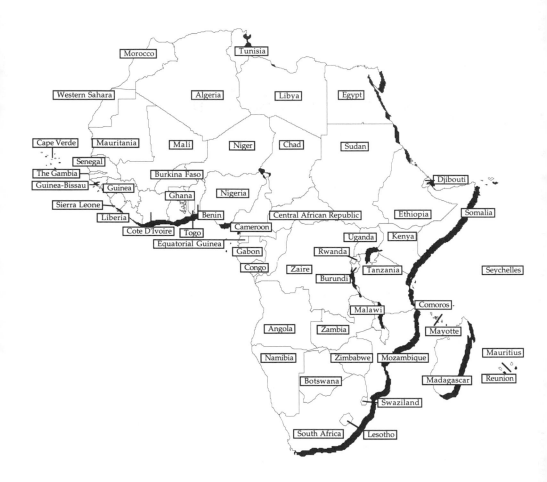

JENNIFER A. WIDNER

Introduction

Between 1989 and July 1992, roughly half the countries of sub-Saharan Africa either installed multiparty governments or embarked on a move toward multiparty rule. The press received freer license to report domestic political events. In almost every country, newspapers, broadsides, and newsweeklies began to appear on street corners in the capital, while audio and video cassettes containing political material found their way into their countryside. In some cases, such as Benin, Cape Verde, and Zambia, incumbent heads of state lost at the ballot box and surrendered the reins of government to the leaders of new opposition movements. In other instances, governments initiated or were forced to convene national conventions—broad-based assemblies to redraft constitutions and to prepare plans for transition governments. Many more reluctant leaders, such as Daniel arap Moi of Kenya, initially sought to stem the tide of overt popular opposition through repression but found themselves forced by a combination of domestic and international pressures to legalize some forms of opposition, even if they did not schedule elections.

This wave of political change took place at a time when governments and peoples in other parts of the world had moved to support greater political openness. Levels of public contestation, or ability to challenge public policy, increased, as did the inclusiveness of participation—the willingness to allow new categories of citizens to engage in voting and other aspects of political decisionmaking. Preceding the wave of protest and change in Africa in the mid-1970s, the authoritarian governments of Greece, Portugal, and Spain collapsed. Latin America was the locus of political reform shortly thereafter. Brazil began its *abertura*, or opening, in 1974, a process it completed in 1985. New civilian regimes emerged in Ecuador in 1979, Peru in 1980 (later reversed), Bolivia in 1982, Uruguay in 1984, and Chile in 1989.

The most proximate cases of political liberalization were those that occurred in the former Soviet bloc, most visibly expressed in the fall of the Berlin Wall. Hungary engaged in a transition to a multiparty system beginning in 1988, at the same time pressures for political change were building in Africa. Solidarity captured electoral votes in parliamentary elections in Poland in 1989. The collapse of the hard-liners' August 1991 coup attempt against Mikhail Gorbachev, the subsequent rise of Russian reformer Boris Yeltsin, and the splintering of the Soviet Union into independent states took place after many Africans had already started to lobby for stronger voices in the division of public resources and formulation of public policies. Thus this wave of change was concurrent with that in Africa, and although the events in Europe may have encouraged African opposition groups, most of the key changes in the former Soviet bloc occurred too late to be models. The changes in Africa were already in progress.

Characteristics of Political Liberalization in Africa, 1989–1992

Most of the chapters in this volume are less concerned with the sustainability or the consolidation of the political liberalization in African states than with the adoption of measures to increase freedom of the press, to legalize opposition parties, and to institute elections. The evidence suggests that political liberalization can take place in settings long considered hostile to liberal democratic ideas; it says nothing about the durability of the new institutions created. It remains quite arguable whether the new regimes can survive absent an independent commercial class, elevated literacy rates, and higher levels of per capita income.

The political liberalization that took place in sub-Saharan Africa in 1989–92 had several distinctive characteristics and these are the focus of this book. As Robert Bates notes in chapter 1, these political openings contained three paradoxical features. First, although demanded domestically, political openings usually took place only in conjunction with international pressure. That is, foreign governments, international organizations, and transnational professional associations used the threat of media attention and reduced economic or military assistance to force incumbent heads of state to embark on the changes the citizens championed. Second, although reformers sought new political beginnings, these men and women were, themselves, often older politicians, once members of the government and now outsiders. Their numbers also included professionals, especially lawyers, also once closely connected with established governments. Third, in many instances, the reforms were initiated by the very governments that were the object of demands for change. In Côte d'Ivoire, for instance, the government of Félix Houphouët-Boigny chose to respond to the dissatisfaction with proposals for the higher taxation of urban salaries by legalizing opposition parties and calling for elections. Bates seeks to explain these paradoxes.

The reforms had other distinctive features as well. Political scientists have long considered an independent commercial class an important prerequisite to the kinds of changes observed in Africa and posit an association between higher levels of socioeconomic development— including per capita gross domestic product, proportion of urban to rural population, and literacy rates—and support for "democratic ideas." Yet in few countries of sub-Saharan Africa do these conditions exist. Again, paradoxically, political openings have taken place in settings where social science theory suggests they were least likely to occur.

The following chapters indirectly address this puzzling feature of the 1989–92 period of regime change. Robert Bates offers a "human capital" argument to explain this characteristic as well as the other three he discerns. That is, old politicians, lawyers, and some other groups demanded political liberalization in part because their skills and resources were usable only in their own countries and to be unable to operate in those contexts threatened their livelihood and that of their families. Chapter 3, on patterns of change in Francophone and Anglophone Africa, and several of the case studies suggest that pressure for greater political competitiveness came from elites who found that public offices they held suddenly stopped yielding the rents they used to supplement their incomes. Where these elites could organize general strikes, incumbent heads of state often tried to preempt their demonstrations by legalizing such opposition while maintaining control over critical electoral resources.

The third puzzling feature of the 1989–92 period was the proliferation of national conferences as vehicles for drafting new constitutions and creating new institutions in Francophone Africa and in some countries of Portuguese colonial heritage—and the near absence of corresponding forms in Anglophone countries. Under pressure from street demonstrations in capital cities and from discontent in general, many Francophone governments initiated (or abdicated to) sovereign national conferences—broad assemblies of representatives from different *couches sociales* (walks of life). Chapter 3 examines this phenomenon, introduces competing explanations, and tries to show that differences in the political economies of Francophone and Anglophone countries accounts for the patterns observed.

Forms of Explanation

The aim of this book is to offer hypotheses about the relationship, if any, between the economic crises of the 1980s and patterns of regime change in sub-Saharan Africa. From the outset, then, this book addresses a subset of concerns and theories. It does not purport to present and discuss the full range of perspectives social scientists might examine in trying to understand the events of 1989–92.

The task the conference organizers set the authors was strictly delimited. The contributors were asked to explain patterns of political liberalization—specifically, why some countries legalized opposition political parties, created transition governments, or held multiparty elections while others did not. This definition of the dependent variable sets these essays apart from those on the consolidation of democracies. This volume posed the more restricted task of analyzing when and why countries move from one type of regime, as defined by the level of public contestation and the inclusiveness of participation, to another—and specifically from political systems that afford few opportunities for citizens to debate policy to those that create more such occasions.[1]

Contributors were asked to consider the economic crises of the 1980s as independent variables (or causes) of the events and behaviors observed. The writers go to great lengths to specify in exactly what respects economic difficulties affected political outcomes, however. All of the chapters share a recognition that standard economic indicators, such as inflation rates and rate of growth of GDP, explain little of the political change observed. Michael Bratton and Nicolas van de Walle note in an excellent, earlier essay that "there is little or no correlation between the intensity of political unrest on the one hand and the severity of economic crisis or austerity measures on the other. Some countries with very deep economic problems, such as Tanzania, Guinea, or Guinea-Bissau, witnessed little or no unrest by 1990, yet riots and strikes shook relatively wealthy countries."[2] The analysis presented in chapter 3 of this volume corroborates Bratton and van de Walle's earlier observation.

Instead, the authors focus their attention on the ways the political economies of African countries shaped the pressures on incumbent governments. Specifically, they consider how (1) changes in rent-seeking opportunities, (2) differences in the ways incumbent authoritarian governments distributed the costs of declining terms of trade or economic shocks, or (3) alterations in the relationships between farmers and their urban kin shaped the abilities of heads of state to maintain past strategies for maintaining political order. The emphasis in most of the case studies—but especially in Richard Westebbe's discussion of Benin and Nicolas van de Walle's analysis of Cameroon—is on the loss of opportunities for some members of the political elite to collect the rents to which their jobs in the public sector had accorded them access. Holders of public office throughout the world often supplement their salaries by exacting "tolls" from those who need their signatures to secure licenses, services, foreign exchange, or documents. Where countries practice import licensing, foreign exchange rationing, or other kinds of market intervention, unproductive rent seeking tends to increase, although it does not have the same consequences for economic growth in every society. Chapter 2 offers a development economist's perspective on (1) the ways the distribution of costs and benefits of adjustment vary and (2) the implications of these differential effects for evolving general theories about political liberalization. Most of the authors adopt some version of the first hypothesis or a combination of the first and second. Several authors claim either that the economic reforms imposed by multilateral development agencies or long-term economic decline eliminated such rent-seeking opportunities, sometimes severely jeopardizing the standards of living of key elites. In the late 1980s, many older politicians excluded from these spoils of office, as well as new generations worried about their futures, took to the streets to protest their lack of influence over policy.

The relationship between structural adjustment and the collapse or alteration of rent-seeking opportunities in Africa is not straightforward, however. The effect of the privatization of public enterprise, devaluation, and trade liberalization on the opportunities for elites to exact tolls for their services, and the consequences of these measures for urban standards of living, depend heavily on the sequence of reform. In chapter 2, Barbara Grosh examines the consequences of sequencing for political outcomes from the point of view of an economist, providing an important caution to political scientists against overgeneralizing the effects of structural adjustment programs. She elaborates upon a concern expressed by many of the economists present at the conference that gave rise to this book: namely, the mistaken assumption that the mere existence of rent-seeking opportunities is

necessarily growth dampening and the related belief that, with structural adjustment, rent seeking disappears. It is the form of rent seeking
and the distribution of opportunities for noncompetitive rent seeking
that are critical to understanding political outcomes.

The way governments distributed the costs of economic adjustment, coupled with the character of associational life in the countries
concerned, may also explain some of the variation in political outcomes
observed between 1989 and 1992. In their earlier essay, Bratton and
van de Walle remark that they "place the weight of [their] . . . interpretation on contingent factors, such as the skill of state elites at using
available political resources, the coherence of opposition coalitions,
and the relative strengths of elite and opposition groups."[3] In his
chapter on Zambian politics in this book, Bratton devotes considerable
attention to the unusual degree of coherence among members of a
key interest group: the unions. Unlike most Anglophone countries,
Zambia tolerated the growth of a strong mine workers' union capable
of quickly organizing a grass roots campaign and of using its economic
gatekeeping position to force the government to adopt reforms. Chapter 5 points out that this degree of coherence was unusual in Anglophone sub-Saharan Africa, where many incumbent leaders had
succeeded in fragmenting independent producers' associations. It
suggests that the corporatist, or more centralized, union structures
of Francophone Africa made it easier for dissatisfied groups to stage
general strikes and to force governments to accede to demands. It
also cautions that these more centralized interest groups, usually explicitly incorporated into government, may prove less effective guard-
ians of political reform than their more independent, if fragmented,
counterparts in many parts of Anglophone Africa. Two case studies—
of Ghana by Jeffrey Herbst and of Tanzania by Mwesiga Baregu—
devote considerable attention to the kinds of barriers that associations
and political oppositions long faced in those two countries.

The conference organizers also challenged the authors to consider
the consequences of changing urban-rural ties for patterns of regime
change. Political science theory emphasizes that pressure for greater
political competitiveness usually comes from urban dwellers, not from
farmers. Collective action is difficult to initiate and sustain where there
are many farmers with holdings of roughly equal size spread over a
considerable area, for there is little way for them to monitor one
another's contribution to broad-based political action. Under these
conditions, collective action is rare. In urban areas, by contrast, people
of different cultural backgrounds live close to one another, have access
to mass media, and have lower transportation and organizing costs.

They may also be able to monitor one another's contributions to collective political activity more easily. The rapid growth of urban areas and the inability of governments to provide jobs and amenities for urban newcomers may increase frustration and trigger political competitiveness.

Moreover, urban life brings with it an explosive mix of, on the one hand, new challenges to identity and survival and, on the other hand, more rapid communication. Samuel DeCalo emphasizes the significance of this problem for the regime changes sweeping Africa: "With urbanization in several [countries] . . . up by 300 per cent, modern urban expectations rise, and when unfulfilled lead to social frustrations. This in turn leads to impatience and decline in respect for national political leaders . . . At the same time there is a vastly expanded number of educated young people . . . which further complicates employment prospects and adds to the undermining of the legitimacy of the political system."[4] This hypothesis is potentially powerful, although rates of urbanization are uniformly very high across Africa, while patterns of regime change vary. In these essays, changing, urban-rural ties are of secondary importance.

Finally, the chapters in this volume depart from the usual focus among Africa specialists and development agencies on the likely consequences of regime change for economic reform or structural adjustment processes. Indeed, they reverse the dependent and independent variables. Although the consequences of political change for structural adjustment programs are important, political liberalization is so new that there is little clear Africa-based evidence to test generalizations. Thus to contemplate the effects of political change on economic reform remains a theoretical and speculative enterprise at this stage. Only comparative analysis based on evidence from countries of other regions can address those concerns.

The Cases

The volume attempts to provide broad comparative and theoretical discussions, case studies, and a brief examination of sustainability. The cases introduce the process of political change in several key countries. They include discussions of countries that held multiparty elections early in the 1989–92 period as well as some that long were holdouts.

There are three cases of rapid legalization of political opposition and conduct of multiparty elections. Richard Westebbe examines the sources and sequence of political reform in Benin, the first sub-Saharan country to hold multiparty elections and to oust an incumbent head of state. The changes in Benin occurred half a year before the meeting at la Baule, France, at which French foreign policymakers announced they would no longer automatically intervene to support incumbent heads of state. Thus pressure from donor countries cannot account for the dramatic liberalization in Benin. Westebbe's discussion focuses attention on the effects of international economic pressures on the behavior of civil servants and urban groups. He also notes the important role of the Catholic church as a broker of change. Two other cases of multiparty elections receive attention, one in the chapter on Zambia, by Michael Bratton, and the other in chapter 3, where the case of Côte d'Ivoire is contrasted with the case of Kenya, long a holdout in the wave of political liberalization.

The chapters on Cameroon by Nicolas van de Walle, on Tanzania by Mwesiga Baregu, and on Ghana by Jeffrey Herbst, as well as the brief discussion of the Kenya case in chapter 3, examine instances in which governments legalized opposition only with great reluctance and under international pressure. These authors faced the difficult task of trying to understand the processes of change that were under way as they wrote. They focus on the kinds of barriers that opposition groups encountered in bringing pressure to bear and on the ways political economies limited the bargaining power of these groups.

The Sustainability of Political Reform

The contributors conceptualize patterns of regime change in sub-Saharan Africa either as *political liberalization,* as defined above, or *democratization.* In the colloquium at Harvard University, some scholars argued that the difference in terms is merely semantic and that both refer to a process of political opening. Others suggested that *democratization* implies that the changes have a particular end point, namely, the creation of regimes that social scientists and citizens recognize as democratic, with open elections, broad rights to associate and to run for office, freedom of speech, and a clear link between the results of elections or the views of elected representatives and the public policy choices that governments pursue. Given the great uncertainty that the political openings in sub-Saharan Africa will endure, most of the conference participants preferred the term *political liberalization,* believing that many of the changes would stop short of creating democratic governments. As Bratton and van de Walle write, "Cracks in the edifice of autocracy should not be mistaken for fully fledged transitions to democracy."[5] For the same reason, the term *transitions from authoritarian rule* also received infrequent use.

The main focus of this volume is explaining what triggered the patterns of political change in Africa between 1989 and 1992. To many of the African participants in the Harvard colloquium, this emphasis seemed misplaced, however. Their real interest lay in estimating the sustainability of the measures adopted in Africa and in institutionalizing multiparty political systems—that is, in the public policy implications of the analyses. Although that is a different conference and a different book, the concluding chapters address some of these concerns. Donald Rothchild proposes ways of creating an enduring base for political reform, and Crawford Young seeks to place the events described in earlier chapters in broad historical perspective.

Finally, the authors each contribute to the way political scientists think about microlevel politics, or individual behavior, and macrolevels, such as the international system. For example, the chapter by Robert Bates explores individual responses to shortages of economic opportunity, where differences in laws and political systems among countries render legal expertise and coalition building skills nontransferable. Chapter 4 highlights the influence of World Bank conditionality on individual calculations about political involvement in Benin. In his epilogue, Ernest J. Wilson draws out some of the conceptual issues these analyses raise.

Notes

1. The colloquium at Harvard and most of the chapters in this volume use this framework for defining types of regimes. It is borrowed from Robert Dahl, *Polyarchy: Participation and Opposition* (New Haven: Yale University Press, 1971). It departs from the typology of regimes that appears in the volume *Governance and Politics in Africa,* edited by Goran Hyden and Michael Bratton. Hyden distinguishes four types of regimes (statist; market based or libertarian; corporatist; and communitarian) according to (1) the degree of citizen influence or oversight, (2) the responsiveness and responsibility of leadership, and (3) the character of social reciprocities (degree of political equality, level of intergroup tolerance, inclusiveness of associational membership, etc.) See Goran Hyden, "Governance and the Study of Politics." In *Governance and Politics in Africa,* ed. Goran Hyden and Michael Bratton (Boulder, Colo.: Lynne Rienner, 1992), 15.

2. Michael Bratton and Nicolas van de Walle, "Toward Governance in Africa: Popular Demands and State Responses," in Hyden and Bratton, *Governance and Politics in Africa.*

3. Ibid., 45.

4. Samuel DeCalo, "The Process, Prospects, and Constraints of Democratization in Africa," *African Affairs,* no. 91 (1992): 7–35, 16.

5. Bratton and van de Walle, "Toward Governance," 29.

PART 1

THEORETICAL PERSPECTIVES

ROBERT H. BATES

One

The Impulse to Reform in Africa

Africa is in the midst of a sweeping movement of political reform. Incumbent presidents have been voted out of office. Others have retired, most notably Julius Nyerere. Still others have been challenged to broaden their ruling coalitions, open up their political institutions, and tolerate opposition and dissent. Authoritarians, such as Hastings Banda, Daniel arap Moi, and Mobutu Sese Seko linger on. But even they face strong challenges. As analyzed by Claude Ake, Richard Joseph, and others, the democratic impulse now runs strong in Africa—a fact long ago discerned by Richard Sklar.[1]

Africa thus joins what Samuel Huntington celebrates as the "third wave" of democratization: the political reforms that began in Iberia in the mid-1970s, then swept through Latin America and Asia, culminating in the late 1980s in the downfall of Leninist parties in Eastern Europe and the Soviet Union. In analyzing this current of political reform, Huntington, like others, notes that democratization tends to "break out" in middle-income countries, countries whose per capita incomes range from $1,000 to $3,000.[2] Only a handful of countries in black Africa fall in this range: Gabon, South Africa, and possibly Mauritius and the Congo. In contrast to other parts of the world, the political impetus to reform in Africa thus operates in the midst of poverty.

In this respect, the reformist movements in Africa are distinguished by several paradoxes:

—While demanded domestically, they are often supplied internationally.
—While calling for new political beginnings, they are often led by old
politicians.
—The reforms they call for are often initiated by the very governments
they are attacking.
This chapter seeks to resolve these paradoxes.

The Development Commitment

The "year of democratization" in Africa—1991—followed by three
decades the "year of independence"—1960. Characteristic of the drive
for independence was the demand for the use of political power for
economic purposes, a demand that ran parallel to deeply held political
convictions and ideological commitments.

The nationalist movement mobilized a wide array of economic interests. One segment was drawn from the white-collar workers who
staffed the bureaucracies that managed the governments and firms
created by the European occupiers. Articulating their demands in the
language of political liberalism and racial equality, they condemned
the superior conditions of service accorded expatriates: higher salaries,
better housing, larger transport allowances, and so forth.[3] Their demands drew support from all who aspired to salaried employment:
students in the universities and secondary school and their parents,
who were investing in the education of their children. These shared
economic interests gave impetus to broader political demands for racial
justice.

Business and commerce also backed the nationalist movement.
Because of the collusion of the large, expatriate firms in western Africa,
indigenous businessmen were able to attribute inflation in the postwar
period to machinations by the colonialists. Condemning price gouging
and monopoly profits by imperial firms, they mobilized popular sentiment for nationalist attacks on foreign economic domination, on the
one hand, and nationalist appeals for public support for indigenous
entrepeneurs, on the other.[4]

An analogous pattern appears in eastern Africa. Michael Cowen
and Nicola Swainson trace the origins of nationalist politicians in
Kenya to indigenous competitors of colonial firms. Many entered
politics to protest the administrative barriers that protected foreign
firms and increased the cost of entry for those who, like themselves,
sought wealth through commerce. A. L. Epstein notes a similar pattern
in Zambia, where businessmen—the so-called hawkers—helped or-

ganize nationalist political parties in the urban townships.[5]

The examples could be multiplied. Robert Bates, Lionel Cliffe, Goran Hyden, and others stress the economic demands of the peasantry; Richard Sandbrook, Richard Jeffries, Epstein, and others stress those of urban labor.[6] The nationalist movement thus introduced a core political expectation: that in Africa the road to prosperity ran through politics, a point perhaps best made by Kwame Nkrumah when he enjoined his contemporaries: "Seek ye first the political kingdom, and all else shall be added unto you."[7]

In the postindependence period, the nations of Africa took different branches in this road. Those who triumphed in Kenya and Côte d'Ivoire constructed a postindependence political economy that privileged the fortunes of multinational corporations and export agriculture.[8] The postindependence governments of Ghana and Zambia seized the revenues of exporters and channeled them into a multitude of government-owned import substituting firms.[9] Nigeria's government, by contrast, used its control over capital markets to subsidize investments by private businessmen and local corporations, thereby promoting the formation of an indigenous (if politically dependent) bourgeoisie.[10] While differing in their developmental trajectories, African governments were virtually all activist. Each sought to overturn "the market solution": to alter incentives and relative rates of return so as to channel resources from activities to which they gave a higher priority than did the market. The result was a characteristic pattern of market intervention. This policy mix provides a mechanism that helps account for why, in the African case, poor economic performance and demand for political reform go together.

The Economic and Political Consequences: A Simple Model

This section sketches a simple, idealized version of this mechanism and derives from it implications for the economics and politics of Africa. As seen in figure 1.1, given competition, normally behaved forces of supply and demand generate a market equilibrium: they establish a price (P_0) at which the quantity demanded (Q_D^0) equals the quantity supplied (Q_S^0). Governments may seek to alter the market solution, however. For example, for social or political purposes, they may lower the price to a point below that generated by market forces (say to P_1).

In their attempts at state-led growth, African governments frequently adopt policies that generate such distortions in markets. In agriculture, for example, they have sought to lower the price of food

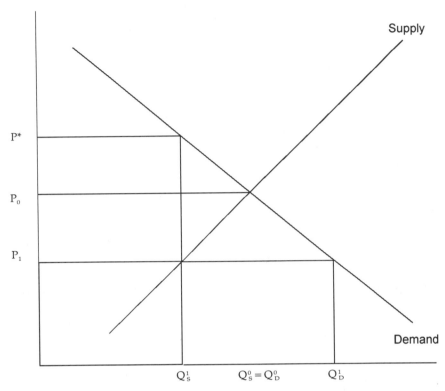

Figure 1.1 A stylized market

for urban consumers, the price of raw materials for urban industries, and the price of inputs for farmers.[11] For industry, they have sought to lower the prices charged for electricity and petroleum products. For consumers, they have subsidized the prices of essential commodities: cooking oil, paraffin, processed foods, and clothing, for example.[12] In credit markets, they have sought to lower interest rates, and in markets for foreign exchange, they have sought to lower the exchange rate, thereby reducing the costs of importing from abroad.

Such interventions are often targeted at a specific market or industry. In practice, they are carried out by agencies leaders create to mobilize resources so as to fulfill development objectives. While defined at the level of a specific market or industry, the impact of these interventions soon registers at the macro level. This is true by definition of controls imposed upon the exchange rate and interest rates: the impact of such measures is economywide. But it is also true of market- or industry-level distortions. When summed over all programs, their costs contribute to the macro level imbalances characteristic of Africa's economies. They also lead to characteristic political patterns: clientelism and patronage politics, corruption, and the privatization of public institutions, resulting in a loss of legitimacy by the activist governments that captured power at the time of independence.

The mechanics that link the microdistortions to macrolevel effects can readily be outlined. The new price, P_1, is not an equilibrium price. At the lower price, less efficient producers cannot profitably supply goods, and consumers will demand more goods than the remaining producers can supply. The quantity demanded therefore exceeds the quantity supplied, putting an upward pressure on the price. To render the price sustainable, the government must therefore subsidize the costs of production such that the less efficient producers find it profitable to supply the good at the reduced price; the result is fiscal pressure on the state. Alternatively, the government must import the good; the result is loss of foreign exchange.

It should be stressed that the interventionist policies pursued by governments in Africa have been pursued elsewhere. As revealed in Indonesia and Thailand, such policies can in fact be compatible with economic growth. Unlike Indonesia, however, most African nations have failed to maintain stable macroeconomic policies; they have pursued populist economic programs, using their budgets to purchase public support, to finance large military establishments, or to construct elaborate monuments for the sake of national pride. Unlike Thailand, most African governments fail to pursue positions of advantage in global trade; most often, they adopt trade or commercial policies that separate their economies from international markets. In the context of such macroeconomic policies, the interventionist policies of African governments inflict great damage on Africa's economies, contributing to Africa's budgetary deficits and mounting international indebtedness. Insofar as the legitimacy of any incumbent regime is tied to the performance of its economy, they also weaken Africa's governments.

The characteristic pattern of government intervention not only affects Africa's economic performance, it helps to define Africa's characteristic patterns of politics, as well. Interventionist policies can transform economic markets into political machines. Interventions help to create a form of politics that has been termed *personalistic*: one in which those who hold power exchange personal benefits for political loyalty.[13] The logic can be seen in figure 1.1: at the official price (P_1), the quantity demanded exceeds the quantity supplied; the value of the commodity then rises to P^*—a price that high demanders of the good are willing to pay. The excess demand therefore creates new value, but it also creates the opportunity for discretion. With demand exceeding supply, those who command power over the allocation of the good give it to some and withhold it from others. Government intervention in industries and markets can thus be used to create organized followings—groups of persons who owe their individual fortunes to discretionary or personalistic acts by those in power.

In Africa, the interventions also help to create a form of politics that has been termed *patrimonial*: one in which those who hold power derive their incomes from the state.[14] In the situation just described, the political leader gives away the scarce commodity at subsidized prices and reaps political service in exchange. There exists a second possibility, however: the leader can use his command over the market or industry to secure the good at the government price, P_1, and sell it at the market clearing price, P^*, thereby reaping a higher income from his public office.[15]

Interventions help create a third form of politics in Africa, one that has been termed *rent seeking*. In this interpretation, the origins of government programs do not lie in the political or economic ambitions of leaders, but in the actions of interest groups. Political leaders intervene in markets in response to political pressures by lobbyists who seek to secure the good or service at the privileged price, P_1. In response, government officials maintain the program by offering subsidies that make the policy attractive to politically salient special interests.[16] The result is the use of government power to underpin the economic fortunes of a privileged segment of civil society—private groups that possess influence over public programs.

Thus far, I assume that leaders control the programs they govern and either give the economic benefits of the program to individuals or groups or consume it themselves. Naturally, however, the bureaucrats who run these programs are less than perfect agents of the leaders' will: they themselves can privatize the benefits of the public programs, selling goods under the counter at black market prices. And the staffs of these public agencies survive in part off the proceeds of these sales. This fourth pattern of politics in Africa is bureaucratic *corruption*.

Governments pursue policies that are economically not sustainable, contributing to public deficits and shortages of foreign exchange. These policies also promote characteristic patterns of politics in postindependence Africa. Africa's economic crisis thus shares a common origin with Africa's political crisis. The consequence is that the need for—and demand for—reform originate in the midst of economic misery.

The Delay of Reform: The Weakness of the Bourgeoisie

Personalism, patrimonialism, rent seeking, and corruption have long provoked condemnation within Africa. Writers as diverse in style and orientation as Ayi Kwei Armah, Chinua Achebe, and Ngugi wa Thiong'o dramatize the relative wealth of those who have seized power in postindependence Africa.[17] Ordinary citizens cheer the military coups that toppled civilian governments and then turn against the military as well. Their condemnation of their governments is fueled by their growing recognition that government policies undermine their economic well-being, even while promoting the well-being of those in politics.

Given the breadth, depth, and duration of public opposition to prevailing political practices, why, then, has reform been so delayed? There are several reasons, all of which share a common attribute: the lack of economic incentives for interests, and especially bourgeois interests, to oppose African governments.

Notwithstanding numerous public statements to the contrary, Africa possesses an active and powerful private sector. The markets and trading routes of Africa have long histories, strong institutions, and highly professionalized cadres.[18] These commercial networks thrive even in the midst of the interventionist policies of the postindependence period; they provide the framework for the black markets that have burgeoned even as public institutions decayed.[19] While a major force in the real economies of Africa, this market economy has nonetheless failed to provide the focus for a coherent, reformist political movement.

Participants in this informal economy have failed to act as a coherent bourgeoisie—failed to provide the political impetus necessary for sustained economic reform. One reason is that, instead of being oppressed by the gap between official and market clearing prices, traders in Africa profit from it. A portion of their profits results from arbitrage between official and unofficial markets, especially in international trade, where traders benefit from smuggling and profit from the arbitrary valuation of national currencies.

Rather than turning to protest, then, "marketeers" turn to trade and seek to benefit from the very policies that destroy the business environment for firms in the formal sector.

Another way of characterizing the behavior of African marketeers is that they resort to "exit" rather than to "voice," in the words of Albert Hirschman.[20] But Hirschman's distinction does not quite serve, for it overstates the passivity of the entrepreneurs and understates the degree to which they are active participants in the old order. Rather than retreating from the distorted economy, they instead dwell creatively within it, profiting from the opportunities for arbitrage.

But what of those whose interests lie not in commerce and trade but rather in physical capital? There are ports, utilities, mines, textile plants, food processing firms, manufacturing establishments, and so on in Africa. Why do those whose fortunes are attached to these industries not voice their opposition to the policies that weaken Africa's economies and public institutions? One reason is that their fortunes are not attached to the value of the capital embodied in these activities; capital is often owned by foreigners or the government. The major portion of the nontrading bourgeoisie is managerial, not capitalist; its members receive payment in the form of salaries rather than earnings from shares.[21] The squeezing of quasi rents from these investments and their dissipation by inefficient regulatory policies may offend the sensibilities of these talented cadres, but they do not violate their private economic interests. The losses imposed constitute losses to the national treasury rather than to their personal fortunes.

As a managerial elite, these cadres seek to do their jobs, which involves solving production problems under highly adverse conditions. It also involves giving policy advice to directors of enterprises, many of whom are bureaucrats or party personnel who vote but do not own the shares of government. As those of us who have done research in Africa know, much of the counsel the managers offer constitutes a stinging indictment of government policies and a plea for the freeing of markets. But the reformist impulse of many of these cadres has been stilled by the governance structure of Africa's firms, in which industrial authority often rests in the hands of political elites. By hiring and firing managerial personnel, making judicious use of transfers, and rationing access to credit and foreign exchange, public directors quickly stifle the protests of disaffected managers and their opposition to the prevailing way of doing business in Africa.

Activist governments in Africa intervene in markets and regulate industries, contributing to the macroeconomic imbalances that weaken African economies and generate demands for reform, but also strengthening the capacity of incumbent regimes to neutralize the reformist opposition. The result is deadlock, as those who oppose the prevailing political-economic order are stifled by it. While the poor economic performance of African governments and the distributive impact of their policies undermine their moral right to govern, there is little in the way of a coherent middle class to oppose these policies.

Africa's economic elite fails to become a coherent opponent for an additional reason: it is divided along ethnic lines. It is easy to comprehend how ethnic loyalties provoke internal division; but it is also important to realize that ethnic rivalries can be manufactured by politicians who use them for political ends. Often, incumbents use ethnic sentiments to stymie attacks on the old order. If a reformer advocates merit promotions instead of patronage, for example, incumbents point out the potential for discrimination against those who are historically deprived.[22] If reformers call for a reduction in subsidies, incumbents from poorer regions condemn the proposal. And if reformers call for a more competitive political regime, incumbents point to the threat of ethnic violence, even while inciting some violence to lend credibility to their contention.

Ethnic ties are deeply meaningful to many Africans. To gain social standing in their communities, elites often invest their material wealth in local causes, building schools, clinics, or public works, for example. They often marry locally, build a second home in the village, and send their children to live there. Some seek traditional titles and sacrifice major portions of their incomes from the modern sector for traditional prestige. Appeals to ethnic loyalty by politicians who feel threatened by reformist agendas thus can easily divide Africa's economic elite and undermine the potential for forming a coherent opposition.

The reformist impulse is thus weak in the African bourgeoisie. Merchant capital depends upon, or even benefits from, government interventions. Industrial capital is publicly owned. The managerial bourgeoisie is silenced by public authorities. And the loyalties of the economic elites are divided by political manipulation.

The Organization of Reform

From whom, then, does the reformist impulse emanate? One source is fixed and specific human capital, those people who have invested in skills that are but imperfectly transferable elsewhere. Among these are the old guard politicians and those who people the ranks of local, community-based hierarchies: lawyers, community activists, and church leaders.

A lawyer in Ghana, for example, especially one at the peak of his career, is unlikely to find a comparable position in London. Although he might join an international agency, his career path is not international. Unlike finance capital or people with general, as opposed to community-specific, skills, professionals cannot readily defect abroad. Therefore, in the face of declining welfare, rather than exit, they may find it preferable to give voice.

Such people have paid; they have used family savings to gain an education. After others left school, they remained to train professionally. In the early stages of their careers they continued to train, undertaking low-paying apprenticeships. Only later did they begin to reap the rewards of their sacrifices. To reap these rewards, they need—and demand—a future: a period of time in which arbitrary and capricious acts by political leaders do not deprive them of a return on their investment. As heads of families, moreover, they seek a prosperous future for their children, one based on the life-style of the professional middle class. The value of their sacrifices depends on the future prosperity and political stability of their country. These people, then, want good government.

In addition to their willingness and ability to give voice to their demands for reform, professionals possess another advantage: access to independent associations—the church or the law association, for example. Within these associations, they practice the arts of self-governance, organizing activities, developing tactics, canvassing for membership, raising funds, making rules, and so forth. In addition, they use these associations to develop, debate, and make public an alternative vision of national governance. Their associations provide lines of communication, some of which are privileged (the relationship between lawyers and their clients or between the clergy and their congregations, for example). These associations afford their members international ties, linking prominent dissidents with professionals in other nations, while enabling the latter to monitor African governments and defend the liberty of their African colleagues. Professional associations thus provide the organizational infrastructure for dissident movements in Africa.

The human capital of old guard politicians is also geographically specific. Defeated in previous political struggles, the opposition waits on the sidelines for an opportunity to reenter the fray. Abroad, they would join those who, once at the center of events, have been thrust to the political margins, swelling the dejected ranks of political refugees. Unknown in, say, Paris, they remain famous at home. They can transfer neither their reputations nor their political capital: their knowledge of who hold grudges against the old regime or who believe their ambitions could be realized more rapidly by toppling the existing government rather than by ascending through its ranks. It is characteristic of African reformist movements that they tend to be led by old guard politicians. For the reasons given here, it is also not surprising.

Thus from a human capital framework, along with the theory of exit and voice, one can derive the characteristics of those who people the reform movement in Africa. I now add two refinements.

The decision to join the reformist opposition constitutes a gamble; the uncertain value of the prospect must exceed the certain value of the status quo. All else being equal, then, the less attractive the prevailing conditions, the greater the willingness to gamble on reform. Two implications follow. One pertains to the conditions under which reform will take place: we would expect to see reformist political gambles being taken in countries subject to economic stagnation and poverty. Another pertains to the composition of the reformist leadership: economic elites have the most to lose and therefore would choose risky political gambles only when convinced that the "certainty equivalent" will remain intolerable. For this reason, too, reformism is linked to poverty.

The decision to initiate reform movements is also a strategic decision: the value to an individual of the gamble to demand political reform is determined in large part by the decisions of others. When protesting politically, it is safer to be a member of a crowd. The implication is that coordination is essential to the politics of reform. Knowing that others have acted or will act decreases the perceived risks of acting. If reformism appears to be sweeping through the continent or assumes the status of a force of history, then being a reformer becomes less dangerous. The strategic nature of initiating reforms thus helps explain the pronounced element of contagion in reformist politics. It helps explain the diffusion rate of reformist movements and their geographical patterns. It also helps explain the significance of external actors. Increasingly, international agencies demand domestic political reforms in Africa. In responding to these external demands, some African governments themselves become reformist. And the interventions of these agencies encourage individuals to enter the reformist ranks, both by reducing the threat of reprisal and by convincing them that, rather than being isolated dissidents, they are part of a concerted movement.

The impetus for reform, then, rather than originating in the ranks of commercial or industrial capital, originates within the ranks of Africa's embattled professionals. Reform movements are also organized by old guard politicians who have lost out in earlier political struggles but who prefer to try their luck once again at home rather than suffering anonymity abroad. Finally, the incidence of reform is patterned: its location is influenced by the extent and duration of economic decline and its timing by forces that give assurance that, if reform is initiated, others will join.

Top-Down Reform

This chapter began by noting that the behavior of African governments in the postindependence period both weakened their economies and shaped the nature of Africa's politics. It ends by demonstrating that the very policies that made reform necessary and desirable help as well to define one of its most characteristic attributes: that reform tends to be top-down, that is, to be led by the very governments whom the reformers attack.

The demand for political reform possesses strong domestic roots. While the demand comes from the bottom up, however, the "supply" is often top-down. Governments often initiate reform—and not, as in other regions, because they are on the verge of being toppled by massive, organized movements of political opposition. There governments do not rest upon mass parties or strong bureaucracies; they rest upon markets and industries that have turned into political organizations. This form of political organization generates a need for borrowing, and lenders seek political reform as the price for continued credit. To buy time for their regimes, governments introduce political reforms to secure these loans from foreign donors and creditors, who have underpinned the economies of Africa and who now insist on political liberalization as the price of further lending.

Creditors became political reformers in part because of changes in international political alignments. During the cold war, competition among the big powers led to a search for friends, even among morally corrupt nations; the big powers therefore extended financial aid even to these governments. Now that the cold war has ended and the great power rivalries have abated, creditor governments are freer to act in accord with political principles, and they choose as their political friends those who practice good government. In addition, Africa has friends within the development agencies, even if African governments do not. Institutions such as the World Bank have an institutional commitment to lending in Africa. But the Bank and other lenders must raise money from donor governments, most of which are democratic. Given the present international realities, if donor governments can choose between lending to authoritarian governments or lending to newly democratic governments, they are likely to choose the latter. Friends of Africa, therefore, view political change as a necessary requirement for continued funding for development assistance, and they prod recipient regimes to open up to political reformers or to initiate reform themselves.

Domestic reform in Africa thus presents an odd spectacle. While demanded domestically, it is supplied internationally; it is also supplied by the very governments whose behavior led to the demand for reform in the first place.

With governments taking the lead, political change in Africa could simply yield the recreation of the old order. Features of the dynamics give hope, however, that change will result in something more than that. Political reform has been undertaken as part of economic reform. The reduction of controls and the movement toward market prices eliminates rents; and indeed, protests over the losses of these rents, particularly by civil servants, help fuel political opposition. But if governments succeed at this task and create strong economic bureaucracies in their efforts at economic reform—bureaucracies able to resist distributive claims and to minimize economic distortions—then the beneficiaries of the old order will not be able to recolonize the new. They will have been disinherited. Possibilities thus exist for political realignment, rendering a return to old practices less than inevitable.

Conclusion

Why, in Africa, do democratic reform and poverty go together? I argue that economic decay and political instability share a common origin: the interventions that yield clientelism, patrimonialism, and corruption promote as well fiscal deficits and trade imbalances.

In further probing into the economic base of political reform, I argue that, however passionate may be the domestic political impetus for reform, it is nonetheless weak. While Africa is racked with economic disillusion, few mass movements have arisen demanding less government intervention, fewer social programs, less spending, or less regulation. There is little by way of a rights-oriented opposition in Africa or movements of bourgeois liberalism. The very policies that create the prevailing economic and political order in Africa divide the middle class, an outcome strengthened by the ethnic and cultural diversity of Africans.

Reformism in Africa thus possesses distinctive characteristics. It is passionately championed by the articulate wordsmiths of the professional classes, but it is led by the old war-horses—politicians discredited by their previous complicity with the old order. Reformism has strong domestic roots, but it is powerful because it is backed by international agencies and foreign capital. It opposes Africa's governménts, but it is often initiated by them. A major purpose of this chapter is to account for these paradoxical characteristics.

Notes

I would like to thank Jennifer Widner, Samuel Huntington, Thomas Callaghy, and Catherine Elkins for comments on this chapter.

1. Claude Ake, "Rethinking African Democracy," *Journal of Democracy* 2, no. 1 (1991): 32–44; Richard Joseph, "Africa: The Rebirth of Political Freedom," *Journal of Democracy* 2, no. 4 (1991): 11–24; Larry Diamond, Juan J. Linz, and Seymour Martin Lipset, *Democracy in Developing Countries: Africa* (Boulder, Colo.: Lynne Rienner, 1988); and Richard L. Sklar, "Developmental Democracy," *Comparative Studies in Society and History* 29, no. 4 (1987): 686–714.

2. Samuel P. Huntington, *The Third Wave: Democratization in the Late Twentieth Century* (Norman: University of Oklahoma Press, 1991), 62.

3. See, for example, David Abernethy, "Bureaucratic Growth and Economic Stagnation in Sub-Saharan Africa," in *Africa's Development Challenges and the World Bank,* ed. Stephen K. Commins (Boulder, Colo.: Lynne Rienner, 1988).

4. See P. T. Bauer, *West African Trade* (London: Routledge and Kegan Paul, 1964); Dennis Austin, *Politics in Ghana, 1946–1960* (London: Oxford University Press, 1970); and A. G. Hopkins, *An Economic History of West Africa* (New York: Columbia University Press, 1973).

5. Michael P. Cowen, "Capital and Household Production: The Case of Wattle in Kenya's Central Province, 1903–1964," Ph.D. diss. University of Cambridge, 1978; Nicola Sainson, *The Development of Corporate Capitalism in Kenya, 1918–1978* (Berkeley: University of California Press, 1979); see also Gavin Kitching, *Class and Economic Change in Kenya* (New Haven: Yale University Press, 1980); John Spenser, *The KAU* (London: KPI, 1985); and A. L. Epstein, *Politics in an Urban African Community* (Manchester: Manchester University Press, 1958).

6. See Robert H. Bates, *Essays on the Political Economy of Rural Africa* (Berkeley: University of California Press, 1983), chap. 4; Lionel Cliffe, "Nationalism and the Reaction to Forced Agricultural Change in Tanganyika during the Colonial Period," *Taamuli* 1 (July 1970): 1–15; Goran Hyden, *Beyond Ujamaa in Tanzania: Development and the Uncaptured Peasantry* (Berkeley: University of California Press, 1980); Richard Sandbrook, *Proletarians and African Capitalism: The Kenyan Case, 1960–1972* (Cambridge: Cambridge University Press, 1974); Richard Jeffries, *Class, Power, and Ideology in Ghana: The Railwaymen of Sekondi*

(Cambridge: Cambridge University Press, 1978); and Epstein, *Politics in an Urban African Community.*

7. Thandika Mkandawire, in his comments on this chapter, reminded me of a contrasting current in African nationalism: a willingness to incur economic costs in order to gain political liberty. Figures as diverse as Hastings Banda and Sekou Toure illustrate his point, the first by taking Malawi out of the Central African Federation and the latter by breaking ties with France. As noted by Mkandawire, Sekou Toure proclaimed: "We would rather be poor on our feet than rich on our knees." These orientations toward politics, while clearly less materialistic than those stressed in this chapter, would of course also contribute to the impoverishment of Africa.

8. See, for example, Colin Leys, *Underdevelopment in Kenya* (Berkeley: University of California Press, 1975).

9. See the superb analysis in Tony Killick, *Development Economics in Action: A Study of Economic Policies in Ghana* (New York: St. Martin's, 1978).

10. Sayre Schatz, *Nigerian Capitalism* (Berkeley: University of California Press, 1977).

11. See, for example, Robert H. Bates, *Markets and States in Tropical Africa* (Berkeley: University of California Press, 1981).

12. See Killick, *Development Economics;* Scott R. Pearson, Gerald C. Nelson, and J. Dirck Stryker, "Incentives and Comparative Advantage in Ghanaian Industry and Agriculture," Stanford University, 1976, typescript; and Robert H. Bates and Paul Collier, "The Politics of Economic Reform in Zambia," in *Political and Economic Interactions in Economic Policy Reform,* ed. Robert H. Bates and Anne O. Krueger (Oxford: Basil Blackwell, 1993).

13. Robert H. Jackson and Carl G. Rosberg, *Personal Rule in Black Africa* (Berkeley: University of California Press, 1982).

14. Richard Joseph, "Class, State, and Prebendal Politics in Nigeria," *Journal of Commonwealth and Comparative Politics* 21, no. 3 (1983): 21–38; Thomas Callaghy, *The State-Society Struggle: Zaire in Comparative Perspective* (New York: Columbia University Press, 1984).

15. See Richard L. Sklar, "The Nature of Class Domination in Africa," *Journal of Modern African Studies* 17 (1979): 531–52.

16. See Anne O. Krueger, "The Political Economy of the Rent-Seeking Society," *American Economic Review* 64, no. 3 (1974): 291–303.

17. Ayi Kwei Armah, *The Beautyful Ones Are Not Yet Born* (Boston: Houghton Mifflin, 1968); Chinua Achebe, *A Man of the People* (Garden City, N.Y.: Anchor Books, 1967); Ngugi wa Thiong'o, *Petals of Blood* (New York: Dutton, 1978).

18. See, for example, the contributions in Claude Meillassoux, ed., *The Development of Indigenous Trade and Marketing in West Africa* (London: Oxford University Press, 1971); Richard Gray and David Birmingham, *Pre-Colonial African Trade* (London: Oxford University Press, 1970); and the superb overview in William O. Jones, "Agricultural Trade within Tropical Africa: Historical Background," in *Agricultural Development in Africa: Issues of Public Policy,* ed.

Robert Bates and Michael F. Lofchie (New York: Praeger, 1980).

19. Jerry Jenkins, ed., *Beyond the Informal Sector* (San Francisco: ICS, 1988).

20. Albert Hirschman, *Exit, Voice, and Loyalty* (Cambridge: Harvard University Press, 1979).

21. For a discussion, see Richard L. Sklar, *Corporate Power in an African State* (Berkeley: University of California Press, 1975).

22. See, for example, the discussion in Nelson Kasfir, *The Shrinking Political Order* (Berkeley: University of California Press, 1976); and Donald Rothchild and Victor A. Olorunsula, *State versus Ethnic Claims: African Policy Dilemmas* (Boulder, Colo.: Westview, 1983).

BARBARA GROSH

Two ◈ Through the Structural Adjustment Minefield: Politics in an Era of Economic Liberalization

Since independence in the 1960s, virtually every sub-Saharan African country has pursued policies of substantial regulation and control by planners. These policies include (but go beyond) the complex of practices that have been discussed in the semi-industrial countries since 1973 under the rubric of *financial repression*.[1] The countries of the region have experienced the sluggish (even negative) growth predicted by the economists who began the critique of such policies.

In the 1970s and 1980s most of these countries were forced by their low growth and increasing balance of payments problems to turn to the multilateral and bilateral agencies for help. This help comes with strings attached, in the form of programs for stabilization and structural adjustment, the thrust of which is the dismantling of significant parts of their apparatus for regulation and control. For shorthand, I term these policies *programs of economic liberalization*.

Also in the late 1980s and early 1990s, massive political change came to Africa, following dissent both from old politicians who could no longer be contained within the one-party system and from professional groups not previously politically active (in some cases because of the repression). This change has taken various forms, including the retirement of heads of state, coups, civil wars, and the end of one-party rule. The sequence of these events—economic liberalization followed by regime change—gives the impression that structural adjustment is a minefield and that heads of state who attempt to cross it are likely to lose their positions, if not their heads. From a social science standpoint, there are four questions. To what extent is the political liberalization linked to the programs of economic liberalization that preceded it? How does recent economic history influence political change in Africa? What will be the nature of these new regimes? And what will be the economic consequences of political liberalization? It is evident from recent experience that a wide range of outcomes is possible.

The object of this chapter is to develop a conceptual framework from the vantage point of development economics that will help us answer these questions. To do that, we must distinguish among the programs of economic liberalization that have been followed so far, since the conditions under which they have been undertaken, the consistency with which they have been pursued, and the results they have produced vary dramatically. The following section explores the different conditions under which economic liberalization has been undertaken and the varying effects of such liberalization on politics. In particular, I distinguish between countries that have experienced economic collapse and those that have not. I argue in the second section that the political transitions they experience are likely to be quite different.

Though the economic starting point of liberalization matters, it is not deterministic. There is room to mediate the political effects of economic liberalization, the subject of the third section.

Liberalization: The Decisionmaking Process

To assess the political consequences of structural adjustment, it is helpful to begin by recalling who wins and who loses under prevailing policies as well as the incidence of burdens and benefits under reform. This section first introduces the main elements of policies of financial repression and their effects on different economic groups. It then suggests that political scientists consider the sequence of reform policies, the broad redistributional effects of economic liberalization, and the way benefits and costs accrue to key parties.

Most of the countries in Africa follow policies of financial repression, including the use of usury ceilings that depress interest rates below market clearing rates.[2] As a consequence, credit is allocated through bureaucratic means. To stem the capital flight that would result from efforts to avoid low returns on domestic financial assets, exchange controls must be introduced.

Financial repression usually stems from the need to finance fiscal deficits. Rather than levying and collecting taxes, which is a politically (and in Africa's relatively less monetized economies, economically) difficult process, deficits are financed by borrowing from the banking system at low controlled rates. Reserve requirements are high, and the banks are forced to keep a large portion of their portfolios in the form of government securities, which pay low real rates of return. This system is often accompanied by borrowing from the central bank—in effect printing money—which then leads to inflation. The combination of interest rate ceilings and inflation leads to very low (often negative) real rates of return on deposits in banks. Savers avoid banks, looking instead for inflation hedges, such as real estate, inventories, and various other investments of low social productivity. Real deposits in the banking system grow slowly or even shrink.

The effects of financial repression on the real economy are that the financial sector cannot play its normal role in channeling investment to high-return activities. Investors must rely on self-finance and may make investments with very low rates of return simply because they are better than negative rates available in the financial system. As the quantity and productivity of investment declines, real growth slows.

In Francophone Africa, macroeconomic policy has been less repressed because of membership in the Communauté Financière Africaine (CFA) franc zone. These countries have lower inflation rates and higher growth rates than their Anglophone neighbors due to restraints on money supply growth imposed by the collective central banks: the Central Bank of West African States (BCEAO) and the Bank of Central African States (BEAC). While these "agencies of restraint"[3] help avert (or at least postpone) the worst effects of economic repression, they make the politics of structural adjustment less tractable. The CFA franc has become overvalued. Since nominal devaluation requires the unanimous agreement of all members of the monetary union, devaluation has never occurred in the postindependence era. Without devaluation to reduce the real salaries of the formal sector, thus forcing these workers to share in the economic adjustment, it becomes necessary to reduce their nominal salaries directly, a much more politically contentious process.[4]

In Africa the effects of policies of financial repression are compounded by other policies, which are less common or less severe in other parts of the developing world. (1) The public and parapublic sectors constitute a large part of the formal sector in Africa. The claims of these large public sectors are relatively rigid. Civil servants and parastatal employees are difficult to dismiss, and declines in their living standards often give rise to political unrest. (2) Further, many

African governments also engage in extensive agricultural price stabilization, even where the defense of price floors and ceilings leads to large losses for state marketing boards. (3) African economies also make extensive use of protective trade barriers, including tariffs, quotas, import licensing, and foreign exchange rationing. In the process of allocating scarce foreign exchange, priority is normally given first to the pubic and parastatal sector and then to formal sector manufacturing firms that need capital equipment, spare parts, and intermediate inputs for processing. The lowest priority is given to consumer goods.

The effect of this complex of policies is that internal terms of trade move strongly against the unprotected sectors, especially agricultural exporters and informal sector manufacturing. It is possible to run a repressed economy that has a low but positive rate of growth without serious problems of external balance.[5] However, prolonged use of policies of economic repression often leads to implosion, defined as "a disastrous cumulative contraction in the economy."[6]

These policies have been characterized as tactics for rent extraction and redistribution. In fact it yields *quasi rents*; these are rents only in the short run, when fixed factors represent a sunk cost. For example, once a farmer has planted a tree crop and cultivated it through the initial gestation period, his income from the crop over and above the annual costs of maintaining it can be extracted like rent via low producer prices without causing the supply of the crop to decrease. Eventually, however, the fixed factors have to be replaced. If the farmer's returns are depressed over the long run, these fixed factors will be allowed to depreciate, production will fall, and there will be no more rents to extract. Tree crops in Ghana and Tanzania were exploited in this way.

The possibility of implosion is more likely in countries with large state sectors, rigid claims, and a high degree of economic repression. When the economy experiences shocks, all the burden of adjustment is on those without rigid claims, who face disproportionately large contractions in income. The unprotected part of the economy contracts, and the economy enters a downward spiral.

In an imploding economy, the base from which resources are extracted—through either explicit or implicit taxes—contracts. Eventually, the formal sector's claims erode, since even with very high tax rates, the yield is insufficient to satisfy the claims of the formal sector and the public employees, commonly the main base of support for African regimes. Eventually, the regime may change, and the new government faces the same question, whether to liberalize or not.

This was the scenario in Ghana before 1983, in Tanzania in the mid-1980s, in Benin in the late 1980s, and in Zaire in the early 1990s and is probably typical of the consequences of extreme and prolonged economic repression.[7]

At some stage, the regime may try liberalizing its economy. Liberalization is a complex process. It involves many separate changes, and the order in which these changes are made matters a lot, as do external market conditions. If the changes are made out of order, or if important steps are missed, or if the world economic climate is unfavorable, things may easily become worse. In this case, the regime is likely to reverse its reforms. Zambia provides two instances of such reversals, after it tried to remove cereal subsidies and after it liberalized its foreign exchange regime without bringing its budget deficit under control. It retreated from these liberalizations in the belief they would not work. Each time a country unsuccessfully tries to liberalize, it is likely it will go deeper in to debt, as it draws tranches from the IMF and borrows from other lenders. This debt then exacerbates the problem, as most debt is usually nonnegotiable. Thus unsuccessful attempts at liberalization will ultimately speed economic collapse.

Some countries that try liberalization do get the order essentially correct, and they begin to see the benefits of liberalization, including economic growth. This growth is inevitably accompanied by redistribution, since stabilization and structural adjustment necessarily involve relative price changes—which by definition hurt some while they help others. This redistribution may be perceived as a transfer of resources from one region to another, with possible ethnic implications, or from consumers to producers, with a possible rural-urban dichotomy as well as possible income-level differences.

It is not only the order of reforms and their redistributional effects that matter in assessing who wins and who loses in economic liberalization. To make matters more complex, the benefits and costs of these policies need not accrue to the same parties. A simple thought-experiment helps clarify the dilemma regimes face: one might distinguish between the regime in power (and the political base that allows it to remain in power) and everyone else. On the one hand, if the regime in power bears most of the cost and reaps few of the benefits from liberalization, it is likely to try to reverse the liberalization process. If it succeeds in reversing direction, the economy will return to its path of stagnation or decline. If liberalization cannot be reversed fast enough, there is a prospect of a regime change led by the beneficiaries of the reforms or by those who believe the incumbent government sacrificed their interests. On the other hand, if the incumbent leaders and their supporters capture most of the benefits and bear few of the costs of liberalization, the government may continue the policy at the risk of substantial opposition from those who do bear the burdens. If disaffected groups join together and lobby for a voice in policymaking, the result may be greater political openness, probably accompanied by struggles over whether to continue economic liberalization. Reversion to financial repression may occur, but if these policies are sufficiently discredited by many years of stagnation and decline, an about-face may attract little support.

There are two other possible cases. The chances that the regime neither captures the benefits nor bears significant costs are probably negligible. Almost by definition, regimes that have employed financial repression suffer from liberalization, especially because the main way to balance the budget is to cut civil service wages or employment. (The situation where the regime bears significant costs but also captures significant benefits is the most difficult to predict. I return to it in the third section, below.)

How can we predict when the regime will benefit from liberalization and when it will bear the costs? In general, most structural adjustment programs are designed to increase the relative prices of traded goods, both exports and imports, versus nontraded goods. This means that those who produce exports or who import competing goods gain, while those who consume either exports or imports suffer. We can predict then, that when the regime in power owns and operates export producing farms or manufacturing firms that compete with imports, the regime will capture much of the benefit. When the regime is controlled by ethnic groups from regions without export agriculture, or when the regime's supporters are hurt more by consumer price increases than helped by producer price increases, the regime will suffer. If members of the regime have engaged in capital flight over the years preceding liberalization (for example, via transfer pricing or embezzlement in foreign trade), members of the regime may stand to profit handsomely from devaluation and the liberalization of foreign exchange rules.

Economic Liberalization and Politics

Clearly, there is a tremendous range of possible interactions between economic liberalization and political liberalization. Let us begin by considering countries suffering from economic stagnation or decline as a result of a failure to liberalize.

It has become the conventional wisdom to understand repressive economic policies not as economic mistakes made by policymakers who have not had the benefit of economic training in Harberger triangles but as a rational response from a political economy perspective.[8] Although repressive policies create deadweight losses, the argument goes, they also create large rents, which can be transferred to parties of the regime's choosing, permitting the regime to create a patronage network and stay in power—to say nothing of enriching those in power. The argument is appealing, and it is easy to think of cases where the description seems apt, including places as diverse as Zaire and the Philippines. But the paradigm has outlived its usefulness in much of Africa. It really makes sense only in countries that have managed to run "compatible control regimes," where policy distortions were mild enough and consistent enough to permit a sustainable, if grossly suboptimal, equilibrium.[9] Much of Africa has experienced incompatible control regimes, with economic implosion as a result. At some stage, as the economy shrinks, it becomes irrational on the part of the regime to persist in repressive economic policies, even if we impute to them (which I do not) the most venal motives of self-enrichment. As the economy shrinks, hefty shares of a shrinking pie become smaller than small shares of a growing pie. The leaders of Ghana, Tanzania, and Zambia, for example, ultimately gained little from persisting in their repressive economic policies.

This argument applies with even more force to formal sector employees, who are important beneficiaries of the rents generated and who are often politically potent in blocking reform at earlier stages. With many of these workers either seeking to emigrate or scrambling to earn money in the informal sector—raising chickens, driving taxis— we cannot cling to theories that see the strangulation of their economies as still being in their self-interest. The labor force in Ghana, for example, was far more drastically affected by reforms under the economic recovery program than by the budgets of 1961 and 1971, yet the latter provoked a large amount of worker unrest, while there was little protest following the recovery program.[10] One reason for this is the sheer fiction of formal sector controls. So few goods were traded, anyway, at official prices, that the lifting of official price controls under the recovery program had little impact on people's well-being. As liberalization took effect, real income started to rise for the first time in over a decade. While it was not able to enforce official prices or the use of official channels, the control regime was potent enough to force transactions into the parallel market, so removal of controls permitted economic activity to flow back into official markets, where transactions costs were lower. This example suggests that, if governments wait long enough to liberalize, there are so few economic rents still generated and distributed that political opposition to economic liberalization disappears.

Even the interests to which regimes cater become malleable as decay sets in. In Tanzania, Ali Hassan Mwinyi has worked steadily to dismantle the policies of Julius Nyerere, with no real opposition; Tanzanian civil servants have much more to gain from being allowed to buy and sell things freely than they have to lose from devaluation. New regimes may reshape populist rhetoric to both focus on peasants and the informal sector and delegitimize the sinecures of the public servants, as Jerry Rawlings did in Ghana. With little resistance left from the remnants of the formal sector, it is then possible to persist with reforms that previously were blocked by the opposition.

I suggest, then, that economic collapse is likely to lead to a change in leadership or personnel of some sort. This is because the collapse of the economy leads to a collapse of the rents with which the previous government constructed its alliance. There is no inherent reason that such a political change need entail greater consultation or democratic participation. In Ghana, Tanzania, Somalia, and Liberia, where the economies had disintegrated by the early 1980s, the regime changes that followed economic decay were quite undemocratic. In Ghana and Tanzania, leaders implemented structural adjustment in an old-fashioned, authoritarian way, although both countries later moved to introduce multiparty systems.[11] In countries that suffered economic collapse later in the 1980s, like Zambia, Benin, and Côte d'Ivoire, political reform had a far more democratic character.

The timing of these events suggests that (1) economic collapse does lead to political change but not necessarily to democratic regimes or styles and (2) there must be another source of pressure for political liberalization. I suggest that the collapse of the authoritarian regimes of Eastern Europe is the second factor. Most African countries were one-party states, a form of government that drew political legitimacy as well as some financial support from Eastern Europe. The unity these systems promised seemed essential to generating fast growth in backward economies. But to retain one-partyism in the current era would require far more political repression than it previously did, precisely at a moment when regimes in Africa are weak due to economic collapse and cannot afford a larger security apparatus.

What can we expect from political openings brought on by economic collapse? Because of the collapse of rents, it is politically possible to liberalize economically where it was impossible before, and the result is likely to be higher rates of growth. In a world that demands greater democratic participation, it should be possible, then—with the pie beginning to grow for the first time in years—to gain some political breathing space. Perhaps as the economy grows again and is increasingly channeled back into formal, legal markets, regime legitimacy will improve and challenges to political survival will diminish. Regimes may then tolerate greater political openness.

This process may have a fairly short life span, however, depending on the economic astuteness of government policymakers. In the initial phases of economic liberalization, as rehabilitation is undertaken, growth can be very rapid. Rates of return on capital invested in spare parts may be extremely high as past investments are returned to service. For example, in Ghana in 1982, 70 percent of vehicles were grounded due to lack of spare parts.[12] Eventually, such easy options will be exhausted, and future growth will have to be fueled by savings and investment. New institutions must be created to facilitate this growth—a process that will not always go smoothly.[13]

What sort of political institutions will develop as these collapsed economies rebuild? Presumably, the new regimes will have to find new ways to amass political support, since without the rents generated by the old repressed economy policies they will not be able to rely so heavily on patronage politics.[14] Can we learn from the experiences of countries that avoided extreme repression and collapse, such as Kenya, Côte d'Ivoire, and Cameroon? These countries actually moved more slowly toward economic liberalization than the countries that suffered economic collapse; their formal sectors did not atrophy to the point where opposition to liberalization from the urban employed disappeared. The urban employed could still impede change. With democracy sweeping the world, it is hard to repress their dissent. In the absence of pressure from donors one might expect that the increase in political pluralism will give rise to inflationary spending, as previously repressed groups succeed in gaining benefits via the public budget. Clearly, such demands cannot get far within the confines of structural adjustment loans and standby agreements. However, when political openness precedes the elimination of the old rent-creating institutions, it may lead to bitter struggles for control and an inability to reach consensus within the constraints of a sound economic framework. Severe political instability, leading to economic instability, seems a real possibility.

It may be possible for clever politicians to find a political base by articulating discontent with corruption and past repression, both economic and political. They may be able to sell liberalization as benefiting the many and costing only the discredited politicians of the past. In Sahelian countries, with their mass peasant movements preaching self-help, such political-economic regimes could have some staying power.[15] But although transitions based on such appeals may be possible, I fear that they may not be able to stay the course as parties proliferate and the temptation grows to generate rents for patronage distribution. The future may be more fragile for countries that have heretofore averted economic crisis than for their neighbors who have not.

Countries that succeed in liberalizing, whether they implode or not, will have to fashion a new politics based less on distribution of rents. What groups will come to the fore under such conditions? Certain ethnic groups have traditionally prospered in business, whether for reasons of culture or endowments (including rights to high-potential land or a colonial legacy of greater educational achievement). These are the groups (the Kikuyu in Kenya, the Chaga and Haya in Tanzania, etc.) that will blossom economically and provide bases for political support. One can imagine more free-wheeling liberal regimes wherein institutions that distribute rents to groups of lesser business accomplishment are dissolved, paving the way for increasing inequality of income and wealth. Eventually, there will probably be backlash, as in Tanzania, where complaints about the dominance of Asians are increasingly common. The tendency toward backlash may be especially strong in countries where the economies do not actually collapse under the repressed economy policies, and hence the policies are not totally discredited.

Grabbing Benefits, Shedding Costs

The initial process of economic liberalization is a complicated one, involving many steps. Although it is often convenient for regimes to pretend they have no choice and that the measures for dismantling the rent-generating apparatus of the repressed economies are imposed by donors, in fact there is substantial leeway in how liberalization is carried out. In this section I discuss various means by which the political fallout of economic liberalization can be minimized.

Dismantling Public Enterprises

Public enterprises in Africa are supposed to generate profits for reinvestment; they are considered necessary because peasants are not considered capable of saving or investing. But most African public enterprises in the 1990s have failed to generate any savings and in fact run chronic deficits, which must be financed from the government budget.[16] Thus, while there are nationalistic or patronage reasons for keeping some public enterprises, many governments prefer to cut back the parastatal sector. They are hindered from doing so by parastatal employees, a vocal and organized group that often articulates discontent in the face of austerity and is able to generate public sympathy.

In the face of such opposition, some governments conduct wars of attrition on their public enterprises. Although workers cannot be terminated, the enterprises, which usually run at a loss, are left to languish. Without the subsidization of losses, the enterprises collapse in on themselves, failing to meet payrolls or payments to suppliers. One survey of privatization finds that 70 percent of liquidations were achieved in this way.[17] Furthermore, of enterprises privatized through sale, about half were in this condition. In Togo, "state-owned industrial operations were crippled by lack of imported inputs, nonpayment for products supplied to the government, and inability to meet employee payrolls. . . . Many SOEs ceased to exist as productive entities."[18] This form of state contraction certainly involves inefficiencies, as plant and equipment are underutilized and deteriorate. However, it is often the only politically tractable way of retreating from untenable commitments of the state. Eventually, employees get fed up and leave. The policy is less wasteful when their departure can be speeded with severance pay, though this may not be feasible if the government is in default for services or supplies already rendered.

The withering of state enterprises can be accelerated by removing their monopoly power. For example, in Kenya during the 1970s private firms were allowed to enter the meat industry for the first time. Both the Kenya Meat Commission and the Uplands Bacon Factory were financially troubled parastatals. When suppliers were able to take their animals elsewhere, these parastatals withered rapidly, and by the time they were closed there was virtually no protest.[19] Another example comes from Mali, where the marketing of cereals was liberalized at the same time as members of the cereals marketing board, OPAM (Office des Produits Agricoles du Mali) were laid off. Who was better placed to enter the newly private trade than former OPAM employees, who knew the trade well? The policy was implemented with a minimum of protest and resulted in improved market performance.[20]

The policy of removing monopoly power to accelerate the withering of state enterprises has the advantage of setting the stage for a privatization consistent with the goals of structural adjustment. Buyers of state enterprises assume that they must compete with either imports or other domestic producers, and they buy these enterprises only if they believe they are efficient enough to be profitable in such a competitive environment. Where grants of monopoly are not removed before privatization, the results can be inimical to the goals of structural adjustment. For example, when Togo leased its money-losing steel mill to a foreign investor, it agreed to retain a 41 percent import duty on steel. The lease payments cover less than 5 percent of the enterprise's annual debt service, but the lessor receives management fees and profits, which he can remit freely out of the country. The payback period on the ten-year lease was calculated at less than six months, though the deal could not have gone through if the firm had been required to compete with imports.[21]

It is often necessary to remove the state from the role of guarantor of high agricultural prices and low food prices. This has been especially true where structural adjustment included increases in producer prices that transformed marketing boards from revenue generators to sinks. A retreat from this obligation can be achieved gradually if the board is left to languish without subsidies; the board then fails to buy crops, and farmers turn parallel markets. Once the board has withered sufficiently, it can be liquidated or reorganized with little protest, since it no longer distributes significant rents. The private traders who replace the board are generally more efficient, function without protection, and will certainly be more susceptible to adjustment pressures in the future.

Making Policies Public

Some rules of thumb for successful adjustment violate theoretical norms of fairness or rationality. For example, transparency is usually seen as a virtue—rules should be clear, understandable, known, and applied consistently.[22] Transparency generally requires a public announcement of a policy change, which can precipitate debate and opposition. But many governments are finding that, by not announcing a policy, they can shed costs. For example, privatizing of public enterprises is always contentious. When Kenya wanted to privatize Kenatco (a trucking firm), it took several years and several rounds of tendering before the sale went through. Later, it privatized several manufacturing firms with no announcement and no delay. One suspects that the terms were very favorable to the buyers, and this might be looked at askance as a form of patronage politics, if not outright corruption. However, it can be a successful means of shrinking future formal sector claims, inasmuch as the private sector's demands are considerably less rigid than those of the public sector. Côte d'Ivoire also made use of secretive privatization.[23] Much of the political block-age of liberalization consists of intrastate rivalry among a disunited elite.[24] Nontransparent privatization could be a way to compensate groups that might otherwise stand to lose from liberalization, buying them off so that they withdraw their opposition and allow the econ-omy to move to a truly Pareto improving allocation.

Of course, nontransparency carries numerous political risks. What is nontransparent in the short run may become better known in the long run, as information leaks out. Even where the facts never become known (e.g., the buyers and the terms), the mere fact of secrecy may imply wrongdoing. The regime that uses nontransparency to achieve reform may earn itself a reputation for corruption, which may harm it in the long run.

Nontransparency can be distinguished from policies designed to avoid providing a focus for protest. For example, many very small price adjustments may be used to accomplish a desired end, where one large one would raise a storm of protest. When Egypt wanted to remove bread subsidies and announced that the price of a loaf would double, riots broke out. It then began to gradually shrink the size of the loaf until it reached half the original size, introducing a new jumbo loaf (the original size) at twice the original price.

The foreign exchange rate is clearly an area where making many small changes is the best policy. In countries with fixed exchange rates, devaluations can set off marches in the streets, but in countries like Kenya, with its floating peg, the exchange rate is reported on the last pages of the newspaper rather than the first. It never changes enough to be noticed, and there have been no protests, despite a cumulative nominal devaluation of some 300 percent.

Cost Sharing

One of Africa's most promising options for achieving fiscal balance is cost sharing, that clever 1980s euphemism for user fees. With Af-rica's relatively egalitarian income distribution, arguments for free public provision of education, health care, water and sanitation, and so on are not nearly so compelling as in more highly polarized so-cieties. Africans have proven willing and able to pay for such ser-vices.[25] To persist in their nonprovision or suboptimal provision in the face of such willingness to pay is clearly inefficient.

Of course, user fees sometimes attract opposition—and sometimes on a large scale. Here again, the policy of having no policy can be very useful. In Tanzania user fees are being introduced piecemeal, with no announced policy. When opposition appears, the state can temporarily withdraw the fees on one front without reversing the general policy and, at a later date, reintroduce them. Such piecemeal cost sharing has greater legitimacy if the revenues stay in the institution concerned, for example, the school or the hospital. Then users of institutions that charge user fees will receive better service than users of institutions that do not, which increases the acceptability of user fees. If the fees are not retained at the local level but are sent to some higher level, for example, the ministry budget or even the national exchequer, the result will be a perception of unfairness as some people are charged for services that other people receive free.

Populist Privatization

While nontransparent divestiture can be useful in buying off opposition to liberalization and in withdrawing from further state obligations, transparent divestiture can also be used to good effect. An example of this is Kenya's floating of new shares, equivalent to 40 percent of the ownership, in the Kenya Commercial Bank, a bank with a history of profitable performance and good management. The flotation was heavily oversubscribed, so shares were allocated using formulas that ensured that every district received a certain portion, with a ceiling on the number of shares any individual was allowed to purchase. The shares were issued at a price that ensured later appreciation.

This clever move accomplished several things. First, it garnered good feelings toward the regime. More important for the long run, it created a constituency with a strong interest in a sound banking and business regulation and sound parastatal management. It also demonstrated the demand of the Kenyan public for financial assets not subject to the reduced returns of deposits in the banking system, with its interest rate ceilings. It helped build political support for financial liberalization. Finally, it mobilized, through voluntary channels, new capital for what the public saw as a sound investment.[26] This device obviously has limitations in Africa. It can probably be used to good effect only in countries with stock exchanges—a small minority in Africa. And it can be done only with well-run, profitable enterprises. Nonetheless, it demonstrates an ability to manipulate the liberalization process to build political support.

Emergency Social Funds

Senegal, Benin, Sudan, and Ghana established social funds to help ease the human cost of transition to liberalization.[27] Typical is the Programme of Actions to Mitigate the Social Costs of Adjustment

(PAMSCAD) in Ghana, which "seeks to address the needs of vulnerable groups who are in a precarious condition due to the adjustment program or due to the earlier period of economic decline. Projects were included in the proposed portfolio if they had a strong poverty focus; high economic and social rates of return; modest institutional requirements to ensure ease and speed in implementation; and in sensitive areas, high visibility to enhance confidence in and sustainability of the ERP."[28] These social funds have been underfunded in Africa, and have probably not lived up to their full potential (as they have in Bolivia[29]). However, their existence on even a small scale gives governments a flexibility for coping with particularly urgent (especially politically urgent) hardship cases, which may prevent the development of more serious opposition.

Conclusions

I distinguish two kinds of states, those that used repressed economy policies long enough to cause their economies to collapse and those that used the policies less severely and whose economies grew slowly but positively. Economic collapse changes the interest group structure, so that eventually liberalization is in virtually every sector's self-interest. Most of those economies that reached this condition before the wave of democracy experienced regime transition, which permitted liberalization to begin. These states experienced greater pressures for political openness. They are well placed to tolerate such openness, since their economies are growing and much of the formal sector that previously blocked liberalization now supports it. These countries can probably expect an era of relatively good economic performance and popular political participation.

States whose economies never collapsed have not succeeded in liberalizing, so their economic growth will continue to be slow. Significant rents are being collected and redistributed, and hence there is significant political opposition to liberalization. To introduce new forms of political contestation in such an environment is likely to lead to pressure for more redistributive economic policies. Redistribution could lead these countries to enter the cycle of collapse, which is frightening because of their high debt levels. Debt service (especially to the International Monetary Fund and the World Bank, which hold a high portion of Africa's debt) is a rather rigid claim. If economies contract too much, their infrastructure deteriorates to such an extent that supply response becomes very difficult. Thus, with high levels of debt, these economies could become paralyzed.

Eventually, the formal sector's resistance to liberalization weakens as the economy implodes. With good leadership, low debt levels, access to grant aid, and favorable export prices, it is possible to halt the free fall, liberalize, and begin to grow. At this stage, regime change can be accomplished peacefully even with the new political openness, because the beneficiaries of past rent-creating policies realize they no longer have anything to gain from past policies and their contention is muted. Growth may also create new interest groups with vested interests in liberal, private sector, growth facilitating policies. If so, there can be a virtuous circle of success: sound policies create constituencies that ensure their continuation. It is also possible that old interest groups may reemerge to press again for rent redistribution and perhaps to undo the budget balance.

This scenario may be too deterministic, however. Capable leaders can negotiate adjustment in economies that have not yet entered free-fall. I suggest several techniques, including (1) dismantling public enterprises, (2) withdrawing from such state commitments as guaranteed prices, (3) cost sharing, (4) populist privatization, and (5) emergency social funds. In the present world climate, economic liberalization has a new political legitimacy, which should make adjustment easier. However, in the current world political climate, continued political repression and lack of transparency in policymaking will also be difficult. Between the difficulties of cutting off former recipients of rents and the challenges of managing new demands that follow from greater political openness, regimes engaged in economic reform will find it difficult, but not impossible, to stay in power. The danger is that they will be swept out by populist movements, which will return the country to the rent-creating repressed economic policies of the past. Given the high indebtedness of these countries, the risks are grave.

Notes

I would like to acknowledge helpful comments on a draft of this chapter by Jennifer Widner, Howard Brill, Stephen Younger, Tom Selden, Larry Schroeder, Ali Galaydh, Michael Roemer, and Mark Gallagher.

1. Ronald I. McKinnon, *Money and Capital in Economic Development* (Washington, D.C.: Brooking Institution, 1973); Edward S. Shaw, *Financial Deepening in Economic Development* (New York: Oxford University Press, 1973).

2. See McKinnon, *Money and Capital in Economic Development*; Ronald I. McKinnon, *The Order of Economic Liberalization: Financial Control in the Transition to a Market Economy* (Baltimore: Johns Hopkins University Press, 1991); Shaw,

Financial Deepening in Economic Development; Maxwell Fry, *Money, Interest, and Banking in Economic Development* (Baltimore: Johns Hopkins University Press, 1988).

3. See use of term in Paul Collier, "Africa's External Economic Relations, 1960–90," *African Affairs* 90 (1991): 339–56.

4. For a discussion of the CFA franc zone, see Nicolas van de Walle, "The Decline of the Franc Zone: Monetary Politics in Francophone Africa," *African Affairs* 90 (1991): 383–405; and Santayanan Devarajan and Jaime de Melo, "Evaluating Participation in African Monetary Unions: A Statistical Analysis of the CFA Zones," *World Development* 15, no. 4 (1987): 483–96.

5. David Bevan, Paul Collier, and Jan Willem Gunning, *Controlled Open Economies: A Neoclassical Approach to Structuralism* (Oxford: Clarendon, 1990), 7; McKinnon, *The Order of Economic Liberalization*, 112.

6. Bevan, Collier, and Gunning, *Controlled Open Economies*, 3.

7. For Ghana, see Tony Killick, *Development Economics in Action: A Study of Economic Policies in Ghana* (New York: St. Martin's, 1978); Stephen D. Younger, "Ghana: Economic Recovery Program—A Case Study of Stabilization and Structural Adjustment in Sub-Saharan Africa," in *Successful Development in Africa: Case Studies of Projects, Programs, and Policies*, EDI Development Case Studies 1 (Washington, D.C.: World Bank, 1989); for Tanzania, see Bevan, Collier, and Gunning, *Controlled Open Economies*.

8. Robert H. Bates, *Markets and States in Tropical Africa* (Berkeley: University of California Press, 1981).

9. Bevan, Collier, and Gunning, *Controlled Open Economies*.

10. Jeffrey Herbst, "Labor in Ghana under Structural Adjustment: The Politics of Acquiescence," in *Ghana: The Political Economy of Recovery*, ed. Donald Rothchild (Boulder, Colo.: Lynne Rienner, 1991).

11. See Richard Jeffries, "Leadership, Commitment, and Political Opposition to Structural Adjustment in Ghana, in *Ghana: The Political Economy of Recovery*, ed. Donald Rothchild (Boulder, Colo.: Lynne Rienner, 1991); and Andrew Kiendo, "The Nature of Economic Reforms in Tanzania," in *Tanzania and the IMF: The Dynamics of Liberalization*, ed. Horace Campbell and Howard Stein (Boulder, Colo.: Westview, 1992).

12. Younger, "Ghana: Economic Recovery Program."

13. For an account of some of the pitfalls in the case of Ghana, see Stephen D. Younger, "Aid and the Dutch Disease: Macroeconomic Management When Everybody Loves You," *World Development* 20 (1992): 1587–92.

14. Jeffrey Herbst, "The Structural Adjustment of Politics in Africa," *World Development* 18 (1990): 949–58.

15. Pierre Pradervand, *Listening to Africa: Developing Africa from the Grassroots* (New York: Praeger, 1989).

16. John Nellis, *Public Enterprises in Sub-Saharan Africa*, Staff Discussion Paper 1 (Washington, D.C.: World Bank, 1986).

17. Elliot Berg and Mary Shirley, *Divestiture in Developing Countries*, Staff Discussion Paper 199 (Washington, D.C.: World Bank, 1987).

18. Robert A. Barad, "Privatization of State-Owned Enterprises: The Togolese Experience," in *State Enterprise in Africa*, ed. Barbara Grosh and Rwekaza Mukandala (Boulder, Colo.: Lynne Rienner, forthcoming).

19. Barbara Grosh, *Public Enterprise in Kenya: What Works, What Doesn't, and Why* (Boulder, Colo.: Lynne Rienner, 1991).

20. Phillip Steffan, "The Structural Transformation of OPAM, Cereals Marketing Agency," in Grosh and Mukandala, eds., *State Enterprise in Africa*.

21. Berg and Shirley, *Divestiture in Developing Countries*.

22. Ibid.

23. Ernest J. Wilson III, "The Political Economy of Economic Reform in the Côte d'Ivoire: A Micro-Level Study of Three Privatization Transactions," in Grosh and Mukandala, eds., *State Enterprise in Africa*.

24. Nicolas van de Walle, "The Politics of Public Enterprise Reform in Cameroon," in Grosh and Makandala, eds., *State Enterprise in Africa*.

25. World Bank, *Sub-Saharan Africa: From Crisis to Sustainable Growth: A Long-Term Perspective Study* (Washington, D.C.: World Bank, (1989), 68; Randall P. Ellis and Bermano M. Mwabu, "The Demand for Outpatient Medical Care in Rural Kenya," 1991, typescript.

26. Grosh, *Public Enterprise in Kenya*.

27. Mary Shirley, *The Reform of State-Owned Enterprises: Lessons from World Bank Lending*, Policy and Research Series 4 (Washington, D.C.: World Bank, 1989); and Kwame Ninsin, "The PNDC and the Problem of Legitimacy," in Rothchild, ed., *Ghana: The Political Economy of Recovery*.

28. Quoted in ibid., 61.

29. Steen Jorgensen, Margaret Grosh, and Mark Schacter, *Bolivia's Answer to Poverty, Economic Crisis, and Adjustment: The Emergency Social Fund*. Regional and Sectoral Studies 9 (Washington, D.C.: World Bank, 1992).

PART 2

CASE STUDIES

JENNIFER A. WIDNER

Three ◈ Political Reform in Anglophone and Francophone African Countries

The regime transformations in sub-Saharan Africa, 1982–92, took place in two distinct waves, or clusters. The first transformations early in this period were often ushered in by national conferences and usually happened in Francophone countries. The second wave took place over the persistent objections or resistance of incumbent heads of state. Domestic demands for political change existed before the changes in Eastern Europe and before the flirtation of donor agencies with political conditionality. Although international aid flows and overseas public opinion influenced the liberalization process, particularly in Zambia and Kenya; domestic pressure triggered the reforms.

Why did some countries acquiesce quickly to demands for reform while others held out? At first glance, there are no clear correlations between reform and standard measures of economic composition or condition. Countries similar in resource endowment, in dependence on export agriculture, and in economic policies and performance show different political tendencies. There is also no association between political liberalization and such standard economic variables as GDP growth, per capita food production, government spending as a proportion of GDP, defense expenditure as a proportion of government spending, development assistance as a proportion of GDP, inflation rates, and proportion of the labor force engaged in agriculture. Further, there is no distinction between countries whose economies experienced windfalls—oil or metal profits or foreign aid—and those that depended heavily on taxation of small-scale farming for revenues. Thus revenue base has no effect on political reform in sub-Saharan Africa, contrary to many explanations of regime change in Middle Eastern countries.

To account for the national conference phenomenon, so early and so widespread in Francophone countries and so rare in Anglophone countries, some scholars offer a version of contagion theory. For example, Pearl Robinson argues that close relationships between French and African political actors and intellectuals provided opposition leaders with a common cultural referent: the bicentennial of the French Revolution in 1989 and the metaphor of the *états-généraux* of 1789, at which the Third Estate appointed itself the National Assembly, replacing the monarchy. Linked not only by this common referent but also by a shared exposure to the short-wave radio broadcasts of Radio France Internationale and print media such as *Jeune Afrique,* political dissidents learned from one another.[1]

Although a compelling explanation, especially for the choice of vocabulary of the national conferences, this hypothesis does not account for important aspects of the observed political changes. Not all of the Francophone countries where political liberalization took place held national conferences, even though they legalized opposition parties during the first wave of change. In Côte d'Ivoire, for instance, there was no such assembly, and the language of the French revolution and the estates-general was little in evidence among either incumbent politicians or opposition groups. The leader of Burkina Faso also rejected calls for a conference. Further, although shifts in French aid policy to favor greater political openness is often credited with triggering change, French policy lagged behind actual events and so could not have shaped the initial patterns of political liberalization.[2] Finally, although arguably less strongly tied to a metropolitan intellectual community (certainly the Magna Carta and the American Revolution figured less strongly in political rhetoric), opposition groups and incumbent politicians in Anglophone countries had similar access to news media. They, too, heard about the changes taking place in Eastern Europe and other parts of Africa. *West Africa, Africa Events,* and *New African* reached English-speaking readers of roughly the same social groups as those to which French readers skimming the pages of *Jeune Afrique* belonged. The contagion theory does not work.

This chapter offers an interpretation of these patterns on two levels. At one level, it suggests that, behind the general indicators, four independent variables distinguish the countries in the first and second waves. The first variable is the change in rent-seeking opportunities forced by economic reform; in some instances, recovery programs pushed political elites to oppose incumbents in order to protect their own sources of income. The prior distribution of rents significantly influenced the political behavior of elites during adjustment. The second variable is whether a segment of the political elite or the popular classes controlled economic "gatekeeping" positions with significant countervailing power. Where elites could not command an economically significant sector, they could not force authoritarian governments to reform. The capacity to muster countervailing power varied with the structure of parallel associations (whether corporatist or decentralized). Where producers' groups were independent of government but fragmented, general strikes were difficult to organize. Third, the electoral rules of single-party states affected the linkages between the urban elites and the grass roots. These linkages, when present, reduced the opposition's cost of campaigning and increased the incumbent's risk in liberalizing. The fourth variable is the extent of the incumbent's control of critical electoral resources.

At a second level, this chapter suggests that, whether a country has an Anglophone or a Francophone heritage has affected (1) the way rents are distributed in the polity, (2) the organization of parallel associations, (3) the use of single-party list voting or multicandidate elections and the consequent extent and character of elite bases of support among urban and rural grassroots, and (4) the degree of central control over critical electoral resources, such as radio, print, and television. Thus, the Anglophone-Francophone distinction is a proxy for a cluster of variables that affected regime change. Although common economic and demographic pressures have helped create patrimonial regimes out of the parliamentary systems in place at independence, there are important variations in institutions among them that influence patterns of regime change. The distinctive Francophone and Anglophone patterns of political reform, based on the political structures and traditions that the colonial powers put in place, may also have affected the sustainability of liberalization under new multiparty governments.

The chapter is divided into three parts. It begins with a brief theoretical discussion that introduces the four variables in greater detail. It then considers the paths of political change in two comparable countries: Côte d'Ivoire, which liberalized in May 1990, and Kenya, which did not liberalize until November 1991. This section examines the significance of the four variables in understanding the divergent paths taken in these two countries otherwise so comparable in economic base, openness to international investment, and cultural heterogeneity. The third section probes the fit between the hypotheses and patterns of regime change in sub-Saharan Africa, generally. The concluding section observes that the institutional differences in Francophone Africa may render reform more rapid but less sustainable than in Anglophone Africa, where it is likely to come more slowly and perhaps with greater violence but where the bases for multiparty competition may be stronger.

Institutions and Paths of Political Change

From the late 1970s until the late 1980s, much of the literature on African politics focused on the rise of patrimonial rule and posited the emergence of relatively undifferentiated neopatrimonial systems. Crawford Young's seminal study, *Ideology and Development in Africa*, found little association between the rhetoric of rulers or the governments they installed and policy outcomes. Other political scientists took this finding to mean that the economic and demographic conditions particular to Africa gave rise to similar patterns of political behavior, regardless of the structure of governing institutions. With a few exceptions, such as the studies of Zaire by Thomas Callaghy, Michael Schatzberg, Crawford Young, and Thomas Turner, political scientists focused on explaining the apparent similarities between these new political systems, whatever their ideological tone or colonial heritage. Following Robert Jackson and Carl Rosberg, scholars have produced numerous studies of personal rule, patrimonialism, and neopatrimonialism.[3]

Although many of the insights generated by this literature advance our understanding of political change in Africa, the contributions on the whole overstate the degree of homogeneity. In particular, they overlook the long-term institutional legacies of colonial rule. Colonial experiences figure in analyses of contemporary African politics mainly through the patterns of elite recruitment they inspire or through the way African countries are incorporated into world markets. In contrast, this chapter advances the claim that the continent's differing colonialisms created institutional legacies that are apparent in patterns of regime change.

Distribution of Rents and Preference for Commodity Stabilization

In general terms, but with local variations, Francophone and Anglophone countries have differed in the way their polities distribute

rents. Major rent-seeking opportunities are created by the use of tariffs, credit rationing, foreign exchange rationing, domestic monopolies, and monopsonies.[4] There were broad differences in the way
Anglophone and Francophone countries used these policy tools and
organizations in managing their economies during the period 1960–
90. The supranational currency boards of the colonial era survived in
most of Francophone Africa, for a long time limiting the overvaluation
of currencies and the deficit financing of government.[5] Membership
in the CFA franc zone created an external agency of restraint and
constrained the rent-seeking opportunities available to the elites of
these countries. In Anglophone Africa, equivalent boards did not
survive the independence period, and governments faced less powerful budgetary restraints. The consequence was that "budget deficits
created excess demand for imports: this was restrained by import
controls. Import controls shifted the problem from the balance of
payments to inflation: this was restrained by price controls."[6]

Elites of Anglophone countries thus had different rent-seeking
opportunities available to them. Rents from public enterprises,
for example, offered a comparatively more important source of income
for elites in Francophone Africa than they did in many Anglophone
countries, where the relatively greater reliance on tariffs, licenses,
and credit rationing provided additional opportunities. In Francophone Africa competition among elites for rents centered more on
public enterprises, than in Anglophone Africa. When international
donors conditioned their loans on reductions in the number of public
enterprises and public sector employees or wage bills, Francophone
elites felt the differences in their incomes and options more severely
than did their Anglophone counterparts. Unable to engage in deficit
financing as easily as their Anglophone neighbors, the "pays d'expression française" either fired public employees or stopped their paychecks. In Anglophone countries, governments simply allowed inflation to reduce the wage bill.

Further, between 1960 and 1990, these countries differed with regard to the use of centralized commodity price stabilization schemes
versus systems that pass fluctuations in prices on to farmers. As a
general rule (to which there are exceptions), Francophone countries
favored stabilization schemes that paid farmers stable prices for their
harvests, using savings from boom years to subsidize producer prices
when international prices drop. Indeed, in the late 1940s and 1950s
French officials were often the moving force behind the creation of
these boards, and French farmers in the metropolitan country made
stabilization a focal point for their demands in the midtwentieth century. A higher proportion of the Anglophone countries favored sys-

tems that passed some risk to farmers, in most cases offering variable premiums above a floor payment.

Interest Group Organization

Few governments in either Anglophone or Francophone countries tolerated much independent formal associational life or interest group organization. Nonetheless, many of the Anglophone countries did tolerate employers' unions, farmers' unions, and other semiautonomous groupings, usually on a regional-, crop-, or industry-specific basis. In most cases, these groups remained outside of the ruling party and had no formal representation in government decisionmaking.

By contrast, and consistent with the organizational style of the colonial power, Francophone countries tended to use corporatist structures for interest representation. That is, producer organizations were part of a centralized system of peak associations, which approximated representational monopolies.[7] Pearl Robinson calls these systems "neotraditional corporatism," which she defines as "interest-representation organized by the state and held in check by participatory structures [created by governors]."[8] Interests were organized through syndicates, often with government subsidy or sponsorship, and met with decisionmakers at intervals and in forums designed for that purpose. These were highly centralized systems of representation, often tied to membership in the ruling party. Drawing on data that appeared in *Africa South of the Sahara*, a yearbook for the African region, the research reflected in this chapter found that the numbers of producers' associations in 1988 differed between Anglophone and Francophone countries. Of Anglophone countries, Ghana had twenty-five; Kenya, seventeen; Nigeria, twenty-five; Sierra Leone, seventeen; Zambia, twenty-five; and Zimbabwe, fifty-eight. Of Francophone countries, only Côte d'Ivoire, with twelve, and Burkina Faso, with nine, had more than seven such groups; many had only one.

The corporatist structure of interest representation in Francophone Africa reduced the kinds of collective action problems that interest groups typically encounter, while increasing their vulnerability to government control. Their hierarchical structures may have limited their propensity to free ride and therefore increased the odds of a general strike or other organized action. The national membership of these organizations also granted them a greater ability to paralyze an economic sector or service and conferred greater bargaining leverage in negotiations with governments. Their corporatist structure made them easier targets for government surveillance, however, and their dependence on government-granted access to policy and sometimes to public funds rendered them fiefdoms of patrons, themselves allies of rulers. Thus, where parallel associations had this character, interests could organize quickly to make their views known, but they were, similarly, less resilient when they met with official displeasure. Further, because of their centralized structure, they could be brought into a transition process like a national conference with greater ease and speed than is possible when unions and interest groups are highly fragmented.

Electoral Rules and Opposition Bases of Support

Prior to the recent period of regime change, most sub-Saharan African countries were de facto or de jure single-party systems. Electoral rules in Anglophone countries supported multicandidate, single-party elections in single-member districts. In Francophone Africa, where elections took place they usually did so according to a system of single-party list voting. Party list voting in a single-party system meant that the name of only one candidate appeared on the ballot in legislative elections. Usually, competition for party office was also limited.

Each system had distinct consequences for the bases of support that political elites built. In Anglophone Africa, machine politics tended to flourish at the grass roots level. To secure election against other aspirants, a candidate had to convince voters that he or she could deliver more to the local community—usually water projects, cattle dips, new schools, and so on. Candidates who set themselves up as patrons fared better than those who made broad class or populist appeals.[9] In Francophone Africa, the incentives and outcomes were quite different. Single-party list voting, where the selection of party candidate is not open to popular choice, provides little motivation for politicians to cultivate support among voters and to make legislators or party officials responsive to local interests or to the demands of an interest group, other than those of the bureaucratic class of which they are members. Indeed, these rules lead politicians to invest in support from party elites, which eventually divides the party leadership from the masses.

As a result of this difference, the linkage between politicians and constituents in Francophone Africa was much less than that in Anglophone Africa. More important, the grass roots networks so vital for conducting campaigns existed in many parts of Anglophone Africa but were poorly developed in Francophone Africa.[10] The existence of such networks and a lively tradition of drumming up campaign support at the local level lowered the costs of a serious electoral battle to the challenger and thereby increased the incumbent's risk of losing office. On these grounds, then, one might reasonably expect that leaders of Anglophone countries would be much less willing than leaders of Francophone countries to pursue a transition to a multiparty system.

Central Control over Critical Electoral Resources

Until 1989, Anglophone and Francophone countries differed in the degree of central control over such electoral resources as building licenses, telephone permits, zoning variances, and printing presses. These resources are all important to opposition leaders in waging electoral campaigns. They were much more vulnerable to intervention by the chiefs of state of Francophone countries than by those of Anglophone countries, although certainly having a few well-placed clients in local government could have disrupted provision of these services in Anglophone Africa as well.

More important, central government control of the media tended to be somewhat greater in Francophone Africa than in Anglophone Africa. Television, in both areas, was predominantly a central government operation, and few opposition leaders used it effectively as a medium of communication. A higher proportion of Anglophone governments tolerated multiple newspapers than did Francophone governments. In 1988, the reluctant liberalizers of Anglophone Africa included Ghana, with twenty-eight newspapers (including government owned) and weeklies; Kenya, with sixteen; Malawi, with eight; Nigeria, with sixty-four; Sierra Leone, with nine; Zambia, with fifteen; and Zimbabwe, with thirty-three.[11] By contrast, media control was much more concentrated in the Francophone countries: Benin had only five newspapers, Central African Republic had four, Congo had nine, Côte d'Ivoire had six, Gabon had eight, Guinea had six, Mali had eight, Mauritania had three, Niger had three, and Togo had six.[12] Although most of the independent newspapers displayed substantial self-censorship, they did provide some competition for government and party dailies and could occasionally voice points of view at odds with those of the head of state. Again, this difference may well have appeared to reduce the campaign costs of opposition leaders and to increase the risk to the incumbent, making Anglophone heads of state more wary of political reform than their Francophone counterparts. After the initial wave of liberalization, between 1989 and 1991, these differences disappeared, however. Greater press freedom in both Anglophone and Francophone countries resulted in a proliferation of weeklies and dailies across the continent.

Kenya and Côte d'Ivoire as Paradigmatic Cases

The broad analytic approach used in this chapter borrows the notion of path dependence from Douglass North's work on institutions and institutional change in the economic sphere. North suggests that "once a developmental path is set on a particular course, the network externalities, the learning process of organizations, and the historically derived subjective modeling of the issues reinforce the course."[13] That is not to say that profound changes and dramatic shifts cannot occur in the structure of an economy or a polity. Rather, it means that history matters—and matters in specific ways. To North, the effect of institutions on transaction costs is the source of path dependence. This logic is useful in understanding regime change in Africa.

I use North's theoretical framework to show the puzzling, if possibly temporary, divergence of political paths between two countries quite similar in economic base and colonial and immediate postcolonial history: Côte d'Ivoire and Kenya. During the 1960s and 1970s, a combination of smallholder and plantation agriculture fueled economic growth in both countries and generated significant foreign exchange earnings. Moreover, both were subject to similar changes in terms of trade; that is, both produced beverage crops (cocoa and coffee in Côte d'Ivoire and coffee and tea in Kenya), and neither had significant exploitable petroleum reserves. Their governments pursued interventionist economic politics, but both adhered to policies and practices substantially more market conforming than those of most other countries of sub-Saharan Africa, and both allowed significant latitude to local private sector entrepreneurs and foreign investors. During about twenty years of fairly steady growth, they built extensive road systems and infrastructure, more than on most of the rest of the continent. Between 1965 and the late 1970s, under the leadership of Jomo Kenyatta in Kenya and Félix Houphouët-Boigny in Côte d'Ivoire, citizens of the two countries were governed by single parties that were comparatively weak as vehicles for aggregating and channeling interests and as instruments of control. Power resided in the head of state and in an increasingly technocratic administration. Political suppression of opposition groups and critics were lower than in neighboring countries. Finally, both countries were demographically diverse, with no single cultural community accounting for more than 20 percent of the population. For many years, the policy world recognized Côte d'Ivoire and Kenya as the success stories of Africa.

Beginning in 1980, the two countries took quite different political paths, highlighted by the first multiparty legislative and presidential elections in Côte d'Ivoire's history (November–December 1990), on the one hand, and the repeated jailing of opposition figures and the rejection of demands for political reform by the government of Daniel arap Moi in Kenya, on the other. At independence, Côte d'Ivoire had a single-party system, in which President Félix Houphouët-Boigny retained effective power over policy, while the Parti Démocratique de la Côte d'Ivoire (PDCI), the sole legal political party, a loose association of political elites, had few functions except as facilitator of intraelite bargaining. A system of party list voting, in place until 1980, meant that PDCI officers effectively selected the *députés* from each electoral *circumscription*. Only in 1980 did the government sanction multicandidate single-party competition, with elections in 1980 and 1985. At the end of April 1990, after the onset of a severe economic crisis that rendered many of the country's banks illiquid and forced cuts in government wage bills—and in the wake of street disturbances—the president announced the move to a multiparty system. Legislative and presidential elections took place in November and December 1990, respectively, only a few months after opposition political parties were allowed to form.

Kenya started with a multiparty system at independence. Through a series of maneuvers, the Kenya African National Union (KANU) became, under Kenyatta, the dominant party, with functions similar to that of PDCI. As Houphouët-Boigny did in Côte d'Ivoire, Kenyatta resisted efforts to make the political party a forum for creating a political platform or for generating policy proposals, although he tolerated the effective expulsion of the populist faction within KANU. After Kenyatta's death and Daniel arap Moi's accession to the presidency in 1978, the regime curtailed political participation by stages. Ethnic welfare societies, the springboards to political careers and vehicles for constituency building, became illegal in 1980. In 1982, the Moi government won rapid passage of a change in the constitution, making Kenya a de jure single-party state. In 1985, the office of the president moved to strengthen the watchdog role of KANU and to eliminate potential opposition both through intervention in the selection of senior party officials and through replacement of the secret ballot with a queuing system. Detentions of public defenders and opposition leaders and killings and arrests of demonstrators followed, accompanied by resolute statements that Kenya would not liberalize. Only under overwhelming pressure from donors at the end of November 1991, including an agreement to suspend further international assistance to the country, did the Moi government finally agree to legalize opposition political parties. The president and his party used their privileged access to state resources to ensure electoral success in 1992.

Any theory that attempts to explain the patterns of political liberalization that developed between the last quarter of 1989 and the last quarter of 1992 in Africa must shed light on the divergent paths in these two cases. Certainly, further political change is likely in Kenya, as is a period of intensified civil strife in Côte d'Ivoire. A solid theory must account for the initial variation in outcomes, however. The important, if transitory, differences between the cases are rooted in more than the acumen or style of the respective leaders; the way the institutional legacies of the colonial period shaped the perceived costs and risks to incumbents is critically important.

The two countries differed in three key respects.[14] First, they differed in the favor given different systems for distributing the effects of commodity price shocks and for allocating rents. The strong preference of the top Ivorian leadership for central control provoked, in different ways, two important threats to the economic status of elites. The decision to stabilize commodity prices on behalf of farmers, managing revenues through a special *caisse* in Abidjan instead of indexing producer prices and allowing farmers to bear at least part of the burden of changing terms of trade, precipitated an economic crisis of unprecedented proportion. Likewise, the decision to restructure public enterprises, in part to recentralize control over patronage resources, set in motion a series of layoffs, pay cuts, and reductions in rent-seeking opportunities that severely affected elite incomes. Although the Houphouët-Boigny government also launched new public enterprises, the initial restructuring nonetheless reduced and made more uncertain the incomes of many politicians and civil servants.

Second, the organization of a few critical sectors of the economy into centralized syndicates made the Ivorian government initially more vulnerable to countervailing power than did the more decentralized structure of Kenyan civil society, the unity of whose producers was more easily shattered. Third, the centralization of control in Côte d'Ivoire over critical electoral resources, including the media, may have lessened the threat of defeat of the president at the ballot box, making tentative steps toward reform possible.

Elite Incomes, Rents, and Reform Movements

Because the base of political opposition in both Côte d'Ivoire and Kenya is largely elite, any analysis of the differences between cases must pay attention to changes in the economic or political status at the end of the 1980s of what Irving Leonard Markovitz calls "the

organizational bourgeoisie."[15] In both countries, the boundaries between the political elite and the business elite are indistinct.[16] Prominent businessmen often accumulate capital for their enterprises by
first working in the civil service or gain entrée to the private sector
by holding positions on the boards of public corporations. The households of civil servants, politicians, and well-to-do businessmen usually
receive income from several sources. Elite incomes in Côte d'Ivoire
declined for two reasons. First, the effects of changes in the terms of
trade for primary commodities were intensified by the marketing and
price stabilization systems. Second, structural adjustment reforms reduced the income elites and civil servants received from the public
sector portion of their portfolios, in the form of salaries and rents,
and their standards of living came under threat, triggering disgrun-
tlement and political action. An exact measurement of these effects
is difficult, but it is possible to gauge rough differences in magnitude.

Stabilization Schemes and Elite Incomes   The terms of trade for beverage
crops such as coffee, cocoa, and tea—which lie at the heart of the
export sectors of the Ivorian and Kenyan economies—turned against
producers in the 1980s. However, the structures in place for accom-
modating commodity price fluctuations determined how severely
these changes affected elite incomes in each country; Ivorians endured
more dramatic reversals of fortune than Kenyans.

Although the declining price of cocoa on world markets affected
Côte d'Ivoire in the early 1980s, it was not until 1987 that crisis struck.
The Ivorian government and its colonial predecessor had stabilized
the prices of coffee and cocoa, offering farmers a predictable, stable
real producer price by taxing producers more heavily when prices
were high and using these proceeds to support future subsidies. This
system was the undoing of the Ivorian elite, in two respects. First, it
proved extremely difficult to sequester the funds collected during
periods when world prices were high; some well-connected *fonction-
naires*, politicians, and businessmen benefited, but many others lost.
During the 1970s, the government borrowed heavily from the stabilization fund to finance investments in the north of the country, mainly
in sugar refineries, which promised no economic return, because sugar
was then in international oversupply. Overbilling became such a problem that the president eventually removed the three ministers most
directly involved and launched a public campaign against corruption.
Although the country's cocoa farmers were the principal long-run
losers (their earnings had financed the projects), the economic effects
of squandered investment funds also hurt those who derived their
incomes from other activities.

Second, the 1980s saw a prolonged deterioration in the price of cocoa, as new suppliers came into the market. In the late 1980s, the government subsidized farmers at a rate of one dollar per kilogram of cocoa beans, borrowing to do so. It then withheld cocoa from the world market to force the price of cocoa to rise (with a nearly one-third market share, the country was not necessarily a price taker). Traders who had financed their purchase of the crop from the farmers with funds they had borrowed privately in anticipation of government reimbursement (as was the norm) found they could not repay their loans on time. The collapse of several Ivorian banks followed and produced a liquidity crisis in several banks with French connections.

In the crisis, elites thus lost money both directly, as growers, transporters, and exporters of cocoa, and indirectly, through the liquidity crisis in the banking system, on which they depended for business loans and operations. Many were unable to withdraw funds from bank deposits during this period. Further, the president's personal funds, from which he might have dispensed largesse, had dwindled because of the expenses incurred in constructing Notre Dame de la Paix, the Florentine basilica constructed at Yamoussoukro, Houphouët-Boigny's birthplace. There were few patronage resources left in the late 1980s to ease the effects of the collapse of cocoa.

The economic crises of the 1980s did not affect Kenya in quite the same way as it did Côte d'Ivoire. Kenya had eschewed a commodity stabilization system that fully buffered farmers from the effects of world market fluctuations. Instead, it had instituted a pass-through system, in which farmers shared in the variation in prices. Farmers received a stable base price; the actual producer price then provided farmers, in addition, a portion of the world price. When world market prices dropped, so did the indexable portion of the producer price. When prices rose, farmers shared the windfall. Under this system, surpluses in large part accrued to farming households, not to a central government-managed fund where the government could have borrowed against them.[17] This system for administering producer prices, combined with a hesitance to manipulate world prices through cartelization and differences in trade financing systems, meant that changes in the terms of trade had a less negative impact on elite incomes in Kenya than they did in Côte d'Ivoire.

Restructured Public Enterprises and Elite Incomes   As structural adjustment programs went into effect, governments came under pressure to reduce the public sector wage bill either through reductions in wage rates or through layoffs and hiring freezes. During the early part of the 1980s, Côte d'Ivoire's government expenditure on wages and salaries averaged about 26 percent of total expenditure.[18] In 1984, Houphouët-Boigny announced sharp pay cuts for parastatal employees—in some cases by as much as two-thirds—to bring their salaries in line with those of the civil service.[19] Jean-Pierre Lachaud estimates that, for slightly over 25 percent of parastatal employees, base salaries diminished, and for about 13 percent, salary reductions were more than 50 percent.[20] In 1980 in Côte d'Ivoire, wages were 36 percent higher in the private sector than in the public sector.[21] Civil service salaries were frozen between 1984 and 1986 and rose only slightly after that time, until further freezes and a substantial new income tax came under discussion in 1990. The government cut benefits as well, reducing housing allowances and selling over a third of the fleet of official cars, even those allotted to senior elites and long-time allies of the president.[22] These actions, coupled with an announcement of a 30 percent income tax on employees of public and private organizations and of a possible 20–25 percent reduction in teachers' salaries and benefits, provoked university students, civil servants, and teachers in 1990 to join street demonstrations in Abidjan. In 1991, a worried government merely froze compensation levels in consequence.

Côte d'Ivoire also restructured the parastatal sector, eliminating employees from some enterprises and liquidating or privatizing whole organizations. The program began in 1980, at the same time as the country's first steps toward political liberalization, and was quickly recognized as more than just window dressing, although the actual extent of some of the changes remains in dispute.[23] In 1979, 43 parastatals were totally public, in 52 others the government was principal shareholder, and in 110 the government maintained a financial interest but did not hold controlling shares. The World Bank estimates that, between 1983 and 1987, the government privatized (sold its shares in) 14 enterprises and liquidated (sold the assets of) 24 others.[24] During the same period, the government also created a few new enterprises, however. In 1992, the estimate of the number of parastatals, of one type or another, was 150.

One consequence of these changes was to eliminate some employees from the payroll, reducing household incomes of elites. Lachaud estimates that, between 1980 and 1984, 10,679 people lost their jobs in the public enterprise sector—roughly 10.5 percent of all employees in the sector. The general unemployment rate in Abidjan tripled, rising from 7.7 percent in 1980 to 22.8 percent in 1986.[25] After 1985, however, the public enterprise sector began to increase its share in total formal sector employment, rising to about 37.4 percent in the late 1980s.[26]

A more important political consequence was the reduction of rent-seeking opportunities for members of the political elite. Patronage was tightly controlled by the president during the 1960s and into the very early 1970s. Expansion of the parastatal sector, however, provided new ways to create clientelistic relationships, including not only relatively high-paying jobs but also the ability to collect rents through manipulation of quotas, licenses, access to credit, and so on. Initially, Houphouët-Boigny dispensed positions in the sector both to technocrats and to *anciens*, those who had helped in the preindependence period, especially to keep the latter in the political fold at a time when the party and ministerial posts were opening to a younger generation or a "development faction." The senior elites used the opportunity to build support networks of their own, however.[27] For example, in a celebrated case, the mayor of Abidjan manipulated a program to house civil servants by purchasing or renting buildings owned by other elites at above-market rates. One of the domestic rationales for restructuring the sector in the 1980s and for the accompanying attack on corruption was to contain the power of the new barons who had taken advantage of the president's largesse. The restructuring forced a number of key political elites, including the mayor, to stand trial and to pay considerable sums of money.

Accurate measures of the reduction in elites' incomes due to these reforms are difficult to calculate. Mark Gallagher offers an index with four components: (1) the value added by manufacturing multiplied by the effective tariff; (2) the effects of price distortions, measured by the nominal protection coefficient multiplied by the value of agricultural exports, (3) the difference between black market rate and the official rates of exchange multiplied by exports in U.S. dollars (as a measure of rents available from foreign exchange allocations), and (4) the below-zero real interest rate multiplied by domestic credit (to measure nonmarket allocation of capital).[28] For lack of complete data, Gallagher does not calculate rents before and after the policy reforms of the 1980s. Foreign exchange rents, resulting from the overvaluation of the CFA franc, increased through much of the period, as did manufacturing rents resulting from tariff protection. The latter dropped significantly in 1990–91, however, as radical reductions in tariff protection took place.

Elite incomes fared better in Kenya than in Côte d'Ivoire. Throughout the 1980s, Kenya typically spent roughly the same proportion of its total expenditure on wages and salaries as Côte d'Ivoire, but it expanded public spending at the same time, incurring large deficits and generating a 25 percent average annual inflation rate. Wage employment in the public sector increased during the 1985–90 period, with the number of people employed in the central government rising from 252,000 to 269,000; in parastatals, from 241,000 to 317,700; and in enterprises in which the state held controlling shares, from 35,600 to 54,700. Unlike Côte d'Ivoire, however, the Kenyan government did not seek to reduce nominal wages but allowed inflation to take its toll, diminishing wages in real terms. During the 1990–91 period, overall government expenditure increased.[29]

Kenyan elites also did not suffer a reduction in rent-seeking opportunities through parastatal reform. The failure of the Kenyan government to follow through on its promised reforms of the public sector contrasts with the Ivorian case. Between 1980 and 1990, the Moi government began negotiations for the privatization of one parastatal but added eight new public enterprises, including the Nyayo Bus Services and Nyayo Tea Zones. In the period under study here, it created yet another enterprise—to produce automobiles with high domestic content—and called for a rural development parastatal. Trade liberalization lessened the protection afforded the public sector and reduced the rents available there, but these efforts stopped short of what was promised.

Countervailing Power and Parallel Associations

Another key respect in which Côte d'Ivoire and Kenya differed was in the structure of parallel associations. Interest group organization in Côte d'Ivoire took place largely through national syndicates, whose leaders the president consulted in occasional "days of dialogue." In Kenya, interest group organization was less centralized, more independent of government, and often more vocal, except in the case of formal sector wage labor, which the government had sought to co-opt during the Kenyatta era. Ironically, although there were more parallel producers' associations in Kenya than in Côte d'Ivoire— and, in some respects the country had a livelier associational life— the character of interest group organization made collective action at once more difficult and more threatening to the incumbents in the short run. The degree to which opposition leaders in the two countries could draw upon the bargaining power of dissatisfied producers' groups differed, as did the ease of sustaining pressure for change.

Although students and teachers were perhaps the most visible participants in political demonstrations in Côte d'Ivoire, their actions were preceded by that of the country's transporters. Transport was the economic sector typically both more independent of government than other sectors and more vital to the continuation of trade. In

Africa, it was one of the few potential sources of countervailing power. Myriad entrepreneurs equipped small pickups with a few seats to convey passengers or developed small cargo transport services. In some cases, members of the organizational bourgeoisie (administrative elite) invested in this sector, too, developing small trucking businesses or long-distance bus services. Without these enterprises, trade would have slowed considerably, and most important, food would not have reached urban areas. Where this sector remained substantially in private hands, transporters could amass considerable bargaining leverage vis-à-vis the central government.

In Côte d'Ivoire, road transportation was substantially a private sector industry—and a deconcentrated industry at that. The Société des Transporteurs Abidjanais (SOTRA), the capital city's bus system, was a public enterprise, owned 60 percent by the government in combination with Renault. Most of the other bus systems, taxis, and transport companies were privately held, often by entrepreneurs owning one to seven vehicles. These owners belonged to a syndicate, which reduced collective action costs by assuming organizational functions. Transporters have long participated in the president's periodic days of dialogue. As economic conditions deteriorated during the late 1980s, transporters sought to defend their interests outside of this forum. In early 1990, truckers and taxi drivers went on strike to oppose the many road blocks manned by the military, customs, and police. At the road blocks, which proliferated during the 1980s, drivers and passengers often had to pay bribes in order to continue along their routes. They might have to stop every five to ten minutes along heavily traveled roads, which significantly increased the cost of transportation. The strike was successful, and by the end of June—two months after the protest—the number of roadblocks was dramatically reduced. Further, the government pulled the army off the streets, where it had been posted to maintain public security.

In the Ivorian case, the teachers' syndicate held comparable countervailing power, but other groups were more subject to government control. Farmers' unions were illegal until mid-1991, and growers were unable to bring direct pressure to bear on policymakers. They could exercise indirect influence through *groupes de ressortissants*, or urban-based relatives, whose members could more easily push their demands in appropriate ministries and advance claims during the days of dialogue. As long as world prices for major export commodities remained low, the bargaining power that attached to crop burning or crop holdups was limited, however. Withholding food crops promised to send a more powerful message, but the many small producers heavily dependent on such cash staples as manioc and yams provided a poor base for concerted political action. Teachers were well organized, by contrast, and could call out their students to support street demonstrations. Teachers and transporters, along with students, brought Houphouët-Boigny's government to account and prompted a shift to a competitive party system.

Kenyan elites had less short-run bargaining power (although they may have posed a more credible long-run threat) than their Ivorian counterparts. Their greater numbers and the absence, in most cases, of centralized, panterritorial organizations, made mobilization against policies or incumbent politicians difficult. The higher costs of organizing producers meant that, initially, it was difficult to stage a general strike or to stop operations in a critical sector of the economy. The general strike was more often a phenomenon of the Francophone than the Anglophone countries during the early part of the period of regime change.

Although public protests against the government in Kenya were frequent, they did not demonstrate significant countervailing power, except when the business community got the legal profession and the churches to draw international attention to their plight. The transport sector, however, demonstrated on several occasions, before KANU and the president took steps to counteract its power. In 1986, the government announced that it would enforce a No Standing rule against vehicles and drivers of the Kenya Bus Service, Ltd., a partly British-owned company and the principal provider of bus transportation between the capital and periurban areas. Typically, these buses carried as many passengers as could crowd in. The company responded to the ruling by briefly withdrawing bus service from the routes around Nairobi, stranding many thousands of government workers. So great were the disorder and the public outcry that the government relented, temporarily. Within three months, KANU began to run *nyayo* buses on many routes (*nyayo* is a Swahili word meaning "following in the footsteps" and was among the slogans of the Moi government). The *nyayo* vehicles were contributed by European donors, and the drivers were drawn from the National Youth Service, a government-run vocational training program. Moi took the decision to launch the service at a KANU parliamentary group meeting shortly after the initial protest. Two years later, in 1988, the Nyayo Bus Services Corporation was established as a public enterprise partly directed by the party.

The main alternative to bus transport was the *matatu* system, a relatively unregulated, low-cost form of travel in converted pickup trucks. This part of the sector proved to have strong bargaining power.

In 1990, the government moved against owners and drivers on suspicion that some were broadcasting seditious tapes to their passengers—protest songs about the razing of Nairobi shantytowns, Kenyatta's early speeches, and songs about such men as Kenneth Matiba, a wealthy businessman who had led a public bid for multiparty rule and had been detained, and J. M. Kariuki, a populist who was assassinated during Kenyatta's reign. Many of the tapes were played in advance of the multiparty demonstrations and riots of mid-1990. The president deregistered the offending vehicles and the Matatu Vehicle Owners Association, making it difficult for the sector to organize.

Growers of export crops were also organized in Kenya and had considerable bargaining power because of the government's heavy dependence on the revenues from these crops as a source of foreign exchange. These growers were possible advocates of multiparty government, because government-run agricultural services and pricing procedures had deteriorated in both fairness and quality. The Moi government defused the threat from farmers' unions by reorganizing or proscribing these groups. For example, it introduced the Nyayo Tea Zones, a new parastatal, which limited the bargaining power of Central Province tea farmers by flooding the tea factories with cheap leaves from new, government-controlled land, thus rendering smallholder's leaves less valuable. Similarly, Moi moved to take the direction of their coffee cooperatives away from Central Province farmers, who threatened opposition.

If interest group associations were less centrally organized in Kenya than in Côte d'Ivoire and, therefore, subject to more severe collective action problems, they nonetheless inspired sufficient fear in the president for him to take steps to weaken them further. Moi shifted access to rent-seeking opportunities to his supporters, especially Kalenjin backers, shattering the community of interests among the country's business and government leaders.[30] He also tried to establish central control over the women's movement by absorbing it into KANU and over the legal profession by interfering in the elections of the Law Society of Kenya. These measures made collective action by parallel associations, especially producers' groups, still more difficult.

Electoral Rules and Constituency Building

By limiting the government's ability to spread the costs of economic downturns and by providing or tolerating industrywide rather than enterprise-specific organization of unions and parallel associations—which by their very structure could command greater economic clout than small, voluntary associations—the Ivorian political regime was more vulnerable than its Kenyan counterpart. By the same token, however, it was much easier for Houphouët-Boigny to control the resources necessary to ensure his reelection and the maintenance of PDCI as an important political force. Political acumen played a role in his decision to liberalize, but so did central control over building permits, meeting permits, telephone service, printing presses, information systems, and so on. As long as he called elections early, before opposition groups could devise ways around the limitations the centralized political and social system imposed, Houphouët-Boigny could be fairly confident that we would carry the vote.

Until 1980, the electoral rules and party system of Côte d'Ivoire militated against the rise of politicians with strong local constituencies, because the constitution provided only for single-party list voting. PDCI leadership held the right to screen and appoint nominees for both party office and legislative seats. In this system, those who aspired to become *députés* to the National Assembly in Abidjan needed to curry favor not with the electorate but with the party hierarchy. That meant appealing first to the *secrétaires généraux*, the men and women who acted as links between the PDCI leadership (the party's Political Bureau) and the small party *comités* in the villages and urban *quartiers*, which replaced the official ethnic associations that ran local party affairs until 1972. In reality, however, members of the party's Political Bureau itself wielded ultimate nominating power, and ambitious candidates sought to establish ties directly with this elite, sometimes bypassing the local officers of PDCI.

Although political aspirants had to lobby hard for the leadership's backing, this system provided little incentive to cultivate support among voters and to make legislators or party officials responsive to the interests of farmers or entrepreneurs. Indeed, it promoted division between the party leadership and the masses. Although the electoral system changed in 1980, by the 1990 elections, few local political leaders had emerged with the kinds of clienteles or constituency bases that many of their Kenyan counterparts had developed.

The Kenyan situation was quite different. A longer history of multi-candidate local elections and of decentralized local development initiatives enabled some elites to gain broad regional constituencies and limited national followings. These Kenya politicians as a group were far more habituated to the demands of political competition, even though their actions were increasingly constrained by the regime. Many of those clearly outside the Moi camp—men such as Kenneth Matiba and Charles Rubia—commanded significant incomes and influence in both private and public sectors and could amass patronage independent of government coffers. Further, Kenyan politicians had sponsored *harambee,* or local self-help development projects, to persuade voters to lend their support. They invited senior members of the government to contribute and often found government monies to staff the schools and dispensaries that were constructed, at least in the early years. In Côte d'Ivoire, on the other hand, the distribution of finance for local projects and the control over patronage networks were tightly managed from the center. When Houphouët-Boigny observed what he considered excessive use of the spoils system—using party resources or public sector jobs and equipment for building followings—he usually relieved the would-be patron of major responsibilities. In consequence, by 1990 no political leader in PDCI or any opposition party commanded the public attention or the networks that Kenyan underground opposition leaders like Charles Rubia, Kenneth Matiba, Oginga Odinga, and Martin Shikuku had. When Philippe Yacé attempted to build such a network in the 1970s, the president limited his access to resources.

Further, during the extended period of multicandidate competition, senior Kenyan politicians learned to broker party platforms and broadly representative slates of candidates in order to win a majority of the party or popular vote. Former Vice President Mwai Kibaki (who launched his own political party when the government legalized opposition in late 1991) and others had direct experience of the process of forging compromises and cutting deals in order to win office. They engineered the victory of Daniel arap Moi in 1978, a fact of which the president was well aware when he resisted calls for a multiparty system. Their experience posed a threat.

Central Control over Campaign Resources

The two countries also differed in the organization of the media and other resources important for waging political campaigns, although high levels of censorship existed in both systems. Through its hold on government, PDCI controlled radio and television news, the two daily newspapers, *Fraternité Matin* and *Ivoire Soir,* and the weekly, *Fraternité-Hebdo.* These media carried little local political news or coverage of meetings attended by candidates. During the campaign, opposition leaders complained that they could secure coverage of their campaigns only in late-night television slots, when most people were asleep. In the end, they produced and circulated their own audio cassettes. New newspapers proliferated, but the manifestos of the new parties often appeared very late and in limited copies, because the government or PDCI officials controlled the printing presses.

Kenya had a livelier tradition of critical journalism. The government controlled the *Kenya Times*, the party newspaper, and could suspend publication of other magazines and newspapers when they overstepped government-prescribed limits. The existence of multiple newspapers, with independent, often foreign-based owners, meant that the editors of each had to differentiate their products from the others or lose a market. Although most were careful to avoid direct criticism of the president, they also competed to cover meetings at which politicians and senior civil servants were present. When the country's major publications engaged in self-censorship, transient broadsides often filled the breach, including photocopied Sunday sermons. Although vilified by some members of the opposition, the *Weekly Review*, edited by Hilary Ng'weno, offered much more coverage of issues and disagreements among key political figures than did *Fraternité-Hebdo*, its counterpart in Côte d'Ivoire. Ng'weno ventured occasional criticism of the president's policies, something Ivorian publications did not do prior to 1990.

The new presses that grew up in the two countries after the periods of political opening were also dramatically different. Abidjan's streets saw the sale of a new satirical genre and weeklies with political party backing, while Nairobi's residents could pick up substantial newsmagazines, such as *Society* or the *Nairobi Law Monthly*, independent of the political parties, whose pages carried extended exposés and discussions of political issues, grist for the development of political platforms.

There is substantial evidence that Houphouët-Boigny retained stronger control over the distribution of patronage than Moi. Houphouët-Boigny installed Antoine Cesario, an Antillese, to direct *grands travaux* (public works), which during the early 1980s approved all major expenditures. Although the president's control over resources may have attenuated slightly after Cesario (a man much hated by the Ivorian elite) left the country, the president nonetheless had significant knowledge of who had secured what resources and how. The skillful use of such resources during the brief campaign of 1990 is believed to have caused several key defectors to return to PDCI, including Lanciné Gon Coulibaly, son of a prominent political family in the north—the man the opposition coalition hoped would oust Konan Bédié, president of the National Assembly and the man who succeeded Houphouët-Boigny in 1993.[31] By contrast, and in a departure from the tradition established by his predecessor, Daniel arap Moi had lost control over such practices. Nicholas Biwott and other Kalenjin appointees skimmed an estimated 2 percent of the country's GDP. People in some parts of the opposition had independent access to funds. Again, the uncertainty about the resources that potential opponents could tap contributed to the president's unwillingness to engage in an electoral competition.

Summary

The differences between Côte d'Ivoire and Kenya have roots in the character of the institutional legacies of colonial rule in the two countries. There may be distinctively Francophone and Anglophone patterns of political reform, based on the political and economic structures the colonial powers put in place.

First, the strong preference of the top Ivorian leadership for central control provoked, in different ways, two important threats to the economic status of elites. The decision to stabilize commodity prices on behalf of farmers—managing revenues through a special *caisse* in Abidjan instead of indexing producer prices and thereby allowing farmers to bear at least part of the burden of changing terms of trade and to acquire a larger share of the surplus during booms—helped precipitate an economic crisis of unprecedented proportion. Likewise, the decision to initiate a restructuring of public enterprises, in part to recentralize control over patronage resources, caused layoffs, pay cuts, and less access to noncompetitive rents, which severely affected elite incomes.

Second, the organization of the critical sectors of the economy into centralized syndicates made the Ivorian government more vulnerable in the short run to countervailing power than did the more fragmented structure of Kenyan civil society.

Third, the electoral rules that prevailed in single-party Kenya spawned local political machines and networks, as well as skills, that reduced the costs of opposition campaign activity, increasing the risk that the incumbent might lose a multiparty contest. The electoral rules in effect in Côte d'Ivoire between 1960 and 1980 loosened the ties between elites and the grass roots and made the costs of opposition campaigns much higher.

Fourth, the centralization of control over critical electoral resources, including the media, lessened the threat of the president's defeat at the ballot box, making possible steps toward reform in Côte d'Ivoire, whereas in Kenya the international community helped force change.

Testing the Generalizations in a Larger Context

An argument of this chapter is that the patterns observed in the Côte d'Ivoire and Kenya comparison hold across a larger number of cases: that the 1990–92 pattern of regime change in countries with a Francophone institutional legacy differs systematically from the pattern in countries with an institutional legacy from Britain. Quantitative analysis is constrained by the numbers of cases and the quality and completeness of the available data. Because the p-values used to test significance of effects is greatly influenced by the number of cases, it is not likely that statistical analysis will reveal many significant effects at p-values of .05 or .01. Thus, this analysis focuses on determining whether inclusion of variables that are part of the hypothesis advanced improves the goodness of fit of more standard models, accepting p-values of .1. Further, available data on changes in the rents available to elites in the public sector were relatively poor. Measures of rents were unavailable for as many as seven cases. Finally, the data for analyzing patterns of regime change in Africa lag considerably; I was unable to include in the analysis changes in the public sector wage bill or in the number of public sector employees. With due regard for the limits these conditions impose, it is nonetheless possible to use statistical techniques to explore and test the generalizations.

The data set this analysis employed contained thirty observations. The research excluded countries of sub-Saharan Africa (1) that already had de facto multiparty systems (Botswana, Gambia, Senegal, and Mauritius), (2) that were in the middle of civil war (Angola, Somalia, Chad, Sudan, Mozambique, and Ethiopia), and (3) that were under the influence of South Africa (Swaziland, Lesotho, and Namibia). The resulting group of thirty countries were coded *Anglophone, Francophone,* or *other,* according to colonial heritage. Cameroon was coded in the *other* category; former Belgian colonies were coded *Francophone.*

The data set included a number of economic variables: the annual rate of inflation for 1988, the year before the wave of political change; the proportion of the labor force engaged in agriculture; urbanization rates; the average annual rate of GDP growth for 1984–88 and 1988; the change in exchange rate overvaluation from 1987 to 1988; overseas development assistance as a proportion of GDP (1988 and the 1980–87 average). It also included several measures of rents, including foreign exchange rents (the 1980–86 average and the 1987–88 level); manufacturing rents (the 1980–86 average and the 1987–88 level); and import duties (the 1980–86 average and the 1987–88 level).[32] I used logit techniques to assess the effect of colonial heritage on regime change, which was treated as a dichotomous variable (that is, whether a country held a national conference or legalized opposition parties before September 1991). The preliminary results suggest that a model incorporating measures of the four parts of the theory performs better than a model that uses standard economic variables and understands regime change as a straightforward response to deteriorating economic conditions. A clear test of the theory must await better data, however.

As expected, the logit results suggest that standard economic variables, such as rates of inflation could not explain patterns of regime change. Initially, only one standard economic variable appeared to have any explanatory power: lower rates of 1988 GDP growth were at first moderately correlated with either a national conference or the legalization of opposition political parties. This effect disappeared when the analysis controlled for colonial heritage, however. Further, although Anglophone countries displayed higher overall rates of GDP growth in the year prior to the first wave of change, unlike many Francophone countries, their GDP growth rates in 1988 were generally below the average annual GDP growth rates for 1984–88. Francophone countries and countries with mixed or Portuguese colonial heritage, on the other hand, generally had higher GDP growth rates in 1988 than during 1984–88. Thus, a sudden downturn in rates of growth also lacked explanatory power.

After the analysis controlled for colonial heritage, only one standard economic variable exercised a significant effect on patterns of regime change. The proportion of the labor force engaged in agriculture showed a negative relationship to political liberalization when this variable was included with a dummy variable indicating heritage. Because rurality usually implies lower education levels and less exposure to media, this finding coincides with political science theories that posit political liberalization as a concomittant of urbanization and industrialization.

Separate tests of the four parts of the theory advanced in this chapter indicate that the system of electoral rules dominant since independence is the strongest single predictor of the pattern of regime change. A tradition of single-party list voting made political liberalization more likely in the first wave of change. By itself, centralization of electoral resources as measured by concentration of the print media proved to have little causal effect. Fragmentation among parallel associations also lacked significant explanatory power.

Goodness of fit improved when a measure of the fourth variable, change in rents, was included in the analysis. Although change in import duties, change in foreign exchange rents available, and change in manufacturing rents available did not improve the goodness of fit or exercise significant effect, the inclusion of a measure of public enterprises in 1986 privatized or liquidated by 1990 did improve the fit.

Conclusion: Regime Change versus Sustainability

This chapter aims to explain patterns of regime change. The problem of consolidating the base for competitive politics (or *consolidating democracy* in the larger political science literature) features more frequently in public policy discussions and in much current academic research than the problem of explaining why regimes altered as they did in the 1989–92 period, however. In these final paragraphs, therefore, I assess the implications for understanding the long-term survival of these new multiparty systems.

Four main factors account for patterns of regime change: First, where multicandidate, single-party voting dominated between independence and 1989, the grass roots ties of politicians were more extensive, the possibility of mounting a campaign to dislodge the incumbent was greater, and leaders resisted political liberalization more strongly than where single-party list voting prevailed. In the latter, the costs of building an electoral base were greater, and heads of state were less concerned that they would lose an election (rightly or wrongly; some were ousted in the actual event).

Second, where parallel associations, especially producers' associations, were centralized a corporatist structure of interest intermediation, as in Francophone countries, the costs of mounting a general strike to force a government to liberalize were lower and incumbent governments more vulnerable. But given such centralization as well as a tradition of government consultation with the leaders of these groups, it was feasible to try to control the process of change; that is, the centralized structure of these interest groups made national conferences possible. Thus, the inclination of heads of state in these countries was to bend to pressure for greater political openness, given the immediate high cost to the economy and to social harmony of not doing so and the prospect of being able to control the process once launched. In Anglophone countries, although producers were often less dependent upon government, they faced short-run collective action problems, and their autonomy and more limited dependence on government may also have raised the specter, in leaders' minds, of a political opposition more difficult to control over the long run.

Third, where governments were restricted from going over their budgets or of overvaluing their exchange rates, the economic crises of the 1980s forced cuts in pay, disbursements of IOUs instead of paychecks, layoffs, and other measures that affected the incomes of political elites. Thus, elites in the countries of the CFA franc zone were more immediately and severely affected than their counterparts in Anglophone Africa, where inflation was allowed to erode wages and where there was little restructuring of public enterprises. In this instance, again, incumbents in Francophone Africa were more vulnerable in the short run than were their Anglophone counterparts.

Fourth, control over resources important in waging political campaigns was also more centralized in Francophone than in Anglophone Africa. Thus, costs to opposition groups of waging political campaigns in Anglophone Africa were lower than they were in Francophone Africa. That meant that incumbents in Anglophone Africa reasonably feared loss at the ballot box more than their Francophone counterparts did. Opposition to liberalization was a rational response on their part, given the formal and informal political rules in place.

Each of these factors has implications for the sustainability of competitive political systems and for the measures that supporters of multiparty systems must take to consolidate the changes that occurred.

First, the meager network of relationships between politicians and the grass roots in Francophone Africa may have made a competitive political system easier to introduce (because less threatening to incumbents) but more difficult to sustain. The tendency of politicians to invest in developing ties to party elites rather than to electors under single-party list voting was long responsible for the generational fights that plagued Francophone countries. It also created distrust of debate among voters. Indeed, an analysis of election returns in Côte d'Ivoire suggests that voter turnout in 1985 and 1990 was lowest where the number of candidates was largest and that turnout negatively correlated with competitiveness.[33] (Returns in Kenya from earlier multi-candidate, single-party elections do not show this pattern.) Candidates in Francophone Africa have to learn new rules of behavior, as do their constituents, in order to reduce the gap between voters and the political elite. New politicians of Anglophone Africa—who come not from the old political class but from the ranks of lawyers and intellectuals—may need to do the same.

Second, if the ability of producers' associations to exert countervailing power over government is critical to sustaining government respect for constitutional rules, then the independence or autonomy of these parallel associations is critical for consolidating multiparty systems. Centralized corporatist associations that are part of the dominant political class and that have been co-opted through participation in transition governments or conferences (and so are vulnerable to government control) may be less likely than fragmented groups to exercise countervailing power over the long run. The evidence available from Africa to date is mixed, however. In Côte d'Ivoire, for example, political liberalization encouraged followers dissatisfied with their leaders to break away from other syndicates and organize their own interest groups, creating a flourishing associational life outside the reach of the state.

Third, although the political economies of Francophone countries may force new governments to make the layoffs and wage cuts that destabilized the ancien régime, triggering more political upheaval, their Anglophone counterparts may also have a difficult time. Pressure on them from aid donors to stop using the public sector as a source of patronage may place countries of both heritages on a similar—difficult—footing.

Fourth, control over resources critical to campaigning became, in the short run, dramatically less concentrated in Francophone Africa after political liberalization. New newspapers and magazines flourished, making it easier for opposition leaders to get their message out to urban elites. Nonetheless, the legacy of concentration and strict media control plagued journalists, who had to forge new contacts with sources of information and build their own news gathering skills.

At first glance, there is reason to think that, although these regime changes came more slowly, over greater resistance from incumbent heads of state, and often with greater violence in Anglophone countries, they may be easier to sustain in these countries than in Francophone Africa. Regime change itself rapidly eroded some of these differences, however, and all of the newly competitive regimes will face severe tests throughout the 1990s.

Notes

1. See Pearl T. Robinson, "The National Conference Phenomenon in Africa," July 17, 1992, typescript.
2. Jean-François Bayart, "La Problématique de la démocratie en Afrique noire: 'la Baule et puis aprés?' " *Politique africaine* 43 (October 1991): 5–20, 5.
3. Crawford Young and Thomas Turner, *The Rise and Decline of the Zairian State* (Madison: University of Wisconsin Press, 1985); Thomas Callaghy, *The State-Society Struggle: Zaire in Comparative Perspective* (New York: Columbia

University Press, 1984); Michael Schatzberg, *The Dialectics of Oppression in Zaire* (Bloomington: Indiana University Press, 1988); and Robert H. Jackson and Carl G. Rosberg, *Personal Rule in Black Africa* (Berkeley: University of California Press, 1982).

4. For a lengthier discussion of this subject, see Mark Gallagher, *Rent Seeking and Economic Growth in Africa* (Boulder, Colo.: Westview, 1991), 57–61.

5. Paul Collier, "Africa's External Economic Relations: 1960–90," *African Affairs* 90 (1991): 339–56, 340.

6. Ibid., 340–41.

7. This definition is one component of the concept of *corporatism* that Peter Katzenstein employs in his book on the way the positions of small countries in international markets shape domestic politics. See Peter J. Katzenstein, *Small States in World Markets* (Ithaca: Cornell University Press, 1985), 89–90. Note that, according to Katzenstein's theory (not discussed here), domestic political economies of small states—presumably including those of African countries—should converge. Katzenstein's thesis suggests that the differences used as explanatory variables should in this instance disappear with time.

8. Pearl T. Robinson, "Niger: Anatomy of a Neotraditional Corporatist State," *Comparative Politics* 23 (1991): 1–20, 4.

9. For detailed arguments about the logic of this conclusion, see the discussions in Robert Bates, *Beyond the Miracle of the Market* (Cambridge: Cambridge University Press, 1990), and Jennifer A. Widner, *The Rise of a Party-State in Kenya: From Harambee! to Nyayo!* (Berkeley: University of California Press, 1992).

10. For a discussion of other aspects of the electoral systems of these countries, see Ruth Berins Collier, *Regimes in Tropical Africa: Changing Forms of Supremacy, 1945–1975* (Berkeley: University of California Press, 1982).

11. Zimbabwe was a de jure multiparty system, although a de facto single-party system, at the time of this study. During the 1989–92 period, in contrast to political rhetoric in many other countries, Zimbabwe's president, Robert Mugabe, indicated an interest in moving the country to de jure single-party rule. He backed away from that sentiment in later public statements—but not in actions.

12. Throughout this analysis, Cameroon is counted neither as Francophone nor as an Anglophone country. Cameroon has a mixed colonial heritage. Although it remains part of the CFA franc zone, it bears greater similarity to Anglophone countries than to Francophone countries in degree of central control over the media and in patterns of interest group organization.

13. Douglass C. North, *Institutions, Institutional Change, and Economic Performance* (Cambridge: Cambridge University Press, 1990), 99.

14. This analysis differs from, but is compatible with, the observations of Jean-François Médard, who also focuses some of his recent work on this two-country comparison. See Jean-François Médard, "The Historical Trajectories of the Ivorian and Kenyan States," in *Rethinking Third World Politics*, ed. James Manor (Harrow, England: Longman Group U.K., 1991); and "Autoritarismes et démocraties en Afrique noire," *Politique africaine* 43 (October 1991): 92–104.

15. Irving L. Markovitz, *Power and Class in Africa* (New York: Free Press, 1970).

16. There is a difference of opinion about the degree to which an independent business class exists in these countries. For more on this subject, see Ernest J. Wilson III, "Strategies of State Control of the Economy: Nationalization and Indigenization in Africa," *Comparative Politics* 22 (1990): 401–19.

17. For a more extensive discussion of the Kenyan system, see David Bevan, Paul Collier, and Jan Willem Gunning, *Peasants and Governments* (Oxford: Clarendon, 1989).

18. United Nations Development Program and World Bank, *African Economic and Financial Data* (Washington, D.C.: World Bank, 1989), 117.

19. Economist Intelligence Unit, *Côte d'Ivoire: Country Profile, 1991–92* (London: Business International, Ltd., 1992), 9.

20. Jean-Pierre Lachaud, *Le désengagement de l'état et les ajustements sur le marché du travail en Afrique francophone*, International Institute of Social Studies, Research Series 96 (Geneva: International Labor Organization, 1989), 54.

21. Jacques van der Gaag, Merton Stelcner, and Vim Vijverberg, *Public-Private Sector Wage Comparisons and Moonlighting in Developing Countries: Evidence from Côte d'Ivoire and Peru*. Living Standards Measurement Study, Working Paper 52 (Washington, D.C.: World Bank, 1989), 27.

22. Economist Intelligence Unit, *Quarterly Report on Côte d'Ivoire, 1990*, no. 3 (London: Business International, Ltd., 1990), 12.

23. There is a lively debate between Ernest J. Wilson and French scholars Bernard Contamin and Yves Fauré on this subject. Wilson's views were first presented in a manuscript entitled "Privatization in the Ivory Coast: Three Case Studies," Kennedy School of Government, Center for Business and Government, December 1987, typescript. Contamin and Fauré present their analysis in *La Bataille des entreprises publiques en Côte d'Ivoire: l'histoire d'un ajustement interne* (Paris: Karthala, 1990). *Année africaine 1990*, includes a debate between the two parties.

24. United Nations Development Program and the World Bank, *African Economic and Financial Data*, 180.

25. Lachaud, *Le désengagement de l'état*, 15, 36.

26. United Nations Development Program and the World Bank, *African Economic and Financial Data*, sec. 10-4.

27. See the interesting discussions of this process in Contamin and Fauré, *la Bataille des enterprises publiques en Côte d'Ivoire*, 219–39; and Richard C. Crook, "Les Changements politiques en Côte d'Ivoire: une approche institutionelle," in *Année africaine, 1990–1991* (Paris: Pedone, 1991).

28. Mark Gallagher, *Rent Seeking and Economic Growth in Africa* (Boulder, Colo.: Westview, 1991), 89–93.

29. U.S. Agency for International Development, unclassified telegram on policy reform in Kenya, October 1991.

30. For an extensive discussion of such attempts to control political action in Kenya, see Widner, *The Rise of a Party-State in Kenya*.

31. Yves Fauré, "L'Economie politique d'une démocratisation: élements

d'analyse à propos de l'expérience récente de la Côte d'Ivoire," *Politique africaine* 43 (October 1991): 31–49, 37.

32. Data from United Nations Development Program and World Bank, *African Economic and Financial Data*; Gallagher, *Rent Seeking and Economic Growth in Africa*; *Africa South of the Sahara, 1989* (London: Europa Publications Ltd., 1990).

33. Fauré, "L'Economie politique d'une démocratisation," 42.

RICHARD WESTEBBE

Four ◈ Structural Adjustment, Rent Seeking, and Liberalization in Benin

This chapter analyzes how structural adjustment affected rent seeking in Benin and how such rent seeking on the part of government officials contributed to perhaps the most dramatic and earliest shift in Africa from a military, Marxist dictatorship to a multiparty political system. In late 1989–90, under political pressure generated by a severe economic crisis, the government of Mathieu Kérékou permitted the formation of a National Council to redraft the country's constitution and then ceded power to newly elected governors. I suggest that the structural adjustment process was partly responsible for this outcome.

Government programs had created protected havens for officials who, not being subject to the pressures of economic competition, of performance-based promotions, or of the scrutiny of a democratically elected parliament and a free press, used their positions for personal aggrandizement. These activities slowed economic growth and caused "the few" instead of "the many" to benefit from growth and to have access to the assets of the public sector. The structural adjustment process affected the way many Beninese understood the sources of economic stagnation; it also focused discontent among both government elites, some of whom found their sinecures less remunerative as the economic crisis deepened, and many other members of Benin society. Thus, economic reform played a role in precipitating political change, even though the World Bank and the International Monetary Fund themselves did not attach political conditions to loans. The chapter concludes with comments about the role of the Bank and the degree to which Benin's trajectory is comparable to that of other African countries.

The Institutional and Policy Settings

Benin (earlier, Dahomey) became independent in 1960, after some seventy years of colonial rule. Much of the country had a several-hundred-year-old history as independent kingdoms; Abomey resisted French dominance in fierce warfare until 1890, when the last warrior king was forced to surrender. Benin was also profoundly influenced by centuries of contact with the West, dating back to the Portuguese trade era, and by the growing influence of the Catholic Church (by 1980, about one-fourth of the population was Catholic). These influences created a stratified society and altered earlier forms of property rights and social obligations, even in the northern regions, where the dominant role of the elders was much reduced.[1]

The country experienced significant political instability in the 1960s. Three civilian governments came to power, led by dominant leaders from the south, center, and north. The tenure of each government was interrupted by military intervention, followed by a brokered return to civilian control, sometimes with the involvement of the French. The 1969 election produced a stalemate between the leaders of the three regions. In order to resolve the impasse, a Presidential Council was created, within whose framework the presidency was rotated among the three leaders every two years.

Continued unrest and attempted military mutinies prompted the senior officer corps to terminate the Presidential Council in 1972 and to appoint Mathieu Kérékou, a military officer from the north, as president.[2] Initially, the new regime was welcomed, or at least regarded as benign. Stability was restored. The government stressed national unity as part of an independent economic and social identity. Popular participation in political life increased.

The subsequent shift to a Marxist-Leninist ideology and a socialist command economy took place two years later and was forced by at least three major radical elements long present: the trade unions, the teachers and other intellectuals influenced by socialism in France, and some militant members of the younger generation called *liguers*, who came from the Savelou region and who were heavily influenced by the student riots in Paris in 1968. These three groups were joined by young officers attracted by the prospect of breaking postcolonial ties and adopting a new, unifying philosophy that attributed the country's economic woes to the influence of the West. The new system banned participation by former political leaders and by military officers who had led coups in the past. The new government suppressed participation by students—and by many other groups, as well.[3]

Coupled with a falling out with the former colonial power, this change in elites and policy led the government to seek close ties to the communist bloc. In the contest between cold war rivals, the Soviet Union saw Benin as a useful ally, as a prospective base for aircraft flying to Angola, and as a naval base on the west coast of Africa. The Party of the People's Revolution was created. In 1975, the name *Dahomey* was changed to *People's Republic of Benin.* The party and its Central Committee retained all key policymaking authority and dominated the Council of Ministers, which was the nominal governing body. A new constitution was adopted in 1977, and elections were held in 1979. Governments after this period were largely civilian, although at different times military officers held key posts throughout the 1980s in education, public enterprises, and finance.

After 1975, the process of transforming Benin into a mini Marxist state on the Eastern bloc model began. The rationale was to use the state to promote the welfare of the people by preventing their exploitation by domestic and foreign capitalist interests. The objective was to accelerate economic growth and development by state dominance of the means of production. Most formal sector activity was brought under state control, including distribution, secondary-sector enterprises, and financial institutions. Public enterprises were created throughout the economy, with large industrial investments financed with foreign borrowing. This was particularly the case with the large sugar and cement clinker complexes owned jointly with Nigeria, which have never produced positive returns. State farms were set up with Bulgarian, East German, and Soviet Union support. The marketing of export crops was entrusted to state monopolies. What was not owned was tightly controlled by a pervasive regulatory system, including prices, import licenses, quotas, and wages. The output of the formerly enviable education system was greatly increased at the secondary and university levels, and the increasingly less well-trained graduates were guaranteed jobs in the expanding public sector. The number of civil servants tripled between the 1960s and the 1980s.

Benin's strategic course was not unusual for Africa. The conditions and conventional development theories prominent in the independence era were quite different from those that prevail today. The path Benin pursued in creating a postindependence political system and in promoting development was paralleled by many other African states. At independence, many Africans believed that their new governments had to intervene to mobilize resources in order to compensate for the lack of developed private sectors and to prevent private rent seeking. They cited market failure and deficiencies in basic infrastructure in defense of this approach.

African socialism, which took root in such diverse countries as Guinea, Congo, Benin, Guinea-Bissau, São Tomé and Príncipe, and Tanzania, was consistent with the development theory that favored allocating resources to public enterprises and controlling foreign exchange, prices, and capital. Development was to take place through the mobilization of capital for industry, which would benefit from protection against well-developed economies. Economic planning was to be a means of achieving internally oriented, rapid economic growth; and the state was the instrument of such planning.[4] Tanzania adopted socialism after 1971 partly because of the ideology of the ruling party but also because of the failure of private investment in industry during the First Five Year Plan, compounded by a shortfall in external public investment financing.[5] Even such mixed economies as Côte d'Ivoire, Cameroon, and Mauritania adopted planning and substantial state intervention in agricultural marketing, public enterprises, labor markets, import licensing, and building of infrastructure. Togo invested heavily in the mid 1970s in a host of ill-conceived public (mainly consumer) goods industries financed from the windfall gains from the short-lived boom in phosphate prices and from large-scale foreign borrowing.

Not only was development theory compatible with socialist and other forms of command economies adopted by newly independent Africa, but the lessons of economic history appeared to support an entrepreneurial, if not controlling, role for the state in promoting economic development. In Russia, Prussia, and the United Netherlands, the state played an indispensable role in promoting entrepreneurs with policies, financing, infrastructure, and supporting institutions to overcome their relative backwardness in the industrialization process.[6] The more recent examples are Japan, South Korea, and the other newly industrializing Asian countries, with their rapid-growth industrial policies and limited popular participation. Neither the Western nor the Asian model is, of course, transferable to Africa. Newly organized governments do not necessarily have the capacity to play an entrepreneurial role. Nor do societies with the same kinds of institutional structures and opportunities behave similarly. Indeed, the colonial legacy in former French Africa was one of complex bureaucracies, centralized state control, and central control and guidance of communities within the state.[7]

The Beninese economy, which grew at an estimated 0.7 percent per year between 1972 and 1976, saw accelerated growth of between 4 and 5 percent in real terms, between 1977 and 1982. A substantial degree of internal and external stability accompanied this expansion. A principal factor in this growth was the public capital investment program, which was 40 percent industrial. During this period, it grew 12 percent annually. Public services, mainly new employment—which rose by 15 percent annually in this period—grew by 8 percent. Fixed investment rose by 20 percent annually in real terms between 1976 and 1981 and reached a peak of 33 percent in 1981. National savings declined, so that about 90 percent of investment was foreign financed, mainly borrowed on commercial terms. The other main source of growth was the transit trade, which was based on reexporting Benin imports to Niger and Nigeria. Nigeria was undergoing an oil-induced import boom and lacked adequate physical facilities to handle the volume of traffic; Benin with its well-developed class of traders was well placed. Public revenues benefited from the taxes on these imports, and the private uncontrolled transit sector thrived.

By the end of the 1970s, Benin had a population of some 3.5 million people with a per capita income of about $270. Three-fourths of the population were engaged in traditional farming. Industry accounted for some 10 percent GDP and consisted of import substitution and agricultural processing plants. Small amounts of oil were discovered offshore, and sugar growing was undertaken on an industrial basis.

Trouble was in the offing, however. The oil and uranium booms that drove the transit trade ended in 1983, as did unsustainable spending for public investments. Much of the earlier investment proved to be of low quality and was unable to produce reasonable returns, let alone service the debt incurred for its financing. The economy entered a period of low growth and financial decline. Real GDP growth between 1983 and 1987 averaged under 1 percent. Moreover, because the population growth rate exceeded 3 percent per annum, Benin's real per capita income was declining. The public finance gap rose to 9 percent of GDP and the balance of payment gap to 7 percent, both financed by growing internal and external arrears. Declining productivity in agriculture due to a shortage of modern inputs and the presence of subsidized imported grain made output insufficient to meet the demand for food in growing urban centers, so that cereal imports rose from 34,000 tons in 1976 to 110,000 tons in 1981. Palm oil was produced in important quantities, some 20,000 metric tons of palm kernels a year, but declining rainfall adversely affected long-term yields.

In the 1980s, with World Bank encouragement, the government altered some of its agricultural policies. Cotton output rose sharply, from 20,000 tons in 1982–83 to 130,000 tons in 1986–87 and 170,000 tons in 1992, due to the introduction of incentive pricing, better input distribution, and an efficient extension system under tightly supervised projects financed by the World Bank and other donors. This was the one bright spot in an otherwise dismal picture, but it was difficult for the authorities to accept as a model because it had everything to do with farmer incentives and efficient market-oriented distribution and very little to do with collective farming and state control.

The Emerging Crisis

The government's initial response to these economic problems in its Second Five Year Plan (1983–87), which it presented to donors in March 1983, set forth a critique of past performance and a strategy for future development. It referred to excessive centralization, inadequate management and technical training, and the need for better planning. Specific corrective actions included price increases and a reduction in the hiring of new college graduates by the civil service, better project analysis, and a gradual elimination of agricultural subsidies. In return for taking these steps, the government requested assistance in external debt management, project analysis, and planning.

In 1983, the World Bank opened a resident mission in Cotonou in order to deepen its relations with the country. It attempted to address the basic structural and management issues facing Benin in its 1984 *Country Economic Memorandum*, which served as the principal instrument for its economic policy dialogue with the authorities. The memorandum assessed Benin's comparative advantage in agriculture and industry for the domestic and large neighboring markets. Benin's low labor costs and the public sector's sharply reduced role in economic activity prompted this emphasis. The memorandum suggested that the prospects for cotton, corn, and yams were good and that further investments in transit facilities were in line with Benin's comparative advantage. It also suggested improvements in human resources as a basis for future growth. To succeed, the strategy required concrete reforms of planning, public enterprises, and public finances. The memorandum stressed the need to reform loss-making public enterprises on the grounds they not only were badly managed and subject to considerable rent seeking but were also greatly overstaffed (they had become the main vehicle to meet the governments' commitment to hire recent university graduates). The memorandum also recommended a complete overhaul of budgetary controls and procedures, including linking current and capital spending decisions. Finally, it contained a devastating critique of project preparation and planning. Despite the Marxist state's focus on central planning, it could not properly assess the technical merits of projects, nor did its planning permit it to set priorities, define policy options, or estimate the budgetary consequences of policy decisions.

Although the memorandum was well received by the president, who welcomed its frank analysis—saying he was tired of people congratulating him for things that were not true—no real policy reform took place. The World Bank was unable to mount a macro reform program and, instead, negotiated a project to rehabilitate eight specific public enterprises. The dialogue between the World Bank and the Kérékou government on economic policy, which began in 1982, did not result in a decision to accept a broad-based adjustment program until 1986–87, when the Political Bureau dropped its opposition in the face of overwhelming evidence that *dirigiste* policies had failed.

Part of the difficulty of negotiating a reform package stemmed from the structure of the political system. Benin was organized as a one-party state. The president was the chairman of both the party's Political Bureau and Central Committee and the head of government. As president, he exercised his authority through a National Executive Council selected in consultation with the Political Bureau and consisting of the ministers, and prefects of the six provinces. There was also a National Revolutionary Council of elected representatives, which met infrequently and had little real power. Despite the centralization implied by this structure, the president acted more like a chairman of a coordinating committee and usually made decisions based on consensus. The result was a long period of political stability but also a government unable to act decisively in crisis.

Between 1985 and 1987, a period of government incapacity, real GDP fell. Investment declined below 13 percent of GDP, compared with over 20 percent a decade earlier. The overall budget deficit remained at some 6 percent of GDP only because rising personnel expenditures were offset by falling investment outlays; the wage bill rose substantially because of two general increases in the 1980–82 period. Revenues declined to below 12 percent of GDP, compared with some 15 percent earlier. The government drew down its deposits in the banking system to finance the deficit, and by 1984, it was a net debtor to the banks. By the end of 1987, it was some 70 billion CFA francs in domestic arrears. Delays in meeting the government payroll began in 1986 and were as long as three months by 1988. By late 1988, as revenues fell below 10 percent of GDP, a financial crisis was at hand.

This situation was disastrous for the entire government-owned banking system. The banks were a primary source of official rent seeking through insider loans to important officials, the financing of loss-making public enterprises, and outright theft by banking officials. By 1988, the three banks (commercial, development, and agricultural) were bankrupt, with some three-quarters of their consolidated port-folio, of 150 billion CFA francs nonperforming. At that time, this amount was the equivalent of $500 million, or over $120 per capita. The regional central bank in Dakar had refinanced some 70 billion CFA francs of this sum, which had to be consolidated. The money supply contracted, as central bank credit was restricted and the banks were illiquid.[8] External arrears reached over $240 million on debt service, which neither the government nor its enterprises could ser-vice. Domestic depositors, including business and official depositors, found their deposits frozen and could not pay their bills. A massive flight of available liquidity, particularly bank notes, took place, thus further exacerbating the crisis.

Although banking system losses were the most obvious result of such activity, official rent seeking was pervasive and increased during the later years of the Kérékou regime. It was reliably reported in Cotonou that high-level agents in the customs and internal revenue services had developed a system of complicity in which fixed per-centages of importers' and taxpayers' taxes were discounted upon payment of bribes. The revenue that was collected was shared by the collection agents and the public treasury. The sharp contraction in officially recorded import and customs revenues in 1989 over 1988 (more than 12 percent) is at least partly ascribed to such rent seeking.

A highly questionable contract to manage the huge Benin-Nigeria sugar complex was awarded to an operator close to members of the Political Bureau, who stripped the enterprise of an important part of its movable machinery, failed to pay workers, and introduced serious financial irregularities. Political interference in cotton sales was also used to seek rents. The social security fund paid an exorbitant amount from its reserves to construct fifty villas, which it could not sell for enough money to cover costs. The fund showed excessive operational costs; and it awarded disproportionately high pensions to some mem-bers of the previous regime.

The most ubiquitous form of rent seeking was the inflation of the civil service and military payrolls by the former government. In all of Francophone Africa, salaries as a proportion of revenues were highest in Benin; they left inadequate financial resources for vital economic and social programs. Many of Benin's adjustment problems stem from past hiring of poorly prepared school leavers to reward political allies and buy peace—at the expense of the rest of the economy.

Rent seeking was a primary cause of the economic collapse that precipitated political change. A country without a banking system cannot maintain economic activity, and depositors who have lost their money cannot buy goods and services. Bankrupt public enterprises can provide neither jobs nor growth. A tax system that diverts significant amounts of revenue to personal gain cannot maintain government priorities, let alone pay public servants, sustain loss-making public enterprises, or pay for scholarships in a bloated system of higher education.

The Benin government's response to the crisis was relevant but inadequate and included measures for resource mobilization, investment programming, the elimination of irregular salary payments, agricultural producer pricing, public enterprise reform, and the liberalization of transport and public utility pricing. The domestic problem was compounded by a growing lack of competitiveness abroad; as export prices fell, the U.S. dollar depreciated, and regional trade slumped. Benin's real exchange rate appreciated at the very time when domestic policy should have been promoting the expansion of tradable sectors through increases in productivity, switching expenditures to productive sectors, compressing demand by fiscal and monetary measures, and introducing appropriate incentives for the expansion of exports and the production of import substitutes. It was clear that only a sweeping reform in economic policy would enable Benin to get through the financial crisis and restore growth. The Political Bureau conceded its incapacity to govern and turned economic policy over to a coordinating committee of ministers mandated to begin the time-consuming process of preparing a structural adjustment program with the World Bank and, later, the International Monetary Fund.

The World Bank and Governance

In 1989, the Benin government embraced a radical program of structural reform that represented a fundamental shift in development strategy. It moved toward economic liberalization and private sector development while substantially reducing the role of the public sector. The program received substantial World Bank and IMF support. A first structural adjustment loan (SAL) for $45 million was approved by the World Bank Board of Directors in May 1989, followed by an IMF structural adjustment facility (SAF) and significant financing from France, the European Economic Community, Switzerland, and West Germany. The objective was to raise real GDP growth over the medium term to some 3 percent annually in order to reform the current budget and general public sector management, improve investment programming, deepen public enterprise reforms, restructure the banking system, reform trade policy, and deregulate markets.

The steps taken by the government and the issues raised by the World Bank mission reflected a deepening awareness that governance had to be a central concern in promoting growth. In order to work, structural adjustment lending required not only the fulfillment of technical efficiency conditions but also a political commitment by the leadership to implement sweeping reforms and, therefore, an acceptance by the governed of the reforms. The World Bank's 1989 report on sub-Saharan Africa refers to a crisis in governance on the continent.[9] Politics had become personalized and the leadership had assumed broad discretionary authority and had therefore lost its legitimacy. Because of an absence of countervailing power, officials were not accountable. Moreover, political repression had caused imperfections in the market and an absence of the voluntary associations needed to support a dynamic economy. In essence, the World Bank acknowledged a relation between the state and economic performance.

This recognition caused considerable concern and discussion within the Bank. In a study of the relevance of the governance issue to the Articles of Agreement of the Bank, the general counsel of the Bank cited the *Long-Term Perspective Study* and its call for "political renewal." He noted that the *LTPS* was a staff study, not an official Bank perspective, and that, unlike the European Bank for Reconstruction and Development (EBRD), the World Bank was prohibited from engaging in political activities or from being influenced by the political character of its members in its decisionmaking. The Articles permitted only economic considerations to be taken into account in the Bank's decisionmaking. "The Bank as coordinator of foreign assistance to a country should not act on behalf of donor countries in influencing a recipient country's political orientation or behavior." The Bank was only concerned with aid effectiveness and efficiency; it might advise a government about the current thinking of donors but could not convey political messages.[10]

The general counsel also recognized the ambiguity in the Articles

Agreement, however. The major objective of adjustment lending—
"unleashing the forces of growth, reducing the obstacles to investment, and making government more efficient"—prompts resort to
conditions that affect public administration. The justification for structural adjustment lending is based on special circumstances that permit
the Bank to undertake operations that assist countries in creating the
conditions and incentives needed for the investment of capital for
productive purposes. The Bank does so by helping reduce the serious
deterioration in balance of payments or by meeting financial needs
resulting from the reform process. Therefore, economic considerations
extend to the way a state manages its resources, "and thus [it] may
be difficult to isolate from political considerations, especially in policy
based lending." The Bank cannot ignore political instability, which
affects a country's economic prospects.

The issue for the Bank was not whether one form of government
was preferred over another: *governance* is not a synonym for *democratic
decisionmaking* or *representative politics.* Although there was certainly
widespread preference for political choice and competition not only
in the West but also in Africa, from the point of view of many in the
Bank, competitive politics—as much as repressive political systems—
raised the specter of economic mismanagement. Economic efficiency
and political liberalization were not necessarily consistent: politicians
in a democracy could also pander to special interest groups, including
ethnic subgroups in relatively young nations.

Governance, in the Bank's parlance, meant (1) improving public
sector management in order to raise returns to investment, reduce
poverty, and achieve growth, (2) increasing economic and financial
accountability, (3) enhancing predictability and the rule of law, particularly as they affect business and redress of public sector abuses,
and (4) developing information and transparency to promote private
sector efficiency and as safeguards against corruption.[11] Two experienced World Bank officials defined the Bank's view of governance
as "the use of political authority and exercise of control over a society
and the management of its resources for social and economic development."[12] They point out that the definition allows for the indispensable and creative role of the state in development, both by providing an enabling environment to economic operators and by
determining how assets and benefits are distributed. Governance, of
course, includes a political dimension, as it must, because it also refers
to a system of politics and how people are ruled—or, as the 1989 *Long-
Term Perspective Study* says, the "exercise of political power to manage
a nation's affairs."

The role of the state in economic development is multifaceted. In one interpretation, good governance may be seen as the opposite of privatizing official rents by using the instruments of state power. "Good governance depends on the extent to which a government is perceived and accepted by the general citizenry to be legitimate, committed to improving general public welfare and responsive to the needs of its citizenry; competent in assuring law and order and in delivering public services; able to create an enabling policy environment for productive activities; and equitable in its conduct, favoring no special interests or groups."[13] Donors increasingly condition their aid on progress toward improving governance on the grounds that aid cannot promote development where these criteria are not met.

The Bank recognized the risk in proceeding with a major reform program under the circumstances prevailing in Benin, with its dismal record of governance, but it decided to proceed with the SAL because it concluded that it could support the policies of the Kérékou government and the programs it proposed to carry out these policies. The Bank's dialogue with Benin had been under way for years, and in 1988 it began to show substantial payoffs in the willingness and capacity of the Kérékou regime to undertake structural reforms. Specifically, Kérékou demonstrated a willingness to address macro and sectoral issues by going beyond investment projects and economic and sector work. In 1986 the National Commission to Implement the Structural Adjustment Program (CNSAPAS) was created, which removed macro policy from the Political Bureau and transferred it to line ministers, who reported to the president. (In the Political Bureau, the president had been only the first among equals on economic policy matters.)

The CNSAPAS was chaired by the minister of finance and included the ministers of planning, industry, energy and public enterprises, commerce, rural development, labor, and social affairs. As a result of this shift in power, the government was able to implement a substantial number of actions prior to the presentation of the SAL and the policy framework paper (which must precede an IMF SAF program) to the boards of directors of the World Bank and the IMF. These actions included changes in import tax valuation, a census of the civil service, an end to the automatic recruitment of graduates, reductions in civil service and military housing allowances, the adoption of economic rate of return and least-cost criteria for public projects, a new law defining government-public enterprise relations, the liquidation of twelve public enterprises, the dissolution of the failed banks and a plan to establish a sound banking system, the liberalization of food and export crop marketing and the removal of quantitative restrictions, and a reduction in price controls.

The creation of the CNSAPAS and the adoption of reforms in public sector management and the banking system greatly increased transparency and reduced patronage and opportunities for rent seeking. The preparation of the SAL was greatly facilitated by the willingness of unions and other private associations to join in the reform process as a way to address the governance issue and restore the fortunes of their country. In short, these groups correctly saw the SAL as a way of empowering the reform-minded segments of society without having to take on the entrenched military and political hierarchy, at least in the first stage. The subcommissions of the CNSAPAS, consisting of Beninese civil servants, did most of the work on the program. In this new context, the World Bank was seen as a valuable ally, and its resident mission and visiting staff were warmly received at the senior levels of government. This relationship stood in marked contrast to the hostility shown by ministers to Bank policy missions in the mid-1980s, when the regime was defending its ideology following student demonstrations that it had severely repressed.

The Bank's prior assessment of risk also pointed up the possible resistance of those who would be vulnerable to any adverse social effects of austerity, including public sector layoffs and reduced privileges and rents. The reform program thus included measures to reduce the impact on the vulnerable. Civil service departures were entirely voluntary, and those leaving were given such generous indemnities that the program was oversubscribed. Public enterprise employees who lost their jobs were also indemnified by law, and they and civil servants received redeployment help. Civil servants knew that, in the absence of the program, their chances of receiving regular salary payments would be low. For the lowest income groups, the Bank added a labor-intensive public works component to one of its urban infrastructure projects. The program also provided for budget allocations for health and education. As resources did not permit a shift to nonwage spending on primary health and education, a social fund to buy medicine and primary schoolbooks was set up, directly financed by a World Bank and SwissAid health project.

In short, there was substantial internal ownership of the program and a number of safeguards against adverse social impacts, which augured well for the sustainability of the program. These social impacts would have been far worse had economic decline been permitted to continue, with no prospect for restoring growth in per capita incomes and essential public services, particularly the health and education of the poorest classes.

Economic Crisis and the Political Opening of 1989

The immediate cause of the political crisis that erupted in late 1989 was the failure of the regime to pay civil service workers' and teachers' salaries. Three months of salary arrears had been incurred by May 1989, just after the SAL to Benin was launched. Teachers were already on strike, and civil servants joined them intermittently, beginning in December, when arrears reached six months. The administrative apparatus was at a standstill; an entire school year had been lost, and another one was a risk.

The success of the SAL was predicated on the achievement of budgetary targets. Specifically, the Kérékou government had to maintain salaries and vital public services as well as meet the conditions for the release of the exceptional financing that would cover budget and balance of payments gaps. The government maintained reasonable discipline in restraining expenditures, but the overall deficit widened as a result of a 30 percent shortfall in expected revenues. The causes of this shortfall were several. The collapse of the banking system froze deposits and made tax payments and business activity difficult. Domestic demand contracted, in part because of the non-payment of civil service salaries, the flight of capital as confidence declined, a decline in transit trade as merchants shifted to more stable areas, and lower revenue collections as a result of strikes and customs fraud.

The situation was exacerbated by the government's inability to meet the conditions for the disbursement of foreign budgetary aid; these conditions included amassing import invoices and customs declarations. As a result, only about half of the projected foreign budgetary aid of 50 billion CFA francs was disbursed, and project financing for investment fell short because of a lack of government counterpart funds. Domestic arrears rose to 75 billion CFA francs ($230 million), higher than budgetary revenues. External arrears fell, due to a June 1989 Paris Club rescheduling of Benin's debt. Real GDP fell by about 2.6 percent in 1989, compared to a program target of a 2.5 percent increase.

The crisis pushed Kérékou, in August 1989, to appoint Robert Dossou, a prominent law professor and human rights activist, to join the government as minister of planning. Dossou agreed on the condition that political prisoners be given amnesty and steps be taken towards multiparty democracy. This appointment did not forestall a sharp increase in public pressure for more fundamental change, however. The economic and financial crisis became a crisis of governance in the last part of 1989, when profound dissatisfaction with the regime erupted throughout the country, reaching into churches, local neighborhoods, and diverse ethnic groups. Influential nongovernment leaders sent the regime a message that, unless it did something, Beninese society would break down. Bilateral donors voiced similar concerns. Kérékou urgently requested donor aid to pay the three months' salary arrears for 1989 (the other three months' salary arrears were for 1988) before civil service workers went on strike.

Kérékou's speech of November 29, 1989, referred to the serious economic difficulties facing the nation and the new era of liberalization and private sector activity that the SAL had launched. He announced that this new era required a moralization of political life and that the new political realities required that the power of the people supersede all special interests.[14] But the president still lacked a detailed reform plan, and donors rejected the Beninese request to pay salary arrears and provide other emergency aid.

The World Bank and the IMF made it clear that Benin's structural adjustment program was off track and that they therefore could not meet Benin's request for special assistance. It was also evident that the structural adjustment program would not succeed without popular support. To receive the support of the Bretton Woods donor agencies, the Benin government would have to reduce corruption, reopen schools, restore stolen revenues, reform the banking system (including collecting nonperforming loans), and maintain the civil service departure program.

On December 6 and 7, 1989, Kérékou called called a meeting of the political and military leadership. He posed four rhetorical questions for discussion and resolution: (1) Is Marxism-Leninism consistent with economic liberalization and private sector promotion? (2) Do the principles by which the party controls the state guarantee the effective participation of those Beninese who do not share the Leninist ideology? (3) Do the structures and operation of the state safeguard efficiency in the conduct of public affairs? (4) Do the constitutional principles allow for initiative and harmonious development in the private sector? The president asked the assembled representatives to consider the political changes necessary for people to accept the order and discipline required by "our" structural adjustment program. He alluded to the factors that had delayed the structural adjustment program, including school closings, strikes, and the drop in revenues. He concluded with a declaration that no longer would Marxism-Leninism be the official ideology of the nation. The term *camarade* to refer to fellow citizens would no longer be obligatory.

The president said he would convene a national conference in early 1990 of all elements of society to decide on "democratic renewal" under a new constitution. Henceforth, party and state would be separate. The new constitution would provide for a prime minister as head of government and would make the government subject to the authority of the National Assembly. The declaration reaffirmed the liberal economic and private sector emphasis of the structural adjustment program signed in June 1989. As part of the new moralization of economic life and public service, the leadership was to create a National Commission to investigate the sources of illicit wealth. Examples would be made of flagrant corruption, particularly in the customs service and the tax collection departments.[15]

The World Bank mission leader in Cotonou issued a statement referring to these measures and the assurances of the head of state that the government would take action to ensure the success of the structural adjustment program. A meeting of donors was to be held in Paris to mobilize funds to pay the 1989 salary arrears.[16] The Bank's mission chief quickly made clear that neither the Bank nor the IMF had made political change a condition of the payment of salary arrears. The statement pointed out that the meetings with the president concerned the measures required to relaunch the structural adjustment program, not the design of a new political system.[17]

But although the World Bank's Benin mission established no political conditions, many Beninese did. In the wake of the president's speech, a major demonstration took place that drew thousands into the streets of Cotonou and Porto Novo. A subsequent antiregime protest turned violent when the guards accompanying Kérékou on a walking tour of Cotonou opened fire and killed several youths who had thrown stones. It was the only case of killing recorded during the transition to more democratic government. The crowds destroyed all the symbols of the regime and burned the shroud of the undedicated statue of Lenin. The latter demonstration extended far beyond Cotonou; reportedly, almost every person and vehicle up to the Togo border carried a branch of leaves in solidarity with those protesting the regime. The promise to pay back salaries and the leadership's commitment to political change stabilized the situation until the national conference could be held.

The national conference in February 1990 established an interim government under a transitional prime minister, Nicephore Soglo, a former World Bank executive director and a graduate of the elite French École National d'Administration (ENA). Soglo's mandate was to restore the structural adjustment process and create a consensus for its implementation. Soglo was committed to cleaning up corruption and introducing institutional reforms. His was a government committed to morality in public life, the rule of law, efficient use of public resources, and raising revenues to finance vital expenditures. A supreme council of the republic was created to act as the final authority, equivalent to a legislature. It was headed by Monseigneur de Souza of the Catholic Church, who played a remarkable role, along with others, in persuading the Political Bureau and the military to accept the peaceful demolition of the ancien régime.

President Kérékou stayed on, although with sharply reduced powers, in recognition of the positive role he had played in restraining the more extreme elements among his supporters. This conference and the Soglo government pursued a deliberate nonconfrontational policy with respect to Kérékou, who was allowed to preside over cabinet meetings, even though Prime Minister Soglo was making all the decisions. A year later a new constitution was voted in and a multiparty election held for a new president. Although he had no formal party, Soglo won an overwhelming victory over Kérékou and several leaders from the past. Kérékou retired with dignity and lives in relative obscurity.[18]

The new government restored the momentum of reform. The public finance targets for 1990 and 1991 were met, leading to a small primary budget surplus at the end of 1991; salaries were paid on time; and the stage was set for the departure in 1992 of close to 10 percent of civil servants. At least half of these, including some from the army, chose to leave voluntarily. The government reopened the schools and started preparations for an education loan from the World Bank and other donors, with the aim of fundamentally reforming the educational system. The reforms were to focus on primary education, including expanded education of girls and a reduction in and reorientation of the university's curriculum, with a view to restoring the university as a center of excellence.

The World Bank's second SAL led to substantial additional donor aid. Growth in 1990–91 averaged 3.5 percent in real terms, a good sign that reform had taken hold. This new SAL was fully debated in parliament and reported on in the free press. Visiting Bank officials were invited to respond to questions from television interviewers and to meet with business and labor leaders, and key ministers began to explain their programs in television interviews, too.

Conclusion

Few other African countries are likely to follow precisely the Beninese path to a more open political system: application of the rule of law, transparency and accountability in public affairs, and sweeping decontrol and disengagement of the state from the economy. Even fewer will achieve such a fundamental and peaceful transfer of power from an entrenched, ideologically driven, military control system based on extensive noncompetitive rent seeking. The reason is that not many have suffered such severe economic mismanagement and human distress. Few may be so lucky as to have the leadership of a National Commission or an elected president with the confidence to tell his people the truth about their circumstances. Zaire may be comparable in terms of despair, and neighboring Togo has certainly been influenced by the capacity of the Beninese to remove their oppressive regime. But Togo is also different in that its army is predominantly from the same northern ethnic group as the president and is much more prepared to defend his regime than was the Beninese military.

Rent seeking was a major reason for political change. Politicians discounted the future and extracted rents in such volume and in such manner as to produce economic crisis, including the destruction of such major economic institutions as the banking system and the public enterprises, which, after the government, were the major employer of school leavers. The diversion of the nation's financial savings and the corruption and inefficiency of the major revenue collecting services made regular payment of salaries impossible, leading to a closing of the school system and to public sector strikes. Most such opportunities for private gain lost their value during the crisis, and others, such as existed in the tax system, were the object of reform programs. Given the economic and social consequences of the crisis, it was probably inevitable that the public would turn from passive to active resistance to the regime. In short, pervasive rent seeking was incompatible with sustained economic growth, as it diverted scarce resources to non-economic uses and even forced the formal private sector into complicity with the rent seekers, thus further reducing legitimate economic activities and driving business into the informal sector.

The structural adjustment program required by international donors played an important role in Benin's political liberalization, despite the program's avowed purely economic and social objectives. By requiring reform of public sector management, it created expectations among senior civil servants and the business community, and later among the population at large, that their economic and social prospects would improve. It is noteworthy that the SAL was internalized in the public sector and endorsed by the Kérékou regime, which first shifted control over economic policy to technocratic ministers and then cited the failure to achieve SAL objectives as a major reason for the abandonment of the Marxist economic and political system. Finally, the national conference and the new government adopted the structural adjustment program as their basic economic policy.

Governments of excessive size and influence can be a major negative influence on economic and social development. Benin is not alone in this respect, nor in the socially and politically destabilizing impact of an inflated higher education system, which absorbed a major part of the education budget and public revenues to graduate many poorly qualified, unemployable youths, who were guaranteed careers in public service. This kind of higher education spending was not only inefficient, but it was done at the expense of primary education, especially of girls. Large military establishments consumed funds that could have provided better health care and education. Marxist Benin was such a case, but the same can also be said for non-Marxist regimes.

The World Bank in its lending policy must tread a delicate line between economic considerations and political interference. Where a country's political mismanagement and rent seeking leads to a misuse of resources, the Bank has a legitimate right to withhold support and to recommend that other donors withhold assistance until reforms are implemented, particularly when the Bank has been entrusted with monitoring economic performance on behalf of donors—a role that donors have come to expect the Bank to play as coordinator of foreign aid. Donors do have other agendas, including supporting democratic processes and human rights, that also influence their willingness to contribute.

Economic reform is more sustainable if there is an effective mechanism to inform opinion makers and the population about the objectives of reform and its consequences for them. Contrary to conventional wisdom, adjustment and political liberalization can go together. In Benin, the free clandestine press was an important factor in destroying the credibility of the regime after 1988 and became an accepted forum for criticism of and information about government policy. In addition, in 1991 the government conducted a full debate in parliament on the content of SAL II, which delayed policy implementation by several months but ensured political support for the reforms requested. Subsequent governments also will have to debate each phase of the reform in parliament. Moreover, the economic program provided relief for the urban and rural poor, who compose the majority of the population. SAL II provided some relief for those most affected by past mismanagement, paying indemnities to those leaving public service, buying medicines and schoolbooks for primary clinics and schools, mounting special programs for the unemployed, and rehabilitating run-down basic social infrastructure.

Notes

I am indebted to Emmanuel Akpa, Shigeo Katsu, Ismael Serageldin, Antoinette Sayeh, Eduarado Locatelli, and others who shared the Benin experience in the World Bank and who contributed to the dialogue leading to reform. The views expressed in this chapter are those of the author and do not represent those of The World Bank.

1. Robert Cornevin, *La République populaire du Benin* (Paris: Maisonneuve and Larose, 1981), 506–25.

2. See Dov Ronen, *Ethnicity, Ideology, and the Military in the People's Republic of Benin*, Discussion Paper 5 (Cambridge, Mass.: African-American Issues Center, 1984).

3. Ibid., 14.

4. Mark Gallagher, *Rent Seeking and Economic Growth in Africa* (Boulder, Colo.: Westview, 1991), 5–7; and Robert Klitgaard, *Adjusting to Reality* (San Francisco: ICS, 1991), 3–4.

5. Joshua Doriye, "Public Office and Private Gain: An Interpretation of the Tanzanian Experience," August 1991, typescript.

6. Alexander Gershenkron, *Economic Backwardness in Historical Perspective* (Cambridge: Cambridge University Press, 1962); and Richard Westebbe, "State Entrepreneurship in the United Netherlands, 1815–1830," *Explorations in Entrepreneurial History* 8 (1956).

7. Deborah Brautigam, *Governance and Economy*, Working Paper 815 (Washington, D.C.: World Bank, 1991), 8.

8. The central bank, the BCEAO, is a regional bank with national branches owned by seven countries; it controls monetary policy and domestic credit, including credit to governments.

9. World Bank, *Sub-Saharan Africa: From Crisis to Sustainable Growth: A Long-Term Perspective Study* (Washington, D.C.: World Bank, 1989), 60–61.

10. World Bank, *Issues of Governance in Borrowing Countries: The Extent of Their Relevance under the Bank's Articles of Agreement* (Washington, D.C.: World Bank, 1991).

11. Dunstan M. Wai, "Governance, Economic Development, and the Role of External Actors," paper prepared for the Conference on Governance and Economic Development in Sub-Saharan Africa, Oxford, May 2–4, 1991; and *Managing Development: The Governance Dimension*, Discussion Paper (Washington, D.C.: World Bank, 1991).

12. Ismael Serageldin and Pierre Landell-Mills, "Governance and the External Factor," paper prepared for World Bank Annual Conference on Development Economics, Washington, D.C., April 25–26, 1991.

13. Ibid., 11–12.

14. President Kérékou, "Message de la Nation," Ehuzu, Cotonou, December 1, 1989.

15. *Final Communiqué of the Special Joint Session of the Central Committee of the Popular Revolutionary Party of Benin, the Permanent Committee of the Revolutionary National Assembly, and the National Executive Council,* Cotonou, December 7, 1989.

16. IBRD Mission Chief, press statement, Cotonou, December 8, 1989; World Bank press release, Paris, December 14, 1989. The meeting was held at the Ministry of Cooperation.

17. IBRD Mission Chief, press statement, Cotonou, December 11, 1989.

18. The new government did not represent the political elites of the past, although all of its senior members were from the same classes that produced past political leaders. No members of the cabinet were members of past cabinets, although a few held technocratic jobs in the civil service or public enterprises.

MICHAEL BRATTON

Five ◈ Economic Crisis and Political Realignment in Zambia

Give us rain. Give us bananas. Give us sugarcane. Give us plantains. Give us meat.
Give us food. You are our king, but if you do not feed us properly, we will get rid of
you. The country is yours; the people must have their stomachs filled. Give us rain.
Give us food.
   —Accession rite of a Shambaa king, quoted in Steven Feierman, *Peasant Intellectuals*

In October 1991, voters in Zambia's presidential and parliamentary
elections got rid of Kenneth Kaunda and his ruling United National
Independence Party (UNIP). They handed trade unionist Frederick
Chiluba a sweeping victory, with more than three-quarters of the
vote, and granted his Movement for Multiparty Democracy (MMD)
125 out of 150 seats in the National Assembly. After two decades of
monopolistic one-party rule, there was a peaceful succession of civilian
governments in a competitive election that international observers
declared "free and fair."[1] In the current wave of political change in
Africa, Kaunda was the first nationalist founding father to be displaced
and Zambia the first Anglophone country to undergo a democratic
regime transition.[2]
   The results of the 1991 elections (see table 5.1) reveal a remarkable
consistency in voting behavior, with Zambians in every part of the
country except Eastern Province strongly favoring MMD over UNIP.
There was no discernible difference in the pattern of party preference
between urban and rural areas.[3] Whereas MMD won over 89 percent
of the parliamentary vote in the industrial Copperbelt Province, it

Table 5.1.   *Results of Parliamentary Elections, Zambia, October 1991* (percentage of total valid votes)

Province	MMD	UNIP
Central	73.07	26.93
Copperbelt	89.77	10.23
Eastern	26.08	73.92
Luapula	86.27	13.73
Lusaka	77.03	23.03
Northern	85.97	14.03
Northwestern	70.33	29.67
Southern	84.10	15.91
Western	80.56	19.44
Total	75.31	24.69

Source: Calculated from Zambia Independent Monitoring Team, "Summary of Parliamentary Election Results" (Lusaka: ZIMT, November 1991). These unofficial data do not include votes for independent or small party candidates.

also attained more than 84 percent in the rural constituencies of Luapula, Northern Province, and Southern Province.[4] Nor, for the most part, did voters express ethnic preferences through the ballot, with MMD running well in Bemba-, Tonga-, and Lozi-speaking areas. The only exception to MMD's countrywide ascendancy was UNIP's strong showing at the polls in Eastern Province.

Why was Kaunda so broadly defeated? In this chapter, I argue that a national economic crisis led to political realignment, as a ruling coalition of diverse classes and regions emerged to oppose the incumbent regime. A severe economic downturn in Zambia after 1975 seriously affected a wide range of social groups, including, most critically, urban wage earners, who had previously benefited from UNIP's patronage and welfare policies. UNIP's statist development strategy created a monumental national debt and drastically undermined living standards. When UNIP supporters could no longer afford the price of maize meal and were reduced to eating a single meal a day, they blamed Kaunda. The government's loss of legitimacy was marked by a series of urban food riots, which by 1990 had turned political. MMD—a loose alliance centered on the labor movement but including business and professional leaders—took advantage of the popular upsurge by blaming the economic distress on UNIP's mismanagement and corruption.[5]

Of course, Zambia was not the only African country to suffer economic crisis or political protest, but few moved as far and as fast down the path of political reform. What, then, distinguishes the Zambian case? This chapter offers an explanation centered on domestic rather than international factors, on civil society rather than the state. This is not to claim that the Zambian transition took place in international isolation from democratic initiatives in Eastern Europe or elsewhere in Africa, or that the government's desperate need for financial credits did not make it pliable to pressures from external donors and lenders. In marked contrast to the case of Kenya, however, Zambia's international development partners never attached explicit political conditions to their assistance and hence were not major players in the transition to multiparty politics.[6] Nor was the transition driven primarily by divisions within the ruling elite or by leadership defections to the opposition. Most UNIP defectors joined MMD well before the political transition began in April 1990, and once the transition was under way, the top hierarchy of the ruling party closed ranks.[7]

Thus, rather than regarding political reform as a top-down process promoted by interventionist donors or calculating elites, this chapter stresses the dynamics of state-society interactions. By 1990 in Zambia, the initiative for political reform lay outside the state in the actions of mass protesters and an increasingly unified opposition movement. Previous research demonstrates a direct relationship between demand and supply for political reform in African countries, with reform occurring in all sixteen countries that experienced civil protests between late 1989 and mid-1991.[8] Commonly, however, protests were not sustained, thus enabling state incumbents to truncate the reform process and to retain power with piecemeal concessions. Under what conditions, then, does the momentum of protest break through the resistance of entrenched leaders and lead to open and competitive elections?

One-party regimes submit to competitive elections only where there are sources of countervailing political power. These include a mobilized citizenry, a free press, civic watchdog groups, a unified political party, a professional civil service, and an independent judiciary.[9] This chapter focuses on the first factor: the emergence of a mass social movement in Zambia. In this case, the independent trade union congress and MMD provided channels through which economic grievances could be expressed and organized into an electoral bid for state power. The heart of this chapter is a narrative that traces how economic crisis led to political realignment and electoral transition.

The presentation is based on four main points. First, the Zambian government favored a development strategy marked by acute economic distortions and symbolized by the politically charged policy of subsidizing staple foods for urban consumers. The rebalancing of

Zambia's maladjusted economic structure required "a truly heroic reform effort,"[10] which the Zambian government undertook with vigor only belatedly, in 1985. Second, economic contraction and austerity policies had a profound social impact, in which poverty "trickled up" to most social classes in Zambia. But, whereas UNIP's patronage machine had always protected its key constituency of urban wage earners, by 1985 it had exhausted its resources. Previously privileged elements in society came to bear a share of the adjustment burden once the government committed itself to a serious reform effort.

Third, the existence of powerful interest groups in Zambia—especially organized labor, which enjoyed an unusual degree of autonomy—meant that economic grievances could be translated into political action. The trade union confederation played a catalytic role in directing mass opposition against the perceived incompetence and dishonesty of UNIP leaders and the authoritarian strictures of the single-party state. Fourth and finally, the emergence of MMD as a cohesive opposition party both reflected and enabled a fundamental political realignment among Zambian voters, in which urban wage earners changed from supporters to opponents of the UNIP government. Recognizing this shift, the ruling party sought reelection by bidding for the rural vote, only to discover that, after years of neglect by government, peasant farmers had also defected to the opposition.

The Zambian Economy: From Boom to Bust

For a decade after independence, Zambia was one of the most prosperous countries in Africa, with a balanced external trading account based on the export of copper. Providing 90 percent of foreign exchange earnings and 53 percent of the government budget, copper revenues enabled major public investments in health, education, and transportation. Opportunities for wage employment in the mining economy prompted outmigration from rural areas, making Zambia one of the most urbanized countries in sub-Saharan Africa. By 1990, urban dwellers accounted for 42 percent of the total population.[11] From the early colonial period onward, the agricultural sector was expected to provide a reliable supply of cheap food for the labor force in Copperbelt Province. Despite plentiful uncultivated land of reasonable agronomic quality, policymakers did not fully exploit agriculture's potential to contribute to a diversified economy.

UNIP's development strategy was guided by Kaunda's welfarist philosophy of Humanism that emphasized state ownership and administrative control. In a wave of nationalizations in the late 1960s, the government purchased majority shareholdings in all major mining and industrial enterprises. By the end of 1970s, the parastatal sector spanned the economy, accounting for 30 percent of GDP, 60 percent of investment, and 37 percent of formal sector employment. The strategy was motivated as much by political as by economic considerations and was aimed at the creation of patronage jobs. The Zambianization of the mines and civil service rectified racial inequalities in employment but at the cost of losing the best-qualified personnel. Overstaffing became a conspicuous feature of public institutions during the 1970s, with jobs in parastatal companies increasing twice as fast as production. And through control of trading licenses, the party ensured that access to opportunities in petty commerce was reserved for the party faithful.

Because the center of gravity in Zambian politics lay in the towns, the UNIP government granted urban wage earners a privileged position in Zambian society. The Brown Commission of 1966 unified urban wage scales at levels established for non-Africans. These developments pitched Zambian wages, particularly those in the mining sector, at "very high levels" and included numerous benefits: pensions and leave pay; housing, transport, medical, and educational allowances; loans and advances for special purchases; and access to canteens, clinics, and recreational facilities.[12] In 1968, a miner's average annual earnings were twice those of any other urban employee and over nine times those of a peasant farmer.[13]

The UNIP patronage machine did not completely overlook the rural areas. During the 1960s, copper earnings fueled a handout of public resources. Through a program to promote agricultural cooperatives, UNIP distributed jobs, loans, and trading licenses with the aim of building local political support for the ruling party and undermining opposition parties.[14] To guarantee a national supply of staple grains, the government provided fertilizer subsidies and panterritorial prices for controlled products. It established an unwieldy marketing bureaucracy known as the National Agricultural Marketing Board (NamBoard), which purchased all the grain that peasants chose to sell. The government's willingness to absorb the costs of transporting and storing grain from outlying regions helped to build popular support for UNIP among peasant farmers far from rail lines (in Central, Copperbelt, Lusaka, and Southern provinces).

But the government clearly favored urban over rural voters. The centerpiece of its economic policy was a subsidy of basic commodities consumed by townsfolk, principally maize meal (the staple starch), but also cooking oil, salt, milk, matches, and soap. Subsidies had been first introduced by the colonial authorities in the 1920s as a means to stabilize the labor supply; over time, the UNIP government used them to purchase political quiescence from potentially volatile urban constituents. The subsidization policy had many perverse effects: it was so broadly targeted that even high-income workers came to regard affordable food as an entitlement, it helped displace traditional grains from farmers' fields and from the Zambian diet, and it induced parastatal managers to rely on the government to make up deficits in the trading accounts of price-controlled products.

Politically, consumer price subsidies led the state to "align itself with the organized work force and the bureaucracy and . . . cut itself off from the poor peasantry."[15] Although Kaunda was rhetorically committed to a policy of rural development, he allowed agriculture's share of the public budget to decline from 7 percent in 1966–70 to 3 percent in 1975–80 and spent heavily on prestige projects in the capital city. Between 1965 and 1980, the terms of trade for rural dwellers deteriorated more than 5 percent per year.[16] Peasant producers experienced a decline in purchasing power as a direct result of the government policy to fix producer prices of major crops well below border price equivalents. As a consequence, food production declined and smuggling became rampant, with up to one-third of the national crop crossing the borders into Zaire and Malawi. By 1980 Zambia supplied only 79 percent of its food needs, and food imports were on the rise.

Moreover, copper proved to be a curse as well as a blessing. The world copper price slumped in the mid-1970s, and copper output began to dwindle as high-grade ore deposits were exhausted.[17] The Zambian economy entered a prolonged economic downturn, shrinking by an average 2.1 percent per year between 1965 and 1988.[18] Zambia was demoted from a middle- to a low-income economy, as annual per capita GNP slumped from $540 in 1964 to $290 in 1988.[19] The downward spiral resulted not only from external shocks but also from economic mismanagement. To offset losses in export revenues, the government borrowed heavily in domestic and international capital markets, leaving "a onerous legacy of overindebtedness and rapid inflation."[20] By 1988, the country's external public debt stood at 117 percent of GNP, and debt servicing had fallen seriously behind schedule. During the 1980s, the fiscal costs of maintaining consumer subsidies became unbearable. To counter the growing budget deficit (which stood at 30 percent of GDP by 1986), the government resorted to printing money. As a consequence, inflation rose during the 1980s to an average 50 percent per annum and, by 1990, to 120 percent. The economic crisis had arrived.

Economic Reform: Halting and Reluctant

The Zambian government was forced to confront the need for economic reform once it began to seek loans from international financial institutions. Standby agreements were negotiated with the IMF on four occasions between 1971 and 1981,[21] and program loans were taken from the World Bank in 1973 and 1976. The lenders attached policy conditions aimed at helping the government stabilize and adjust the economy. The conditions included devaluation of the national currency (the kwacha); increases in agricultural producer prices, especially for maize; wage freezes in the public sector, including mining; and elimination of some subsidies for basic consumer goods. At least in the short run, the economic reform program "challenged long-held fundamental assumptions about the relationship between . . . government and society,"[22] in particular the popularly held belief about an African ruler's responsibility to provide for his people.

The Zambian government's commitment to such reforms was lukewarm, and its half-hearted implementation efforts led repeatedly to arrears in loan repayments and breakdowns in international loan agreements. The government, by continuing to honor its patronage obligations, declined to make its promised reforms in agricultural policy and trade tariffs and failed to get public spending under control. For example, at the end of the 1970s, senior civil servants and parastatal managers received salary awards to maintain the real value of their incomes. Their perquisites—such as transportation, entertainment, and housing allowances, which amounted to at least half their salaries—were indexed for inflation. The IMF agreements in 1976 and 1978 called for a restructured mining industry, including mine closures and worker layoffs, but these measures were never implemented.

Guided by considerations of political feasibility, the government chose to reform agriculture first. It liberalized markets in 1982 by removing price controls and marketing restrictions on nonessential commodities like wheat and beef. In January 1986, restrictions were removed on who could sell maize and fertilizers, but the government retained an effective monopoly by fixing prices so low that private traders did not enter the market. Nor did policy reforms address persistent institutional problems such as the deteriorating state of farm-to-market roads and the inefficiency of NamBoard. As always, a good proportion of the crop was lost each year as harvested maize remained uncollected or was inadequately protected from the rains.

As the national economic crisis deepened, the government haltingly adopted a more serious commitment to economic reform. In October 1985, on the advice of technocrats in the Ministry of Finance, the government launched its most ambitious reform effort by auctioning foreign exchange, the first such experiment in Africa. The auction's main effect was to set in motion the most rapid devaluation of the kwacha in Zambia's history.[23] The reform program called for additional adjustment measures: decontrol of interest rates to tighten the money supply, removal of import licensing requirements to liberalize trade, and reduction of public expenditure through layoffs of state employees. The government's evident sincerity enabled Zambia to buy time with international donors, who, meeting in the Paris Club, agreed to reschedule the country's debt on three occasions between 1983 and 1986. In the final analysis, however, donors failed to honor all their pledges to support the reform program, and shortages of funds to finance the auction contributed to its eventual demise.[24]

The reform effort was also jeopardized by mass political opposition to the government's plan to remove maize meal subsidies over a two-year period beginning in 1986. The first target was the subsidy on superrefined breakfast meal, the preferred repast of the urban elite, followed later by the subsidy on coarse-ground roller meal, the daily diet of the urban poor. Perhaps panicked by a runaway budget deficit, the government removed the breakfast meal subsidy in one fell swoop in December 1986, and the price of breakfast meal doubled overnight. At the same time, roller meal disappeared from the market, as millers stopped producing the cheaper commodity for fear that the government would soon stop reimbursing the costs of the remaining subsidy. Faced with the choice of buying expensive meal or doing without, the urban poor rioted. In a weekend of fierce street fighting in Copperbelt Province, fifteen people were killed. Rattled, the president reinstated the full subsidy and nationalized the milling companies, accusing them of trying to destabilize his government.

Thus, even though he launched major economic reform initiatives, President Kaunda never put his full political weight behind them, responding instead to protests from UNIP's key urban political constituencies. He made a further sharp political reversal in April 1986 by appointing a team of doctrinaire socialists to key financial management positions. They gradually set about manipulating foreign exchange allocations. In January 1987, Kaunda suspended the auction and in May abandoned it entirely. Breaking off relations with the IMF, he introduced an indigenous New Economic Recovery Programme (NERP), in which Zambia would seek to "grow from its own resources." Its key measures were the limitation of debt payments to 10 percent of export earnings, a fixed and overvalued exchange rate for the kwacha, and controls on consumer prices.

Table 5.2.   *Labor Force and Paid Employment, Zambia, 1975–1990*

Year	Labor Force	Paid Employees	Percent Employed
1975	1,479,000	393,490	26.6
1980	1,758,810	384,090	22.0
1985	2,104,000	361,520	17.2
1990	2,527,000	358,430	14.2

Sources: Central Statistical Office, *Monthly Digest of Statistics* (Lusaka: Government Printer, 1989); Beatrice Liatto-Katundu, "Social Consequences of Structural Adjustment: Effects on Zambian Workers and Workers' Coping Strategies" (Lusaka: University of Zambia, Department on African Development Studies, November, 1991), typescript.

At first, the NERP was politically popular, enabling UNIP to win the 1988 single-party elections without significant reductions in voter turnout or in the president's margin of victory. After the election, the government allowed the price of maize meal to rise significantly but compensated low-income formal sector workers with coupons to cover part of the cost increase. The NERP resulted in new distortions: hoarding by wholesalers, price control evasion by petty traders, and real hardship among informal sector workers excluded from the maize meal coupon system.[25] Faced with the curtailment of funds from Western bilateral donors, Zambia had no choice but to reopen negotiations with the IMF. In preparing the ground for a new loan agreement, the government removed price controls on all consumer goods except maize meal. Thus the stage was set for a showdown over the role of maize meal subsidies in the Zambian political economy.

Social Impact: Trickle-Up Poverty

The brunt of economic crisis and adjustment was borne by ordinary producers and consumers. In particular, low-income urban dwellers encountered shrinking employment opportunities, a rapidly rising cost of living, and the virtual collapse of social services. Together, these trends precipitated "an *extremely large* fall in living standards, incomparably larger than anything experienced in the industrial countries and among the largest in developing countries in recent years."[26]

The labor market dried up. Between 1975 and 1990 the number of paid employees decreased by 9 percent while the number of job seekers rose by 71 percent (see table 5.2). By 1984, the government could no longer resist calls for a restructuring of the mining industry. In return for guaranteed flows of foreign exchange, Zambia Consolidated Copper Mines (ZCCM) agreed to close three mines and several processing plants, trim management ranks, and dismiss 4,000 workers.

By 1989, an estimated 60 percent of the men in the mining center of Mufulira were unemployed.[27]

For those who retained jobs, favorable wage rates could not be upheld. The government first introduced ceilings and freezes on wage increases in the 1970s, the worst effects of which were moderated by cost of living adjustments to lower-paid employees. But by 1983, real earnings for formal sector workers dropped below preindependence levels for the first time, with mine workers absorbing the largest losses. Expenditure on public service salaries declined by 26 percent in real terms between 1975 and 1985, leading to resignations from the civil service, difficulty in recruitment, and low employee morale.

Inflation became the biggest bugaboo. The devaluation of the kwacha and the government's failure to stem its ballooning budget deficit led to unprecedented price rises in the 1980s. Between 1980 and 1986, the consumer price index for low-income urban households (which had doubled in the previous five years) leapt 260 percent. In 1985 alone, at the outset of the foreign exchange auction effort, the purchasing power of urban consumers fell by two-thirds,[28] and a whole range of prices rose in concert: maize meal, petroleum, and interest rates. The shock of inflation was compounded when the liberalization of import controls sent a flood of luxury consumer goods from Europe and South Africa into the display windows of long-empty stores. These niceties were beyond the reach of most consumers and raised political criticism about previously hidden income gaps.

The erosion of real incomes hurt rural dwellers, too. By 1980, roughly 80 percent of rural households "did not have sufficient income to satisfy their minimum private consumption needs."[29] Given the severe shortages of consumer goods in rural outlets, there was little to buy anyway. Periodically, the press reported on cases of extreme distress in outlying rural areas where hunger-stricken communities were subsisting on wild tubers and relief efforts were hampered by lack of transport.[30]

Access to social services also deteriorated as the government, under pressure to prune the budget deficit, cut back drastically on social expenditures. At first, the authorities resisted laying off personnel in service ministries and instead targeted other recurrent expenses. All government departments, especially rural extension agencies, experienced shortages of fuel to operate vehicles and materials for routine repairs. Schools found themselves without textbooks, and health clinics ran out of essential drugs. There was a marked physical deterioration in roads, buildings, and equipment and an interruption of development projects and programs, even where matching funds were available from foreign donors. In short there was "a wholesale deterioration in the productivity of the government machine."[31]

The nutritional and health status of the Zambian population slipped during the 1980s, accompanied by a sharp increase in child mortality.[32] The estimated proportion of malnourished rural children varied from one-third in Eastern Province to two-thirds in Northern Province.[33] Major outbreaks of cholera in 1990 and 1991 were directly linked to the collapse of water and sanitation facilities in low-income, high-density urban areas. The press reported an increase in illegal abortions, which were attributed to the prohibitively high cost of feeding children. And the incidence of HIV infection continued to rise, with about half of all hospital beds occupied by AIDS and HIV-infected tuberculosis patients. At the same time, the government introduced cost recovery measures such as service fees at hospitals and clinics. This change in policy radically challenged the popular assumption that government would automatically provide for basic human needs. By 1990, virtually the only welfare program still offered by the UNIP government to the Zambian people was the consumer subsidy on maize.[34]

In response to declining living standards, Zambians devised various coping strategies. The most common response was to reduce household consumption. A 1987 survey of one hundred households in Lusaka revealed that, as prices rose, poorer households stopped buying meat, chicken, and fish and cut back on bread and vegetables.[35] Some families reduced the number of daily meals; others borrowed money from family or employers to make ends meet. Under these circumstances, there was a marked decline in the practice of families helping relatives. Workers also reduced expenditures by walking to work, a practice that, along with moonlighting (holding a second job), contributed to absenteeism and reduced productivity.

With the loss of paid jobs, workers left the formal sector. Many took to petty trading on city streets, eking out a living by hawking miniscule quantities of retail goods: single cigarettes, oil by the cup, salt by the spoon. Although the number of people working in the informal sector expanded—to an estimated 42 percent in Lusaka[36]— earnings fell as consumer demand shrank and more sellers entered the market. Other exit options included return migration to rural areas, as the quality of urban life began to crumble. Professionals with marketable skills left Zambia entirely, usually finding jobs elsewhere in southern Africa. The brain drain was most pronounced in the medical sector, where dwindling real incomes and lax professional standards led to vacancies in almost half the established posts for doctors in the government health service.[37]

Economic reforms created new categories of winners and losers. The foreign exchange auction released a flow of imports to manufacturers and traders but neglected agricultural producers. In urban areas, foreign companies and Asian businessmen, who could deploy vast reserves of kwacha, did well in the bidding war for foreign exchange. The imports they purchased enabled a modest recovery in the use of factory capacity but also led to a politically indiscreet orgy of conspicuous consumption. Parastatal companies and the small Zambian business class were ill-prepared to prosper in a more competitive environment. The biggest losers were party leaders and government officials, who saw their rent-seeking opportunities diminish with the abolition of administrative rationing of foreign exchange, a process widely believed to have been corrupt. They vigorously lobbied against the adoption of the auction and were the main advocates of a return to a fixed exchange rate.

In sum, an upward trickle of poverty gradually affected all social classes. Soaring inflation did indiscriminate damage, "reduc[ing] the working class to subsistence level and sharply alter[ing] the expectations of the non-political middle class."[38] This is not to claim that the costs of economic contraction were distributed evenly. Increases in the prices of basic consumer goods hit the poor more severely than the rich and urban households more than self-provisioning rural households. What was new, however, were the costs of economic adjustment to the urban bureaucratic bourgeoisie and the aristocracy of mine labor, who had earlier benefited from UNIP's largesse. During the 1980s, urban wage earners saw their economic advantages dissipate.

Political Impact: Upsurge in Civil Society

Deservedly or not, Zambians are stereotyped as "notoriously passive, even lethargic," displaying an "unusually high . . . threshold at which public tolerance of economic conditions is broken."[39] But popular frustration with the deprivations of everyday life periodically burst into open political protest. Major incidents of civil unrest occurred on three separate occasions in postcolonial Zambia: November 1974, December 1986, and June 1990. On each occasion, riots were precipitated by food price increases following a government decision to reduce food subsidies.

Before 1990, however, the protests fizzled out, the government revoked its subsidy cuts, and political opposition did not cohere or persist. In 1990, these conditions changed. The Kaunda government had become so dependent on international assistance that it could not easily back away from its commitments to shrink subsidies. Equally important, an alternative ruling coalition emerged within Zambia's civil society, with a nascent political organization aimed at ending single-party rule.

Political organization in Zambia has always been rooted in urban areas. In the colonial era, workers formed burial societies, dance clubs, and welfare associations to ease the transition from rural to urban life.[40] Mine workers pioneered techniques of mass political confrontation with wage strikes in 1935 and 1940. Only with the accession of power of a Labour party government in Britain, however, did the governor of Northern Rhodesia permit the formation of trade unions in 1946. At first, the Trade Union Congress limited its demands to workplace issues and failed to rally behind the nationalist political campaign against the Central African Federation.[41] By 1956, however, miners initiated rolling strikes and boycotts of tribal administration and white businesses.[42] A close relationship was established between the trade union movement and nationalist political parties (first the African National Congress, later UNIP) around the issue of African economic advancement. When the colonial government permitted political rights, the labor movement became the organizational machine through which UNIP turned out the vote. Nationalist leaders implicitly promised their followers that they would reap the material rewards of political independence: they would be "fed."

After independence, Kaunda came to regard the party as the instrument to consolidate state control over society, including the labor movement. The UNIP government promulgated the Industrial Relations Act in 1971, which made strikes illegal in strategic industries, inserted government into negotiations between labor and management, and granted government powers to remove and appoint union leaders. In the same year, workers formed the Zambia Congress of Trade Unions (ZCTU), whose base rested in eighteen affiliated unions, including the Copperbelt-based Mineworkers Union of Zambia (MUZ) and the nationwide Zambia National Union of Teachers (ZNUT). The concentration of mine workers in company townships in Copperbelt Province—in contrast to dispersed workplaces and residential patterns of manufacturing workers—led mine workers to develop a relatively cohesive and militant class consciousness.[43] The organized labor movement grew steadily; by 1980, ZCTU membership stood at

380,000, almost double the party's paid membership.

At first, both state and labor regarded ZCTU as an official channel of communication, with UNIP's allies taking union leadership positions and workers gaining representation on the UNIP National Council. Yet, ironically, the Industrial Relations Act of 1971 helped to strengthen the independence of the trade union movement. It stipulated that there would be only one union per industry and that ZCTU would be the only recognized umbrella body. Moreover, the act provided that, once a union organized 60 percent of the workers in an industry, union dues would automatically be deducted from workers' paychecks, with 20 percent of the dues going to the union. Thus, because approximately 90 percent of Zambia's formal sector workers were organized, the unions were unusually well financed.

With the election of Frederick Chiluba as ZCTU president in 1974, the union began to flex its muscles. Chiluba was convinced that the labor movement could best represent its members if it was constituted as an independent interest group. In a situation where the government was the largest employer of labor, the interests of workers in collective bargaining were undermined when the unions were directed by the ruling party. ZCTU asserted its independence through the election of leaders, rejecting those who accepted patronage posts offered by UNIP. Chiluba and ZCTU Secretary-General Newstead Zimba refused repeated offers to join the UNIP Central Committee, saying they would serve the party only if they were sent by union members.

Political interests in rural Zambia were less well organized. UNIP had incorporated the Zambia Cooperative Federation, the umbrella body for cooperative societies and unions, to the point that farmers came to regard it as a parastatal rather than their own organization. It executed government's agricultural marketing policies rather than representing members' on policy or political issues. The only independent pressure group in the agriculture sector was the Commercial Farmers' Bureau (CFB), initially the redoubt of white estate owners, but which racially integrated its leadership and which by the 1980s had added to its 1,700 membership over 1,000 small-scale black farmers. While CFB became an increasingly vocal and articulate critic of state-managed agriculture (for example in annual producer price negotiations with the Ministry of Agriculture and through editorials in its mouthpiece, *Productive Farming*), it leaders sought to remain nonpolitical. Thus, when the opportunity came to organize an opposition alliance to challenge the ruling coalition, rural interests were either emasculated or chose to stay on the sidelines.

Leadership within civil society therefore fell to urbanites, predominantly in the labor movement but also among entrepreneurs and professionals. Business leaders, like Emmanuel Kasonde and Elias Chipimo, discouraged by UNIP's *dirigiste* economic approach, were among the first to split from UNIP. When in 1980 Chipimo, a banker, was bold enough to imply that multiparty competition might forestall military intervention in politics, he was stripped of his job and publicly vilified.[44] UNIP politicians like Arthur Wina and Vernon Mwaanga, who fell out of Kaunda's good graces, took refuge in commercial enterprise and accumulated financial resources independently from the state. Zambian businessmen found themselves disadvantaged under regimes of both state-regulated allocations and radical market experiments like the foreign exchange auction. Thus, together with professional colleagues in the Zambia Economic Society and the Law Association of Zambia, they began to develop a critique of UNIP's mismanagement.

The discourse of political opposition in Zambia had a strongly economistic slant, influenced heavily by ZCTU's commitment to the protection of jobs and the maintenance of living standards. The party and labor first drew apart on economic issues in November 1974, when the government announced substantial consumer price increases and proposed to remove subsidies on bread and cooking oil. ZCTU organized vigorous street demonstrations in Lusaka and Copperbelt, forcing the government to back down. And wildcat strikes proliferated at the turn of the decade in response to ceilings on wage increases imposed under Zambia's early agreements with the IMF.

Confrontation between state and labor turned explicitly political in the early 1980s over reforms to decentralize administration. The government proposed to merge the administration of urban centers and mine townships, thereby diluting the quality of welfare services available to mine workers. The government also restricted the election of local government councillors to party members only, thus weakening the voting rights of Zambian citizens. ZCTU and MUZ opposed both measures, leading to the expulsion of seventeen of their leaders from UNIP. Four senior labor leaders, including Chiluba and MUZ Chairman Timothy Walamba, were detained for several weeks on charges of conspiracy to overthrow the government. Miners reacted with a series of protest strikes during 1981, leading the government to back down: it removed the threat to services for miners, accepted a court ruling to release the union leaders, and offered them seats on the boards of directors of parastatal companies. These events signified "the power of the labor movement in the one-party state, and the weakness of the party at the local level."[45]

In reaction to the government's program of economic reform, MUZ used its influence to delay the closing of unprofitable mines and to ensure that personnel cuts were not as deep as the government first proposed. And in 1984, MUZ called upon the government to introduce new machinery to upgrade mine productivity. The chairman of MUZ claimed that the miner fed "every other citizen" and sustained the political and industrial infrastructures and that he "must not be the easiest target of cost-saving measures while those who live from his sweat and toil have an easy life."[46] ZCTU's secretary general even challenged Zambia's foreign policy, suggesting importing essential commodities from South Africa.

The government's hesitant approach to economic reform derived in part from its failure to bring the trade unions to the negotiating table with the international financial institutions. For example, under the April 1983 IMF standby agreement, there was to be a 10 percent wage ceiling, which the union accepted only after the government agreed not to eliminate mining jobs.[47] In April 1985, however, the government acceded to an 18 percent wage rise for unionized workers when it found itself confronting ZCTU over escalating prices for essential commodities. Notably, mine workers did not participate in the 1986 food riots because the Zambia Consolidated Copper Mines protected its employees from the increase by providing its own subsidy on maize meal.

The frequency of industrial protest increased toward the end of the decade and, significantly, spread to the public service sector. From January to April 1985, the state was gripped by a series of illegal strikes, which included doctors and nurses. Such events recurred throughout 1987, 1988, and 1989, usually led by administrative and parastatal employees dismayed at the erosion of the purchasing power of their wages and salaries. The defection of lower-level public servants to the opposition camp was prompted by the trickling up of poverty into formerly middle-class ranks. Once the middle classes joined the opposition in large numbers, the nature of protest shifted qualitatively from narrow economic concerns to a broad-based political critique.

Building on a growing reputation as the only national leader capable of challenging Kaunda, Chiluba embraced the multiparty cause. At a labor union rally, he queried, in reference to Eastern Europe: "If the owners of socialism have withdrawn from the one-party system, who are the Africans to continue with it?" Calling for a referendum on party pluralism, Chiluba announced that "ZCTU believes that the one-party system is open to abuse; it is not the people in power who should direct political change, but the ordinary masses."[48] Later, a ZCTU workshop on economic recovery condemned the closed deliberations at UNIP's national conventions and drew attention to the volatility of the economic situation, "which needs to be corrected without delay."[49]

This chapter does not enumerate the events in Zambia's political transition, since this information is available elsewhere.[50] Suffice it to say that, during 1990, President Kaunda made a series of concessions to the escalating demands of the opposition camp: first for a referendum on multiparty politics, then for a multiparty election, and finally for international election observers. The decisive event was the resurgence of mass civil unrest in June 1990, sparked by the doubling of maize meal prices. Angry protesters in Lusaka sent pointed political messages to Kaunda not only by setting ablaze a national monument commemorating his leadership role in the nationalist struggle, but also by singling out state-owned retail stores as the main target of looting. Citizens now explicitly blamed the single-party system for their economic plight.

It was in this context of deep public alienation that an alternative ruling coalition made its first appearance. The National Interim Committee for Multiparty Democracy, created in July 1990, drew together the various organized interests in civil society and represented all ethnic subgroups.[51] The committee was chaired by Arthur Wina (businessman and former UNIP finance minister), supported by two vice-chairs: Frederick Chiluba, in charge of organization and operations, and Vernon Mwaanga (businessman and former UNIP foreign minister), responsible for publicity. The committee saw its mandate as the rapid restoration of accountable politics. It argued that a referendum was unnecessarily expensive and time consuming, especially given the patent public sentiment for pluralism. Kaunda tried to delay the referendum for a year, using his opponents' own argument for a national registration of voters prior to any election. But the president was soon faced with huge urban crowds chanting the opposition slogan, "The Hour Has Come!" These peaceful rallies—"the first in Africa on the scale of Leipzig and Prague"[52]—left Kaunda with little choice but to accede to the opposition's main demand to move directly to multiparty elections.

The 1991 Election Campaign

The election campaign began in earnest after MMD was registered as a political party in January 1991 and Frederick Chiluba was elected party president at the founding MMD Congress in February. The campaign revealed that all political parties relied on the distribution of patronage resources to get out the vote, though UNIP had major advantages.[53] And the election results confirmed that the Zambian electorate had shifted it partisan preferences.

MMD concentrated its voter mobilization effort in the towns by continuing to hold mass rallies. While the crowds, predominantly young men, grew smaller after the heady days of spring 1990, they were still large. The fledgling MMD structure was built around the local branches of ZCTU's member unions, especially in the towns served by railroads, but also in provincial and district capitals. Unionized workers disseminated the MMD message, occupied local party leadership positions, and recruited party members. Turning patronage policies on its head, some public service workers did organizing work for the opposition on government time and using public vehicles.

Chiluba ostensibly encouraged unions to remain independent of all political parties in order to concentrate on pressuring any new government to improve workers' wages and living standards.[54] Accordingly, six senior ZCTU leaders had to resign from the union before they could run on the MMD ticket. But other ZCTU leaders retorted that their members had already abandoned UNIP; MUZ Chairman Jonathan Simakuni asserted publicly that UNIP could not hope to win a majority at the polls without support from workers.[55]

In an effort to expand its urban, working-class base into a cross-regional, multiclass coalition, MMD formed branches in the countryside. The civil servants' and teachers' unions were critical conduits, and rural schools and government extension offices became centers of MMD support. Local businessmen contributed campaign resources and occupied party leadership positions. In Northern, Southern and Western provinces, MMD picked up support from the adherents of former regional opposition parties that had been banned or absorbed by UNIP. The local MMD party apparatus, such as it was, was assembled rapidly in a two-month period leading up to the first party congress. In this process, and during the selection of parliamentary candidates, MMD headquarters often pushed local preferences aside, creating an unfortunate precedent of arbitrary, patrimonial decision-making. Top MMD leaders grabbed safe seats in Copperbelt Province, and regional MMD bosses allegedly bought party cards en masse to boost their own local followings.

UNIP made systematic efforts to hamper opposition political organizing. Undercutting the key source of MMD funding, the government promulgated the Industrial Relations Act of 1990, which made it unlawful for trade unions to use workers' subscriptions to foster any political party, unless a separate voluntary fund was set up for that purpose.[56] And in a sharp reversal of UNIP's previous policy to politicize the bureaucracy, the prime minister's office announced that civil servants owed their allegiance to the nation and not to a party — and henceforth should be politically neutral.[57] In practice, this directive was addressed only to supporters of opposition parties; the prime minister threatened dismissal of workers in the civil service, local government, and defense and security forces if they did not show loyalty to UNIP. The civil servants' union retorted that it was folly to expect its members to stand on the sidelines when the country's future was being determined.[58] The secretary general of ZCTU challenged the government to dismiss any public workers it deemed disloyal, threatening that the unions could in turn "disrupt everything."[59]

Kaunda acknowledged that the towns had swung to the opposition and concentrated UNIP's campaign on the rural areas, dispatching senior leaders to tour all provinces. UNIP's rural strategy was symbolized by the choice of a hoe as the party's ballot symbol. The heart of its approach was to woo to UNIP Zambia's 280 hereditary chiefs, whose endorsement would supposedly induce their followers to remain loyal to the ruling party. Eleven chiefs were included among UNIP's parliamentary candidates, and UNIP leaders supported proposals to give chiefs decisionmaking positions in the National Assembly and the party hierarchy.[60] In 1990, the UNIP government increased the salaries of traditional rulers and in 1991 distributed Toyota Land Cruisers to senior chiefs, notably in Eastern Province.

Throughout the campaign, observers in the capital city were unclear about the political alignment of rural dwellers: Which way would they vote? There was much speculation that, being poorly educated and assumed to lack political sophistication, they might be inclined to vote for the best-known party. But UNIP's organization had atrophied in most rural areas within a decade of independence,[61] and by 1991, local party organizers were able to recruit only schoolchildren to attend UNIP election rallies in rural areas. By contrast, knowledge of MMD (if not its party organization) had quickly penetrated to even remote villages. In three rural provinces I visited during the campaign, people openly flashed the MMD finger-and-thumb sign and hollered its slogan. When questioned about the popularity of the chiefs, rural respondents (especially younger voters) argued that the chiefs had lost the respect of their subjects and that, rather than advocate the ruling party, chiefs should be neutral arbiters whom anyone in the community could turn to for guidance.

Kaunda also made special appears to women, a majority group in rural areas. In previous elections, women had been active voters and loyal UNIP supporters, being willing to turn out and to wait in long lines at the polls. By 1991, however, female support for UNIP was questionable, probably because women had shouldered most the costs of coping with economic austerity.[62] UNIP Womens' League was still able to orchestrate rituals of support at UNIP rallies in the urban areas, but in a notable act of defiance, the market women of Kabwata shouted down the UNIP slogan, "One Zambia," with a chorus of "No sugar!" MMD promised to liberate market women from "the iron fist of the UNIP market committee" by releasing them from requirements to purchase party cards, to support party "vigilantes," and to adhere to party commands on the opening and closing of markets.[63]

The election campaign was highly vituperative and centered on personalities rather than issues. Perhaps unsurprisingly after thirty years of one-man rule, the election became a referendum on the performance of Kaunda himself. All candidates resorted to character assassination, most often involving charges and countercharges about dishonesty in the use of public funds. To the extent that issues were discussed at all, Kaunda built his campaign on the issue of political stability. He raised the inflammatory specter of civil war if MMD won and threatened to "deal ruthlessly" with those known to vote against UNIP. Eastern Province became the epicenter of a UNIP intimidation campaign to burn houses, crops, and granaries.[64]

Young MMD supporters retaliated in kind, mainly in Copperbelt Province. Kaunda charged that MMD would do anything to overturn a UNIP victory, including challenging election results in the courts and inciting mutiny among the junior ranks of the army. Chiluba responded with claims that UNIP was harboring a secret commando unit in Malawi and called for an international peacekeeping force to supervise elections and the transition.[65] These outbursts probably contributed to voter cynicism about all politicians and almost certainly frightened some voters away from the polls on election day.

The opposition capitalized on the real issue of the campaign: the shattered economy. A hard-hitting MMD media campaign, featuring pictures of potholed highways and fetid water supplies, drew attention to the decline in public services. MMD candidates harped on the shortage of basic commodities but were careful not to attack UNIP for removing price subsidies. An MMD district official in Northern Province told me that "UNIP campaigned for us: inflation was our best weapon in recruiting support for MMD."

The opposition attributed Zambia's woes to UNIP's mismanagement and corruption. While hospitals and schools were "in dire need

. . . UNIP and its government officials were driving expensive imported cars without regard for the welfare of citizens."[66] MMD promised to remove party salaries and expenditures from the public budget, requiring instead that "each political party . . . make adequate arrangements for the sustenance of its officials."[67] At a rally in Ndola, Vernon Mwaanga charged that Parliament had granted 1.3 billion Kwacha of taxpayers' money for the UNIP election campaign and for a UNIP leaders' retirement scheme.[68] UNIP leaders were also alleged to have raided parastatal companies to swell family bank accounts abroad. MMD promised that, if it won the election, it would repossess UNIP properties and prosecute leaders who defrauded the state.

MMD promised a liberal economic policy. A manifesto released in February 1991 declared that the state would not be a "central participant" in the economy and encouraged "a wider spectrum of entrepreneurship"; it would cooperate with international donors to convert debt obligations and regain creditworthiness; and it would control inflation, but not through "an unbalanced suppression of worker earnings." On agricultural policy, Chiluba promised to shift subsidies from consumption to production.[69] He warned supporters to "brace for hard times" and prepare for "sacrifice and hard work."[70] MMD's advocacy of economic liberalization, however, contradicted the demands of its followers for price controls. Some local MMD party cadres adopted a more populist line, holding out the prospect of cheaper maize meal and the removal of fees for services. Such unrealistic expectations, readily embraced by MMD supporters, presaged almost certain popular disillusionment after the election.

For the most part, UNIP tried to dodge debate on economic issues, asserting that MMD's economic platform was a carbon copy of UNIP's own programs for debt management and privatization. Instead, UNIP resorted to the tried-and-true tactics of patronage politics, promising to reward voters in return for votes. Kaunda reminded Zambians that UNIP had "taken care of the poorest of the poor by subsidizing mealie-meal" and promised grinding mills and infrastructure repairs for the rural areas.[71] He claimed that UNIP was the only party to enjoy the backing of the international donor community. Appealing to the nation to allow time for the party to finish its "program of action" to revive the economy, Kaunda launched his campaign by announcing new spending programs for microindustrial enterprises and womens' projects. The party doled out T-shirts to attendees at UNIP rallies, bribed local party officials to prevent them from crossing over to the opposition, and issued bad government checks for school repairs at rural campaign stops.

UNIP also tried to deny patronage to supporters of the opposition.

For example, maize meal coupons were withheld from those who could not produce a UNIP membership card. A UNIP district governor openly threatened that non-UNIP members could not live in council houses, ride on public buses, or enter markets.[72] The courts subsequently ruled this type of campaigning illegal.

Once the electoral campaign began, the UNIP government abandoned any pretense of further economic reform. At first, the government's decision not to revoke price increases on maize meal following the 1990 food riots appeared to bespeak a new commitment to fiscal discipline. But the official price of maize meal was kept constant from the time the election was announced in August 1990 until polling day in October 1991. With inflation more than halving the purchasing power of the kwacha every year, consumers thus experienced a drop in the price of this staple commodity relative to all other prices. In addition, the government offered massive pay hikes—85 percent in 1990 and 100 percent in 1991—to public service and parastatal workers. And the parastatal mining companies introduced their own maize meal subsidies for workers, as did the army for the troops.

By this time, political leaders were responding more to the exigencies of electioneering than to the warnings of the international financial agencies. As the election approached, maize meal subsidies rose to an unsupportable US$1.5 million per day, and subsidies to parastatals ballooned to approximately 30 percent of the public budget. In September, when Zambia again defaulted on loan payments, the IMF and the World Bank broke off relations. At the same time, due to a shortfall in domestic maize production in the 1991 season, Zambia faced the prospect of running out of maize meal before election day. As an emergency measure, the government contracted with suppliers in South Africa to deliver enough maize to carry the country through to March 1992, with payment guaranteed from future copper returns after the election.

Thus, MMD's overwhelming victory—in which it won more than three-fourths of the vote in the October 1991 general elections—was also bitter, for the new government inherited a bankrupt economy and an electorate who continued to look to the state to feed it. More than a single competitive election would be required to dismantle the legacy of economic crisis endowed by a single-party patronage regime.

Conclusion

The literature on the political economy of economic reform reflects the perspectives of states and donors. A top-down framework is warranted because African societies contain few organized interests that initiate, support, or understand a call for economic liberalization. Not so with political reform. Recent political openings have been prompted by mass political protest. The analytic challenge in accounting for political reform outcomes, therefore, is to develop a perspective that allows for the inclusion of bottom-up influences from within civil society.

The economic crisis in African countries is a fundamental cause of the demand for political reform, more so than political rights abuses per se. After all, the recent flush of political protests in Africa have occurred in a context where economic conditions were rapidly deteriorating but where the degree of central political control has remained constant for many years. Thus, the popular demand for political accountability seems to be largely instrumental, aimed at restoring economic equilibrium. Moreover, most ordinary Africans do not seem to attribute declining living standards to ill-advised economic policies but rather to elite corruption. Hence they are inclined to change leaders rather than policies.

Let us expand this point. Leader-follower patronage ties are the defining characteristic of African politics and the thread of continuity in African political history. In traditional societies, the political survival of the chief depended on his ability to guarantee regular rains and bountiful harvests. A new social compact was struck in the nationalist era, with the leaders of anticolonial struggles basing their claim to authority on promising to deliver the material advantages denied to ordinary people under colonial discrimination. And, after independence, the same political leaders constructed personal networks through which they traded the goods and services of "development" in return for political loyalty. These postcolonial regimes were durable as long as the patron could deliver the goods, but they became brittle when the flow of public funds began to evaporate. Such regimes became doubly vulnerable if state elites were perceived to be living high on the hog while the populace suffered.

The demise of the UNIP party-state in Zambia was a logical outgrowth of the politics of patronage by which its leaders maintained power. At the outset, when copper revenues were flowing, Kaunda was able to demonstrate concretely that "it pays to belong to UNIP." Because this accommodative style of politics did not rely heavily on coercion, and because the persuasive power of his ideology of Humanism was soon exhausted, Kaunda came to rely for political survival almost exclusively on the distribution of material inducements. Ultimately, however, the UNIP patronage machine ran out of fuel due to a deadly combination of external shocks and internal mismanagement. Economic reform was politically volatile in Zambia because it was attempted "in a context in which the powerful organized interests that had benefitted from earlier policies were still fundamentally in place."[73] The activation and political realignment of these interests was triggered by the government's gradual withdrawal of subsidies, especially for food.

As poverty trickled up and deprivation touched every social class in Zambia's urbanized society, people began to blame the occupants of the commanding heights: the party-state leaders themselves. While political parties were banned, dissidents expressed opposition through labor unions and professional associations; later, when a political opening enabled the registration of political parties, a broad coalition of social interests cohered around MMD. Even though Kaunda tried to deflect attention elsewhere, MMD succeeded in making UNIP's mismanagement of the economy the underlying theme of its successful 1991 election campaign.

The case of Zambia draws attention to characteristics of civil society that facilitate electoral transitions. First, high levels of urbanization and industrialization meant that Zambia had an unusually well-educated, well-paid, and class-conscious population. The extent and rapidity of contraction in the national economy—among the most precipitous in Africa—provoked a particularly keen grievance among urban wage earners. Zambia's characteristics as an socioeconomic outlier help to explain why it was one of the first African countries to undergo an electoral transition.

Second, the opposition alliance was broad, spanning the politically relevant cleavages in society. It included both urban and rural dwellers, mine workers, and the unemployed, businessmen and civil servants, plus representatives from most regions of the country. This inclusive coalition contrasts with narrower opposition movements in other African countries, which, for example, are predominantly urban in Côte d'Ivoire, ethnic in Kenya, and Islamic in Algeria. Third, social forces possessed an organizational framework upon which to build a bid for state power, namely the labor unions. In most African countries, independent national associations do not exist or, as in the case of the Christian churches in Kenya and Zaire, are wary of partisan involvement in electoral politics. The cohesion of social forces behind MMD meant that Zambia was able to avoid the fragmentation of the opposition into multiple parties that is so characteristic of other liberalizing African countries.

But the emergence of a newly dominant movement in Zambia raises a cautionary note about the persistence of patronage in African politics. Single-party politics reinforced a patrimonial political culture, in which people believe that their well-being depends upon attaching themselves to the coattails of powerful leaders. In the aftermath of the election, opportunists are abandoning UNIP and flocking to MMD in the hope, as one MMD cabinet minister put it, that government will be an "eating post."

The new government thus faces unrealistic popular expectations about its ability to rapidly improve living standards. On the one hand, the election mandate endows Chiluba with the legitimacy he needs to promote realistic consumer prices. The absence of political protest in the wake of the announcement of the halving of roller meal subsidies in December 1991[74] is a sign that democratically elected governments are not necessarily weaker than authoritarian regimes at pushing economic reform. On the other hand, the still-powerful unions have shown themselves willing to turn against their erstwhile political leader on issues like civil service retrenchment and wage controls. Within a year of taking office, Chiluba was already confronting the highest rate of industrial strikes in Zambia's history. Over time, the capacity of a democratically elected government to contain such expressions of economically driven political protest is likely to decline.

Notes

1. National Democratic Institute for International Affairs/Carter Center of Emory University, *The October 31, 1991, National Elections in Zambia* (Washington, D.C.: National Democratic Institute, 1992).

2. Similar transitions took place during 1991 in Benin, Cape Verde, and São Tomé and Príncipe. In the multiparty elections in Gabon and Côte d'Ivoire, the incumbent president and party were returned.

3. An initial analysis suggested a significant difference (at the .001 level) in urban-rural voter preferences, with MMD securing 83.4 percent in major urban constituencies against 71.1 percent in rural constituencies. But this distinction did not hold countrywide; instead, it was accounted for almost entirely by results from Eastern Province, a predominantly rural area.

4. Without Chiluba's favorite son status in Luapula (his birthplace) and Copperbelt Province (where he built his political career), the vote spread between urban and rural provinces would have been even narrower.

5. Guillermo O'Donnell and Phillipe Schmitter, *Transitions from Authoritarian Rule: Tentative Conclusions about Uncertain Outcomes* (Baltimore: Johns Hopkins University Press, 1986).

6. Interview, senior economic adviser to the president of Zambia, Lusaka, October 1991.

7. The last major defector to MMD was Humphrey Mulemba, former UNIP party secretary general, several months before Kaunda made his first major concession to allow a referendum on party pluralism.

8. Michael Bratton and Nicolas van de Walle, "Popular Protest and Political Reform in Africa," *Comparative Politics* 24 (1992): 419–42. In five countries, political reform occurred without protest—that is, at the initiative of the political elite—but this was clearly a minority pattern.

9. Michael Bratton, "Zambia Starts Over," *Journal of Democracy* 3, no. 2 (1992): 81–94.

10. Ravi Gulhati, *Impasse in Zambia: The Economics and Politics of Reform* (Washington, D.C.: World Bank, 1989).

11. Republic of Zambia, *1990 Census of Population, Housing, and Agriculture: Preliminary Report* (Lusaka: Central Statistical Office, December 1990).

12. Gulhati, *Impasse in Zambia*, 28.

13. Kenneth Good, "The Reproduction of Weakness in the State and Agriculture: Zambian Experience," *African Affairs* 85 (1986): 239–66.

14. William Tordoff et al., *Politics in Zambia* (Manchester: Manchester University Press, 1974), 12.

15. Good, "The Reproduction of Weakness," 261.

16. International Labor Organization, *Zambia: Basic Needs in an Economy under Pressure* (Geneva: ILO, 1981).

17. World Bank, *Commodity and Trade Trends* (Washington, D.C.: World Bank, 1988).

18. World Bank, *World Development Report, 1990* (Washington, D.C.: World Bank, 1990).

19. In March 1988, Zambia applied to the U.N. General Assembly to be granted least developed country status and, thereby, access to concessionary international assistance. The United Nations rejected the application, reportedly because Zambia's economic straits were attributable to government mismanagement of the economy. Income figures are in 1980 prices.

20. Gulhati, *Impasse in Zambia*, 7.

21. These loans began with a loan of SDR 19 million in 1971 and peaked with a loan of SDR 800 million in 1981.

22. David Gordon, "Zambia: The Political Economy of Economic Reform," memorandum (Nairobi: USAID/REDSO/ESA, January 1991), typescript.

23. The rate of the kwacha in relation to the U.S. dollar slipped from 2:1 to 7:1 within two weeks, stabilized for a while, then slipped to 21:1 by early 1987.

24. Tina West, "The Politics of Implementation of Structural Adjustment in Zambia, 1985–1987," in *The Politics of Economic Reform in Sub-Saharan Africa* (Washington, D.C.: Center for Strategic and International Studies, 1992), 15–17.

25. Robert H. Bates and Paul Collier, *The Politics and Economics of Policy Reform in Zambia*, Papers in International Political Economy, Working Paper 153 (Durham: Duke University, 1992), 56–60.

26. International Labor Organization, *Basic Needs in an Economy under Pres-*

sure: Findings and Recommendations of an ILO/JASPA Mission, (Addis Ababa: ILO, 1981), xxv.

27. John Clark and Caroline Allison, *Zambia: Debt and Poverty* (Oxford: Oxfam, 1989), 23.

28. West, "The Politics of Implementation," 5.

29. ILO, *Zambia: Basic Needs,* 47.

30. *Times of Zambia,* December 25, 1990.

31. Gulhati, *Impasse in Zambia,* 16.

32. F. Javaheri, *Soyabean: Combatting Malnutrition in Zambia* (Lusaka. Government of the Republic of Zambia, 1990), 2; and G. J. Bhat and R. S. Patel, "Maternal and Child Health in Zambia," 1987, typescript.

33. Clark and Allison, *Zambia: Debt and Poverty,* 47.

34. Even though the government maintained subsidies long after agreeing to remove them, by 1990 they had phased out subsidies of milk, cooking oil, sugar, salt, and candles.

35. Dorothy Muntemba, "Impact of the IMF/World Bank on the People of Africa, with Special Reference to Zambia" (Lusaka: National Commission for Development Planning, 1987), typescript. See also Beatrice Liatto-Katundu, "Social Consequences of Structural Adjustment: Effects on Zambian Workers and Workers' Coping Strategies" (Lusaka: University of Zambia, Department of African Development Studies, November 1991), 17, typescript; and Clark and Allison, *Zambia: Debt and Poverty,* 30.

36. Guy Mohne, "Employment and Incomes in Zambia in the Context of Structural Adjustment" (Lusaka: ILO/SATEP, 1987), typescript.

37. Economist Intelligence Unit, *Zambia: Country Profile* (London: Business International Ltd., 1987), 11.

38. West, "The Politics of Implementation," 18.

39. *Africa Confidential,* October 16, 1985.

40. A. L. Epstein, *Politics in an Urban African Community* (Manchester: Manchester University Press, 1958).

41. Liatto-Katundu, "Social Consequences of Structural Adjustment," 10–11.

42. Robert Bates, *Unions, Parties, and Political Development: A Study of Mineworkers in Zambia* (New Haven: Yale University Press, 1971), 18–22; and Cherry Gertzel, "Labour and the State: The Case of the Zambia Mineworkers' Union," *Journal of Commonwealth and Comparative Politics* 13, no. 3 (1975): 290–304.

43. Gilbert Mudenda, "The Process of Class Formation in Contemporary Zambia," in *Beyond Political Independence: Zambia's Development Predicament in the 1980s,* ed. Klaas Woldring (London: Mouton, 1984).

44. *Africa Confidential,* May 21, 1980.

45. Cherry Gertzel, Carolyn Baylies, and Morris Szeftel, *The Dynamics of the One-Party State in Zambia* (Manchester: Manchester University Press, 1984, 95.

46. Good, "The Reproduction of Weakness," 256.

47. *Africa Contemporary Record,* 1985.

48. *Times of Zambia,* December 31, 1989; March 16, 1990.

49. *News from Zambia,* March 1990.

50. Michael Bratton, "Civil Society and Political Transition in Africa: Kenya and Zambia Compared," paper prepared for the Conference on Civil Society in Africa, Harry S. Truman Institute, Hebrew University, Jerusalem, January 1992.

51. Akashambatwa Mbikusita-Lewanika and Derrick Chitala, eds., *The Hour Has Come: Proceedings of the National Conference on the Multi-Party Option* (Lusaka: Zambia Research Foundation, 1990).

52. *Africa Confidential,* October 12, 1990. The demonstrations in Benin and several other countries were prior, however.

53. Bratton, "Zambia Starts Over."

54. *Times of Zambia,* September 28, 1992.

55. Ibid., December 25, 1990; and *Sunday Times of Zambia,* December 30, 1990.

56. *Africa Confidential,* February 8, 1991.

57. *Times of Zambia,* January 1, 1991.

58. Ibid., January 7, 1991.

59. Ibid., January 22, 1991.

60. *Weekly Post,* October 20, 1991. The most powerful chiefs, including the Chitimukulu of the Bemba and the Litunga of the Lozi, had previously been drafted into the UNIP Central Committee.

61. Michael Bratton, *The Local Politics of Rural Development: Peasant and Party-State in Zambia* (Hanover: University Press of New England, 1980).

62. In his concession speech, Kaunda blamed the "mothers" for not turning out to vote. In rural western Zambia, women were in a clear majority in voter lines, though other observers cited otherwise in urban areas. The other notable social cleavage in party affiliations was generational: whereas UNIP polling agents were often in their fifties and sixties, those from MMD were commonly twenty to thirty years old.

63. *Weekly Post,* October 26, 1991.

64. Ibid., October 11, 1991.

65. *Times of Zambia,* October 10, 1991; October 22, 1991.

66. Ibid., January 21, 1991.

67. Mbikusita-Lewanika and Chitala, *The Hour Has Come.*

68. *Times of Zambia,* January 13, 1990.

69. *Daily Mail,* October 7, 1991.

70. *Times of Zambia,* October 4, 1991.

71. *Daily Mail,* December 28, 1990.

72. *Sunday Times of Zambia,* November 11, 1990.

73. Gordon, "Zambia: The Political Economy of Economic Reform," 10.

74. *News From Zambia,* December 10–30, 1991.

NICOLAS VAN DE WALLE

Six ◈ Neopatrimonialism and Democracy in Africa, with an Illustration from Cameroon

Since late 1989, the African continent has been gripped by a protest movement demanding the democratization of the region's one-party dictatorships. The importance of this movement and the government's response has varied from country to country;[1] the resources available to both the state and the opposition largely determine national outcomes. In some countries, already weakened leaders quickly gave in to demands for democratization and competitive elections. In others, stronger, more resourceful leaders were able to repress the movement or manipulated it, often by calling for elections that they knew they would win. Nonetheless, the democratic movement left virtually no country untouched, and its impact on African politics has been enormous.[2]

This crisis of the one-party state is clearly linked to the economic crisis raging in these same countries, but the precise nature of the link is ambiguous. Many observers argue that political stability was threatened by increasing economic hardship throughout the 1980s and by subsequent government efforts to achieve macroeconomic stabilization and structural adjustment.[3] When the protests began in late 1989, many observers interpreted them as responses to adjustment, with Africans venting their frustration at austerity and declining living standards.

But an analysis of the protest movements in the countries in which organized action occurred reveals a mixture of economic and political demands.[4] Many protests started as economic protests and only later became more overtly political. Typically, the protests began when civil servants protested structural adjustment-mandated cuts in their housing allowances, students protested delays in the disbursement of their stipends, schoolteachers and university professors protested cuts in their budgets, or consumers protested price increases for basic goods. There is no correlation between the severity of the recession and political protests, however. Large-scale protests occurred in rich countries like Gabon and Kenya but not in Malawi or Tanzania, where the economic crisis lasted longer and hit harder. A comparative analysis across Africa reveals that, although the economic crisis featured centrally in the political crisis that shook these regimes, an economic explanation does not suffice to explain the political dynamics across the continent.

Other observers, notably in the donor community, link the economic and political from the opposite direction. They argue that fundamental changes in the manner in which African countries are governed are a prerequisite to any real progress on the economic front and sustained long-term growth. As the World Bank put it with unusual bluntness, "better governance requires political renewal."[5] The term *governance* is of course normative rather than descriptive.[6] Nonetheless, these observers suggest that the political and economic liberalization in Africa today are largely complementary. They interpret the protests as directed less at structural adjustment than at the government incompetence and venality that resulted in the crisis.[7] The main obstacles to successful economic reform are the state and the elites that control it, not the social groups that suffer from the economic austerity programs. Evidence supports this contention; it is undeniable that corruption in high places is a central theme of the protest;[8] it is also true that the protests mark the political emergence of a "good government" constituency: lawyers' groups, consumer associations, human rights associations, and so on.

These two broad perspectives on the relationship between Africa's economic and political crises provide us with useful insights. At the same time, the fact that these perspectives are essentially contradictory suggests a third, more nuanced perspective is necessary to fully understand the dilemmas in African political economy. This chapter seeks to reconcile these two views and to present a more sophisticated analysis of the economic and political crisis in Africa. First, I describe African political systems as neopatrimonial and investigate the implications of this method of rule. I argue that state power in Africa is built on rent seeking and prebendalism, in which political alliances within the national elite are fashioned on the basis of access to state resources.[9] I show that such political systems are economically inefficient and politically unstable. I then examine the impact of economic and political liberalization on these regimes and argue that the disruption of rent-seeking networks caused by the economic crisis brought about a crisis within the state elite before popular protests erupted in late 1989.

Structural adjustment programs are a last-ditch effort to save African regimes from themselves and from the economic crises that undermine them. Because they typically serve to reassert presidential control over rent-seeking, adjustment programs attack the power and wealth of the political class, which responds by defending its interests. In many respects, the real threat to these regimes is this elite crisis rather than popular opposition, because the latter lacks organization and resources. Regime transitions are most likely where elite cohesion breaks down and disaffected members of the political class seek to manipulate popular discontent to destabilize the regime. Finally, I illustrate the argument with the case of Cameroon, which allows me to investigate which variables account for cross-national differences.

The Nature of Neopatrimonial Regimes

Max Weber defined *patrimonialism* as a type of government organized as an extension of the ruler's own household.[10] The ruler makes no distinction between his own private property and that of the state's. His rule over the territory is personal and arbitrary, without recourse to law or administrative predictability; political authority is based on clientelism. Weber distinguished patrimonialism from rational-legal authority, in which power is exercised in accordance with explicit legal structures specifying procedural rules and norms and serving to promote well-defined public goals. Patrimonialism is most appropriate to small, traditional kingdoms, in which the affairs of state are sufficiently simple to allow the ruler to govern without an institutionalized administrative structure.

Following several scholars of clientelism, I designate as *neopatrimonial* those states—found notably in contemporary Africa—in which patrimonial logic coexists with the development of bureaucratic administration and at least the pretense of legal-rational forms of state legitimacy.[11] It would, for example, be an exaggeration to call Côte d'Ivoire a patrimonial state: an increasingly well-trained bureaucratic class administers complex policies, including state revenue and expenditure programs. The rule of law, while imperfect, is not completely arbitrary. Yet it is an open secret that President Félix Houphouët-Boigny keeps at least a tenth of the country's cocoa export revenues in his personal bank account for redistribution to his followers and cronies as political logic dictates.[12] He similarly regularly disregards his government's own budget to order investments or consumption expenditures he feels are more important. Members of his family and clan routinely benefit from tax and tariff exemptions, high-level state jobs, subsidized credit for their businesses, and state harassment of their competitors.[13]

Much the same can be said of the administrative and political practices of the overwhelming majority of African states, as well as many regimes elsewhere in the Third World. The degree to which rational legal and patrimonial forms of authority coexist varies and depends on such factors as the degree of state formation, the technical skill level of the administration, the strength of bureaucratic traditions, and the nature of civil society. Neopatrimonialism is easily identified in Equatorial Guinea under Macias Nguema and the Central African Republic under Jean-Bedel Bokassa. In countries like Senegal or Kenya, these characteristics are considerably attenuated, although still present.

Can we distinguish between African neopatrimonial regimes and those political systems in the industrialized West in which rent seeking and patronage exist? In other words, is there a difference between neopatrimonialism and Tammany Hall? Several differences seem important to me. First, the patronage practices of the political machines of American cities follow an electoral logic: votes are bought with services, favors, and jobs. In Africa, similar patronage practices did exist briefly around the time of independence, during which public offices were freely contested. With the end of competitive elections and the rise of repression, access to public resources was increasingly limited to a small circle of elites. Patronage practices persisted, but their political importance dwindled and has been superseded by, for example, prebendal distribution of public offices,[14] which benefits only a few highly privileged people. Contemporary Africa is thus characterized by rapidly increasing inequalities in income and wealth.[15] Thus, unlike the machine politics in Western democracies, neopatrimonial regimes do not maintain broad public support but rather cement an intraelite accommodation.

Second, public corruption is higher in neopatrimonial regimes. The evidence is anecdotal, of course, but it does suggest that African states tolerate levels of corruption that would not go unpunished elsewhere and that public accountability is significantly less well developed in these regimes.[16] This means, for example, that corruption often completely negates the function and objectives of structural adjustment rather than merely reducing its effectiveness. Moreover, such corruption is abetted by the lack of administrative capabilities in these countries. For these reasons, the neopatrimonial systems in Africa constitute a distinctive regime type.

Neopatrimonialism affects policy choices in these countries. Since independence, African rulers have favored expanded public production and state intervention in their economies, not only because they believe a large public sector would provide additional revenues and accelerate development, but also because public ownership and intervention facilitate the consolidation and maintenance of their power.[17] In the neopatrimonial regime, political stability and a minimum of legitimacy is ensured by the patron-client network that extends from the ruler through the civil service, the party, and the public enterprise system to the villages and the peasantry. This network results in clientelist clans and factions within the elite, who are the main players in the political system, rather than in the large social aggregates, such as class, that structure Western political life. Indeed, clientelism attenuates horizontal social identities like class and lessens their political salience. The ruler depends on the state apparatus to control and channel political participation.[18] Just as important, state resources are used to reward political loyalty, to forge the regional, ethnic, and religious alliances necessary for national unity, and to obviate the need for coercion.

Public production, notably through the proliferation of public enterprises, and extensive regulation of the economy are essential aspects of neopatrimonial regimes. From Marxist Ethiopia to pro-Western Kenya, public enterprises sprouted in disconcerting numbers in the years after independence. These enterprises created a large number of (not necessarily well-paying) "jobs for the boys" plus a few lucrative positions of power and prestige for the ruler's political allies. Similarly, most African countries extensively intervened in the economy with import and export taxes, price controls, production subsidies, and so forth. All these policies generate rent-seeking opportunities.

Rent seeking assumes a particular dynamic in neopatrimonial regimes because it is inherent in the system of rule. Given the size and sophistication of the typical African economic system, the ruler cannot control all the levers of economic power, and he comes to depend on a class of regime barons to help him manage the political system and its clientelist pyramid, in exchange for which they are allowed to keep a portion for themselves. These barons are typically recruited among political allies, personal friends, family and kin, and even erstwhile enemies. Their privileges and position make them clients of the ruler. The institutions they head typically include all the state agencies that collect government revenues through taxation, regulation, and foreign aid plus agencies whose role in regulating society provides the barons with opportunities for rent seeking and fraud. Such prebendal control is often necessitated by the weakness of the formal institutions of state, such that the ruler gives up a part of this revenue to one or a few individuals in order to make sure he can collect the bulk of it.

The degree to which rulers resort to such clientelism depends on a number of factors. One variable is the state's extractive capabilities, or its ability to collect revenues without resorting to clientelism. A related factor is the ruler's grip on power and his need for political allies. The less contested he is, everything else being equal, the less he needs clients. A third factor is the sources of state revenues; clientelism is likelier if these sources are diverse and multiple than if there is a single source, like oil, which is easier to control centrally. The relationships between patrons and clients have a clear, albeit usually implicit, contractual character: in exchange for being allowed to steal a little from the public till, the client does not steal too much and looks after his patron's interests in the institution the client manages.[19] Given current public norms, such practices can rarely be conducted in the open in most Third World countries, so it is difficult to know how explicit these contracts are. For such relationships to be lasting— and many of them are—patron and client must come to some understanding. Yet the instability of so many of them suggests that these agreements are left vague and ambiguous enough for multiple and changing interpretations.

Even if there is a fairly precise understanding between a patron and his rent-seeking clients, such arrangements can be undermined by information asymmetries. It is easy for the client to skim profits, underreport production, and overreport costs. He has enormous possibilities for corruption and presumably the means to disguise it, particularly since his understanding with his patron includes some profiteering. Thus, African leaders use information gathering and monitoring to police their subordinates.[20]

Crises of the Neopatrimonial State

Many scholars emphasize the inability of the neopatrimonial state to promote capitalist development.[21] There are several overlapping reasons for this. The state discourages productive investment by (1) systematically favoring redistribution over accumulation, (2) preying upon productive activity for the very rents that are essential to attract and maintain entrepreneurial activity, and (3) creating uncertainty by the arbitrariness of its policy.

Less noticed is the inherent inefficiency of such regimes. Not only are clientelism and rent seeking more likely to flourish in weakly institutionalized regimes, they also tend to prevent their institutionalization and to create what one scholar calls the "underdeveloped state."[22] Corruption, poor administrative capability, and hidden decisionmaking processes reinforce each other. The need for discretion and secrecy to conduct the illicit or unsavory aspects of clientelism thwarts the keeping of written records, the promotion of bureaucratic competence, and the free flow of information. The absence of transparency also undermines long-term stability, neopatrimonial contracts are vague and ambiguous, subject to frequent renegotiation, and largely dependent on short-term contingencies and the changing political fortunes of the partners. Given these elements, neopatrimonial regimes are characterized by factional infighting and alliance switching, making them highly unstable even though their rulers may remain in power for long periods of time.[23] These regimes have a structural tendency for fiscal crisis, in part because their rulers cannot control or monitor their clientelist networks. Over time, as clients develop their own power bases and networks, and as state institutions proliferate and the older ones take on more rent-seeking activities, the ruler's control becomes even more problematic.

In addition, exogenous shocks to the economy, notably in the context of the economy's foreign transactions, upset rent-seeking arrangements and impose the need for renegotiations between patron and clients. As a result, these regimes have little flexibility to deal with international price swings, even when they are positive. This may help explain why countries like Nigeria and Côte d'Ivoire—two of Africa's biggest debtors—accumulated the bulk of their debt during the commodity boom of the late 1970s.[24] The inevitable consequence is endemic fiscal crisis, as the state and its enterprises accumulate chronic deficits. By the early 1980s, only two decades after independence, more than half the nations in sub-Saharan Africa were effectively bankrupt, and most of the others were propped up by Western public capital.[25] However, the industrialized West's recession and its growing impatience with Africa's poor economic performance motivated it to promote economic reform, involving liberalization and privatization. Economic reform is designed to restore macroeconomic equilibrium and to spur faster economic growth through trade liberalization, fiscal retrenchment, and deregulation.

Many scholars argue that structural adjustment programs represent grave risks for state leaders.[26] Policies that change relative prices or that reduce absorption levels in the economy necessarily generate winners and losers and are thus likely to generate opposition. However, rational leaders will not undertake structural adjustment unless they perceive it as less risky than the alternatives, which may be even riskier, given an unsustainable macrodisequilibrium; thus it is important to distinguish the political risks of economic crisis from those of structural adjustment. Because economic crisis entails a slowdown in economic activity, it implies budgetary restrictions, reduced rent-seeking opportunities, and reduced patronage.[27] Rent seeking and corruption continues, however, as the state has access to resources that are not affected by the business cycle; commodity production may provide the state with significant resources, while international aid may also be a significant source of rent seeking. For example, during the 1980s famines, state agents in Ethiopia and Sudan found emergency food aid quite lucrative.[28] The evidence from these countries, as well as countries such as Zaire, suggests that neopatrimonial practices can accommodate disastrous economic circumstances. Moreover, in most countries the parallel economy was not hit as hard by the crisis as the official economy, and it continued to provide lucrative opportunities for state agents.

The political implications of structural reform are somewhat different. In political terms, structural adjustment is designed to allow the state to adjust to a new economic environment while minimizing political instability.[29] Donors help the state with an infusion of capital and debt reschedulings in exchange for a program of economic reform. The adjustment effort threatens clientelism in two ways. First, it usually includes austerity measures that seek to decrease the cost of the state apparatus; ministerial positions are eliminated, or managers of bankrupt public enterprises are dismissed. In Côte d'Ivoire, for example, the cabinet was reduced from thirty or forty members to only nineteen, following IMF demands.[30] Second, economic liberalization is likely to reduce the amount of rent seeking in the system and the amount of patronage available to rulers. Devaluation, tariff reduction, and price liberalization all reduce rent seeking.

The essential problem for state leaders is to maintain control of their clientelist networks during the reform process, even as they decrease the cost of these networks by ousting clients or curtailing their access to state resources. Reform thus threatens political stability because it disrupts long-standing arrangements between rulers and elites. At the same time, reform offers rulers the opportunity to regain control over networks and rents that have escaped their grasp. A privatized parastatal, for example, can be sold to a more trusted client or a relative and thus retain the subsidies that made it profitable before. One of the reasons African states such as Senegal, Côte d'Ivoire, and Cameroon undertook privatization more readily than predicted appears to have been the appeal to their leaders of reasserting control over resources.[31]

Democratizing the Rent-Seeking Society

By the late 1980s, the economic crisis and the implementation of structural adjustment programs in African states had placed a great strain on neopatrimonial political systems. The attempts by state leaders to cut back on rent seeking or to redirect it were resisted by their clients. The old political alliances built on rent seeking were upset by the reform process, opening up a Pandora's box of old ethnic and regional claims, factional infighting, and political maneuvering. An inevitable consequence was corruption and further loss of revenue.

The period of adjustment saw states' abilities to collect indirect taxes, such as import duties, falter. Almost every structural adjustment program across the continent has included measures to increase state revenues in order to rectify the budget deficit and service debt. Anecdotal evidence suggests that, before the crisis, roughly one-half to two-thirds of the import duty owed an average African state was actually collected. The rest was not collected either because the goods were officially exempt or because they were imported fraudulently. With austerity and increasing political uncertainty, the incentive for people to take what they could grew. Revenues tumbled during the adjustment process, as the level of fraud escalated. Many of these regimes underwent a real net decrease in their revenue base.[32] In the late 1980s, Senegal granted official duty exemptions to over a third of all imports, and up to another third of all imports were fraudulent. In Cameroon, a 1989 fiscal study estimated that 670–820 billion CFA francs were lost to the state due to fraud and various exemptions, equivalent to 18–22 percent of GDP.[33]

These countries witnessed the collapse of internal discipline, as rulers were increasingly unable to control rent-seeking networks. In normal times, corruption is bounded by considerations other than the ruler's supervisory and repressive capabilities. Managers of public enterprises and other rent seekers understand that, if they steal too much, they risk bankrupting their individual institutions, if not the entire economy. In some respects, they face a prisoner's dilemma, in which compliance implies smaller gains but better prospects for the economy and the regime as a whole, while noncompliance can lead to a maximization of short-terms gains but a higher risk of regime collapse. The latter is the rational choice for these elites under two types of circumstances: first, if they believe egregious corruption by the other elites makes the system unsustainable, and second, if they believe that rent-seeking opportunities will dry up in the near future. Much depends on whether these elites have staked their future on the ruler and his fortunes and are thus unlikely to survive his downfall with their privileges intact. If they are likely to fall with the ruler, any evidence of instability will lead to an "après moi le déluge" attitude and increased corruption. Likewise, the threat of a major deregulation and price liberalization is likely to result in an increase in rent seeking.

Such was the situation before the latest wave of prodemocracy protests. The economic crisis unhinged many regimes that were propped up only by annual debt reschedulings and biannual infusions of donor capital. Their internal discipline and extractive capabilities were seriously weakened, and divisions, defections, and factionalism within the elite were on the increase. However, until the crisis erupted openly, with civil service and student strikes, it was largely confined to the elites.

The events of 1989 and 1990 thus occurred in very vulnerable states. Why did the crisis peak then? There had been protests against austerity since the first oil crisis; why did they take on an explicitly political coloration after 1989? A combination of factors appear to have played a role, beyond economic circumstances: the changing attitudes of the Western powers in a post-cold war context; the diffusion effects of events in Eastern Europe, Algeria, and South Africa, as well as neighboring African countries; and the miscalculations and clumsy responses of rulers to the initial protests.[34]

My description of neopatrimonial regimes provides a new perspective on the economic roots of the political crisis. I do not suggest that the austerity and structural adjustment programs did not hurt nonelites and encourage them also to voice their unhappiness. Clearly, the *deflatés*—civil service workers, students, teachers—were the foot soldiers of the democracy movement in most of these countries.[35] While the *deflatés* form a privileged group relative to the peasantry, for example, they are not part of the state elite. They were responding to the very real economic hardships that austerity had brought, and they rightfully perceived that corruption and mismanagement had played a role in the economic crisis—that the government's inability to reduce corruption and rent seeking at the top of the state apparatus had made it necessary for the government to attack their own purchasing power.

Nonetheless, the organized groups of these nonelites—unions, business associations, and independent political parties—were too weak, unrepresentative, and dependent on the state to dislodge the ruling elites by themselves. Even a weakened state could use its traditional combination of stick and carrot to restore order. Indeed, in countries like Côte d'Ivoire and Gabon, this is what happened.[36] The government suppressed the protesters while co-opting moderate opposition leaders and pushing for rapid elections—which it was sure to win, given the superior organization of the single party and its control over the local administration.[37] The nature of the state's neopatrimonial crisis largely determined whether the protests were able to produce a regime transition. In both Côte d'Ivoire and Gabon, the leader survived politically because of his ability to prevent widespread defection to the opposition by state elites. Félix Houphouët-Boigny and Omar Bongo maintained enough control over rent-seeking networks to prevent such defections, even if there was extensive factional infighting within the party. Ultimately, only traditionally volatile groups such as university students and staffs and middle-class professionals joined the opposition.

On the other hand, in countries in which the old ruler was forced to resign, key parts of the ruling coalition defected to the opposition. In Congo, for example, the single party and the official union imploded, with the latter openly calling for multiparty elections and less corruption. In Benin, significant segments of the political class turned against Mathieu Kérékou when it became clear that the French no longer supported him.[38] In several countries, political institutions began to fragment, and the official trade union, the student association, the party youth organization, the state-controlled chamber of commerce, or the single party joined the opposition in its call for reform. Similarly, prominent politicians long associated with the ruler suddenly broke with him and added their voice to the chorus of protests. In some cases, elite defections took on a regional or ethnic hue: southerners spearheaded the reform movement in Benin, for example, while Bamileke elites were Cameroon's major defectors. The rise in ethnic conflict at the popular level originated in a breakdown of the accommodation processes that leaders had fashioned among ethnic elites to maintain political stability.

The national conferences in French west Africa should be understood in the context of these intraelite conflicts. Designed to be forums in which national representatives would together design the nation's future democratic constitution, these conferences turned into dramatic events, with hundreds of representatives and wide-open agendas. Their size reflected the weakness of civil society: organizations could not claim to represent substantial portions of their populations, and most individuals could speak only for themselves. Indeed, the criteria for participation were vague and ill defined; the first national conference, held in Benin for ten days in February 1990, was open to all the "forces vives de la Nation" (the nation's vital forces), which seemed to include a large proportion of the country's political and economic elite. The Benin meeting attracted some 500 participants, and subsequent conferences were larger, with 1,200 participants at the Congo sessions and as many as 4,000 delegates at the Zaire meeting.

There is as yet little comparative research on these national conferences,[39] but journalistic accounts of them suggest that participation included the establishment elites of the ancien régime as well as the members of the reform coalitions associated with the social protests.[40] Prominent politicians from both the single party and the opposition, student spokesmen, ethnic and religious leaders, and public sector trade unionists dominated the proceedings. The social categories long excluded from the political life of these countries—most notably the peasantry—were not well represented, if at all. In part, their exclusion resulted from the absence of representative organizations in most of these countries to invite on their behalf. In addition, however, the meetings rarely addressed economic policy issues of concern to underprivileged groups.

Revealingly, the national conferences explicitly fashioned themselves on the estates-general of the French Revolution. On one level, their central purpose was to rewrite constitutions and establish electoral procedures; on a more ambitious level, they were to review the basic ground rules of national politics. Their success was probably limited in this latter objective; many inveighed against official corruption and discussed legal procedures against rulers and specific cronies, but there was little attempt to come to grips with the sociological causes of corruption. To pursue the historical analogy, one searches in vain for the equivalent of the night of August 4, 1789, when the French estates-general, having turned itself into the National Assembly, voted to abolish all feudal privileges.

Economic and Political Crises in Cameroon

In the remaining paragraphs of this chapter, I briefly describe the process of democratization in Cameroon. This serves two purposes;

first, it allows me to put some flesh onto the analytical framework I have developed above; second, it provides material for comparative hypotheses regarding democratization processes in sub-Saharan Africa.

State Formation and Political Dynamics, 1960–1985

The neopatrimonial nature of Cameroon is well described elsewhere.[41] I simply sketch a few points in order to analyze the crisis. Under Presidents Ahmadu Ahidjo (1960–82) and Paul Biya (1982–), Cameroon has undergone rapid growth in employment, number of institutions, and size of the annual budget. Its economic policy has been decidedly interventionist, with the state trying to set most significant prices and protecting national production with a panoply of tariff and nontariff measures. Despite this interventionism and its stated purpose of promoting rapid development, the state was never developmental in orientation; political management was a primary consideration in economic policymaking. Perhaps the best example of that was the slow development of infrastructure in the south of the country, largely because President Ahidjo feared the political implications of the south's wealth. Thus, until the mid-1980s, there was no paved road linking the nation's two biggest cities, Yaoundé and Douala, or Yaoundé and the rich agricultural Western Province. On the other hand, an extensive road network was built in the north, and an international airport capable of receiving wide-bodied jets was bestowed on Garoua, the president's hometown.

The best indication of the patrimonial orientation of state rule in Cameroon is the way both Ahidjo and Biya managed the country's oil wealth.[42] Modest oil reserves were discovered in the mid-1970s and provided the state several hundred million dollars in potential revenues by the early 1980s. Although they were the most important state revenue, Ahidjo kept them in a secret overseas' bank account and did not include them in official revenue totals. Oil revenues were then repatriated to finance state activities as he saw fit. When he came to power, Biya ended that practice and officially integrated the oil money into the national budget, although the existence of a substantial secret offshore presidential oil account is widely suspected. Over the years, hundreds of millions of dollars are said to be unaccounted for.

In the late 1980s and early 1990s, rent seeking and corruption have taken many forms and occupy a large place in several distinct areas. First, rent seeking dominates the market for traded goods; government policies drive a wedge between world and domestic prices that rent seekers can capitalize on. For example, in the mid-1980s, the difference between the international price of rice and the fixed consumer price created $10 million dollars a year in rents.[43] Fraud is made easier by the fact that Douala is a port of entry for landlocked countries such as Central African Republic and Chad and that much of the transit trade that passes through Cameroon is fraudulent. Historical trade networks with Nigeria, particularly among the Fulani traders of the north, take advantage of the arbitrage possibilities, given differences in state pricing policies between the two countries. The market for cheap Nigerian gasoline totals millions of dollars, for example, and could simply not occur without the active cooperation of state agents.[44]

Government contracts provide another area for substantial fraud, such as false invoices, bribery, and misappropriation. It is difficult to know the dimensions of this corruption, but the fact that foreign companies are increasingly unwilling to do business with the Cameroon government suggests the dimensions of the problem.[45] The state also tolerates considerable corruption through the allocation of credit. Politically mediated loans to elites have been so common in the state-controlled banking sector that, by the mid-1980s, a quarter of the total portfolio consisted of unrecoverable loans (120 billion CFA francs).[46] Finally, there is considerable corruption through the selective application of laws and regulations: tax exemptions, land title fraud, payment arrears on public utility services, and so on. In each case, the fraud requires at least the passive complicity of state agents or is made possible by state policies. Much of this activity occurred without the knowledge of Ahidjo, but the centralization of power and the presence of an effective security apparatus suggest that Ahidjo was in a position to control and police the beneficiaries of this state largesse.[47]

In the independence period, the political system exhibited some political pluralism. The one party with a genuinely nationalist orientation, the Union des Populations Camerounaises (UPC), was banned by the French government.[48] The other political parties were essentially clientelist and ethnic and did not claim substantial popular support. The French administration promoted Ahidjo, then an obscure northern politician who opposed the UPC but craftily adopted many of its popular positions. As he consolidated power after independence in 1960, he progressively eliminated all independent associations through co-optation, repression, or manipulation. The single party, the Union Nationale Camerounaise (UNC), absorbed all the other political parties in the first decade of his rule, and Ahidjo induced many of his political opponents to join his party, with promises of lucrative positions the state apparatus. By the mid-1970s, Ahidjo had eliminated all significant opposition and could claim at least the passive support of both traditional and modern elites in all parts of the country. Although he favored his native north, Ahidjo was careful to cultivate ties to every ethnic group and to placate all the provincial elites with access to state resources. This produced remarkable political stability—but unfortunate economic results.

The Economic Crisis of 1987

By the early 1980s, Cameroon was subsidizing parastatal sector losses to the tune of some 150 billion CFA francs a year. State employment growth had accelerated and would mushroom from less than 20,000 employees at independence to as many as 250,000, including perhaps 80,000 in the parastatal sector. The country had impressive natural resources and a diverse agriculture that it could have exploited to fashion an economic growth rate of some 6.5 percent a year between 1965 and 1980, but it was never able to promote either productivity growth in agriculture or the development of a manufacturing sector with substantial value added. As in many other African countries, the cigarette factory and the brewery are among the biggest manufacturing concerns. The economy was incapable of supporting this expansive state for long.

The proximate economic and political causes of the economic crisis that erupted in 1987 can be described very briefly. First, external shocks to the Cameroon economy played a role. The combination of a sharp downfall in commodity prices and the rapid depreciation of the dollar vis-à-vis the French franc resulted in a 45 percent deterioration in the country's terms of trade in 1987–88, after a boom in the early 1980s. Second, the conflict between Ahidjo and Biya in 1982–84 contributed to the economic problems.[49] Several months after voluntarily retiring in late 1982, Ahidjo sought to return to power and displace his handpicked successor, Paul Biya. The latter eventually won this power struggle—but at a tremendous cost, as he had to make promises to various groups and individuals to ensure their support.

From the outset, Paul Biya presented himself to the country as a reformer, who would modernize and liberalize the regime.[50] In explicit contrast to the autocratic and secretive Ahidjo, he promised to fight corruption, to respect human rights, and to reduce the prerogatives of the state.[51] Openly distancing himself from many of the old politicians that had constituted Ahidjo's inner cabinet, Biya brought in a new generation of Western-trained technocrats, who adopted a more managerial and liberal public discourse. He renamed the UNC the

Rassemblement Démocratique du Peuple Camerounais (RDPC) and undertook to democratize its decisionmaking processes. These actions gained Biya much good will, not only in Cameroon but also in the West, where he was widely perceived as an economic liberal and political reformer.

In fact, his precarious position during and after his power struggle with Ahidjo led Biya to expand the use of state resources for political purposes—to please the army, to mollify the north (Ahidjo's base of support), and to meet the heightened expectations of his fellow southerners.[52] As a consequence of an ambitious public investment plan and considerable mismanagement, the budget grew to a level unsustainable when the international environment soured after 1986. Far from reforming the system he had inherited, Biya demonstrated less ability to control corruption and rent seeking than Ahidjo had. In particular, the various political clans led by prominent southern politicians—soon dubbed the *Beti barons*—that surrounded Biya in the mid-1980s increased rent seeking, corruption, and patronage beyond what Ahidjo had ever allowed.[53] The regime itself estimates that fraud involving the state apparatus cost some 1,500 billion CFA francs between 1981 and 1986.[54]

Democratic Protests and Economic Reform

Although he promised he would never accept the conditionality of international aid agencies, Biya signed a standby agreement with the IMF in September 1988 and a structural adjustment loan with the World Bank in May 1989. Cameroon thus began the "ritual dances of the debt game."[55] There has been some progress in the implementation of cost cutting measures, largely because the state simply cannot afford past spending levels, but the implementation of the reform program lags well behind schedule and remains highly uneven.[56] As a result, total debt and various arrears continue to increase, the fiscal situation worsens, and the performance of the state's institutions has all but collapsed. In 1991–92, the government budget was about two-thirds its 1986–89 level of 800 billion CFA francs, but the government was unable to meet its expenditure and revenue targets; its budget deficit was still 207 billion CFA francs in 1990–91.[57] In effect, as expenditure went down, so did the state's ability to collect revenues.

The regime has endured thanks to oil revenues and support from donors. True, the IMF and the World Bank increasingly begrudged their support and delayed adjustment program disbursements because of noncompliance, but they continued providing financial support to the government. Among the bilateral donors, France remained the most important, with some 800 million French francs in assistance in 1989. The United States, the second largest bilateral donor, forgave $73.4 million of Cameroonian debt in 1990. A combined donor package of $1.72 billion was negotiated in late 1990 to restructure the banking sector, largely bankrupt because of its careless and highly politicized lending practices.

Until early 1990, no serious popular opposition to Biya had materialized. Arrears in public sector salaries accumulated despite the government's policy of protecting these salaries from budget cuts, but there were no strikes or public demonstrations against austerity. On February 19, 1990, however, Yondo Black, former president of the Bar Association, was arrested with several others for attempting to form an independent political party. His arrest led to a strike by the Bar Association on March 28 to demand the release of Black. His arrest also resulted in the formation of another new party, the Social Democratic Front (SDF) led by Ni John Fru Ndi in the Anglophone city of Bamenda in western Cameroon. These first protests were at least in part inspired by events elsewhere in Francophone Africa and Eastern Europe. They were quickly reinforced by economic protests by public sector employees and by a series of strikes and demonstrations at Yaoundé University, in which students protested both economic conditions and the absence of democracy.

These developments put Biya in an awkward position, given his promises of liberalization. Had he given in right away and organized quick elections, the strategy successfully adopted by both Bongo and Houphouët-Boigny in the previous year, he might have quelled this threat by a poorly organized and divided opposition. Instead, he hesitated and then clumsily combined repressive actions with partial concessions, which pleased no one.[58] By mid-1991, he had allowed the National Assembly to pass a law legalizing the formation of other parties, committed himself to legislative elections, and promised press freedom. But prominent journalists were arrested and opposition newspapers banned, prodemocracy demonstrations were violently repressed, and several leading opposition figures were arrested and tortured—and released only when several embassies interceded on their behalf. The army was put in charge of administering the most unruly provinces. Faced with growing ethnic tension, Biya named a northerner, Sadou Hayatou, as his prime minister in April 1991, but this did little to calm the north and only exacerbated the unhappiness of the Bamileke-dominated western region.

In May 1991, after Biya refused the opposition's repeated calls for a national conference, the National Coordinating Committee, a group trying to unify the twenty-five or so opposition groups, called for Opération Villes Mortes. In what amounted to a permanent general strike and civil disobedience campaign, people were encouraged to stop working completely, to refuse to pay taxes of any kind, and to take their money out of the formal banking sector. After a dramatic start, in which it more or less closed down the entire economy for a couple days, the Villes Mortes campaign continued unevenly, with little effect on life in Yaoundé, a greater impact on Douala, and a strong and sustained impact in the western region. It nonetheless further undermined the state's extractive capabilities, and by the end of the year the state may have collected as little as 15 percent of the previous year's revenues.[59] Only repeated infusions of capital from France allowed the government to meet its most pressing bills, and government arrears continued to increase.

The ultimate outcome of this confrontation is unclear. In October 1991, Biya accepted the general principle of a negotiation with the opposition, but within a more restricted forum than a national conference, and promised to hold legislative elections on February 16, 1992 (they were eventually held March 1). Part of the opposition refused such a format and boycotted the negotiations that began in November between Prime Minister Hayatou and some forty opposition parties. The most prominent group to refuse to compromise was SDF, which boycotted the elections even though it was assured important representation in the future assembly. Thanks in part to the boycott of the elections by several opposition parties, Biya retained a working majority in the legislative elections of March 1992.

Then, in a televised address on August 24, he tried to surprise the opposition by announcing presidential elections for October 11, 1992, even though they were not scheduled until April 1993. Biya was officially declared the winner, with some 39.9 percent of the vote, ahead of Fru Ndi, with 35.9 percent of the vote, and Bello Bouba Maigari, with 19.2 percent.[60] Significant intimidation, fraud, and violence marred the campaign and the voting and most impartial observers did not believe the results to be an accurate reflection of Biya's popular support.[61] The announcement of these results set off another round of political protests and further polarized the political climate. At the beginning of 1993, a standstill existed between Biya and the opposition, and the future prospects for peaceful democratization seemed dim.

Factional infighting and defections continued to weaken the opposition. In part, Biya skillfully combined the stick and the carrot to divide foes and gain allies. Disagreements regarding political strategy revealed the splits and divergent interests within the opposition. Anglophone opposition groups demonstrated a profound dissatisfaction with the Francophone-dominated unitary state, which transcended their discontent with the Biya regime itself. Other parts of the opposition had a much more ambiguous attitude. Although some opposition members were clearly principled advocates of democratization and long opposed the single-party state, others appeared to be driven by personal ambition and opportunism. Many were politicians who had only recently broken away from the single-party establishment. For example, the head of the National Coordinating Committee, Jean-Jacques Ekindi, was a rising star in RDPC until his defection in May 1991. Samuel Eboua and Bello Bouba Maigari, leaders of the Movement for Democracy and Progress and the United National Democratic party, respectively, were both leading figures under Ahidjo and were purged from the single party after 1984.[62]

As Biya's troubles increased, the Western powers appear to have decided to stick with his regime, which seemed as good as any plausible alternative. In particular, France assiduously lobbied on behalf of Biya's regime in international financial circles. Supposedly with the help of the French government, Biya signed a new agreement with the IMF at the end of 1991 for $39 million in new loans.[63] This agreement opened the way to a bigger adjustment loan from France, and another debt rescheduling by the Paris Club, this time involving $1.1 billion. This international support allowed Cameroon to meet its most pressing obligations and to continue paying civil service salaries through 1992, albeit with increasing delays and exceptions.

Both his supporters and his detractors argued that Biya was a weak and indecisive leader. Few contested the sincerity of his earlier promises of democratization. Instead they argued that Biya was a prisoner of his political class, particularly hard-liners in the army and the security apparatus.[64] Biya's genuine popularity in the early years of his rule may have provided him with real autonomy vis-à-vis state elites, and he could have sought a mandate to pursue more rapid reform even against their opposition. By 1992, although Biya apparently retained real support in his home region in Central Province and among the Beti, he no longer commanded significant support elsewhere in the country. The opposition thus probably had a significant popular base of support.

Biya's real vulnerability, however, was linked to his growing inability to dominate factional struggles within the state elite. Whatever his real inclinations, Biya responded to every crisis during his tenure in power by resorting to tried and true neopatrimonial practices: heavy handed repression combined with rent-seeking opportunities for key allies. Biya's central argument against democratization was that it would divide the country by stirring ethnic demons, but this argument has become increasingly unconvincing given the widespread perception that Biya's rule inordinately favored the Beti ethnic group from the south. Indeed, the regime is perceived to have favored rent-seeking southern businessmen, who displaced the traditional Fulani trading houses and Bamileke entrepreneurs, thanks to their high-level contacts and aggressive business practices. Is this perception correct? The evidence is mixed and anecdotal, tied to the business fortunes of a small number of men. But Biya clearly proved unwilling or unable to rein in some of his cronies, who used the state to quickly build important businesses.

Ultimately, it does not matter whether such perceptions are correct; they soured Biya's relationships with non-Beti elites, as Bamileke and northern elites came to believe that the regime was biased against them. Biya and other leading Beti figures encouraged these perceptions with maladroit acts of ethnic chauvinism.[65] The Bamileke issue was particularly important. Fear of economic domination by the highly entrepreneurial Bamileke was a constant in postindependence Cameroon, but under Ahidjo's careful management such fears were allayed without arousing Bamileke resentment. Under Biya, there was little evidence to suggest that the Bamileke have been more favored than before, yet tensions and accusations of favoritism have increased on both sides. There was some evidence that economic liberalization has been slowed down by the fear that the more entrepreneurial Bamileke would be its main beneficiaries, even though Bamileke widely believed they had not gotten their rightful share of the national pie.[66]

Tensions among the elite increased largely because of the changing patterns of rent seeking under Biya's rule and his inability to control them. The pressures of the economic crisis, with growing uncertainties and a net decrease in economic activity, sharpened these conflicts. As of the end of 1991, deregulation had not got far enough to threaten rent-seeking networks. If anything, growing laxity in the implementation of various policies facilitated fraud. Uncertainty over the possibility of reform created some anxieties, however, and the economic recession hurt rent-seeking activities. Biya's inability to manage these situations contributed greatly to the defections of elites. While I do not suggest that conflicts within the state elite fully explain Cameroon's political crisis, I do argue that they were an important factor.

Concluding Remarks: Comparative Perspectives

African countries show many more similarities than differences when they are compared to the rest of the world. With a handful of exceptions (such as Haiti and, arguably, Bangladesh), countries in Eastern Europe, Latin America, and Asia have attained significantly higher levels of state formation. These states' extractive capabilities are stronger, and their institutions possess more legitimacy. Although corruption and rent seeking exist outside of Africa, they are rarely as central to state processes. The low level of "stateness" in Africa implies that institutional interests are not likely to influence transitions, which are more likely to be driven by personal and factional struggles in the context of an increasingly undisciplined state.

What democratic transitions in the neopatrimonial regimes of Africa share with transitions elsewhere in the world is the critical role of elites, including the ancien régime. The importance of elites in the bargaining that shapes peaceful transitions is a general finding in the transition literature outside of Africa. As long ago as 1970, Dankwart Rustow hypothesized the importance of "a small circle of political leaders skilled at negotiation and compromise for the formulation of democratic rules."[67] The literature on transitions in southern Europe and Latin America confirms this condition of change and uses the term *pact* to describe the deal making among elites that is central to democratic transitions.[68] It is tempting to see the national conferences of Francophone Africa as pacts, but they are not. Unlike in Africa, intraelite compromises in Latin America and southern Europe involved a few individuals who could claim to represent broader social forces. These compromises "are typically negotiated among a small number of participants representing established (and often highly oligarchical) groups or institutions; they tend to reduce competitiveness as well as conflict; they seek to limit accountability to wider publics."[69] The success of the west African national conferences, on the other hand, depended on at least the appearance of transparency and popular participation, because the delegates could not claim to represent significant segments of the population. In many cases, the only organization that possessed the requisite legitimacy for deal making was the church, an organization ill suited to take a leading role in the subsequent transition. Church representatives, nonetheless, often ended up chairing the proceedings.[70]

In Africa, the specific role of elites in democratic transitions is shaped by the relative weakness of civic associations (in particular, nonelite associations such as trade unions), by the absence of a class-based politics, and by the preeminence of vertical ties (such as clientelism). The size of the national conferences reflects the disorganized nature of civil society and the weakness of interest mediating structures. In the Cameroon case, which is typical of sub-Saharan Africa, the opposition does not have organizations that legitimately capture and channel popular opinion. Its strength is due only to the unpopularity of the current government, but opposition leaders lack a base of support on which to lay claim to power and the organizational capacity to grab it. They are essentially free riding on a wave of protests, but with their own, often separate, agenda. These protesters may over time develop their own viable organizations to contest state power, but such organizations (with several noteworthy exceptions) do not currently exist.

Several factors account for variations within Africa. The first concerns the role of the CFA franc and the specificity of the CFA franc zone. As a member of the franc zone, Cameroon shares a currency, the Communauté Financière Africaine (CFA) franc with the other fourteen members of the zone. The CFA franc is pegged to the French franc at the rate of 50:1, a parity unchanged since independence. The members of the CFA zone keep their reserves in the French treasury, in exchange for which France guarantees the convertability of the currency.[71] By choosing to remain in the zone, Francophone countries exclude devaluation as an instrument of economic stabilization. To combat overvaluation and a noncompetitive currency, these states have to pursue depreciation through fiscal and credit contraction. This inability to resort to devaluation undermines a country's prospects for stabilization. Although much of its effect is likely to be short lived without accompanying measures, notably to control inflation,[72] devaluation can be accomplished by the stroke of a pen. Thus by forgoing devaluation, a government puts the burden of adjustment on policy instruments inherently harder to wield, such as administrative controls and import restrictions. Given contemporary African state capacities, the latter accomplish little besides encouraging further rent seeking.

In addition, devaluation offers an indirect but effective way of attacking the purchasing power of the urban bourgeoisie by shifting relative prices in favor of the traded goods sector. In effect, devaluation lowers the real salary of wage earners. Franc zone countries forgo that choice and thus have to lower the nominal wage bill. That this is politically much harder seems clear if one compares the experiences of adjustment in sub-Saharan Africa. After a decade of adjustment, franc zone countries like Cameroon barely made a dent in their civil service wage bills, while countries outside of the zone typically cut the purchasing power of civil servants by more than half. The institutional characteristics of the franc zone thus shaped the nature of the economic and political crisis there. On the one hand, countries like Côte d'Ivoire, Congo, and Cameroon suffer sustained labor unrest as the civil service fights to protect direct attacks on its purchasing power.[73] On the other hand, continued overvaluation and ever more administrative controls in the context of economic stagnation simply fuel intraelite struggles over rent seeking.

The second important factor in shaping transition is the strength of civil society. In Cameroon, it is weak; there are simply no civic associations with significant organizational power, in large part because the state destroyed them all in the first two decades after independence. In consequence, opposition groups cannot mobilize meaningful numbers of people for sustained periods to protest government actions. This not only makes toppling the government problematic, it also has an impact on the nature of transitions, when and if they occur. The weaker a civil society is, the less accountable the groups who take over the state will be after the transition. Although human rights activists, churchmen, and intellectuals may be prominent during the uncertain early transition period, they are likely to be displaced by people with links to the state's revenue and coercive apparatus. These people may concede some liberalization measures, but then they rule much as the previous rulers did. In Cameroon, for example, elites who defected from the Biya regime are well placed to take advantage of his regime's collapse. They are the likeliest to be able to control the state apparatus and to use its power to consolidate their rule. And once the protesters go home, who will prevent them?

Third, the level and sources of state revenues are an important factor in shaping the transition. Biya's ability to retain donor financial support and the guarantee of several hundred million dollars in oil revenues are critical to his survival. These revenues allow him to keep paying the state apparatus and prevent the defection of some political allies, as well as to "grease the squeaky wheel" (devoting resources to crisis areas). As the state's extractive capability weakens, the ease with which the state gets its revenues becomes important. A capital-intensive revenue source like oil is ideal in this respect, whereas states that rely on a diverse and decentralized tax base for revenues are likely to be much more vulnerable to neopatrimonial decay.

Ironically, the civil service has emerged as the leading constituency for good government and democratization in many of these countries.

In the richer states that built up large, professional, civil services during the good years, civil servants have become radicalized and pose a significant threat to entrenched leaders. In Cameroon, Côte d'Ivoire and Kenya, the civil service is perhaps the leading constituency of the regime. In poorer states, the civil service is smaller, less professional, and often pauperized and so constitutes a less significant political force within the ancien régime (which relies on old-fashioned clientelism and coercion to retain power) and is less important to transition politics.

In sum, the popular protests of late 1989 reflected the growing unhappiness of Africans with economic austerity and with the corruption and mismanagement it had brought about. The ability of these protests to shake the regimes in power and to bring about governmental transition had less to do with the actual strength and organization of the protesters, however, than with the nature of the neopatrimonial crisis, which had left governments weak.

Notes

I gratefully acknowledge support from the John D. and Catherine T. MacArthur Foundation for the research on which this chapter is based. I thank Barbara Grosh, René Lemarchand, and Jennifer Widner for their comments on drafts of the chapter.

1. See Michael Bratton and Nicolas van de Walle, "Popular Protest and Political Reform in Africa," *Comparative Politics* 24 (1992): 419–42.

2. *Africa Confidential* (January 10, 1992) argues that only Sudan and Malawi have been completely immune to democratic pressures.

3. See, for example, the contributions in Joan Nelson, ed., *Economic Crisis and Policy Choice: The Politics of Economic Adjustment in the Third World* (Princeton: Princeton University Press, 1990); also see Richard Sandbrook, "Taming the African Leviathan," *World Policy Journal* 7, no. 4 (1990): 673–701; and Carol Lancaster, "Democracy in Africa," *Foreign Policy* 85 (Winter 1991–92): 148–65.

4. See Bratton and van de Walle, "Popular Protest and Political Reform."

5. World Bank, *Sub-Saharan Africa: From Crisis to Sustainable Growth: A Long-Term Perspective Study* (Washington, D.C.: World Bank, 1989).

6. See, for example, Pierre Landell-Mills and Ismail Serageldin, "Governance and the Development Process," *Finance and Development* (September 1991): 14–17.

7. See, for example, Claude Ake, "Rethinking Africa Democracy," *Journal of Democracy* 2, no. 1 (1991): 1–13.

8. See Bratton and van de Walle, "Popular Protest and Political Reform."

9. I define *rent seeking* in the sense first articulated by Anne Krueger and accepted by most economists—as activities designed to benefit materially from the economic scarcities and rents created by government policies, such as

quotas, licenses, price ceilings, and controls. See Anne O. Krueger, "The Political Economy of the Rent-Seeking Society," *American Economic Review* 64, no. 3 (1974): 291–303. A theoretical discussion, with empirical applications to Africa, is Mark Gallagher, *Rent Seeking and Economic Growth in Africa* (Boulder, Colo.: Westview, 1991).

10. Max Weber, *Economy and Society*, ed. Guenther Roth and Claus Wittich (Berkeley: University of California Press, 1978).

11. For an analyses on this point, see Jean-François Médard, "The Underdeveloped State in Tropical Africa: Political Clientelism or Neo-Patrimonialism," and Christopher Clapham, "Clientelism and the State," in *Patronage and Public Power*, ed. Christopher Clapham (London: Frances Pinter, 1982). I do not address the issue of why African states are neopatrimonial. This topic is well addressed by Jean-François Bayart, *L'Etat en Afrique: la politique du ventre* (Paris: Fayard, 1989), among many others.

12. On these practices in Côte d'Ivoire, see Jean-Louis Gombeaud, Corinne Moutout, and Stephen Smith, *La Guerre du cacao: histoire secrète d'un embargo* (Paris: Calmann-Lévy, 1990).

13. See Yves Fauré and Jean-Français Médard, eds., *L'Etat et bourgeoisie en Côte d'Ivoire* (Paris: Karthala, 1982).

14. See René Lemarchand, "The State, the Parallel Economy, and the Changing Structure of Patronage Systems," in *The Precarious Balance: State and Society in Africa*, ed. Donald Rothchild and Naomi Chazan (Boulder, Colo.: Westview, 1988), for a similar argument.

15. See Wayne E. Nafziger, *Inequality in Africa: Political Elites, Proletariat, Peasants, and the Poor* (Cambridge: Cambridge University Press, 1988).

16. For analyses of corruption in Africa from a variety of perspectives, see Janet MacGaffey, *Entrepreneurs and Parasites: The Struggle for Indigenous Capitalism in Zaire* (Cambridge: Cambridge University Press, 1987); Paul Nugent, "Educating Rawlings: The Evolution of Government Strategy toward Smuggling," in *Ghana: The Political Economy of Recovery*, ed. Donald Rothchild (Boulder, Colo.: Lynne Rienner, 1991); David J. Gould, *Bureaucratic Corruption and Underdevelopment in the Third World: The Case of Zaire* (New York: Pergamon, 1980); Richard Joseph, *Democracy and Prebendal Politics in Nigeria: The Rise and Fall of the Second Republic* (New York: Cambridge University Press, 1987).

17. In addition, a large public sector conformed to the development ideologies of donors and others in the West.

18. See Henry Bienen, *Kenya: The Politics of Participation and Control* (Princeton: Princeton University Press, 1974).

19. See Nicolas van de Walle, "The Patron's Problem: Agency and Clientelism in Comparative Perspective," paper prepared for the annual meeting of the American Political Association, Washington D.C., September 1991.

20. Ibid.

21. See Goran Hyden, *No Shortcuts to Progress: African Development Management in Comparative Perspective* (Berkeley: University of California Press, 1983); Joseph, *Democracy and Prebendal Politics in Nigeria*; MacGaffey, *Entrepreneurs and Parasites*; and Thomas Callaghy, "The State as Lame Leviathan:

The Patrimonial Administrative State in Africa," in *The African State in Transition*, ed. Zakis Ergas (New York: St. Martin's, 1987).

22. See Médard, "The Underdeveloped State in Tropical Africa."

23. See Henry Bienen and Nicolas van de Walle, *Of Time and Power: Leadership Duration in the Modern World* (Stanford: Stanford University Press, 1991).

24. The impact of commodity booms on African economies is analyzed in Jeffrey M. Davis. "The Economic Effects of Windfall Gains in Export Earnings," *World Development* 11 (1983): 119–39.

25. See World Bank, *Sub-Saharan Africa*; John Ravenhill, ed., *Africa in Economic Crisis* (New York: Columbia University Press, 1987); Carol Lancaster and John Williamson, *African Debt and Financing*, Special Report 5 (Washington, D.C.: Institute for International Economics, 1986); G. K. Helleiner, ed., *Africa and the International Monetary Fund* (Washington, D.C.: International Monetary Fund, 1986).

26. In addition to the works cited above, see Stephan Haggard, "The Politics of Adjustment: Lessons from the IMF's Extended Fund Facility," *International Organization* 39, no. 3 (1985): 505–34; Ravi Gulhati, *Recent Economic Reforms in Africa: A Preliminary Political Economy Perspective*, EDI Policy Seminar Report (Washington, D.C.: World Bank, 1987); and Richard E. Feinberg and Valeriana Kallab, eds., *The Adjustment Crisis in the Third World* (New Brunswick, N.J.: Transaction Books, 1984).

27. See chapter 2, this volume.

28. See Lemarchand, "The State, the Parallel Economy," 157–59.

29. See Robert H. Bates "The Reality of Structural Adjustment: A Skeptical Appraisal," in *Structural Adjustment and Agriculture: Theory and Practice in Africa and Latin America*, ed. Simon Commander (Portsmouth, N.H.: Heinemann Educational Books, 1989), for a similar argument.

30. Jennifer Widner, "The 1990 Elections in Côte d'Ivoire," *Issue: A Journal of Opinion* 21 (1991): 31–40, 33.

31. See, for example, Nim Casswell, "Autopsie de l'ONCAD: la politique arachidière au Sénégal, 1966–1980," *Politique africaine* 14 (June 1984): 39–73; G. Courade, I. Grangeret, and P. Janin, "La Liquidation des joyaux du prince: les enjeux de la libéralisation des filières café-cacao au Cameroun," *Politique africaine* 44 (December 1991): 121–28; Yves Fauré, "L'Economie politique d'une démocratisation: élements d'analyse à propos de l'expérience récente de la Côte d'Ivoire," *Politique africaine* 43 (October 1991): 31–49.

32. See Karim Nashashibi et al., *The Fiscal Dimensions of Adjustment in Low-Income Countries*, IMF Occasional Paper 95 (Washington, D.C.: IMF, 1992).

33. A U.S. dollar was worth 319 CFA francs during 1989. See Republic of Cameroon, "Etude sur la fiscalité," Report of the Technical Commission of the Mission of Rehabilitation of Public Sector and Parapublic Enterprises (Yaoundé: March 1989), 66.

34. A full discussion of these factors is provided in Bratton and van de Walle "Popular Protest and Political Reform." See also Samuel Decalo, "The Process, Prospects, and Constraints of Democratization in Africa," *African Affairs* 91 (1992): 7–35.

35. *Deflaté* means, literally, "the deflated." The term is used in Francophone Africa to designate the victims of deflationary economic policies in the civil service and the parastatal sector.

36. Zambia, with its long tradition of independent trade unions, is a partial exception to this generalization.

37. For Côte d'Ivoire, see Fauré, "L'Economie politique d'une démocratisation," 41.

38. See Théophile Vittin, "Bénin: du 'système Kérékou' au renouveau démocratique," in *Etats d'Afrique noire· formation, méchanismes, et crise,* ed. Jean-François Médard (Paris: Karthala, 1991).

39. An exception is Pearl T. Robinson, "The National Conference Phenomenon in Africa," July 17, 1992, typescript.

40. See issues of *Jeune Afrique economie* and *Africa International,* for example.

41. See Jean-François Bayart, *L'Etat au Cameroun* (Paris: Presses de la Fondation Nationale de Sciences Politiques, 1985); Jean-François Médard, "L'Etat sous-dévelopé au Cameroun," in *L'Année ufricaine* (Paris: Pedone, 1977); Nicolas van de Walle, "The Politics of Non-Reform in Cameroon," in *Hemmed In: Responses to Africa's Economic Decline,* ed. Thomas Callaghy and John Ravenhill (New York: Columbia University Press, 1993); Michael G. Schatzberg and I. William Zartman, eds., *The Political Economy of Cameroon* (New York: Praeger, 1986).

42. See Nancy C. Benjamin and Shantayanan Devarajan, "Oil Revenues and the Cameroonian Economy," in Schatzberg and Zartman, eds., *The Political Economy of Cameroon;* and Joseph Ngu, "The Political Economy of Oil in Cameroon," in *Conference on the Political Economy of Cameroon: Historical Perspectives,* ed. Peter Geschiere and Piet Konings (Leiden: African Studies Center, 1989).

43. See Nicolas van de Walle, "Rice Politics in Cameroon: State Commitment, Capability, and Urban Bias," *Journal of Modern African Studies* 27 (1989): 579–600, 594.

44. In early 1991, a liter of Nigerian gasoline sold in Douala for 150 CFA francs, compared to an official price of 270 CFA francs. See also Celestin Monga, "Bidons d'essence interdits," *Jeune Afrique économie,* no. 129 (March 1990): 93–97.

45. See Michel Courcelle, *The Private Sector in Cameroon* (Paris: Organization for Economic Cooperation and Development, 1990), 63–67.

46. Ibid., 39–40.

47. The level of centralization is indicated by the widely held belief that, during the 1970s, Ahidjo personally approved of every exit visa granted to a Cameroonian citizen.

48. For the definitive history of the UPC, see Richard Joseph, *Radical Nationalism in Cameroon: Social Origins of the UPC Rebellion* (Oxford: Oxford University Press, 1997).

49. For a full description, see Jean-François Bayart. "La Société politique camerounaise, 1982–1986," *Politique africaine* 22 (June 1986): 5–36; Victor T. Le Vine, "Leadership and Regime Changes in Perspective," in Schatzberg and

Zartman, eds., *The Political Economy of Cameroon*; and J. P. Biyiti Bi Essam, *Cameroun: complots et bruits de bottes: quelque données pour ébrouiller l'écheveau* (Paris: l'Harmattan, 1985).

50. Biya's liberal ambitions were forcefully put forward in his vanity press book, *Pour le liberalisme communautaire* (Paris: Pierre Marcel Favre, 1986). See also Paul Biya, *Le Message du renouveau: discours et interviews du president Paul Biya* (Yaoundé: Sopecam, 1984).

51. See Jean-François Bayart, "Un printemps camerounais," *Marchés tropicaux*, September 29, 1983; Gilbert Moutard. "Cameroun: au rythme lent du 'renouveau,' " in *Afrique contemporaine* 143 (1987): 52–57; and Gilbert Moutard, "Quelles chances pour la politique du President Biya?" *Afrique contemporaine* 139 (1986): 20–35.

52. Significantly, one of Biya's first acts as president was to declare generous salary increases for the public sector; see Biyiti Bi Essam, *Complots et bruits de bottes*, 19.

53. Biya is a member of the Beti ethnic group, probably the largest in southern Cameroon. See "The Beti Barons," *Africa Confidential*, July 28, 1989.

54. This estimate, by the government press agency, included 600 billion CFA francs in customs fraud, 500 billion in fake billing on government contracts, 300 billion in salaries to fictitious state employees, and 150 billion in bad bank debts. See "Chronique d'une séparation," *Jeune Afrique economie*, no. 128 (February 1990): 129.

55. Thomas M. Callaghy, "Africa's Debt Crisis," in *Journal of International Affairs* 38, no. 1 (1984): 61–79.

56. See van de Walle, "The Politics of Non-Reform."

57. See "Avec un nouvel accord du FMI, le Cameroun amorce un tournant décisif," *Marchés tropicaux*, January 3, 1992.

58. These events are reviewed in Pierre Englebert, *Cameroon: Background to a Crisis*, CSIS Africa Notes, 130 (Washington, D.C.: Center for Strategic and International Studies, 1991), 1–8. See also "Cameroon: Crisis or Compromise?" *Africa Confidential*, October 25, 1991.

59. This claim was made by *Africa Confidential* in "Cameroon: Crisis or Compromise?" The government officially maintained that the campaign had a negligible impact, although in private interviews many officials conceed that it exacerbated an already dismal revenue situation.

60. See "La cour suprême a annoncé le réélection du président Paul Biya," *Le Monde*, October 25, 1992.

61. The National Democratic Institute for International Affairs sent an international team to monitor the election; its report argues that "widespread irregularities during the preelection period, on election day, and in the tabulation of results seriously calls into question, for any fair observer, the validity of the outcome." See National Democratic Institute for International Affairs, "Cameroon Presidential Elections of October 11, 1992: An NDI Interim Report of the International Observer Mission" (Washington, D.C.: NDI, October 28, 1992), typescript. See also Celestin Monga's interesting account of the cam-

paign in "La recomposition du marché politique au Cameroun, 1991–1992" (GERDES, December 1992), typescript.

62. See "Les Grandes manoeuvres," *Jeune Afrique,* April 9, 1991. Even Fru Ndi was a respectable notable of Bamenda in the not so distant past and had, for example, long held the government contract to supply books to North West Province schools.

63. See *Africa Research Bulletin,* Economic Series (February 16, 1992): 10733; see also "Avec un nouvel accord du FMI."

64. See, for example, various editions of *Africa Confidential* from 1989 and 1990.

65. At the height of the tensions in the fall of 1991, for example, Biya told a rally in Yaoundé, the heart of Beti country, "as long as Yaoundé breathes, Cameroon lives." Beti representatives from the region presented him with a machete, a spear, and a drum—gifts that could only be considered extremely provocative by the rest of the country.

66. See, for example, Piet Konings, "La Liquidation des Plantations Unilever et les conflits intra-élite dans le Cameroun anglophone," *Politique africaine* 35 (October 1989): 132–37.

67. Dankwart A. Rustow, "Transitions to Democracy: Towards a Dynamic Model," *Comparative Politics* 2 (1970): 337–64, 361.

68. On the empirical record, see for example Guillermo O'Donnell and Phillipe Schmitter, *Transitions from Authoritarian Rule: Tentative Conclusions about Uncertain Outcomes* (Baltimore: Johns Hopkins University Press, 1986); and Terry Lynn Karl, "Dilemmas of Democratization in Latin America," *Comparative Politics* 22 (1990): 1–22. On pacts, see O'Donnell and Schmitter, *Transitions from Authoritarian Rule,* chap. 4.

69. O'Donnell and Schmitter, *Transitions from Authoritarian Rule,* 38.

70. See "De Quoi se mêle l'Eglise?" *Africa International,* no. 233 (December 1990): 10–17.

71. The institutional details of the CFA franc zone are explained in Patrick Guillaumont and Sylviane Guillaumont, eds., *Zone franc et développement africain* (Paris: Economica, 1984).

72. The importance of this qualification can not be overstated; devaluations in Africa have typically led to sharp rises in inflation.

73. See Bratton and van de Walle, "Popular Protest and Political Reform."

MWESIGA BAREGU

Seven ◈ The Rise and Fall of the One-Party State in Tanzania

The late 1980s and early 1990s have been a time of very rapid, sometimes dizzying, global political change. Apart from the upheavals
in the former socialist block and the realignment of forces in the
capitalist world, pressures for political and economic change have
been mounting in Africa and elsewhere in the world. The dominant
goal of these latter pressures is variously described as "democratization," "liberalization," or "pluralization." Although these pressures
are concurrent and interconnected, it is hard to say if they arise from
the same causes and constitute a single historical process. It is even
more difficult to predict the ultimate outcomes, let alone the extent
to which they will promote democracy in Africa.[1] Collectively, these
pressures aim at dismantling one-party or military rule in Africa. Colin
Legum describes them as leading to Africa's second liberation, and
certainly another wind of change is blowing over the African continent.[2]

At least four groups are discernible among the countries facing
such pressures. The *reformers* have yielded to organized pressures,
permitted the formation of competing political parties, and held multiparty elections in which new parties have come to power. Benin, Cape
Verde, Mauritius, São Tomé and Príncipe, and Zambia belong to this
group. In countries like Congo and Ethiopia, national conferences
have been set up to work out the details and oversee the transition
to democracy. These countries are the *transitionists*. A third group are
the *resisters*, of which Kenya and Zaire are cases in point. Kenya, for

example, strongly resisted domestic pressure for change, but the government of Daniel arap Moi eventually succumbed to considerable coercive diplomacy from donor countries. A fourth group, to which Tanzania belongs, are the *hesitaters*. In 1990, Tanzania grudgingly allowed an open public debate in the press, while resisting demands for constitutional reform. In March 1991, however, it set up a presidential commission to decide whether to have one party or many, and by May 1992, the national constitution had been amended, setting up a timetable to establish a multiparty system.[3]

This chapter traces the rise and decline of the one-party state in Tanzania. First, it identifies the phases through which one-party rule evolved and analyzes the forces that sustained the government through these phases. Second, it describes and analyzes the issues, actors, and dynamics of the current process of political change. Finally, it looks at the problems and prospects of establishing a lasting democratic order.[4] Its principal argument is that the demands for multipartyism and democracy in Tanzania are the culmination of a long and cumulative (albeit uneven) struggle against authoritarian rule. At the time of independence in 1961, the Tanganyika African National Union (TANU), led by Julius Nyerere, arrogated power to itself, suppressed political competition, and forcefully imposed one-party rule. That move was resisted right from the start and continued to be resisted until 1992. Thus the political legitimacy of the one-party state has been contested throughout this period.[5]

Resistance has assumed different forms over time. In the early 1960s trade unions strongly protested repressive labor laws and the forceful incorporation of the unions into TANU. In the 1970s workers revolted against management, the government, and the party. Productivity declined thereafter. Peasants resisted forced villagization and retreated into subsistence production. Attempted coups d'état and "treason trials" dotted the historical landscape of Tanzania. Finally, Chama Cha Mapinduzi (CCM), the ruling party, was forced to submit to popular pressures for a multiparty system. The legitimacy crisis had come to a head.[6]

The legitimacy crisis of the government in Tanzania (and in Africa in general) has deep historical origins. At least two may be identified. The first is that, at the time of political independence, the social compact, which had mobilized the people in support of the nationalist leadership in the anticolonial struggle, came to an end. The TANU government ruthlessly repressed demands for a new social contract between the rulers and the civil society. Hence the postcolonial state floated above civil society much as the colonial state had. The second source of the legitimacy crisis is that, to the nationalist leadership, the demand for national independence did not, pari passu, embody a commitment to democratic rule. Colonial rule itself was a good school for authoritarianism. By its very nature, colonialism suppressed the rise of nationalist movements and definitely resisted their proliferation. Thus the movements that emerged and survived (such as TANU) not only were molded by the colonial administration but were also forced to be highly centralized, monolithic in thought, and intolerant of dissent.[7] The postcolonial state never departed from the colonial tradition of ruling by coercion, not consent.

Uhuru na kazi—TANU Consolidates Power (1961–1967)

When Tanganyika (Tanzania since 1964) became independent in 1961, there were at least three political parties. The Tanganyika African National Union (TANU) was the most dominant. The African National Congress (ANC) and the United Tanganyika Party (UTP) contested unsuccessfully in the 1960, quasi-free, preindependence elections in which TANU won all the seats. On that basis, TANU claimed that it had obtained an exclusive popular mandate. In an essay published just after the elections, Nyerere provided the first rationale for what was later to become a constitutional one-party state.

The last elections were not based on universal suffrage, although this was what we desired. But the franchise was a wide one, and there was no evidence of any group of non-voters who disagreed with the verdict. The only organized political opposition party lost its deposit and all the seats it contested. . . . The people of Tanganyika are behind TANU. . . . In the future it is possible that a second political party will grow in Tanganyika, but in one sense such a growth would represent a failure by TANU . . . a second party will not need to grow provided that a broad two-way channel of ideas and education is maintained through TANU between the people and the government. It is the establishment and maintenance of this channel which is the real problem of democracy in Tanganyika.[8]

Having so written, however, Nyerere added that it was for the people to decide on the desirability and viability of his "channel." They could show this "only by being free to form and support a responsible opposition party if they wish to do so." But, Nyerere equivocated, "at the moment it is clear that they do not wish to do so."[9] This vacillation between democracy and strong government pervaded Nyerere's thinking in the early period of Tanzania's independence and beyond.

The independence constitution was a compact between Britain and the nationalist leadership. It was not a covenant between civil society and the new state. Thus, although it provided for a Westminster model of government, the political conditions on the ground were against it.[10] In 1962, Nyerere wrote: "Immediately after its formation the new government is faced with a major task—that of economic development of the country and the general uplifting of the standard of living of the people, through the elimination of poverty, ignorance and disease. In order for this objective to be successfully accomplished there is as much need for unity as was required during the struggle for independence. *Similarly there is no room for difference*" (emphasis added).[11]

At the end of 1962, Tanzania adopted a republican constitution with a strong presidency. To prepare the ground for this change to a republican system, traditional chieftaincies were abolished, and ethnic organizations were banned. Two important pieces of repressive legislation were also enacted. One was the Preventive Detention Act, which gave the government the power to arrest and imprison any persons deemed to be threats to national security—broadly and conveniently defined. Some of the first victims of this act were trade unionists (1962–64) and former chiefs.[12] The other was an amendment to the Trade Union Ordinance that outlawed all strikes, prohibited civil servants from belonging to unions, and compelled all unions to affiliate with the Tanganyika Federation of Labor (TFL), which was itself under TANU's control. Trade unions vehemently protested these measures. The president of the Tanganyika Union of Teachers was quite forthright: "We are fast moving into totalitarianism; why force a puppet federation controlled by a minister?"[13]

On January 14, 1963, nearly one month after becoming president, Nyerere announced that TANU's National Executive Committee had decided that, in the interest of national unity and economic development, Tanganyika should become a constitutional one-party state. He never explained why TANU found this move necessary if it believed its own numerous claims that the opposition was very weak if not nonexistent. The contradiction never deterred him. A presidential commission on the establishment of a democratic one-party state in Tanganyika was set up on January 28, 1964, with strict instructions to make recommendations on how—not whether—Tanzania was to become a one-party state. By July 1965, Tanzania had become a constitutional one-party state.[14] In that period, Nyerere took steps to centralize power. Between 1964 and 1966, in the wake of a failed army mutiny, a new army was formed under TANU's control. In addition, two unions were established, sponsored and controlled by the party-state: the National Union of Tanganita Workers (NUTA) and the Co-operative Union of Tanganyika (CUT).[15]

Economically, the open-door import substitution policy of the early 1960s had failed to attract the anticipated foreign capital. On the contrary, in a few of those early years, when the wooing of foreign capital went along with restriction of political freedoms, capital inflows were exceeded by profit outflows.[16] The objectives of both the Three Year Plan (1961–64) and the First Five Year Plan (1964–69) could not be met mainly because the anticipated foreign resource inflows did not materialize. Meanwhile, a new class of rich political leaders and public servants was emerging and becoming a target of popular discontent. A period of disillusionment and introspection set in around 1966.[17]

Ujamaa—Mobilization without Empowerment (1967–1970)

By 1967, the Tanzanian state was experiencing political and economic pressures from a number of directions, and it consistently responded with repression and centralization of power. Tanzania had thus been steadily moving toward authoritarianism since independence.[18] The 1967 Arusha Declaration continued this trend.[19] The famous declaration was an attempt to respond to several pressures.

—The open-door policy under the Foreign Investment Protection Act of 1963 failed to attract foreign resources; hence enterprise creation and expansion were slow and demands for employment and higher incomes could not be met.

—Tanzania came into conflict with Western powers over questions of sovereignty and the liberation struggles in southern Africa and lost their economic support.

—The national consensus that led the country to independence was vanishing rapidly as class differentiation set in with the emergence of the nouveaux riches (wabenzi, naizesheni—beneficiaries of uhuru) in the party and government. A rural-urban divide was evolving as well.

—The moral persuasion that sustained self-reliance projects under the slogan uhuru na kazi (freedom and work) was wearing thin, as many self-help schemes collapsed due to lack of committed government support.

—Workers were agitating for free expression and rejecting the state-sponsored trade union, NUTA. A presidential commission of inquiry appointed in 1966 to look into the affairs of NUTA found that it had "no adequate and visible means of democratic expression."[20]

These conditions provide the background to the Arusha Declaration, TANU's policy on socialism and self-reliance.[21] The declaration is most remembered for the nationalization of banks, buildings, and some industries and the formation of state corporations to run them, the establishment of *ujamaa* villages, and the introduction of education for self-reliance. Most analysts take the "socialist" economic objectives as ends in themselves and judge the success or failure of the political system on the basis of the performance on these broadly economic goals. The program articulated at Arusha had political ends as well, however. The declaration's "socialism and self-reliance" were populist slogans intended to achieve ideological hegemony.[22]

The Arusha Declaration embodied an effort by the ruling elite to address its legitimacy crisis and to protect its class interests. By promising a socialist utopia (*ujamaaland*) and focusing attention on a hostile international environment, the Arusha Declaration was a mobilizational and diversionary mechanism for political adaptation and system maintenance in the face of the social discontent described above. That it achieved neither socialism nor self-reliance should therefore not be surprising. They were never the intended objectives. In Arusha, TANU was seeking to obtain peoples' compliance through the imposition of ideological hegemony. Insofar as *ujamaa* came to be perceived as a form of social covenant, TANU succeeded in enhancing its legitimacy while reinforcing its social control.

Thus the seeming democratic content in the voluntary (collective decision) phase of *ujamaa* villages (1967–70) was not intended to enhance the people's capacity to decide their destiny. Rather, it was intended to obtain their "voluntary" compliance to party policies. Consequently, as soon as local level decisions were in conflict with the policies from above, the party imposed its will by force. That is why the *ujamaa* villages phase, in which each village was to be "a voluntary association of people who decide of their own free will to live together and work together for their common good"[23] was not only short-lived but was succeeded by forced villagization. From there on, TANU abandoned persuasive methods, and coercion became the order of the day. Elected district councils and cooperatives were abolished in favor of teams of bureaucrats and party officials whose task was to enforce directives from above.[24]

Party Supremacy—The Elusive Quest (1970–1980)

In January 1971, the Milton Obote government in Uganda was overthrown by a military coup that brought Idi Amin to power. In the same period, Guinea was invaded by Portuguese forces. The Amin coup revealed that a government claiming to represent the common man could be overthrown by a military coup without the slightest protest, let alone resistance, by the working people. The Guinea incident demonstrated to Tanzania how vulnerable to imperialist aggression left-leaning, liberation-supporting African governments were. A way had to be found to mobilize the workers, and the *mwongozo wa TANU* (TANU guidelines) of 1971 and the formation of workers' councils was the answer.[25] *Mwongozo*, like the Arusha Declaration, had two contradictory faces. One was the "democratization" face, which claimed to strengthen the workers' role in decisions affecting the workplace. To this end, workers were encouraged to openly challenge management decisions and policies. Clause 15 of the document became the workers' rallying cry: "There must be a deliberate effort to build equality between the leaders and those they lead. For a Tanzanian leader it must be forbidden to be arrogant, contemptuous and oppressive."[26]

But the other face of *mwongozo* was restrictive: no move was made to repeal the repressive labor laws. In 1975, the government issued a statement declaring the workers' actions under Clause 15 illegal. Some workers were fired. They had been entrapped and, as was happening in the *ujamaa* village movement, the strong arm of law and order soon clamped down on this short-lived workers' democracy.[27] From that point on, the workers' councils and NUTA became conduits for party and government directives to workers.[28]

A process of militarizing society also began with the formation of a people's militia strongly based on workers' councils and controlled by TANU. Similar groups based on party branches were formed in rural areas. Constituted as vigilantes, the members of these groups organized against internal, "subversive" elements, as well as external enemies. Later, the government mobilized them against the workers during *mwongozo* industrial actions, against the peasants in the forced villagization operations, and in the war that removed Idi Amin from Uganda in 1979. Having established control over virtually all spheres of civil life in 1975, TANU entrenched party supremacy and socialism in the national constitution and placed itself above parliament, whose members it nominated. TANU's executive secretary captured the new constitution succinctly (and approvingly): "The amended Constitution provides that all political activity in Tanzania shall be conducted by or under the auspices of the party; and further that the functions of all the organs of state of the United Republic shall be performed under the auspices of the party. The party is now supreme both in practice and in law."[29]

In 1977, TANU and the Afro-Shiraz party (ASP), the ruling party in Zanzibar, which had followed policies roughly similar to those TANU had followed on the mainland, merged to form the Chama Cha Mapinduzi (CCM). The merger was a formality undertaken to remove the anomaly of having two parties in a constitutional one-party state. The birth of CCM was also intended to seal party supremacy over the union. NUTA and the Workers' Organization in Zanzibar were merged to form a new CCM workers' organization. So were the women's organization and the youth movement.[30]

But party supremacy was more apparent than real. CCM, as a political party, was stillborn. It had no real voluntary and loyal members. The distinction between party and state became so blurred that party and government positions were held by the same people—usually authoritarian bureaucrats. The party was one of the state's coercive instruments. A 1975 act gave the peoples' militia police powers of arrest, and they performed their tasks assiduously and brutally.[31] In a cynical play on Swahili words, party supremacy (*chama kushika hatamu*) became popularly known as *chama kushika utamu* (the party appropriating all the good things). Nyerere became known as Husa—not the one that delivered the Israelis to the promised land but the one who got them lost in the Sinai desert for forty years! Thus by the end of the 1970s, the country was much more conscious of the ambiguous character of state authority and how it added to the insecurity of life. People became more careful about what they said in public places and did the minimum needed to keep on the right side of the authorities. The social order stressed innovation from above, and people waited for changes to come; they had little incentive to innovate for themselves.[32]

Bongoland—The Economic and Legitimacy Crisis (1980–1990)

At the time of consolidating party supremacy, the country was in a deep economic crisis that threatened even the physical reproduction of life. Two years of drought and the oil shocks of 1974 brought the crisis to a head, when international reserves plummeted by 70 percent and current account deficits averaged 14 percent. Everybody in the country was worse off than they had been in the early 1970s. Living standards were reckoned to have dropped by 40–50 percent between 1975 and 1983, owing to rising inflation and stagnant real incomes. When, in 1977, Nyerere boasted of reducing income inequality from 20:1 to 9:1 over the ten years of *ujamaa*, he seemed oblivious of the fact that this was because the whole society had become poorer under a policy of repression without growth.[33]

In this economic crisis, the state was conspicuously unable to provide solutions. All its major economic initiatives (*ujamaa* villages, forced villagization, *mwongozo*, regional integrated development programs, and decentralization) had either failed or exacerbated the problems.[34] The state had also come under growing domination by external governments and multilateral agencies through aid and loan dependence for basic sustenance of the people and its own maintenance. Corruption had become widespread. In December 1976, the minister of home affairs reported that about $4 million had been embezzled in public corporations and government departments. In his review of ten years of the Arusha Declaration, Nyerere said, "We have reached a stage where our greatest danger is a new one. The thing which could now do most to undermine our socialist development would be failure in the battle against corruption, against theft and loss of public money and goods and other abuses of public office."[35]

Under these conditions, party supremacy was at best an illusion. The economic crisis, which peaked in the early 1980s, was both cause and consequence of an enduring crisis of political legitimacy—a crisis of democracy.[36] A local political observer summed up the crisis of legitimacy incisively at the time: "Where corruption is on an increase, all organs of state become suspect just as the economic institutions involved in distribution. Law and justice become matters for sale, and opportunism at all levels ensures that only the corrupt and cynical survive. . . . Meanwhile, for the people the situation becomes increasingly difficult, and no explanation of its causes is any longer valid, because the basic confidence in political, legal, and economic institutions is no longer there. The party, to which the people would normally appeal, is no longer authoritative because it is itself compromised by leaders who use its authority to engage in the same malpractices against which it ought to have been the indefatigable fighter."[37]

After protracted and acrimonious negotiations with the IMF, a failed CCM conceived the National Economic Survival Program, 1981–82, and the government pursued an informally negotiated World Bank structural adjustment program for 1982–85. It signed an agreement with the IMF in 1985, launching an economic recovery program, 1986–89, under which economic liberalization (devaluation, price decontrol, reduction of the state sector, control and balancing of the budget, privatization, etc.) all but eclipsed *ujamaa*. By the beginning of the 1990s, the following trends could be discerned in the Tanzanian economy and polity:[38]

—GDP was estimated to be growing at 4.4 percent—an improvement over the 2 percent of 1980. Almost all the growth came from one sector—agriculture. World prices for the country's traditional agricultural exports fell by 22 percent of the 1981 dollar value, however.[39] Industrial capacity utilization continued to hover around 20–30 percent.

—Social services became the major casualty of reduced public spending. Health, education, and water services—all gained with growing aid receipts in the 1970s—nearly collapsed.[40]

—Price decontrols led to runaway inflation, which hovered at around 30 percent a year over the decade. Imports increased despite higher prices, while public sector salaries were one-fifth of their real 1970s level. This situation fueled corruption and embezzlement.[41]

—An income redistribution effect was visible. Under state controls, parastatal managers floated on monopoly rents. These rents then shifted to the commercial bourgeoisie (mainly Asians), creating potentially explosive racial conflict.

—The loss-making parastatals were in a free-fall, without a corresponding spontaneous rise in private enterprise.

—In the transport sector, a major bottleneck to the economic recovery program, all the economic costs of neglect and postponement converged with a vengeance.[42] In 1990, a $900 million road repair project was launched just to restore 1,000 miles of usable roads—the same figure as 1970!

—Industrial output continued to decline, growing at −1.0 percent a year for the period 1980–89.[43]

The economic crisis persisted during the life of the economic recovery program. The deterioration of social services was especially contentious, because it threatened to reverse all the gains Tanzania had made under *ujamaa*. Politically, this issue created growing tension between the party and the government, between CCM chairman Julius Nyerere and President Ali Hassan Mwinyi, and between the right and left factions in the party and government on the issue of the future of socialism in Tanzania. Generally, the socialist ideologues in the party, led by Nyerere, continued to resist the liberalization policies of the economic recovery program, while the pragmatists—mainly in the government and with the support of the World Bank and IMF—continued to push for liberalization. There was virtual paralysis on a number of key policy issues on which continued IMF support crucially depended, and a delay ensued in the disbursement of the final tranche in the structural adjustment facility. The issues included devaluation, an investment code, the privatization of the public sector, and the liberalization of the financial sector. The logjam was finally broken in

1989, the final year of the economic recovery program, when the pragmatic viewpoint prevailed.[44]

The year 1989 was therefore a turning point in economic policy as well as a political watershed. Economically, the country underwent a devaluation of 22.1 percent, adopted an investment code, started dismantling the parastatals, and introduced cost recovery arrangements in education. Politically, these measures signaled a formal break with the CCM ideology of *ujamaa*, but they also meant the breakdown of consensus in the party and the lack of a sense of direction. That is what finally triggered Nyerere's resignation and caused widespread political dissent.

Political dissent in Tanzania therefore traces back to three main proximate factors: the failure of economic liberalization policies, the capitulation of the state to external economic agents, and Julius Nyerere. The interaction of these factors created a situation in which the locus of political power became openly contested.

The economic recovery program catalyzed demands for political liberalization in two major ways. First, traditional opponents of the World Bank and the IMF in the party, the government, and academic institutions (the left intelligentsia) gradually realized that they could not dissuade the government from adopting these policies, given the deepening economic crisis, the need for continued external support, and the absence of viable short-term alternatives. Instead, these opponents turned their attention to the logical inconsistency in the government's espousal of economic liberalization and its rejection of political liberalization. Thus, in September 1990, the Tanganyika Law Society organized a seminar entitled Party Systems and Democracy, focusing attention on this inconsistency. Participants demanded a new "national consensus."[45] Second, the economic recovery program fueled demands for multiparty democracy through the direct intervention of the World Bank and the IMF in policymaking, which further undermined the government's legitimacy. Until 1980, Nyerere had strongly resisted the imposition of IMF conditions, called out massive anti-IMF demonstrations, and swore publicly never to look back lest, like Lot's wife, he be turned into a pillar of salt! At one meeting, Nyerere said, "We are now telling them that we are not going to accept their manoeuvres. . . . Tanzania will overcome its hardships without compromising her policy."[46] By the mid-1980s, however, after the early National Economic Survival Program was abandoned, the IMF conditions were quietly accepted, and a World Bank structural adjustment program was launched in 1983.

The acceptance of IMF conditions was popularly perceived as capitulation, creating a pervasive belief that neither the party nor the government was in charge. People referred to the country as *bongoland* (a country where you survive by your wits) and CCM as Chukua Chako Mapema (Loot Now!) or Chama Cha Majangili (Party of Crooks). In his 1989 budget speech, Finance Minister Cleope David Msuya captured this mood by declaring, biblically: "Each shall carry his own burden!"[47]

Mageuzi—The Interregnum (1990–1992)

Another external source of pressure for political liberalization emanated from the changed position of the major aid donor countries. Ironically, Tanzania's aid dependency and hence its vulnerability increased under its self-reliance policy.[48] Between 1970 and 1985 the country received nearly $9.5 billion and was easily Africa's highest recipient of aid, particularly from the Nordic countries, which hitherto had not questioned the political system. In October 1991, however, Norway (with $10 million per annum in aid) issued a statement that "future financial aid to Tanzania would depend on its human rights record and the introduction of multiparty democracy in the country."[49]

Perhaps ironically, the most influential proponent of political change in the country was Julius Nyerere. At a press conference on February 21, 1990, while addressing the question of the political events in Eastern Europe, Nyerere stated that Tanzania, like the rest of the world, would inevitably be affected by the changes. He counseled the party and the government to prepare for change in Tanzania: "When you see your neighbor being shaved, wet your head to avoid a dry shave. . . . The one party is not Tanzania's ideology; having one party is not God's will. One party has its own limitations . . . it tends to go to sleep."[50] Nyerere challenged CCM to advance contemporary arguments for continued monopoly of power and not to rely on those advanced in the 1960s or hide behind the protection of the single-party constitution.

Nyerere's statements created considerable tension and anxiety (if not panic) in the party and government. For a while, CCM was in disarray; leaders contradicted each other and sometimes themselves. Secretary General Rashidi Kawawa denied any connection between Eastern European socialism and Tanzania's *ujamaa*. President Mwinyi, the party's vice chairman, argued that multipartyism was diversionary and potentially divisive. He raised the specter of tribalism and the possibility of national disintegration plunging the country into interminable civil strife.[51]

On May 29, 1990, Nyerere announced that he was quitting his party chairmanship, endorsed Mwinyi as his successor, but repeated his challenge to the party. He also insisted that the debate be allowed to continue. Nyerere stepped down from the CCM chair on August 17 at a special CCM conference that elected Mwinyi to replace him. By that time, CCM delegates had begun to accept Nyerere's ideas on political change and was "wetting its head to avoid a dry shave." (In July 1991, the party announced that it had retained Nyerere as elder statesman, complete with an office.)[52]

By September, Mwinyi, now more confident as a party chair and president, conceded the possibility of a multiparty system "if the people wished it" and suggested a referendum as a possible way of establishing the peoples' will.[53] CCM heeded Nyerere's advice and was preparing to manage the transition to its advantage. While the debate continued in the press, CCM launched a membership recruitment campaign and undertook some institutional reforms to revitalize itself.[54] By February 1991, Mwinyi announced the appointment of a presidential commission on "one or many parties" chaired by Chief Justice Francis Nyalali. It was to submit its recommendations within one year.

The details of the commission's report are not the subject of this chapter.[55] A preliminary report was submitted to the president in December 1991. It recommended the adoption of a multiparty system, in spite of its findings that nearly 80 percent of the population preferred one form or another of single-party rule. That finding is not surprising when we realize that practically everybody under forty years of age in Tanzania (about 60 percent of the population) has known no other form of politics. Nyerere stressed this point when he noted that the majority of Tanzanians, in a referendum, would probably support a one-party system. "But what does one do about the minority?" he asked.[56]

In the event, the final recommendations of the committee were adopted. Parliament repealed the one-party clause in the national constitution in May 1992 and adopted a new law setting up a timetable to establish a multiparty political system.[57]

Upinzani—The Opposition

In 1992, the political landscape in Tanzania was confused. It is thus not easy to draw a clear map of opposition groups, much less to delineate their differences. Among the peasants and workers, for example, there were elements both for and against political change.

This is partly in the nature of any political transition, when most people are ambivalent about the change and uncertain about their position, opposition groups are still embryonic, and the political situation is volatile. Even CCM itself was in a state of flux, as the leadership and membership, for the first time, contemplated alternative political options under a multiparty system. A vibrant and bold independent press began to emerge in the late 1980s. Three monthly tabloids played a major role in voicing the views of the opposition, despite government efforts to silence them: *Family Mirror* (English) and *Radi* and *Fahari* (Swahili). They consistently advocated an open political system.

This assessment is of necessity tentative. In the course of the political debate, most proponents of change objected to CCM's monopoly of politics and related that directly to the persistently poor performance of the economy. The opponents of change were divided, however. A proportion of them, while unhappy with the economy, nevertheless opposed change, because they associated national unity, security, stability, and the absence of ethnic conflicts in Tanzania with one-party rule. From this perspective, one-party rule was a necessary evil. A good number of beneficiaries of the political system, particularly under the economic recovery program, also wanted the one-party system to continue. A third group of supporters of one-party rule was made up of skeptics who feared that many political parties could collude to exploit them even more. The most cynical question repeatedly raised at the commission's hearings, for example, was: If one CCM is such a burden in terms of extracting resources (taxes, sundry contributions, chickens, etc.), what will life under many CCMs be like?

Institutionally, some protoparties started to emerge, constituting the embryo of an organized opposition. All evolved largely in defiance of repeated "stern" warnings and intimidation by the government. The National Committee for Constitutional Reform (NCCR) was formally established by a national seminar held in Dar es Salaam on June 11–12, 1991. It had existed informally for nearly a year as a coalition of groups fighting for democracy and human rights. It was mainly composed of the intelligentsia (academics, lawyers, clergymen, students, etc.). Its focus was on the reform of the constitution to allow multiparty politics; it opposed "unconstitutional" moves to establish new parties.[58] In its opposition to the presidential commission, it demanded the convening of a national constitutional conference with representation from various sectors of the society. For this reason it did not visualize itself as a political party until after the approval of the commission recommendations. Its party program was still un-known in 1992, but from the orientation of its leadership it seemed to embrace social democratic ideals.

When the NCCR was created in early 1990, the only known quasi-political organization was the Civil and Human Rights Movement (CHRM) of veteran dissident James Mapalala, which for a while be-came part of the NCCR coalition. Before the NCCR was formally launched, however, the CHRM disassociated itself from the former, protesting its legalistic and elitist approach. Mapalala also believed that the NCCR was a CCM front organization or a representative of a CCM faction he described as CCM-8.[59]

The CHRM claimed to represent "the grass roots," mainly un-employed urban and rural youth. In September 1990, it boasted a membership of 100,000.[60] In November 1991, it launched a political party—Chama Cha Wananchi (CCW), or Civic Movement—claiming a membership of 700,000.[61] Its orientation seemed to be left-leaning populism. Mapalala, still believed in African liberation struggles and the principle of socialist self-reliance, but over time, Mapalala said, he grew to detest growing official corruption and political repression.[62]

A third group broke away more directly from the NCCR. The first NCCR chairman, Abdulla Fundikira (the first minister of justice in the independence cabinet), launched the Union for Multiparty De-mocracy (UMD) in October 1991. Fundikira had earlier differed with the NCCR on the question of the timing for political parties and on relations with dissident political groups outside the countries. On a visit to London in August 1990, Fundikira had announced the for-mation of the Social Democratic Party (SPD) in collaboration with Oscar Kambona, TANU's secretary general and former defense and foreign minister, who had been in exile since 1967. This move was denounced by the NCCR, led by NCCR's secretary, M. Marando. The fate of the SPD is unknown. Its successor, UMD, was opposed to the Presidential Commission, which it perceived as a CCM stratagem to perpetuate one-party rule under a multiparty guise. In its policy state-ment, the party pledged itself to "full employment of our youth and our workers by adopting a fully fledged market economy and sound economic policies." It blamed economic decline on "the wrong policies of the Arusha Declaration." It also wanted to reinstitute the provincial government structure inherited at independence but also to create semiautonomous provincial legislatures to be responsible for district and urban councils. UMD also proposed the promotion of autono-mous labor unions and cooperatives.[63]

As noted earlier, on January 20, 1992, CCM's National Executive Committee "decided with one voice to propose to the party national conference . . . that Tanzania should go multiparty."[64] In the wake of that statement, two other groups were reported. One was the Pragmatic Democratic Alliance (PDA), led by one "Lord" Munuo, and the other was the Zanzibar Special Committee Towards Full Multiparty Democracy (KAMAHURU). PDA and CCW approved of the move and hoped it would lead to an early amendment of the constitution and multiparty elections "before the economy worsens." But NCCR and KAMAHURU expressed grave dissatisfaction with the manner in which CCM was usurping the role of bringing about a multiparty system. In Zanzibar, two other groups were reported: the Movement for Democratic Alternatives (MDA), which supported constitutional reform, and Bismillah, an Islamic fundamentalist group that demanded a full referendum on the union.

Externally, there were rumors of a London-based group, the Tanzania Youth Democratic Movement (TYDM). The party was led by Yassin Membar, a dissident who fled Tanzania in 1990. TYDM demanded a multiparty system in Tanzania and independence for Zanzibar. In June 1991, the TYDM reportedly threatened the use of violence to bring about change, claiming that peaceful means had failed. Another London-based group was the Tanzania Democratic Forum (TDF), led by Kambona. According to Kambona, the group believed in representative government, free and open elections, freedom of the press and association, and individual rights guaranteed under law.[65] As of 1992, none of the external groups had a local presence.

Differences existed between the opposition groups on the nature of the transition. One side wanted to involve the people in the making of the constitution—an effort to create a new social contract. The other side was more interested in amending the constitution and setting up a multiparty system. These were two distinct approaches, and the fact that the latter prevailed may make the process of internalizing and institutionalizing democracy in Tanzania more difficult. There was a tendency for all interest groups at this time to believe that they could or ought to form political parties, creating concern about the possible infinite proliferation of parties, which would result in a relatively ineffective political system.[66]

What follows is a summary of the main issues raised and the arguments advanced by the contending groups, particularly as they relate to two basic and interrelated issues—democracy and the economy. The main arguments may be clustered around four themes.

These are (1) diversion and division, (2) waste of scarce resources, (3) redistribution of resources, and (4) insecurity and uncertainty.

CCM's Arguments

On diversion and division, CCM argued that "the people" were not interested in democracy but in the satisfaction of basic needs. It claimed that demands for an open political system would divert the government's attention from addressing the pressing questions of economic recovery and, further, that these demands emanated from a small minority of disgruntled intelligentsia with personal political ambitions who were likely to undermine national unity. This argument leaned heavily on reasoning similar to that advanced in the early 1960s to justify the establishment of the one-party state. It was an argument for the status quo and was upheld by interests ranging from party socialist ideologues to private commercial entrepreneurs. At a dinner held by the Asian commercial community to commemorate independence day, for example, the chairman of the Asian community, R. S. Patel, was quoted as telling the president that "Asians in Tanzania had enjoyed greatly the country's social and political stability that allowed them to live in peace and harmony."[67]

On waste of scarce resources, CCM consistently maintained that it was a waste of resources to have many parties because it would complicate and render more costly the process of decisionmaking and policy implementation. Nyerere upheld a moderate version of this perspective.

On equity and growth, CCM claimed that it pursued an egalitarian socialist policy and, by so doing, mitigated inequality, tempered social conflict, and maintained sovereign autonomy abroad. It contended that the introduction of many parties and the abandonment of socialism would increase inequality, intensify social conflict, undermine national unity, and ultimately expose the country to domination by foreign interests. In this argument, it was usually alleged that proponents of change were sponsored by external imperialist interests.[68]

On insecurity and uncertainty, CCM contended that, under one-party rule, economic policies were predictable and stable over time — factors considered conducive to a dynamic economic environment. It claimed that the existence of many parties would introduce instability and therefore increase uncertainty, which in turn would create higher risk for investment and hence frighten investors. This argument echoed comparable arguments that CCM advanced in the 1960s, during the rise of the one-party state.

The Opposition's Arguments

On diversion and division, proponents of political liberalization argued that demands for democracy were neither diversionary nor divisive. They posited that Tanzania's economic decline could be explained, at least in part, by the monolithic one-party system. They stressed that, apart from suppressing open political dissent, the system stifled innovative thinking and nurtured conformity, mediocrity, and sycophancy among a self-serving party-state oligarchy, which did not brook criticism. Thus when mistakes occurred, they were big in scope (national) and very costly in terms of their social and economic costs: forced villagization and the dislocation of agricultural production, the dissolution of cooperatives and the disruption of marketing, the abolition of local government and the suppression of participation, and the endless and costly saga of moving the capital to Dodoma. National unity was more threatened by such imprudence under one-party rule than it would be under a democratic system, they suggested.

On waste of scarce resources, proponents of political liberalization pointed out that the single-party system promoted waste by nurturing cronyism, nepotism, and patronage, practices that led to widespread corruption and lack of accountability. Under the one-party rule, the public sector performed dismally, and yet it was impossible to bring anybody to account because the party-state protected its own. Between 1985 and 1990, for example, more than $130 million in credits to rural cooperatives run by party officials disappeared, according to some reports.[69] Having reported numerous cases of arrant corruption and embezzlement, the auditor general concluded that "fraud and embezzlement were beyond government administrative control" and had acquired "a political dimension."[70] The party-state was popularly perceived as kleptocracy.

On equity and growth, the opposition pointed out that, when inequality was tempered up to the very early 1970s, this was accomplished at the price of generalized poverty. After that, with the rise of corruption from the mid-1970s and under the economic recovery program in the 1980s, inequality reemerged with a vengeance along with armed crime—the former feeding the latter.

With respect to insecurity and uncertainty, proponents of change pointed out that both domestic and foreign investors were in favor of a multiparty system, particularly insofar as they associated it with a liberal economic environment.

Conclusions

This chapter explores the evolution of the one-party state in Tanzania, identifying the forces that gave rise to it and that propelled it since 1964. Further, it explains the forces that resisted the one-party state, analyzes contemporary political processes and movements, and projects their most likely trajectory.

Of particular interest is the hypothesized relation between single-party or authoritarian rule, economic development, and democracy. In the early 1960s, Julius Nyerere argued that the inclusive, participatory one-party state could not only bring about faster economic and social development but would serve democracy better by following consensus rather than majority rules and procedures. In examining the record, however, we find that neither economic development nor democracy were positively served over the years. On the contrary, the decline in the economy was accompanied by a corresponding rise in authoritarian rule, and vice versa.

Indeed, periods of economic crisis only reinforced authoritarianism. Four such periods occurred: the early 1960s, the early 1970s, the early 1980s, and the early 1990s. The first period is identified with rising postindependence expectations, which were met with repressive labor legislation and the Preventive Detention Act. The next period, characterized by falling agricultural and industrial production, is identified with forced villagization and the institution of party supremacy. In the third period, a foreign exchange crisis curtailed imports resulting in a shortage of basic commodities. The party-state responded with forced labor legislation and the hunting down of so-called economic saboteurs.

But this rise of authoritarianism led to a crisis of legitimacy in the mid-1980s. Consequently, an attempt was made to temper party supremacy, to reduce the power of the president, and to restore authority to parliament. Although the crisis was, for some time, perceived in economic terms, in the 1990s it became apparent that at the root of the economic crisis was a crisis in the political system—a crisis of democracy. This is what spawned the movement for multiparty democracy.

In the mid-1980s, the argument here suggests, there was no state qua state in Africa.[71] At that time, there was considerable opposition to this view, in fact, the dominant belief was that African states were overdeveloped, bloated, and pervasive. This erroneous belief arose from the confusion between state as social order and state as the totality of coercive apparatuses. Using a Gramscian schema,[72] I try to demonstrate that the state in Africa was only an expression of the monopoly of coercive force in political society (domination) and not a necessary social order (protecting life and property) in civil society (hegemony). Since there was no consensual social contract between the new state and the new society after political independence, the African state had no raison d'être. Hence its inherently coercive behavior arose from the lack of primary legitimacy.

My main contention is that the African state was characterized by a low degree of citizen consent, a high degree of coercion, and hence a low level of political legitimacy. Political society dominated civil society. This is what Antonio Gramsci describes as an "organic crisis," by which, he means "the crisis of the ruling class's hegemony, which occurs either because the ruling class has failed in some major political undertaking for which it has requested, or forcibly extracted, the consent of the broad masses (independence; the Arusha Declaration), or because huge masses (especially of peasants and petty bourgeoisie intellectuals) have passed suddenly from a state of political passivity, to a certain activity. . . . A 'crisis of authority' is spoken of: this is precisely the crisis of hegemony, or a general crisis of the state."[73]

When, in the 1960s, TANU declared a one-party state, its main claim for unity and consent was based on the argument that it was committed to the pursuit of economic development. The suppression of political competition was rationalized on this basis in the absence of an accepted social contract. The commitment to pursue economic and social development was, therefore, a necessary covenant to extract conditional consent from the citizens. The Arusha Declaration had the same purpose. It can be logically postulated, therefore, that the failure to bring about economic development, socialism, and self-reliance is ultimately a failure of the quest for primary legitimacy. The challenge for the future is to reverse the equation: to make democracy the basis of economic development.[74]

Notes

1. See Claude Ake, "Rethinking African Democracy," *Journal of Democracy* 2, no. 1 (1991): 1–13. For a recent global view of waves of authoritarianism and democracy, see Samuel P. Huntington, *The Third Wave: Democratization in the Late Twentieth Century* (Norman: University of Oklahoma Press, 1991).

2. Colin Legum, "The Postcommunist Third World: Focus on Africa," *Problems of Communism* 41, nos. 1–2 (1992): 195–206.

3. For a review of trends see *Africa Demos: A Bulletin of the African Governance Program,* Carter Center of Emory University (various issues).

4. For a review of the early period independence, see Lionel Cliffe, *One-Party Democracy in Tanzania* (Dar es Salaam: East African Publishing House, 1967); Lionel Cliffe and John Saul, eds. *Socialism in Tanzania: An Interdisciplinary Reader* (Nairobi: East African Publishing House, 1972); Cranford Pratt, *The Critical Phase in Tanzania 1945–1968: Nyerere and the Emergence of a Socialist Strategy* (Cambridge: Cambridge University Press, 1966).

5. For a theoretical discussion of political legitimacy, see J. H. Schaar, *Legitimacy in the Modern State* (New Brunswick, N.J.: Transaction Books, 1981).

6. Only 30 percent of eligible voters went to the polls in the 1990 elections. Also, there was a wide divergence between voters and candidates on major policy issues. See Mwesiga Baregu and S. S. Mushi, "Mobilization, Participation, and System Legitimacy," typescript. For a contrasting view, see Goran Hyden, *Beyond Ujamaa in Tanzania: Development and the Uncaptured Peasantry* (Berkeley: University of California Press, 1980); and Issa Shivji, *Class Struggle in Tanzania* (Dar es Salaam: Tanzania Publishing House, 1976).

7. As Gwendolyn Carter states, "In the former British territories the existence of a cohesive political party under a dominant leader was a sine qua non for the transfer of power to local hands." Gwendolyn M. Carter, *African One-Party States* (Ithaca: Cornell University Press, 1962), 3.

8. Julius K. Nyerere, *Freedom and Unity* (London: Oxford University Press, 1967), 133–34.

9. Ibid. Compare Nyere's establishment of one-party supremacy in the 1970s with his current propagation of multiparty democracy.

10. In reference to Africa as a whole, K. A. Busia says: "Neither at the centre nor at the local level can it be said that strong foundations for democratic rule were laid." K. A. Busia, *Africa in Search of Democracy* (New York: Praeger, 1967), 51.

11. Nyerere, *Freedom and Unity*, 157–58.

12. See Issa Shivji, *Law, State, and the Working Class in Tanzania* (London: James Currey, 1986).

13. D. M. S. Mdachi, quoted in A. MacDonald, *Tanganyika: Young Nation in a Hurry* (New York: Hawthorne Books, 1966), 145.

14. See Tanzania, *Report of the Presidential Commission on the Establishment of a Democratic One-Party State* (Dar es Salaam: Government Printer, 1965), and An Act to Declare the Interim Constitution of Tanzania, Act no. 43, 1965 (Dar es Salaam: Government Printer, 1965).

15. For a discussion of the 1964 mutiny, see Henry Bienen, *Armies and Parties in Africa* (New York: African Publishing Company, 1978); and Mwesiga Baregu, *The 1964 Army Mutiny in Tanzania* (Dar es Salaam: Dar es Salaam University Press, forthcoming).

16. Andrew Coulson, *Tanzania: A Political Economy* (Cambridge: Cambridge University Press, 1982), 174.

17. In responding to international constraints and in seeking to diversify its sources of assistance, Tanzania turned to China in 1965. See O. Nnoli, *Self-Reliance and Foreign Policy in Tanzania* (New York: NOK, 1978).

18. See Julius Nyerere, *Freedom and Development* (London: Oxford University Press, 1973), chaps. 12, 36. See also Issa Shivji, ed., *The State and the Working People in Tanzania* (Dakar: CODESRIA, 1985).

19. Tanganyika African National Union, *The Arusha Declaration and TANU's Policy on Socialism and Self-Reliance* (Dar es Salaam: Government Printer, 1967).

20. Tanzania, *Report of the Presidential Commission on the National Union of Tanganyika Workers* (Dar es Salaam: Government Printer, 1967).

21. See also Nyerere, *Freedom and Development*, chap. 36.

22. All eastern African countries had their ideological socialist blueprint. Consider Kenya's Sessional Paper 10, Uganda's Common Man's Charter, and Zambia's Mulungushi Declaration. For a view of *ujamaa* as an instrument of political control, see John R. Nellis, *A Theory of Ideology: The Tanzania Example* (Nairobi: Oxford University Press, 1972).

23. Nyerere, *Freedom and Development*, 67.

24. See J. E. Proctor, *Building Ujamaa Villages in Tanzania* (Dar es Salaam: Tanzania Publishing House, 1971), J. Boesen et al., *Ujamaa—Socialism from Above* (Uppsala: Scandinavian Institute of African Studies, 1977); and R. G. Abrahams, ed., *Villagers, Villages, and the State in Modern Tanzania*, African Monograph 4 (Cambridge: Cambridge African Studies Centre, 1985); Norman O'Neill, "Politics and Development Strategies in Tanzania," in *Capitalism, Socialism, and the Development Crisis in Tanzania*, ed. Norman O'Neill and Kemal Mustapha (Aldershot: Avebury, 1990).

25. See Tanzania, *On the Establishment of Workers Councils* (Dar es Salaam: Government Printer, 1970); and TANU, "Mwongozo wa TANU" (Dar es Salaam: TANU, 1971). The circular was partly a belated response to the findings of the Presidential Commission on NUTA.

26. See *Africa Contemporary Record 1971–1972*.

27. For discussion of the implementation of *mwongozo* see Henry Mapolu, ed., *Workers and Management in Tanzania* (Dar es Salaam: Tanzania Publishing House, 1979); and P. Mihyo, "The Struggle for Workers' Control in Tanzania," *Review of African Political Economy* 4 (1975): 62–84.

28. TANU's 1973 constitution brought NUTA, the Co-operative Union of Tanganyika (CUT), the parents' association (TAPA), and the womens' organization (UWT) under party control. Earlier in 1972, a committee headed by party secretary Rashidi Kawawa curbed press freedom. See *Africa Contemporary Record, 1971–1972*.

29. Pius Msekwa, *Towards Party Supremacy* (Dar es Salaam: Tanzania Publishing House, 1978), 70.

30. *Africa Contemporary Record, 1977–1978*.

31. Even the government newspaper complained of "the brutality of the peoples' militia when enforcing government directives"; *Daily News*, December 23, 1976.

32. Coulson, *Tanzania: A Political Economy*, 223.

33. Nyerere, *Freedom and Socialism*, 385.

34. Jeanne Hartmann, "The Rise and Rise of Private Capital," in O'Neill and Mustapha, eds. *Capitalism, Socialism, and the Development Crisis in Tanzania*.

35. Julius Nyerere, *The Arusha Declaration: Ten Years After* (Dar es Salaam: Government Printer, 1977), 24.

36. In 1987 I was a member of a task force to evaluate ten years of CCM. We found that the party lacked an active participant membership and that a wide gap had emerged between the leadership and members. CCM had inherited only the authoritarian structures of its predecessors. See Article 3 of the CCM constitution; and CCM, *Miaka kumi ya CCM* (Dodoma: CCM, 1987).

37. Fred J. Mdoe, in *Nova*, no. 1 (1981). The government responded to this crisis by launching a campaign against "economic saboteurs" and passing the Human Resources Deployment Act, 1983, under which to be unemployed was illegal. On these two issues, see T. L. Maliyamkono and M. S. Bagachwa, *The Second Economy in Tanzania* (London: James Currey, 1990); and L. Shaidi, "The Human Resources Deployment Act, 1983: A Desperate Measure to Contain a Desperate Situation," *Review of African Political Economy* 31 (1984): 82–87.

38. For an in-house assessment of the economic recovery program, see World Bank, *Tanzania Economic Report: Towards Sustainable Development* (Washington, D.C.: World Bank, 1991).

39. For a good analysis of the agrarian crisis, see Paul Collier, S. Radwan, and S. Wangwe, *Labor and Poverty in Rural Tanzania* (Oxford: Clarendon, 1986); David Bevan, Paul Collier, and Jan Willem Gunning, *Peasants and Governments* (Oxford: Clarendon, 1989); and Tanzania, *The Agricultural Policy of Tanzania* (Dar es Salaam: Government Printer, 1983).

40. *Inter Press Service,* August 30, 1990.

41. Robert M. Press, "Tanzania Faces Slow Growth and Legacy of Socialist Controls," *Christian Science Monitor,* May 30, 1990.

42. Janos Kornai, *Anti-Equilibrium: On Economic Systems Theory and the Tasks of Research* (Amsterdam: North-Holland, 1971). Also see Janos Kornai, *Rush versus Harmonic Growth* (Amsterdam: North Holland, 1972).

43. World Bank, *World Development Report, 1991* (Washington, D.C.: World Bank, 1991).

44. The economic and social action program 1990–93, the successsor program, acknowledges the problem of social service deterioration and adopts a strategy of increasing government revenues through taxation and user fees. Given the generally low level of incomes, it is unlikely to succeed, at least in the short term.

45. *Daily News,* September 30, 1990.

46. British Broadcasting Corporation (BBC), November 6, 1979.

47. Tanzania, *Budget Speech for 1989–90* (Dar es Salaam: Government Printer, 1989).

48. See Mwesiga Baregu, "The Paradox of the Arusha Declaration," *African Review* 14, nos. 1–2 (1987): 1–12. This is a special issue on twenty years of the Arusha Declaration.

49. The *Economist,* August 24, 1991. The Nordic countries had supported

the IMF position and withheld aid to Tanzania during the structural adjustment negotiations in the late 1970s and early 1980s.

50. *Daily News,* February 22, 1990.

51. Economist Intelligence Unit, *Country Report: Tanzania and Mozambique* (London: Business International Ltd., 1990).

52. Xinhua News Agency, July 18, 1991.

53. Radio Tanzania, September 24, 1990.

54. BBC, October 23, 1990.

55. See the complete report, Tanzania, *Tume ya Rais ya Mfumo wa Cham kimoja au Vyama Vingi Vya Siasa Tanzania, 1991, Taarifa na Mapendekezo ya Tume Kuhusu Mfumo wa Siasa Nchini Tanzania,* 3 vols. (Dar es Salaam: President's Office, 1992).

56. Interview with author, New York, November 23, 1991.

57. By this timetable, parties were to register in July 1992, and multiparty elections were to be held for local government councils in 1993 and for parliament and the presidency in 1995.

58. The NCCR also stressed a peaceful transition. See Kamati ya Taifa ya Katiba na Mageuzi (NCCR), "Tunachotaka Sasa: Maazimio ya semina ya mageuzi kuelekea mfumo wa vyama vingi vya siasa" (Dar es Salaam, June 11–12, 1991), typescript.

59. Interview with author, July 1990.

60. Neil Henry, "Daring to Differ in Tanzania," *Washington Post,* September 10, 1990.

61. *Inter Press Service,* March 21, 1991.

62. Henry, "Daring to Differ in Tanzania."

63. UMD policy statement in *Family Mirror,* October 1991.

64. *Daily News,* January 21, 1992.

65. *The Independent* (London) July 13, 1990.

66. Nyerere, for example, expressed this anxiety in his November 23, 1991 interview.

67. *Daily News,* 7 December, 1991.

68. *Inter Press Service,* 26 November, 1991.

69. Neil Henry, "Nyerere Bows out with Tanzania in Deep Decline," *Washington Post,* September 26, 1990.

70. *Sunday News,* September 22, 1991.

71. Mwesiga Baregu, "The State and Society in Africa," paper prepared for the annual African Studies Conference, Stanford and Berkeley, April 1991.

72. Antonio Gramsci, *Selections from the Prison Notebooks* (London: Lawrence and Wishart, 1971). See, in particular, the general discussion of the state and civil society, 206–728.

73. Ibid., 210.

74. See "Africa: Democracy Is Not Enough," *Africa Confidential,* January 1, 1992.

JEFFREY HERBST

Eight ◈ The Dilemmas of Explaining Political Upheaval: Ghana in Comparative Perspective

The current wave of political upheaval in Africa has intrigued those political scientists who have spent many of the years since independence analyzing the persistence of authoritarian states across the continent. However, explaining why many political systems in Africa are being challenged is fraught with difficulties. Indeed, at this writing it is not even clear what should be explained. In addition, the fact that political upheaval in Africa is occurring at roughly the same time that many countries across the world are also overthrowing undemocratic regimes suggests an extraordinarily difficult levels-of-analysis problem. This chapter examines the case of Ghana—a country significantly ahead of the rest of the continent in economic reform and that held elections to inaugurate a Fourth Republic—in order to investigate some of the methodological problems inherent in explaining the change in the course of African politics.

What Must Be Explained

The wave of political unrest sweeping across Africa tempts one to believe that politics in Africa has changed so fundamentally that a reversion by a large number of countries to military or authoritarian rule is simply unthinkable, especially when the rest of the world is also moving, almost uniformly, toward greater political liberalization. However, it is sobering to remember that, between 1954 and 1961, when eleven Latin American countries experienced military disengagement from politics, some claimed that politics there had changed forever. However, in the mid-1960s, there was a "tidal wave" of coups across that continent.[1] Indeed, Jerry Rawlings, Ghana's current leader, warns that the military may intervene even if civilian democracy is reestablished. He notes that "a soldier may be a professional fighter, but does that take away his or her social and political responsibility?"[2]

Indeed, the history of democratization elsewhere in the world should serve as a warning that many of the current attempts at political liberalization in Africa will fail. Democratization in Europe took hundreds of years, and although learning how to create democracies may certainly have spread widely, there is little reason to believe that political liberalization can be accomplished in a very short period of time. Indeed, as Arend Lijphart consistently points out, even European democracies vary widely.[3] For instance, the United Kingdom has a highly centralized political system that encourages a small number of parties to compete for power and has no written constitution. In contrast, Switzerland has a decentralized system of power with a proportional representation system that encourages many parties to operate according to a highly detailed constitution. These nuanced political systems developed in response to the particular political and social conditions of the respective countries. They evolved over decades, partially in response to political failures. African countries, if they are to be successful in democratization, will need equally nuanced political systems, each designed to cope with a unique constellation of political, economic, and social forces. Such complex political arrangements cannot be created overnight and will probably evolve only in response to failure. Indeed, even Indian democracy, one of the notable successes in the Third World, may not yet have developed institutions capable of withstanding the stresses of cultural pluralism.[4]

Attempts at political liberalization may also ignite political processes that threaten the very integrity of the nation and that will doom reform, at least in the short run. In the West, political liberalization is equated with democratization because there is fundamental agreement concerning the nature of the nation-state. However, in Africa, questioning domestic political arrangements may have the effect of reigniting debates as to the desirability of the nation itself. The first question that emerges when politics is liberalized is, What should be the outlines of the political community?

Many groups may in fact emerge in a more liberal political environment to demand that they be allowed to leave the existing nation, join another, or create their own political institutions. In Central Europe and what was the Soviet Union, political liberalization has had the effect of reopening old ethnic conflicts, and as a result, some nations have dissolved. There is no reason to believe that African citizens have a stronger commitment to their nations than people in the Soviet Union, Yugoslavia, or Czechoslovakia. Of course, the potential for political liberalization leading to ethnic divisiveness and wholesale boundary change is especially great given that many on the continent perceive the colonially imposed borders as nonsensical. If boundaries do come under stress, the question of political liberalization in those countries will become moot.

Indeed, that an unprecedented number of African states (Liberia, Somalia, and Ethiopia) collapsed at the same time that there is unprecedented political tumult elsewhere on the continent is not a coincidence. As I discuss below, economic decline caused some countries to dissolve into civil war, while in others it merely forced out their leaders. However, there is reason to believe that, given the frailty of so many central governments in Africa, the stresses imposed by the political tumult of this period could lead to the dissolution of more countries, with all of the accompanying violence we witnessed in Monrovia and Mogadishu. It is important to remember that, between 1960 and 1989, only Museveni in Uganda and Habre in Chad gained power by forming their own guerrilla armies in independent African states. In 1990–91 there were four countries (Chad, Liberia, Ethiopia, Somalia) where rebel armies either shot their way into power or destroyed the state.

Thus, it is not at all certain what patterns of regime change we are studying. It may be that many of the upheavals in Africa are the precursors of more open, viable political systems, but it is far more likely that they are simply the beginning of an extraordinarily complex process from which will emerge a few clear successes, some disasters, but mainly the realization that many countries are only beginning the struggle to design appropriate political systems. It is not currently possible to predict which countries will fall into which category. Thus, we should posit explanations for these events with extreme modesty.

Ghana exemplifies the tentativeness of democratization in Africa. The Provisional National Defence Council (PNDC) led by Jerry Rawlings, after holding power since a coup on December 31, 1981, announced in 1991 a schedule for democratization. It is unclear exactly why Rawlings initiated the liberalization process when he did, because he made all of the key decisions, announced them abruptly, and usually did not explain his rationale. Along with other top leaders, he did believe that the PNDC (a secretive group, in which a very small number of people made all the key decisions) had run its course and was becoming more and more inappropriate for the economic challenges facing Ghana as it began its second decade of economic reform. There probably was also a feeling that the government should try to control the transition process before democratic pressures, stoked by events in Eastern Europe and pent-up resentment against authoritarian rule, got out of hand and threatened the leadership, as had happened in other African countries. Also, Rawlings, at least in 1991, may have seen the liberalization process as a convenient way of giving up power. However, the political liberalization process was done in the typical style of the PNDC. It was very much a top-down affair, with only limited public input accepted.

The liberalization process began with a referendum on a new constitution on April 28, 1992; it was widely supported, despite controversial clauses giving indemnity to the PNDC. However, Rawlings waited until September 17, 1992, three weeks before the election (the deadline), to announce his own candidacy. It is unclear if he was just being coy or if he truly did not know if he wanted to continue to rule Ghana. The opposition was unable to unite against Rawlings in part because those who traced their allegiance back to Kwame Nkrumah had split into three parties. On November 3, 1992, Rawlings, leading the National Democratic Congress (a name chosen, seemingly, to indicate the PNDC without the provisional modifier) won a surprising 58.3 percent of the vote.[5] The opposition, stunned by the magnitude of the victory, argued that the election was fraudulent, citing in particular well-known problems with the voting rolls. However, the Commonwealth Observer Group declared the elections "free and fair," despite what they considered to be inevitable logistical problems. The main opposition groups then decided to boycott the December 29, 1992, parliamentary elections, which NDC won overwhelmingly. Rawlings was sworn in as president of Ghana's Fourth Republic on January 7, 1993.

Thus, Ghana is in the extraordinary position of having elected a former soldier who twice illegally seized power. The country cannot be declared a democracy, because it has yet to prove that its rulers will leave power if the electorate turns against them. However, Ghana's Fourth Republic also cannot simply be declared a continuation of the PNDC. The press is noticeably freer, and opposition political parties, despite the fact that they boycotted parliament, regularly and openly criticize the regime. This is in marked contrast to the 1980s, when the press was muzzled, almost no public opposition was allowed, and political debate was sterile. Therefore, the importance of the transition to the Fourth Republic will only slowly become clear, as Rawlings adjusts to ruling in a more liberalized setting and makes clear the amount of opposition he will tolerate. To define Ghana's evolution too soon after the election would be foolhardy.

Indeed, given the newness of almost all countries on the continent, scholars of African politics always face the possibility of jumping to conclusions before the evidence is all in. Previous analytic disasters — including the rush to judgment on the viability of the initial postindependence political arrangements, the attribution of characteristics to political parties and militaries that turned out to be incorrect, and the failure to understand the determinants of ethnicity—came about in part because scholars let what they wanted to see influence them, in an environment where information was scarce. Obviously, the same pitfalls will impede the analysis of political liberalization, especially given that expectations have risen.

This is not to say that something extremely significant has not happened in Africa. Clearly, the era of the old-style personal autocrat is over, at least for the time being. Fewer Africans acquiesce in the stifling political atmosphere that so many experienced after independence. And the international community is increasingly rewarding countries that liberalize their political systems. However, these changes do not guarantee that African countries will march on to full democratization. For instance, elections may be held, but the results may not be unambiguously democratic. This is especially true in Ghana, where those in power control the transition process and retain the allegiance of the military. Or African military rulers, perhaps in response to national disintegration ignited by attempts at political liberalization, may evolve, as Latin American caudillos did, to being proponents of doctrines of national security prominent in the 1960s and 1970s. Other countries may simply disintegrate or may experience long periods of warlordism as no central authority is able to assert control.

Therefore, the safest path is to seek to explain why the old order has fallen. In and of itself, this is a tremendous analytic task, which will not be answered for years. Indeed, until they were challenged and began to fall, one-party states in Africa were viewed by many scholars as fairly resilient; there were few predictions that Africa would experience much of the political revolution that rocked Latin America. Ironically, Mobutu Sese Seko in Zaire, the leader usually singled out as most susceptible to popular pressure because of his venality and authoritarianism survived at least the first surge of democratic tumult that enveloped so many other regimes in Africa. Thus, to try to estimate the possibilities for democracy is to theorize without the necessary analytic foundation and to risk repeating the mistakes of the past.

International Explanations

Given the worldwide movement toward political liberalization and the enormous changes in the superpower relationship, many suggest that at least part of the explanation for the changes in African politics rests at the international level. For instance, Freedom House began its 1990 survey by citing "global structural change" as a critical element in attempts at political liberalization.[6] Explanations centering on changes in global political systems are highly appealing, requiring relatively little information on specific circumstances. However, understanding what is meant by "global structural change" is very difficult, especially when trying to assess the impact of international factors on a country like Ghana. Freedom House's, list of the global factors actually includes both international events (e.g., the "political renaissance" of the West, which presumably includes the dominance of liberal political and economic ideals worldwide, in light of the fall of socialism), and domestic changes (e.g., the adoption of promarket reforms or the achievement of high income levels) that led to democratization in certain countries.

Samuel Huntington, in one of the first attempts to explain the third wave of democratization, cites three potential international prompts for democratization.[7] First, Huntington notes that the "striking changes in the doctrine and activities of the Catholic Church manifested in the Second Vatican Council" had a profound effect by turning national churches from defenders of the status quo to challengers of authoritarianism.[8] Although liberation theology has begun to have a significant impact on some churches in some African countries, the churches do not appear to have played a direct role in the current efforts at democratization. The Catholic bishops in Ghana were early critics of the excesses of the Rawlings regime, but they were ignored in the early 1980s—and then censored. They do not appear to have gained enough influence to be able to suddenly galvanize a democracy movement. However, churches in many African countries do provide sanctuary and moral support for critics of the regimes. Also, the political upheavals in Africa come after a decade when evangelical Protestants made significant inroads in many countries. The link between these changes, as well as the potential ramifications of the increasing influence of the fundamentalist Muslims, needs to be examined.

Second, Huntington argues that the policies of donors have gradually tilted Africa toward a greater emphasis on democratization. Although it is true that the United States and Western Europe gradually put more of an emphasis on human rights and, occasionally, democratization, it is hard to see that those pressures had much of an effect on Ghana or the rest of Africa. The real emphasis of external actors during the 1980s was on helping African countries adjust their economies. Led by the World Bank and the International Monetary Fund, the preponderance of the dialogue between aid donors and African countries was over how to reform African economies. Countries such as the United States were only beginning to develop policies to promote democratization in Africa. These policies were a clear effort at catch-up, given the extraordinary events that occurred across the continent between 1989 and 1992.

For instance, Ghana received a large amount of aid from bilateral and multilateral donors after it adopted its bold structural adjustment program in 1983. This aid was conditioned on continued economic reform, but little if anything was said about the lack of democracy or even of human rights violations. Indeed, more than a few donors seemed concerned that the democratization process could imperil the substantial progress that the Rawlings regime achieved in structurally adjusting the economy.

Nor is it unambiguously clear that aid donors can be consequential agents for democratization. The World Bank, the largest and most important aid donor in Africa, has as its major mission promotion of economic reform. Its mandate requires it to stay out of politics and its staff, composed almost entirely of economists, interprets that stricture to mean avoiding discussing internal political arrangements. While the Bank examines political factors that affect economic policy (under the rubric of *governance*), it does not know what it wants to do in this area. Indeed, even when the Bank issues a report, it often does not have a mechanism to make sure that its staff in Africa knows how to implement the new policy direction. For instance, the Bank's 1989 report *Sub-Saharan Africa: From Crisis to Sustainable Growth* broke new ground in suggesting that the organization had to become more involved in governance issues.[9] However, Bank personnel in Accra reported that they had no idea how the report was supposed to affect their day-to-day work. Finally, the Bank's structure—a large number of professionals in Washington, D.C., with just a skeleton staff in each African country to service loans and prepare for short staff visits—does not lend itself to developing the kind of country-specific knowledge and the long-term relationships necessary for the delicate task of promoting democracy. Rather, given extremely limited staff in the field, the Bank is much better at monitoring prices and other easily observable macroeconomic aggregates.

Other aid donors may find it easier to adopt policies that explicitly favor democratization, but the impact of these policies may not be significant. Certainly, donors will become much more serious in the future about conditioning aid on the observance of certain basic human rights. Indeed, much of what Huntington cites as pressure for democratization were actually calls for respecting certain human rights. Many donors are anxious about explicitly pressuring African countries on democracy because they fear a nationalistic backlash, which will imperil the very reforms they would like to see implemented. Also, donors fear that tying aid too directly to democratization may doom economic restructuring efforts if, in a few years, some of the political liberalization efforts fail but the successor governments continue to try to adopt economic reform policies. More than a few donors realize that, if the Rawlings coup of 1981 occurred today, there might be considerable hesitation in aiding the regime because it was not elected. Of course, such a decision would be a significant mistake, because the PNDC has proved to be by far the most economically successful in Ghana's history. Certainly, as of yet there has been little explicit attention by donors to developing strong policies to promote democratization, and the current tumult really cannot be explained by the policies of external actors.

The third international explanation that Huntington posits is the demonstration effect. Certainly the events in Eastern Europe and the release of Nelson Mandela in South Africa had a profound effect on many in Africa, who began to question if authoritarian practices in their own countries could also be abolished. Further, the spread of the national conference as a way to make a transition from authoritarian rule in Francophone African countries resulted, at least in part, from close lines of communication fostered by a common language.

However, the demonstration effect as an explanation in and of itself has severe problems. First, to say that, because those who overthrew Eastern European regimes wanted democracy, those in Africa who have also tried to remove tyrants also want to establish democracy is engaging in a potentially dangerous ecological fallacy. We need far more evidence on how the successor African regimes operate in practice before declaring that these changes are a process of democratization.[10] Some people in every African country certainly intend to implement a kind of democracy appropriate for their own country. However, there are others in almost every democratic movement who simply wanted to throw the rascals out or, by participating in these "civilian coups,"[11] attempt to replace a government dominated by an ethnic or regional group with another that is more attractive to them. Or, some authoritarian leaders, possibly including Rawlings, use the veil of democracy to continue to rule pretty much as before. Similarly, the commitment to democracy of many of the other candidates in the Ghanaian election was questionable, especially given the authoritarian practices that routinely occurred in the old civilian regimes in which they served. Indeed, there is almost a palpable chomping at the bit by the urban population and certain non-Ewe-speaking ethnic groups to get back into government not so they can promote democracy but so they can reassert control over government patronage.

Second, the demonstration effect does not explain why African citizens have been successful in challenging authoritarian regimes. Why do authoritarian rulers who have been in power for a considerable time suddenly choose to legalize the opposition and, in at least some cases, to give up power? For instance, during the early years of the economic recovery program, Rawlings suppressed far more violent protests than were present during the two years leading up to the transition. There is simply not enough evidence yet to tie the decisions by government leaders to a demonstration effect.

As a result, the demonstration effect by itself does not explain the heterogeneity of responses to pressures for democratization in Africa. Some leaders gave up power quickly, some (such as in Ghana) instituted a planned transition under the heavy control of the government, while some have so far resisted most calls for a political opening. Demonstration effects can best be seen as sparks with the potential to ignite new political processes. They do not, however, explain why some political systems appear more flammable than others.

Domestic Explanations

If events at the international level do not fully explain the current tumult in African politics, analysts must look to the circumstances in each country to explain political developments. However, it still may be possible to investigate explanations for the threats to authoritarian governments by general category so that an analysis of current African politics does not devolve into telling forty-five different stories.

Huntington gives prominence to "the deepening legitimacy problems of authoritarian regimes in a world where democratic values were widely accepted" and places particular stress on crises (economic or military) that further shook legitimacy.[12] Indeed, an explanation for events in African politics that stresses loss of legitimacy as the critical factor in propelling popular politics and convincing government leaders not to resort to repression is very appealing. The problem is that there is no way of measuring legitimacy, and most informed observers believe that most of the authoritarian regimes that were challenged lost their legitimacy years ago, if they ever possessed it.

The legitimacy argument is particularly difficult to test in Africa precisely because politics has been suppressed for so long. In the vast majority of African countries, there are no opinion polls and there have been very few elections that could be used to evaluate legitimacy. Indeed, in Ghana between 1982 and the 1992, parties were not allowed to compete in the elections the government sponsored at the local level. Therefore, a very significant portion of the adult population (given high population growth rates) had never voted in an election contested by parties before the November 1992 presidential election. As a result, even for the Rawlings government (which has been in power longer than any other postindependence Ghanaian regime), it was exceedingly difficult to judge popular opinion. It was generally believed that there was grudging respect for Rawlings's economic success, although living standards have grown only slowly during the reform period.[13] However, many argued that the population had not forgiven Rawlings for the extreme human rights violations during the first year of the PNDC's rule, when at least some in the government seriously advocated the "Ethiopian solution." Most estimates of whether the PNDC government was legitimate were no more than crude guesses, as proven by the widespread surprise and suspicions over the margin of Rawlings's victory.

More generally, as recent polling experiences make clear, it is very hard to judge public opinion in polities where mobilization has been forestalled for a considerable period of time. For instance, in both the Nicaraguan and East German elections, the results of extensive polling by sophisticated observers turned out to be dramatically wrong. It appears that citizens in countries that experienced authoritarian rule for a long time are unwilling to share potentially sensitive political opinions with strangers. If these efforts at scientific polling can be so wrong, there is little reason to believe that informed hunches concerning the beliefs of African citizens will do much better.

An interesting variation of this argument focuses on loss of legitimacy among the leadership. Faced with significant domestic opposition in a world increasingly hostile to nondemocratic regimes, leaders may have lost faith in their own ability to rule. As a result, rulers in Africa, like those in Eastern Europe, did not seriously attempt to repress the rather weak democratic forces that confronted them. This argument has the same problems of retrospective analysis discussed above. Perhaps as important, it assumes that authoritarian African leaders once did justify their ascension to power in terms of the national interest. For instance, Robert Jackson and Carl Rosberg argue that "politics [in Africa] became a kind of 'palace politics' engaged in by privileged members of a ruling oligarchy and sometimes by a wider circle of elites who at most could only tenuously and unofficially represent the broader interests of social groups and classes."[14] To argue that these elites suddenly gave up power because of a self-perceived loss of legitimacy seems, at the very least, difficult to prove.

Huntington and many other scholars claim that the impressive economic growth that some countries have achieved (especially in Asia) since the 1960s led to an expanded middle class, which demanded democracy.[15] Of course, this explanation is problematic for Eastern Europe, Latin America, and Africa, all of which experienced significant economic downturns during the 1980s, precisely when democratic ferment became more noticeable.

A variant of this argument is presented by former U.S. Assistant Secretary of State for African Affairs Herman Cohen, who claims that "the beginning of the movement for democratic change in Africa coincided with, and was stimulated mainly by, structural adjustment, which realigned economic power from urban elites to rural populations and the business community."[16] However, many of the countries that experienced democratic tumult had not at the time made real progress toward structural adjustment. Also, in Ghana and probably in many other countries, structural adjustment did not immediately yield rural interest groups that could serve as a constituency for reform or pressure for democratization.[17] Indeed, the only region where Rawlings did not win a majority of votes was Ashanti, precisely the area where the positive effects of economic reform—with the reinvigoration of cocoa farms and the dramatic increase in gold mining—were greatest. A. Adu Boahen's New Patriotic Party, in the Danquah-Busia tradition, won 60.5 percent in that region,[18] a clear sign that ethnic tensions between the Ashantis and Rawlings' Ewe-based military government were more consequential in determining votes than economic reform.

In addition, the barriers to peasant organization were simply too difficult to overcome in the short term. Indeed, in Ghana and many

other African countries, in the period 1989–92, democratization movements were mainly urban affairs. Some business groups began to
emerge as strong constituencies for structural adjustment, but they
did not necessarily have a connection to those attempting to unseat
authoritarian regimes. The business community in Ghana actually
worries that political liberalization will cause many of the successfully
enacted economic reforms to falter.

Economic Resources and Control of the Transition

Even though economic growth and structural adjustment do not
explain the fall of African regimes, the effects of long-term economic
decline do provide substantial insight. The economic stress caused
by fifteen years of economic decline in many African countries has
had, not unexpectedly, a profound effect on the state. Indeed, in
Ghana, when economic reform was finally implemented, it was much
easier than expected because so much of the country had adjusted to
the black market and the state had become largely irrelevant. For
instance, except for a relatively few individuals with privileged access
to foreign exchange, devaluation did not have a major effect on consumer prices because almost all imported goods were being sold at
black market prices. Similarly, when Ghana's extensive system of price
controls were lifted, very few were affected because there were no
goods on store shelves being sold at the official price. Indeed, prices
may have gone down for some after the devaluations and the price
controls were removed, because consumers no longer had to pay rents
to black marketeers.[19]

A similar process may have occurred in the political arena in light
of the long fiscal compression that African states suffered. For example, between 1973 and 1984, when the country adopted an economic reform program, the resources available to Ghana's leaders
decreased significantly as Ghana's economy declined. The table below
shows state expenditures as a percentage of GDP for each of these
years.[20]

1973	17.38%	1979	17.46%
1974	18.48%	1980	13.14%
1975	23.05%	1981	13.38%
1976	25.11%	1982	11.99%
1977	24.16%	1983	8.02%
1978	19.69%	1984	9.87%

Although the Ghanaian decline was more profound than most on the continent, it is representative of the kinds of stress that state revenue is under in many African countries.

The growing fiscal stress on African countries has several effects on the political market that parallel the increasing irrelevancy of the state in the economic marketplace. As decline continues, leaders are unable to reward clients because they do not have the resources—be they foreign exchange, local currency, or government contracts—to support patronage networks. As a result, the regime's base of support becomes increasingly narrow. For instance, in Ghana, as the economic crisis increased, the state was not even able to reward those groups upon whose support it depended.[21] Richard Hodder-Williams is perhaps only exaggerating slightly when he claims that, by the early 1980s, "to some extent, Ghana is a state only because the outside world asserts that there is a Ghanaian state."[22]

In particular, regimes under fiscal stress find it increasingly difficult to placate two groups. The urban population defects when schools and clinics run out of money, many government employees (overwhelmingly urban) are no longer paid, and the cheap food provided by the governments to the cities becomes scarce as the regime's food collection system breaks down. As economic decline continues, the regime may not even be able to provide the usual disproportionate benefits to its military and security forces and they can no longer count on them to put down popular protest.

As a result, when opposition does coalesce due to demonstration effects, domestic politics, or some combination of the two, political pressure is placed on the state, and the government collapses surprisingly quickly. The old regime may have had little support for years but because there is no other political force to challenge it, it continues on due to inertia. Indeed, what is striking about many of the political upheavals in Africa is the lack of significant violence as regime after regime is revealed to have feet of clay. In Ghana in 1982, Rawlings was not only able to take control quickly, he was able to change political practices that had been critical to the support of previous regimes. For instance, the reduction of patronage through public enterprises was made easier because many employees of state firms were not being paid regularly anyway.

Within this perspective, the change in the international climate toward authoritarian regimes does play a significant role. In particular, the change in attitude among external actors toward military coups fundamentally changes the nature of the constituency that can be formed to challenge the collapsing regime. In the early 1980s, the international community did not punish military regimes that over-threw civilian regimes, so the fact that Rawlings replaced the old regime through a coup d'état was no problem. Indeed, Crawford Young refers to coups as the "institutionalized mechanism for suc-cession."[23] If there was a demonstration effect at the time, it was of the angry young military man coming to power to try to right the wrongs of the old regime (like Samuel Doe in Liberia or Thomas Sankara in Burkina Faso).

However, now the international community punishes military re-gimes that come to power through coups. The United States, for example, is legally prohibited from aiding military regimes that over-throw elected civilians. It is also unlikely that the World Bank, with its new focus on governance, will be very enthusiastic about new military regimes. Of course, opposition to military overthrow—as opposed to promoting democracy or even enhancing governance—is a relatively easy position to adopt, because coups are easily defined and are clearly against current international norms. Thus, even though the old way of replacing bankrupt, decayed regimes is no longer attractive, civilian overthrow through democratic movements—sparked partly by the demonstration effect of Eastern Europe and South Africa—presents a new way to displace old regimes, especially since the international community has made it clear that it is willing to reward experiments in political openness. This new mechanism may be especially attractive to those who object to the old regime on the basis of its political practices, patronage patterns, or ethnic alle-giances but cannot use a coup to come to power. Indeed, this expla-nation also suggests why there is suddenly so much upheaval across the continent: a new means of political succession is suddenly available to many previously weak groups. Further, many long-standing re-gimes may be particularly susceptible to popular revolts because what few resources (e.g., patronage, intelligence) they possess are devoted to forestalling coups, the old method of political succession.

One hypothesis that emerges from this discussion is that the re-sources available to government leaders determines, at least in part, how much control they will have over the transition process. Leaders with relatively great access to resources can continue patronage net-works and still have security forces to respond to popular protests. They therefore have more flexibility to respond to the new type of political threat. In contrast, leaders of bankrupt states have far fewer resources available and thus not nearly as much flexibility. Certainly, one reason that Rawlings was able to control the transition process is that he "delivered the goods" in terms of economic growth during the eleven years of PNDC rule. Also, due to generous aid inflows, the state has more free-floating resources available than most. For instance, Rawlings was able to boost civil servants' salaries significantly in 1992, which may have helped him control the transition process. Other states with significant resources available (e.g., Nigeria and Zimbabwe) have also been able to control the transition process or largely forestall it. In contrast, many of the Francophone regimes that were rocked by early political upheavals had few resources available, and some—notably Benin, Togo, and Mali—were in advanced states of decay.

This argument is difficult to operationalize and test, but it is certainly easier to evaluate than those propositions focusing on legitimacy or demonstration effects. An important task for researchers is to develop an inventory of the assets available to leaders to stay in power— including foreign exchange, government positions, and other forms of patronage—to see if there is a correlation between decreasing political resources and the success of democratic movements. Such an approach may allow a more sophisticated approach to political upheaval. For instance, many scholars note that national conferences have occurred in many Francophone countries but have been unsuccessful in finding a link between these countries. However, an inventory of state power would immediately focus research on the problems of the massively overvalued CFA franc and its role in weakening Francophone states. Likewise, the ability of Mobutu Sese Seko to stay in power despite the democratic ferment around him might be better illuminated by a careful accounting of the stream of resources under his control. Finally, such an inventory would provide a clearer perspective on the importance of repression for leaders who stay in power.

Conclusion

The developments that started to unfold in Africa between 1989 and 1992 are undoubtedly the most exciting since the heady early days of independence in the early 1960s. Many authoritarian regimes collapsed when faced with their first real political challenges and a new means of political succession. However, there are great uncertainties inherent in political liberalization in Ghana and elsewhere, and further analysis, so early in this period of change, may not be useful. We should be wary of making unwarranted assumptions on the basis of weak evidence.

Notes

I benefited from comments by members of the comparative politics seminar at Princeton and from Jennifer Widner.

1. The phrase is from Alain Rouquie, *The Military and the State in Latin America* (Berkeley: University of California Press, 1987), 343–44.

2. Quoted in Collen Lowe Morna, "Ahead of the Opposition," *Africa Report*, (July-August 1991), 20–23. Rawlings's warning is especially ominous because he initially became involved in politics in 1979, handed power over to a civilian government after a bloody housecleaning of the then current military regime, and in 1981, undertook a second coup d'état, which ended Ghana's third attempt at multiparty democracy.

3. Arend Lijphart, *Democracies: Patterns of Majoritarian and Consensus Government in Twenty-one Countries* (New Haven: Yale University Press, 1984), chaps. 1, and 2.

4. See Atul Kohli, *Democracy and Discontent: India's Growing Crisis of Governability* (Cambridge: Cambridge University Press, 1990).

5. Full election results by region are reported by Ajoa Yeboah-Afari, "Post-Election Thoughts," *West Africa* (November 16, 1992).

6. Freedom House, *Freedom in the World: Political Rights and Civil Liberties, 1989–1990* (New York: Freedom House, 1990), 3.

7. Samuel P. Huntington, *The Third Wave: Democratization in the Late Twentieth Century* (Norman: University of Oklahoma Press, 1991), 45–46.

8. Ibid., 45.

9. World Bank, *Sub-Saharan Africa: From Crisis to Sustainable Growth: A Long-Term Perspective Study* (Washington, D.C.: World Bank, 1989), 60–61.

10. Just as in Romania and in several of the Commonwealth of Independent States countries, the overthrow of the old regime in the name of democracy did not necessarily lead to democracy.

11. I owe the term to Pauline Baker.

12. Huntington, *The Third Wave*, 45.

13. Average economic growth between 1983 and 1990 was between 5 and 6 percent. Given a 3 percent population growth rate and the need to save significant resources for future investment, it is unlikely that per capita consumption increased by more than 1.5 percent a year.

14. Robert H. Jackson and Carl G. Rosberg, *Personal Rule in Black Africa* (Berkeley: University of California Press, 1982), 2.

15. See, for example, Huntington, *The Third Wave*, 45.

16. Herman J. Cohen, "African Political Changes and Economic Consequences," *Dispatch* 2, no. 36 (1991): 675–76.

17. See Jeffrey Herbst, *The Politics of Reform in Ghana 1982–1991* (Berkeley: University of California Press, 1992), chap. 5.

18. Yeboah-Afari, "Post-Election Thoughts," 1963.

19. Herbst, *The Politics of Reform in Ghana*, chaps. 3 and 4.

20. Data from International Monetary Fund, *Government Finance Yearbook* (Washington, D.C.: IMF, various years).

21. Naomi Chazan, *An Anatomy of Ghanaian Politics: Managing Political Recession, 1969–1982* (Boulder, Colo.: Westview, 1983), 338.

22. Richard Hodder-Williams, *An Introduction to the Politics of Tropical Africa* (London: Allen and Unwin, 1984), 233.

23. Crawford Young, "The African Colonial State and Its Political Legacy," in *The Precarious Balance: State and Society in Africa,* ed. Donald Rothchild and Naomi Chazan (Boulder, Colo.: Westview, 1988), 57.

PART 3

DIRECTIONS

DONALD ROTHCHILD

Nine ◈ Structuring State-Society Relations in Africa: Toward an Enabling Political Environment

"Underlying the litany of Africa's development problems," observes the World Bank, "is a crisis of governance."[1] The indicators of this political incoherence are readily at hand: weakening rules of political exchange relations between state and societal elites, overdeveloped state structures, insufficient state legitimacy, and what the Bank calls "the deteriorating quality of government, epitomized by bureaucratic obstruction, pervasive rent seeking, weak judicial systems, and arbitrary decisionmaking."[2] The state's ability to manage the economy must be complemented by a capacity for governance, which I define as the development of political routines by state, societal, and international actors that buttress patterns of reciprocity and political exchange. Unless the flows of political exchanges between state and society are regular and predictable, the resulting environment is not likely to sustain a meaningful national development effort over time.

This chapter examines the possibilities for establishing new political routines and institutions for effective governance. It focuses on political reform as the catalyst for an enabling political environment that ensures stable state-society relations. State repression, so commonly resorted to in the past, is now viewed skeptically by many Africans, as it lacks legitimacy and does not provide structures critical for sustained reform. Repressive regimes often rely on the threat, if not the reality, of state coercive power; as such, they tend to be insufficiently responsive to public demands and to lack the information necessary for economic development over time. Another practice, societal disengagement, would, if carried to its logical conclusion, result in the dissolution of the political community—as it has done in contemporary Somalia and Liberia—and therefore lies outside my focus on regularized state-society interactions.[3] Consequently, this seems an opportune moment to concentrate on some of the emergent "regimes" that hold out promise for a new societal coherence in which development can occur.[4]

At the outset, I ask how the breakdown of the independence "bargain" and the weakening of state-society patterns of reciprocity and exchange occurred, and what is the impact of such trends on the state's capacity to undertake the tasks of economic reform (in particular, programs of structural adjustment). I then examine the internal and external pressures for the adoption of new regimes in Africa in the 1990s, examining majoritarian democracy, elite power sharing, populism, and corporatism. It may not be possible to implement economic and political reforms simultaneously. On the one hand, it may be necessary for political change to precede economic reform, thereby encouraging new interest groups to emerge with a stake in the more open and liberal political system; on the other hand, it may prove necessary to begin with alternative regime forms that reduce the burden on governments by putting some economic reforms into effect prior to a full democratic transformation. Finally, after noting the relative advantages and disadvantages of these four regime types for bringing regularity to the flows of state-society political exchanges, I comment on how political liberalization can, in certain contexts, provide incentives for reconnection and cooperative behavior. Certainly, authoritarian regimes allow some scope for rechanneling competition along cooperative lines. Nevertheless, I contend that majoritarian democracy, where appropriate, makes compromise and mutual adjustment a norm, thereby providing additional incentives for electoral and institutional experimentation.

The Weakening of State-Society Linkages

The search for appropriate regimes for Africa must be seen in the context of the deterioration in state-society routines since independence. For a time, it appeared that the independence bargain between the colonial authorities and various local interests and the resulting pact among a number of those elites would nurture progress toward constitutional governments. In fact, the new ruling coalitions did move swiftly after independence to expand some colonially radiated institutions: the executive, civil service, police, and army. Significantly, the elites perceived all of these institutions as enhancing their managerial capacity. Institutions that they viewed as constraints on their capacity to control society—such as multiparty elections, legislative autonomy, judicial independence, legal protections, constitutional checks on central arbitrariness, and federalism—were restricted or even eliminated. The result was an enormous expansion in central government functions and power at the very time that the political elites were showing a strong preference for state-led economic growth and development.

In the early 1960s, a number of African countries managed to hold to political routines that strengthened reasonably stable state-society interactions; this contributed to steady economic expansion in such countries as Kenya, Côte d'Ivoire, and Cameroon. Responding to public expectations of the good life that would follow independence, the political elites looked to the states and their parastatal organizations as a ready means of addressing poverty, national unity, dependency, and uneven regional development. In an effort to overcome the inheritance of colonial neglect and to achieve their economic objectives, leaders and constituents alike looked to an active state to disentangle, even solve, their economic and social problems. As state elites responded to these appeals by intervening in a broad array of public affairs, a greatly overextended and inefficient state apparatus emerged.

By the late 1960s, the interlinked effects of economic deterioration and state "softness" had become increasingly apparent. At the same time that populations were expanding, exports to world markets were falling, inflation was soaring, international indebtedness was rising, and the rates of annual growth of GNP per capita were in decline. Lacking the finances to meet legitimate public demands, interest group competition for public resources became intense. Thus, as the Nigerian central government gained control of significant oil revenues between 1969 and 1981, "there was a general scramble by the power and bureaucratic elites to control the federal state, obviously to acquire and control access to consumption, wealth making, and social class consolidation."[5] This intoxication with politics rechanneled energies "into the struggle for power to the detriment of economically productive effort," and the "overpoliticization of social life" gravely complicated the already difficult task of state capacity building and economic statecraft.[6] State autonomy was weakened at a critical juncture in history, and the state itself appeared soft—that is, unable to regulate society effectively or to implement its ambitious developmental programs, especially in rural areas. Overexpanded and overstaffed, state bureaucracies all too often misallocated scarce resources, spending too much on their own upkeep and on corrupt activities but too little on encouraging the productive sectors and regions.

The result was considerable societal discouragement. The public, which continued to have relatively high expectations of what the state could achieve, was disappointed by the startling gap between promise and performance. Many countries' unimpressive record of achievement contributed to an erosion of state legitimacy as well as a weakening of connections between state and society.[7] Because the state mobilized the people on the basis of its ability to distribute benefits, "the inability of the state to match this requirement . . . created a credibility gap, which . . . necessitated the delinkage of the people from the state."[8] Particularly in the rural areas, where peasant modes of production were largely insulated from government influences, the population came to view the state as an alien superstructure: "an institution without roots in society and suspended, as it were, in mid-air above society."[9] As state performance lagged more noticeably in the 1970s, and as the state's capacity for effective regulation was seen to be highly circumscribed, this divergence between the claim of formal institutional control and actual societal autonomy became more evident.

The assertion of societal autonomy took various forms, both within and without the state. Although interest group intermediaries continued to compete with one another for public allocations, they also took advantage of the state's frailty and lack of "reach" to reorder their relations with it. Societal disengagement ran the gamut from illegal black market operations to self-help educational and building schemes, and even to unofficial village and urban law enforcement units (such as the Sungu Sungu organizations that have emerged in Tanzania). Thus societal groups responded to state decline by establishing new institutions outside of the formal structures of state. State elites' reactions to this trend varied but include frequent expressions of frustration and reluctant accommodation. In Tanzania, for example, the government variously praised and criticized the Sungu Sungu organizations, making significant (though not entirely successful) efforts to co-opt them into the security apparatus.[10] The soft state, unable to dictate the relationship between state and society, at times had no option but to accept a role more akin to coordination than to regulation.[11]

In addition to these manifestations of societal disengagement, the demand for autonomy has in some cases assumed more formal political expression. Here a distinction must be made between de facto and de jure efforts to gain a measure of self-determination within the state. In a number of countries—Nigeria, Ghana, Kenya, Zambia, and Cameroon—the state elite was responsive to ethnic and regional calls for political autonomy, allowing the administrators in the subunits the legal right to exercise discretion in handling local and regional affairs. In Nigeria, for example, successive military governments expanded the number of states in the federation from three to thirty in an effort to promote national unity, weaken the power of the three main panethnic groups, and broaden local participation and representation.

In other countries, however, the state failed to enter into effective political exchange relations with societal interests. Unable to repress the demand for autonomy, it lost control of the political process. As the center's grip has weakened, local leaderships backed by insurgent elements under their command have managed to acquire a measure of autonomous political control. Thus, during the bitter civil war in Angola, Jonas Savimbi's National Union for the Total Independence of Angola (UNITA) movement maintained a kind of de facto authority in the areas under its control. Setting up administrative structures in its own domain, UNITA took care to provide inhabitants with economic opportunities and basic health and educational services.

Similarly, during its battles with the regime of Mengistu Haile Marriam of Ethiopia, the Eritrean People's Liberation Front established an extensive range of administrative services for the people under its influence, as did the Sudanese People's Liberation Movement, which exercises authority over an extensive part of southern Sudan. Unable or unwilling to negotiate adequate terms with the government, these insurgents seized the opportunity presented by a weakened state apparatus to take matters into their own hands. In contrast to the special case of Eritrea, where fragmentation meant a return to an earlier colonial order, most insurgent movements sought incorporation on favorable terms back into the body politic and, recognizing the difficulties of gaining international validation as separate states, did not demand full sovereign rights (as Biafra did). This may well change in future years, however, if state institutions weaken further and prove incapable of providing the structures for political order and sustained development.

As statist interventions and guidance failed to generate sufficient economic and social benefits, and as the political center was seen to lack the capacity to regulate its society, especially in the hinterlands, increasing societal and political disengagement became evident in the 1970s and 1980s. Moreover, authoritarian one-party regimes proved unable to end poverty and dependency, the main justification for their repressive practices. Africa, then, was caught between a "discredited past" and "a future which refuses to arrive."[12]

The Search for New Regimes

What discredited the past for many African observers was widespread evidence of heavy-handed authoritarianism. All too often, state elites compensated for their diminished control by adopting an array of arbitrary and absolutist measures. They employed repressive mechanisms to cover over or slowly emasculate preexisting authority structures or in other ways to mask the growing incoherence of state-society relations.[13] State elites responded to the weakening of the political center by arresting and detaining rivals, outlawing opposition elements, assassinating and executing political opponents, utilizing a network of informers (what Kenyans call *rogota*—collecting information), refusing to issue licenses for public political meetings or demonstrations, and restricting the press.

More often than not, repressive rule was an outward expression of the weak position in which state elites found themselves. Instead of insulating them from myriad domestic and international pressures, however, their containing strategies led to a substantial misuse of scarce public resources that isolated them further from society. Well might Ghana's Provisional National Defence Council (PNDC) Chairman Jerry Rawlings express concern over "the culture of silence."[14] Public silence reflected the general fear about the possible uses of state power.[15] More ominous, however, was the use of state violence to simulate public acquiescence. "In relying on violent repression, African governments have become disconnected from their people and govern without accountability. As a result of this, public policy is completely dissociated from social needs and even from developmental relevance."[16] When the state is perceived as alien, domineering, and unresponsive, the informal economy regarded as a sphere of burgeoning opportunity, and loyalty is given to local rather than national elites, the links between the state and society become enfeebled. For African intellectuals, it became clear "from the history of the past thirty years that authoritarianism had stifled development."[17] Rather than accelerating economic expansion by cutting through red tape and overcoming the possible *immobilisme* of parliamentary democracy, arbitrary rule had been responsible for misconceived and costly decisions and had undercut the legitimate connections between state and society so essential to a sustained developmental effort.

It was time to try new alternatives, and the stagnation and incoherence of the past had created just such opportunities to experiment with the reorganization of political regimes.[18] Weary of repression and corruption and no longer convinced that authoritarian systems accelerated development, the African intelligentsia and its supporters mobilized, often at considerable risk, to demand political reforms. By the 1990s, the transition (although not the sustainability of this process) was no longer in doubt in many countries; national conferences and elections had set the stage in which regime change could be orchestrated. Certainly external factors—such as the dramatic example of change in Eastern Europe and pressures for human rights and democracy from international donors—had an impact on events in Africa; however, the main force contributing to the reform process was a demand by Africans themselves for political liberalization, participation, accountability, and economic relief.[19] Michael Bratton and Nicolas van de Walle estimate that some two-thirds of their sample of thirty-one authoritarian regimes responded to the 1990s call of predominantly urban and middle-class regime opponents for political reform.[20] Certainly the mystique of power surrounding party-state domination had been dispelled. Yet Bratton and van de Walle's caution against overstating the extent of the change is well taken. Although eight countries in their sample provided for multiparty elections, the reform process in other countries was somewhat hesitant—a partial rather than a full liberalization, which left the ruling elites firmly in control. Subsequent events reaffirm this picture of political experimentation with electoral participation in some countries but resistance to meaningful change in others.

In a situation in which the past is largely discredited and the future unclear, it is appropriate to comment on some ways that African leaders have organized their developmental regimes to promote an enabling political environment. As I regard repression as an imposed (and often transitional) state form that masks incoherence and fails to establish enduring intraelite linkages, I focus instead on majoritarian democracy—the optimal choice for coherent state-society interactions over the long term. By their capacity to settle the legitimacy issue, democratic regimes foster the development of societal connections, the emergence of civil associations with a capacity to limit government excesses, and the availability of better information on which to base public policies. Even so, because of structural adjustment

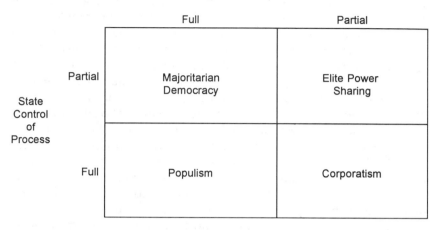

Figure 9.1 Major state options for coping with societal demands

programs that often require central political coordination, because of resistance by elites who benefited from the old order, and because of public expectations unleashed by new democratic institutions, we must also consider one alternative polyarchic regime type and two participatory—albeit essentially authoritarian—regime types that link significant public participation and government effectiveness under conditions of scarcity. As figure 9.1 suggests, these regimes represent four options for coping with public demands and expectations, differing in the extent of societal participation in, and the degree of state control of, the political process. Keeping in mind that experience with some of these has been relatively limited in postindependence Africa, I nonetheless analyze their facilitation of coherent state-society relations and economic development in recent years.

Majoritarian Democracy

The paradox of full democracy in Africa is that, depending on the circumstances, it appears simultaneously to hold the greatest potential for both coherent and incoherent state-society relations, at least in the short term. Democracy, when buttressed by communitywide norms and values, can sanction a healthy dialogue or encourage inclusiveness and state responsiveness. But there is nothing automatic about the development of a societal consensus on these supportive principles and practices. "In those states where representational institutions still exist outside the industrialized democracies," warned Ghana's Committee of Experts in 1991, "universal adult suffrage based on majoritarian philosophy has neither provided a set of *consensual* rules that ensure that leaders are chosen on a regular, meaningful, free and truly competitive basis, nor . . . produced accountable leadership responsive to the basic socio-economic and cultural aspirations and needs of the general public."[21] This somber comment is a realistic caution against undue optimism. Not only must observers be precise about their means and objectives, but they must also be careful to distinguish between formal rules and actual practices. Unless they search painstakingly for appropriate forms of governance in each country's context, structural adjustment initiatives may flounder. Moreover, the risk is ever present that overpoliticization and mobilization based on inflexible principles and commitments will exacerbate existing tensions, leading to a heated rivalry for control.

Let us begin by focusing on the positive potential of majoritarian democracy, reviewing the extensive opportunities such a system offers for making economic reform run parallel with political reform. As shown in the figure, majoritarian democracies have the greatest capacity for combining relatively effective political and economic leadership with extensive societal participation. Put another way, they link a strong state with a strong civil society. Their limited state control over societal participation allows for rivalries to surface at local and national levels, often resulting in the formation of balances of interests at the political center. Moreover, determined to remain in office, state elites have an incentive to be more open and responsive to public demands and accountable for their actions. Majoritarian democracies, then, create their own internal logic, developing rules that facilitate reciprocities and exchanges within an overarching value consensus. By encouraging fairness, inclusiveness, respect for human rights, and sharing, they promote stability and coherent state-society relations, especially as they become accepted and as networks of interactions develop over time.

Up until the 1990s, the countries of sub-Saharan Africa had a decidedly limited experience with majoritarian democracy. In Botswana, Mauritius, Gambia, and Senegal (since 1976), however, politics was structured to promote a two-party or multiparty system. To those countries' credit, elections occurred regularly, and governments remained reasonably responsive to the claims of their citizens. In June 1982, the democratic process reached a high point in Mauritius, when the electorate turned out the party in power.

Yet it seems premature to generalize on the basis of four countries, all small in size or population, whose social makeups have been favorable for democratic experimentation. Senegal's ruling Parti Socialiste, largely backed by the *marabouts,* managed to win substantial successes at the polls in 1983 and 1988; the stability of Gambia's and Botswana's electoral processes is secured by the presence of a preponderant ethnic core group (the Mandinka in Gambia and the Tswana in Botswana); and multiethnic Mauritius's beneficial experience with constitutional democracy and open, competitive elections over the years has been largely assured by its overriding agreement on democratic norms and values. In all four countries, then, democratic forms of governance prevail but the system "legitimates the rule of the powerholders without endangering their continued supremacy."[22]

By the end of 1991, a large proportion of the countries in sub-Saharan Africa caught up in the democratic wave sweeping the continent were either scheduled for or had already pledged themselves to some form of democratic governance.[23] In Namibia, whose leaders voice a strong commitment to democratic values, a still-to-be-tested constitution grants all citizens the right to form or join political parties.[24] Moreover, Benin, Zambia, Cape Verde, and São Tomé and Príncipe have all met the most critical test of a democratic system: the replacement of one set of rulers by another following a general election. Certainly in the African context, severe resource scarcity, weak government institutions, and overpoliticization act as restraints on the development of the interelite and intergroup linkages and reciprocities that lie at the heart of majoritarian democracies. Even though Nigeria's democracy suffered in the early 1980s from intraelite backscratching and corruption, we should not lose sight of the accomplishments of that period: agreement on the revenue allocation formula, the building of inclusive coalitions at the political center, and the application of the "federal character" (proportional) principle in civil service appointments. Democratic regimes have to meet the same test of performance as any other system regarding sustaining political and economic structures over *la longue durée*—and do so under conditions of heady public expectations—or lose the backing of their supporting societal interests.

The difficulties in the way of a smooth transition to democracy are pointed up by the contemporary experiences of Ghana. The Rawlings regime, which seized power from a lawfully elected, civilian regime in December 1981, emphasized (especially during its first eighteen months) the virtues of participatory forms of governance. Seeking to find a new basis of legitimacy, the PNDC mobilized people into organizations such as People's Defence Committees and Workers Defence Committees; exercised popular justice through such newly created quasi-judicial bodies as the Citizens Vetting Committees, the National Investigations Committee, and the Special Military Tribunals; and put a number of price, rent, and transport fare controls into effect.

In mid-1983 a shift of emphasis—from radical populism to a combination of populist rhetoric and pragmatic economic policy—became evident. By the 1990s, the PNDC government, determined to push ahead with structural adjustment and to maintain its influence over the transition process, emphasized the need to include some features of participatory democracy in the emerging political system.[25] It appointed a Committee of Experts, which recommended retaining such populist institutions as the public tribunals in the new constitution, and integrating them into the ordinary court structure.[26] The committee proposed a split executive, modeled to some extent on the experiences of contemporary France and a number of French-speaking African countries, with an eye to ensuring political accountability and the rule of law. Although the president would have an electoral mandate based on direct election by the people, his or her need to consult with the council of ministers was regarded as a restraint on "the exercise of unfettered executive power."[27] The Committee of Experts also favored a proportional representation system, hoping that such a measure would, if implemented fully, reassure minority interests about their place in the political order.

In subsequent deliberations at the Consultative Assembly, the committee's report was revised. The draft constitution that the assembly produced set out a rather standardized form of presidential government, modified by provisions for populist-type institutions (such as public tribunals) and by prohibitions on making the government account for its actions during the early period of its rule. The PNDC then announced the date for a national referendum on the constitution, to be followed shortly after by presidential and parliamentary elections.

Clearly, the guiding hand of Rawlings and the PNDC was evident in the transition process, raising questions as to the genuineness of the democratic process. Not only did the PNDC appoint the members of the Committee of Experts and heavily influence selections to the Consultative Assembly, it controlled the agenda and timetable leading up to the November 3, 1992, presidential election. To be sure, the ban on political parties was withdrawn on May 18; however, by then opposition parties had only a limited time to organize and to get their message to the people. During the election campaign itself, Rawlings had a distinct advantage over his opponents in terms of the extensive state resources at his disposal as well as his ability to create job programs and raise civil service salaries just prior to the voting. In addition, Rawlings's refusal to open up the voting lists to those who had not registered for the referendum on district assemblies in 1987 or the partially updated 1991 register meant, in effect, that hundreds of thousands of regime opponents had no opportunity to participate. The conclusion of the Carter Center mission with respect to these and other irregularities is telling: "Despite the occurrence of serious irregularities in the election process, what we have observed does not lead us to question the validity of the results."[28] Grave irregularities had indeed occurred, but there was no way of ascertaining whether they had affected the outcome.

In the end, Rawlings won a clear majority of over 58.3 percent of the votes cast, eliminating the need for a second, runoff election. This represented a tremendous personal achievement for the new president. Despite the austerity brought on by a structural adjustment program, Rawlings was able to move from a somewhat unpopular and repressive regime arrangement to a popularly elected system of governance, making him the first leader of an African coup regime to win a competitive election. Certainly, his control of the agenda and timetable of the election process established an uneven playing field from the outset. Also important, however, was the public's uncertainty over the prospects of a change in economic policies. It seems likely, for example, that the peasants were extremely wary of a shift in regimes that might involve a reduction in employment, a fall in producer prices for cocoa, or a slowdown in rural road building, electrification, and the provision of potable water.[29] The public might well have recoiled from the austerity measures implicit in structural adjustment, but it nonetheless had strong misgivings over any change of leadership that could result in a significant tampering with the economic recovery program.

However, if the election tallies favored Rawlings, the manner of his victory left many opponents in the urban centers frustrated and angry. Opposition leaders charged that widespread rigging had occurred and refused to accept the validity of the outcome. In Kumasi, where demonstrations led to the imposition of a dusk-to-dawn curfew, people spoke menacingly of an "uprising" and the need to "fight back." The following month, the opposition made good on its threat to boycott the parliamentary elections as a way of demonstrating its lack of confidence in the election process and, most particularly, in the election register.

In brief, then, Ghana's managed election of 1992 enabled Rawlings to remain in power, but it represented something of a setback for political liberalization in the country. With the opponents refusing to play the role of a loyal opposition in parliament, the system had yet to establish rules for competitive elections regarded as fair by all sides. In effect, then, the election proved to be a conflict creating experience, one that hardly facilitated the kind of stable, enabling environment so necessary for sustained economic growth and development.

Certainly, if adjusted to accommodate minority claims, these majoritarian democratic systems—whether representative or combining representative and participatory features—have some potential for reaching mutually beneficial outcomes over time. They hold out the greatest possibilities for channeling state-society conflict along constructive lines, encouraging both societal participation and state responsiveness. And even where their stability rests on having one preponderant ethnic group (as in Gambia and Botswana), the possibilities of change in voter preference and shifting coalitions cannot be precluded, holding out the prospect of alternative regimes in times to come.[30]

But if majoritarian democracies have great potential for promoting regularized patterns of relations, we must recognize that they do not necessarily eliminate clientelist practices, patronage, or overpoliticization. The latter may be exacerbated in part by such democracies' tendency to underrepresent losing parties, leading in the worst cases to the virtual exclusion of political and social minorities. Such exclusion can lead to a loss of legitimacy, with highly destabilizing consequences;[31] hence the appeal in some countries of the logic of guarding against party underrepresentation by controlling the effects of pure democracies. This may entail restructuring factional competition along alternative, competitive lines, or safeguarding minority interests by including mechanisms for proportional representation (South Africa), federalism (Nigeria and Ethiopia), and inclusive coalitions (Mauritius's practice of including the eight losing candidates from underrepresented communities).[32] Majoritarian democracies, then, are not without their complications; yet when carefully attuned to the societies in which are applied, they can become flexible processes that promise both fairness and effective government.

Although many Africans prefer majoritarian democracy, it seems likely to prove fragile in the 1990s and beyond. This fragility stems in part from the tasks facing overburdened democratic regimes in the years ahead: building responsive political institutions, coping with ethnic nationalism and religious fundamentalism, and reversing the economic and social decline of the postindependence decades. In this respect, external donor pressure for political reforms would arouse many sectors of the population through austerity measures, privatization, and interregional differences, which would be likely to result in a determined resistance to change. "The winners of economic reform in Africa are few; they appear only slowly over time and are difficult to organize politically."[33] In such an environment, then, sustained experiments with majoritarian democracy are not easy, making the survival of such systems dependent in no small part on their ability to deal effectively with multiple challenges in an adverse world environment.

When the preferred option is difficult to implement, it becomes necessary to look at alternative forms of governance. To be sure, those alternatives may involve costs in terms of regularized relations between state and societal interests; nonetheless, they may enhance state effectiveness, reducing the short-term burdens on state elites by allowing them greater latitude to launch burdensome austerity programs. The effect may be a greater congruence between what the state can deliver and what the public expects it to deliver. During a transition period at least, the consequence of a "hardened" state may be to facilitate a sequencing process, in this case placing economic reforms before political reforms. In Ghana during the 1980s, for example, the authoritarian regime of Jerry Rawlings, which lacked a firm political base, dampened political participation while moving ahead determinedly to implement a structural adjustment program.[34] Despite a heavy toll in terms of human rights and open political participation, the Rawlings approach secured some acceptance in some quarters by the 1992 election, because it managed to push the process of economic recovery ahead. And if the international community seems likely to frown on an abrupt and violent return to authoritarian rule (as in Zaire and Togo in 1991–93), it can be expected to be more accepting of marginal forms of democracy that link public participation and human rights with central control.

Because experiments with majoritarian democracy are fragile and destabilizing, many states will find it necessary to rechannel popular participation to reduce the burden on governments. "The partial liberalization of authoritarian regimes does not amount to a transition to democracy."[35]

Elite Power Sharing

One alternative charted in figure 9.1 is elite power sharing systems—transitional forms of governance that are amalgams of authoritarian control and consociational democracy (in particular, the principles of inclusive coalitions, balanced recruitment, and proportional allocations). Elites in the political arena, the civil service, and the military, fearful that full democracy will lead to regional, ethnic, and religious strife, may opt for "a pacted democracy" in an effort to limit the uncertainties of majoritarian rule.[36] Viewing "open democratic politics" as potentially "divisive and destabilizing" in contemporary Africa, Kenyan political scientist Meddi Mugyenyi calls instead for "minimalist democracies" that emphasize government effectiveness.[37] Rather than guaranteeing certainty, however, such hybrid systems may themselves prove transitory arrangements for Africa. Depending as they do on an elite culture that facilitates reciprocities and exchanges within a limited circle of interest group patrons and powerful members of the government and bureaucracy, pacted democracies tend to have limited access to information. To the extent that pacts among elites rest on shared norms and values, they may promote conciliatory behavior among diverse interests for a limited time under conditions of resource scarcity; nevertheless, they represent weak forms of governance, which may disintegrate in the event of a regime change.

Pacted democracies can be distinguished from authoritarian systems of control by their openness to power sharing among both state and societal elites; they can be distinguished from majoritarian democracies by their restrictions on full and equal representation in the decisionmaking process. They may allow for one-person, one-vote elections, but they so manipulate their structures and practices as to circumscibe the full participation of the public. In general, these elite power sharing regimes are a form of state-facilitated coordination, in which a somewhat autonomous central government coalition and various interest group representatives engage, directly or indirectly, in a process of bargaining and mutual accommodation.[38] They represent a kind of elite-controlled (at times, authoritarian-inclined) consociationalism that coordinates state and societal interests by adhering to such principles as inclusiveness in forming ruling coalitions; proportionality in allocating resources or recruitment into high government, civil service, or party positions; and autonomy on the part of segmental authorities.[39]

In contemporary Africa, pacted democracy takes various forms, ranging from ad hoc dyadic transactions between state and interest group representatives (regional, ethnic, or religious) to a more encompassing network of political exchanges within an informal cartel of elites. As I am focusing here on the key element of balanced recruitment into the ruling coalition, it will suffice to note two very different variants in the African context: (1) the authoritarian practices of the older elite power sharing systems associated with hegemonic exchange and (2) the 1991 National Party (NP) proposals for power sharing in South Africa. Hegemonic exchange, which links central control with opportunities for state-society political exchange, promotes cooperative behavior among disparate and relatively autonomous interests under conditions of weak institutionalization and resource scarcity. It allows for continual informal bargaining between key state and ethnoregional or other interests within the central government or party arenas. Provided that the genuine spokespersons of the main groups are included in the decisionmaking arena on a roughly equal basis, a hegemonic exchange system can encourage a stable distribution of resources during a transitional period.

During the 1970s and 1980s, African leaders in such countries as Kenya, Cameroon, Côte d'Ivoire, and Zambia made efforts to reconcile single-party rule with the pragmatic inclusion of powerful ethnic notables in the central cabinet and party national executive. These countries differed in their willingness to legitimate the political role of the ethnoregional intermediary in national politics, but including the main patrons and allowing a limited exchange to take place within the central political machine had roughly similar results. Thus, while Zambia's Kenneth Kaunda steadfastly denied claims that ethnoregional champions were active in national politics, he nonetheless was careful to maintain a balance between the Bemba and the Lozi in cabinet appointments and made sure the regions were represented on the national council of the United National Independence Party.[40]

However, in Félix Houphouët-Boigny's Côte d'Ivoire and Paul Biya's Cameroon (and previously in Jomo Kenyatta's Kenya), a more publicly countenanced system of balanced inclusion and interelite reciprocities and exchanges became evident. In the 1960s and 1970s, for example, Houphouët-Boigny, accepting ethnic-based fears as part of the country's political reality, sought to demobilize major ethnic challengers by carefully distributing tangible benefits to key players in the ruling coalition and co-opting important patrons on a generally proportional basis into his one-party government.[41] The resulting cabinet included all major ethnic interests, roughly in proportion to their numbers in the National Assembly. In Cameroon, President Ahmadu Ahidjo, despite his heavy-handed and secretive tendencies, prudently used his ministerial appointments as a means of balancing ethnoregional, linguistic, religious, and economic interests. His successor, Paul Biya, a Catholic from the south-central region, was even more committed to the principle of ethnic and religious proportionality, upholding the north-south balance in high executive appointments and ensuring that a northern Muslim would eventually succeed him as president.

In these cases, initial experiences with elite power sharing led to a widening acceptance of exchange practices and the development of transitory grand coalitions, with their own rules of the game. To be sure, the effects of these ongoing intraelite interactions may have proven inequitable to some ethnic and regional groups and socio-economic classes and may have exhibited the potential for elite exploitation of the masses. Even so, as long as the major actors perceived themselves as at least minimally benefited by the process, conflicts within this dominant class fraction could be kept at manageable levels.

The very different contemporary power sharing proposals of the ruling NP in South Africa call for a kind of centrifugal democracy, which would structure political power to restrain an energetic and possibly abusive central authority.[42] As envisaged by the 1991 NP master plan, the new power sharing system would include the devolution of significant functions to regional and local governments and measures to ensure the participation of minority interests. The latter would be guaranteed by a collective presidency, consisting of the leaders of the three largest parties in the first house; a two-house legislature (the first house elected via proportional representation and the second house, with an equal number of seats allocated to each region, concerned specifically with the interests of the nine regions and the minorities) that must agree on all legislation; and a strong judicial branch having the power of judicial review.[43]

By 1993, NP negotiators had softened their position on the need for a collective presidency and urged, instead, that the conferees agree on "binding constitutional principles" that would be tantamount to power sharing.[44] In an effort to reassure minority groups of their participation in the new ruling coalition, the African National Congress (ANC) agreed to make use of a proportional representation electoral system. The ANC "has been sensitive to a crucial aspect of electoral-system choice: the need to consider not only what is desirable [clear-cut parliamentary leadership], but also what is *possible* given the preferences of others."[45] By enabling NP and other parties to gain a significant bloc of supporters in the legislature through proportional representation, the ANC is in effect facilitating their chances of remaining within the national coalition after the initial five-year period of cooperation.

What the hegemonic exchange and NP centrifugal democracy proposals share is an emphasis on elite consensus in the determination of public policy. In light of Africa's weak institutions and scarcity of resources, further experiments described as democratic but in fact allowing only partial societal participation (including the West Africa concept of diarchy, which is the sharing of political power by civilian and military leaders) can be anticipated. Over time, such pacted systems are likely to prove vulnerable to pressure for democratic governance. Unless these elitist frameworks promote effective economic management while satisfying local demands for state responsiveness and accountability, they do not seem likely to endure.

Populism

Another alternative to majoritarian democracy, radical (or, in contemporary Algeria, conservative) populism, combines substantial societal participation with considerable state capacity to guide this process along desired channels. Regimes such as those of Jerry Rawlings in Ghana and Thomas Sankara in Burkina Faso in the 1980s and of Yoweri Museveni in Uganda in the 1980s and early 1990s were mired in poverty, external debt, and dependency. They turned in indignation and despair to experiments with radical populism, searching for authentic African solutions to the problems of social incoherence and economic decline.[46] Rejecting individualism, acquisitive values, and neocolonial links, these leaders called for a thoroughgoing reorganization of their societies, emphasizing the following goals: social equality and the ending of class privileges, broad citizen participation in government decisionmaking and public tribunals, the reconstruction of state institutions to rid them of people deemed corrupt or unsympathetic to regime goals, and a new, cohesive social order.

Brought to power by military coups or victory in the field, these young military officers—in Uganda's case, an insurgent leader— sought simultaneously to reject the frustrations and resentments of the past and to reorient their societies in communitarian and democratic directions. As Sankara observed, "The primary objective of the revolution is to take power out of the hands of our national bourgeoisie and their imperialist allies and put it in the hands of the people."[47] But if these leaders managed to give their publics a short-term uplift, they were largely overwhelmed by their environments. A populist program proved destabilizing because it led to an expansion of demands, which the government was attentive to but unable to satisfy. In all cases, the tensions between what they promised and what they could deliver became unsupportable, and they were forced to reorder their priorities in more conventional ways.

In a radical populist regime, the state encourages public political participation. Both Ghana and Burkina Faso experimented with committees for the defense of the revolution in urban neighborhoods and villages, established popular tribunals to administer popular justice, and purged the bureaucracy and army of people deemed unsympathetic to the revolutionary cause. Uganda's National Resistance Movement extended the life of the resistance committees after the civil war, linking national political participation to village-based structures that had been created to provide some form of local governance and self-sufficiency at a time of pervasive national disorder.[48] These attempts by the political center to spur participation in defense committees and quasi-judicial bodies were intended to strengthen the state's capacity to cope with societal pressures. By channeling societal activities along desired lines, the populist regime sought to mobilize a support base while it tempered extensive public (especially middle-class) demands.

So long as African states choose to confront economic misery and social incoherence, radical populism seems an option to be reckoned with. In the short term at least, populism can link state and society, increasing the state's capacity for central leadership while broadening citizen involvement in public affairs. Such popular participation in public matters entails mobilizing groups—the lower ranks of the military and civil services, the trade unions, students, market women, and a variety of rural interests—that have been kept on the sidelines under the old elitist, authoritarian order. Involving rural interests in local participatory structures is important to the populist program. To overcome peasants' isolation and sense of alienation, populist regimes try to reconcile central control with a decentralization of decision-making institutions. In 1982 the Rawlings regime, describing decentralization as part of its wider effort to promote Ghana's democratization and efficient administration, set out an eleven-point program for decentralizing policymaking and its implementation. In time, the central service ministries did allow the local authorities limited autonomy to run their own affairs. This process gained in significance in the postpopulist phase, district assemblies elected in 1988 were given the responsibility to "provide guidance and give political direction to, as well as supervise and generally control all other political and administrative authorities in the District."[49]

In Burkina Faso, the Sankara regime combined tight central control with local initiative: it ceased taxing the peasants and encouraged local authorities to build schools, health dispensaries, and movie houses in the villages. In Uganda, the Museveni regime sought to link the self-sufficient resistance committees that emerged during the civil war with the central government's efforts to regain control over society.

As a consequence, there seemed to be little practical alternative to decentralization. In his ten-point program, Museveni envisaged an important role for the people's committees at the village, *muluka*, *gombolola*, and district levels. "These committees would deal with each level's local affairs subject to superior laws. The committees could deal with law-breakers in co-operation with the chiefs and police, take part in discussing local development projects with government officials, but, above all, they would be political forums to discuss relevant issues against the corruption and misuse of office by the chief government officials. . . . They would be a channel of communication between the top and the bottom."[50] Museveni's success in accepting and working with the reality of self-sufficient local governments and bringing them back into the national structure of political authority ensured that Uganda could avoid the further disintegration and anarchy experienced in such countries as Somalia and Liberia.

Yet for all its successes in mobilizing public support for political and economic transformation and in bridging the gap between state and society, populism tends to be rather short term and transitional. It symbolizes the public's demands for reform but fails to come to grips with deeper problems. The reasons are both political and economic. In general, it is difficult for populist leaders to respond to heightened demands or to maintain their support coalitions over time. Sankara encountered strong opposition from not only autonomy-minded trade unionists but also from civil servants concerned about their future employment opportunities and salaries. And in Ghana, where a shift from populism to more pragmatic policies became evident some eighteen months into the regime, restlessness surfaced among its rank-and-file backers in the army, civil service, trade unions, and student organizations. These political support problems were compounded as the different regimes found it necessary to invoke painful deflationary monetary and economic policies, to reduce state subsidies, and to increase taxes and surcharges to satisfy the demands of their urban middle classes and the conditions set by multilateral lending agencies. For a time, revolutionary rhetoric coexisted with increased state control and pragmatic economic policy.[51] Reduced state functions and market economy programs were put into effect but at the cost of disaffection among the ranks of militant supporters of the revolution.[52]

There is reason to hope that Africa's turn toward austerity, market solutions, and a greater concern for human rights and democracy will encourage international donor agencies to contribute generously to its recovery and development in the 1990s and beyond. If, however, structural adjustment provides only a quick and insubstantial lift before these countries are thrown back on their own devices, disillusioned and desperate African states can be expected to attempt new experiments with radical populism. "Movements of rage"[53] arising out of frustration over an inability to achieve productive and equitable societies in the 1990s is a real possibility. Although the Islamic Salvation Front is right wing and fundamentalist in orientation, its December 1991 victory in the first phase of Algeria's parliamentary elections was a notable triumph for an organization championing the cause of the disaffected; it could well be the harbinger of similar events, conservative or radical, in the years ahead.

Corporatism

The third alternative to majoritarian democracy, state corporatism, allows for the limited participation of designated societal interests in a heavily state-regulated political process. The expansion of government capabilities and functions in both developing and developed countries has led to a new intrusion by the state into realms previously reserved for civil society.[54] Hence, as figure 9.1 suggests, a relatively strong state may attempt to organize and legitimate the nature of group formation and the way in which these functionally based groups articulate their interests at the political center. Philippe Schmitter, emphasizing the key role of the state in sanctioning the participation of functionally differentiated interest groups in the political process, defines corporatism as "a system of interest representation in which the constituent units are organized into a limited number of singular, compulsory, noncompetitive, hierarchically ordered and functionally differentiated categories, recognized or licensed (if not created) by the state and granted a deliberate representational monopoly within their respective categories in exchange for observing certain controls on their selection of leaders and articulation of demands and supports."[55] In such a regime, the state elite, determined to promote an enabling environment for economic development, seeks to establish controlled political pluralism. This state elite responds to "the perception of the threat of fragmentation" by using state power to reorganize its relations with interest groups in order to ensure the political center's hegemonic position.[56] For good reason, various authors cast doubts on whether an authentic form of pluralism can develop in such a setting.[57]

Clearly, corporatism requires reasonably strong and autonomous state institutions. Not only must those institutions be able to extract resources from society in an effective manner, they must distribute them in such a way as to maintain support among critically placed interests. In Africa, however, few countries meet this necessary criterion of robust institutional capacity, which limits the relevance of this model at least in the near term. In many African lands, pockets of group autonomy persist, defying attempts on the part of the state to regulate their activities.[58] Moreover, although the powerful and well-organized groups in the formal sector—domestic and multinational corporations and parastatals, employers' organizations, professional groups, trade unions, and cooperatives—may fit into the corporatist plan for group representation, elements in the informal economy—market traders, small businessmen and retailers, repair shops, artisans, and small farmers in the food-producing sector—tend to fall outside of the design.[59] The effect is to leave corporatist governments woefully uninformed about the demands of many of their citizens, raising doubts about the transferability to the African context of the model from the industrialized and state-penetrated societies of Europe, Latin America, and Asia.

Yet despite such reservations about the relevance of the state corporatist model to contemporary Africa, there are in fact corporatist tendencies in certain African settings. In the late 1980s, Ghana's PNDC attempted to structure society along corporatist lines, encouraging those civil associations supportive of government purposes while discouraging those opposed to the regime.[60] In Côte d'Ivoire, the representatives of a wide range of organized interest groups were systematically integrated into the state and the ruling Parti Démocratique de la Côte d'Ivoire (PDCI) during the 1970s and 1980s. Ethnic associations in urban areas, for example, were quickly incorporated into PDCI, often with little change in their authority structures or personnel.[61] State and party control was then extended to a variety of economic interests, including trade unions and tenant organizations. In rural areas, the state and party pursued a similar strategy of incorporating the main socioeconomic groups and achieved considerable success in capturing the peasantry. A retreat into subsistence agriculture is no longer a viable option for the majority of smallholders.[62] In line with its productionist goals, the government maintains reasonable producer prices for cocoa, coffee, and other cash crops and keeps taxes moderate. The effect of such policies is to provide meaningful payoffs for economic enterprises within the modern economy and to form the basis for limited and carefully channeled group participation. Significantly, where desired structures (such as ethnic associations) did not exist, they were created by the state. And where it was not possible to co-opt groups (for example, an incipient organization of the urban unemployed), the state elite systematically undermined them.

In times of strain, Côte d'Ivoire's nascent corporatism kept its balance by means of a system of state-initiated dialogues with its interest groups. After a heavy-handed reaction from state authorities to a strike by secondary school students and teachers and university students over worsening conditions in 1982–83, the government reconsidered its approach and encouraged interest group representatives to meet and submit recommendations to the president. In a process described as "intensified competition among corporatist groups," spokespersons for various government ministries and such PDCI-related interests as the National Union of Parents, Students, and Educators of Côte d'Ivoire and the national labor union assembled for discussions.[63] The upshot was an easing of tensions, for Houphouët-Boigny pardoned the strikers and reopened the university.

In the more serious 1989 crisis, Houphouët-Boigny again attempted to use a state-guided dialogue to encapsulate and control the emerging crisis over demands for political reform and economic relief. At a meeting with some 2,000 government and interest group representatives, the president was obviously startled by the extent of elite dissatisfaction with political and economic conditions.[64] In response to strong pressure for a multiparty system, he gave his approval to contested elections and subsequently guided the country through a closely controlled electoral process; in addition, he appointed a well-known economist, Alassane Ouattara, as prime minister. When demonstrations broke out over a variety of economic grievances prior to the implementation of these measures, Houphouët-Boigny again managed to contain the threat by granting wage increases and job security to various interest groups.

In brief, the relatively strong state in Côte d'Ivoire had managed in the 1970s and 1980s to organize political pluralism in such a way as to allow limited participation and, for a time, impressive rates of economic growth. Backed by a relatively strong economy, it was in a position to promise payoffs to a variety of public and private groups, thereby encouraging cooperation between powerful state and societal interests. However, the linchpin of such an arrangement was a strong economic base. As this base weakened in the late 1980s and early 1990s, the outlook for keeping corporatist practices in place became less hopeful.

Conclusion

Clearly, effective governance is more encompassing than democracy alone. Other regime types such as elite power sharing, populism, and state corporatism can also create political routines that buttress patterns of reciprocity and exchange relations. In weak states, reciprocity and exchange help to avoid destructive conflict by overcoming the distance between state and civil society. They facilitate cooperation by promoting agreement on the nature and limits of political action; hence it is possible to conceive of regularized state-society relations—and the enabling environment they provide—in terms of the four-cell matrix of figure 9.1. Nevertheless, of the alternatives discussed, given Africa's current conditions of scarcity and its brittle institutions, democracy has long-term advantages in providing a sustained basis for regularized relations. Majoritarian democracy offers politicians and constituents an incentive to live by the rules of the game and, because political leaders want to remain in office, to be responsive to the main claims of their constituents. The result over time is likely to be broadened cooperation.

Yet democracy is not easy to put into effect, in Africa or elsewhere—in part at least because it heightens demands and expectations and therefore intensifies competition for public allocations under conditions of severe scarcity. And although the three alternative developmental regime types may provide a temporary reconciliation between government efficiency and societal participation, they are unlikely to prove more than transitory experiments. Power sharing schemes suffer from elitism, populist regimes are perceived as threatening the middle class, and state corporatism is difficult to establish because African state institutions and capabilities tend to be weak and informal interest groups difficult to incorporate. For all its evident frailties and risks, therefore, democracy is the salient goal.

But how is democracy to be encouraged? Although that is a subject for another, longer essay, a key suggestion at this time might be that democratic constitution making be viewed as merely a beginning. As Ghana's National Commission for Democracy astutely observed, "The constitution-making process . . . cannot be constrained to a one-shot effort on the part of a select group."[65] Rather, it is the opening round in an extended learning process. The framing of constitutions is not an end but a process leading to repeated interactions. The national conference or constitutional agreement represents a critically important act, which one hopes binds the participants to an ongoing effort to give fuller meaning to the formal rules. Such iteration may help in developing political norms among organizations favorable to accommodation and give-and-take exchanges, thereby promoting the kinds of cooperative behavior and stable interactions so necessary to democracy. As such encounters lead to an increasing concern with the goals and welfare of other parties, regularized relationships may become an accepted feature of political life, facilitating agreement on the difficult economic and social issues confronting these complex societies.

Notes

I wish to express my appreciation to Jennifer Widner, Ken Shepsle, and Douglass North for their helpful comments on the first draft of this chapter.

1. World Bank, *Sub-Saharan Africa: From Crisis to Sustainable Growth*, a Long-Term Perspective Study (Washington, D.C.: World Bank, 1989), 60.

2. Ibid., 3.

3. For a discussion of these options, see Donald Rothchild and Letitia Lawson, "The Interactions between State and Civil Society in Africa: From Deadlock to New Routines," in *Civil Society and the State in Africa,* ed. John Harbeson, Donald Rothchild, and Naomi Chazan (Boulder, Colo.: Lynne Rienner, forthcoming).

4. By *regimes* I mean the patterns of behavior accepted by the dominant state coalitions and the general public of various countries as the legitimate formula for the exercise of political power.

5. Federal Republic of Nigeria, *Report of the Political Bureau* (Lagos: Government Printer, 1987), 35. Also see Fred Onyeoziri, "Consociationalism and the Nigerian Political Practice," in *Federal Character and Federalism in Nigeria,* ed. Peter P. Ekeh and Eghosa E. Osaghae (Ibadan: Heinemann, 1989), 421–24.

6. See Claude Ake's presidential address to the annual conference of the Nigerian Political Science Association, quoted in *West Africa,* May 25, 1981.

7. Despite the decline in quality-of-life indicators in Ghana in the mid-1970s, expectations of future well-being remained remarkably constant on the whole. See Donald Rothchild, "Comparative Public Demand and Expectation Patterns: The Ghana Experience," *African Studies Review* 22, no. 1 (1979): 127–47; and Fred M. Hayward, "Perceptions of Well-Being in Ghana: 1970 and 1975," *African Studies Review* 22, no. 1 (1979): 110–11.

8. John A. A. Ayoade, "States without Citizens: An Emerging African Phenomenon," in *The Precarious Balance: State and Society in Africa,* ed. Donald Rothchild and Naomi Chazan (Boulder, Colo.: Westview, 1988), 115.

9. Goran Hyden, "Problems and Prospects of State Coherence," in *State Versus Ethnic Claims: African Policy Dilemmas,* ed. Donald Rothchild and Victor A. Olorunsola (Boulder, Colo.: Westview, 1983), 69.

10. Goran Hyden, "The Political Economy of Popular Organizations: The

Case of the Sungu Sungu Movement in Tanzania" (Stanford: Stanford University, Joint Center for African Studies, April 21, 1989), 14–18, typescript.

11. Aili Mari Tripp, "Local Institutions and Grassroots Party Dynamics in Urban Tanzania," in *Governance and Politics in Africa*, ed. Goran Hyden and Michael Bratton (Boulder, Colo.: Lynne Rienner, 1992), 238.

12. Claude Ake, quoted in *West Africa* (October 14–20, 1991): 1717.

13. Thomas M. Callaghy, *The State-Society Struggle: Zaire in Comparative Perspective* (New York: Columbia University Press, 1984), 73.

14. *West Africa* (August 10, 1987), 1528.

15. Albert Adu Boahen, *The Ghanaian Sphinx: Reflections on the Contemporary History of Ghana, 1972–1987* (Accra: Ghana Academy of Arts and Sciences, 1989), 51–52.

16. Claude Ake, "The Case for Democracy," in *African Governance in the 1990s: Objectives, Resources, and Constraints*, ed. Richard Joseph (Atlanta: Carter Center, 1990), 2.

17. Peter Anyang' Nyong'o, "Democratization Processes in Africa," *CODESRIA Bulletin* (Dakar), no. 2 (1991): 3.

18. Manfred Halpern, "Changing Connections to Multiple Worlds," in *Africa: From Mystery to Maze*, ed. Helen Kitchen (Lexington, Mass.: Lexington Books, 1976), 12.

19. For a specification and measurement of the paths by which domestic political conflict may diffuse across state boundaries, see Stuart Hill and Donald Rothchild, "The Contagion of Political Conflict in Africa and the World," *Journal of Conflict Resolution* 30, no. 4 (1986): 716–35, and their chapter "The Impact of Regime on the Diffusion of Political Conflict," in *The Internationalization of Communal Strife*, ed. Manus Midlarsky (London: Routledge, 1992).

20. Michael Bratton and Nicolas van de Walle, "Popular Protest and Political Reform in Africa," *Comparative Politics* 24 (1992): 419–42.

21. Republic of Ghana, *Report of the Committee of Experts (Constitution) on Proposals for a Draft Constitution of Ghana* (Tema: Ghana Publishing, 1991), 90–91.

22. Robert Fatton, Jr., *The Making of a Liberal Democracy: Senegal's Passive Revolution, 1975–1985* (Boulder, Colo.: Lynne Rienner, 1987), 169.

23. Carol Lancaster, "Democracy in Africa," *Foreign Policy* 85 (Winter 1991–92): 148–65, 148.

24. Constitution of the Republic of Namibia, Article 17 (1).

25. See E. Gyimah-Boadi, "Notes on Ghana's Current Transition to Constitutional Rule," 1991, typescript.

26. Republic of Ghana, *Report of the Committee of Experts*, 124, 278.

27. Ibid., 12.

28. See National Democratic Institute for International Affairs/Carter Center of Emory University, *Report of the Carter Center Ghana Election Mission* (Washington, D.C.: National Democratic Institute, 1992), 1–2.

29. Ransford Tetteh and Vance Azu, "The Presidential Election: Who Wins the Race," *Mirror* (Accra), October 31, 1992.

30. In this sense, the description of Botswana as "a *de facto* one-party state" appears to overlook the potential for change in the system. Louis A. Picard, as quoted in Donald L. Horowitz, *A Democratic South Africa?* (Berkeley: University of California Press, 1991), 114.

31. W. Arthur Lewis, *Politics in West Africa* (London: Allen and Unwin, 1965), 60.

32. See James Madison, "The Federalist Number 10," in *The Federalist Papers* (London: Penguin Books, 1987), 125, 127.

33. Thomas M. Callaghy, "Africa and the World Economy: Caught between a Rock and a Hard Place," in *Africa in World Politics*, ed. John W. Harbeson and Donald Rothchild (Boulder, Colo.: Westview, 1991), 60.

34. Richard Jeffries, "Leadership, Commitment, and Political Opposition to Structural Adjustment in Ghana," in *Ghana: The Political Economy of Recovery*, ed. Donald Rothchild (Boulder, Colo.: Lynne Rienner, 1991), 165.

35. Michael Bratton and Nicolas Van de Walle, "Toward Governance in Africa: Popular Demands and State Responses," in Hyden and Bratton, eds., *Governance and Politics in Africa*, 51.

36. Terry Lynn Karl, "Petroleum and Political Pacts: The Transition to Democracy in Venezuela," in *Transitions from Authoritarian Rule: Latin America*, ed. Guillermo O'Donnell, Philippe C. Schmitter, and Laurence Whitehead (Baltimore: Johns Hopkins University Press, 1986), 217.

37. Meddi Mugyenyi, "Development First, Democracy Second: A Comment on Minimalist Democracy," in *Democratic Theory and Practice in Africa*, ed. Walter O. Oyugi et al. (Portsmouth, N.H.: Heinemann, 1988), 185–87.

38. Donald Rothchild, "Hegemonial Exchange: An Alternative Model for Managing Conflict in Middle Africa," in *Ethnicity, Politics, and Development*, ed. Dennis L. Thompson and Dov Ronen (Boulder, Colo.: Lynne Rienner, 1986).

39. On the characteristics of consociational democracy, see Arend Lijphart, *Democracy in Plural Societies* (New Haven: Yale University Press, 1977), 25.

40. William Tordoff, *Administration in Zambia* (Manchester: Manchester University Press, 1980), 14–15; Richard Hall, *The High Price of Principles* (New York: Africana Publishing, 1969), 195; and letter from J. M. Mutti to *Times of Zambia* (Ndola), October 24, 1970.

41. See the data in Tessilimi Bakary, "Elite Transformation and Political Succession," in *The Political Economy of Ivory Coast*, ed. I. William Zartman and Christopher Delgado (New York: Praeger, 1984), 36; and Jean-François Médard, "la Regulation socio-politique," in *Etat et bourgeoisie en Côte d'Ivoire*, ed. Yves A. Faure and Jean-François Médard (Paris: Karthala, 1982), 75.

42. Lijphart, *Democracy in Plural Societies*, 114.

43. Federal Council of the National Party, *Grondwetlike Regering In 'n Deelnemende Demokrasie* (Pretoria: National Party, September 4, 1991), 8–15; and Foreign Broadcast Information Service (FBIS), *Sub-Saharan Africa*, 91-175 (September 4, 1991): 12–20.

44. FBIS, *Sub-Saharan Africa*, 93-24 (February 8, 1993): 19.

45. Timothy D. Sisk, "South Africa Seeks New Ground Rules," *Journal of Democracy* 4, no. 1 (1993): 79–91, 87.

46. For an extended discussion of populist experiments in Africa, see Donald Rothchild and E. Gyimah-Bouadi, "Populism in Ghana and Burkina Faso," *Current History* 88 (1989): 221–44; and Rothchild and Lawson, "The Interactions between State and Civil Society," 15–20.

47. Quoted in Guy Martin, "Ideology and Praxis in Thomas Sankara's Populist Revolution of August 4, 1983, in Burkina Faso," *Issue: A Journal of Opinion* 15 (1987): 77–90, 78.

48. Michael Twaddle, "Museveni's Uganda: Notes towards an Analysis," in *Uganda Now: Between Decay and Development*, ed. Holger Bernt Hansen and Michael Twaddle (London: James Currey, 1988), 318.

49. Republic of Ghana, *District Political Authority and Modalities for District-Level Elections* (Accra: Ghana Publishing, 1987), 3. For data on the 1988 district assembly elections, see Naomi Chazan, "The Political Transformation of Ghana under the PNDC," in Rothchild, ed., *Ghana: The Political Economy of Recovery*, 35–37.

50. Yoweri Museveni, *Selected Articles on the Uganda Resistance War* (Kampala: National Resistance Movement, 1986), 50–51.

51. Nelson Kasfir, "The Tension between Progressive Populism and Democratization in Uganda," paper prepared for the annual meeting of the American Political Science Association, Atlanta, September 1989, 8–9.

52. Donald Rothchild, *The Rawlings Revolution in Ghana: Pragmatism with Populist Rhetoric*, CSIS Africa Notes, 42 (Washington, D.C.: Center for Strategic and International Studies, 1985).

53. The term is from Martin Kilson, "Thinking about African Re-Democratization," paper prepared for the Colloquium on the Economics of Political Liberalization in Africa, Cambridge, March 6–7, 1992.

54. Joan M. Nelson, "Political Participation," in *Understanding Political Development*, ed. Myron Weiner and Samuel P. Huntington (Boston: Little, Brown, 1987), 153.

55. Philippe C. Schmitter, "Still the Century of Corporatism?" *Review of Politics* 36, no. 1 (1974): 93–94.

56. Alfred Stepan, *The State and Society* (Princeton: Princeton University Press, 1978), 47, 58.

57. See, for example, Eboe Hutchful, "The Limits of Corporatism as a Concept and Model," in *Corporatism in Africa*, ed. Julius E. Nyang'oro and Timothy M. Shaw (Boulder, Colo.: Westview, 1989), 28.

58. See Naomi Chazan and Donald Rothchild, "Corporatism and Political Transactions: Some Ruminations on the Ghanaian Experience," in Nyang'oro and Shaw, eds., *Corporatism in Africa*.

59. Hutchful, "The Limits of Corporatism," 32.

60. E. Gyimah-Boadi, "Civil Associations in the PNDC Era: Aspects of the Evolution of Civil Society in Ghana," in Harbeson, Rothchild, and Chazan, eds., *Civil Society and the State in Africa*, 2.

61. Michael A. Cohen, *Urban Policy and Political Conflict in Africa: A Case Study of the Ivory Coast* (Chicago: University of Chicago Press, 1974), 97–101.

62. Jennifer Widner, "The Discovery of Politics: Smallholder Reactions to the Cocoa Crisis of 1989–90 in Côte d'Ivoire," in *Hemmed In: Responses to Africa's Economic Decline,* ed. Thomas Callaghy and John Ravenhill (New York: Columbia University Press, 1993).

63. Cyril Kofie Daddieh, "The Management of Educational Crises in Côte d'Ivoire," *Journal of Modern African Studies* 26 (1988): 639–45.

64. Gerald Bourke, "Day of Truth," *West Africa,* October 9–15, 1989.

65. Republic of Ghana, National Commission for Democracy, *Report on the Evolving Democratic Process,* reprinted in the *Post* (Accra), no. 29 (1991): 2.

CRAWFORD YOUNG

Ten ◈ Democratization in Africa: The Contradictions of a Political Imperative

At the beginning of the 1990s, Africa, from Algiers to Capetown, faced a common conjuncture, an imperative of democratization, broadly defined. Battered by economic decline and weakened by political decay, the African state faced narrowed choices; political opening was no longer an option but an obligation. A political economy where, in the oft-cited aphorism, political man ruled the economy and economic man ruled politics had finally produced an impasse whose sole exit was liberalization, political as well as economic.

The magnitude of the challenge confronting Africa was daunting. No litany of the economic disaster afflicting the continent (in varying degrees, to be sure) is required; no one disputes the depth of the crisis nor its continental scope. The virtual disintegration in 1991 of Liberia and Somalia sent clear warning signals that political decay matches economic decay, even if the health of the polity is less statistically monitored than the health of the economy. Thus, a pathway beyond perpetual crisis and integrating political and economic liberalization wends perilously through uncharted minefields. One cannot dismiss the argument that simultaneous pursuit of democratization and structural adjustment will cause both to fail.[1] Yet no other choice is available; integral liberalization, however risky, is dictated by conjuncture and circumstance. A unique configuration of historical conditions has—

at least momentarily—destroyed all credible alternatives and generated overwhelming pressures, internal and external, in favor of democratization. Yet conjuncture and circumstance are inherently contingent; democratization will be judged by its performance and consequences. Perhaps the mood one encountered in Nigeria in 1991, near the final stages of the third transition to democratic rule, stands as metaphor for the entire continent: relative confidence that power would be transferred to elected civilian politicians but deep skepticism about their capacity to institutionalize the Third Republic. Nonetheless, at a normative level the Nigerian public clearly wants democratization, however uncertain its sustainability.

To set the stage for this argument, a backward glance is necessary at the historical sequences and trajectories that brought Africa to a distressing crossroads—caught between a "discredited past" and "a future which refuses to arrive."[2] Although the significant particularities of individual political economies produced substantial variation among the fifty-two sub-Saharan African states, overarching similarities stand out. It is these patterns I seek to illuminate in this compressed historical overview.

In the aftermath of World War II, the colonial powers—expecting to remain in Africa for an indefinite future—recognized that legitimation of their rule now required a major commitment to economic development. Improving the economic well-being of the dominated would dilute the emergent force of nationalist claims. Thus, for the first time, colonial development plans appeared, a "second colonial occupation" of European agents staffing newly expanded technical and welfare services occurred, and significant public investment financed by metropolitan treasuries took place.

Anticolonial nationalism, however, was not to be denied its historical mission of liberation by the proverbial thirty pieces of silver. Its initial discourse was almost exclusively political; "seek ye first the political kingdom," spake one of its prophets, Kwame Nkrumah, "and all else shall be added unto you." Until virtually the eve of independence, the classic texts of African nationalism (with the possible exception of the 1945 Manchester Pan-African Conference resolutions) were remarkably devoid of economic content.

Once in power, the first generation of African rulers closed the door of politics and co-opted the colonial discourse of "development." "To discourage opposition and perpetuate their power, they argued that the problems of development demanded complete unity of purpose, justifying on these grounds the criminalization of political dissent and the inexorable march to political monolithism."[3] The political kingdom was won; the era of accelerated economic development was at hand. There was a truly extraordinary confidence in the rationality and capacity of the developmental state to plan, organize, and effect rapid transformation, illusions shared by the new political leadership and the new profession of development economics.[4]

During the 1970s, a new round of political battles was fought, this time over control of the economy.[5] The reception in Africa of dependency theory from its Latin American birthplace led to the conclusion, in ruling and intellectual circles, that the political kingdom was incomplete without conquest of the economic realm.[6] A political struggle was engaged to secure economic independence, marked by such events as the economic war in Uganda in 1972, or the 1973–74 Zairianization and radicalization campaigns of Mobutu Sese Seko in Zaire, epigrammatic of a broader trend in their very excesses. The nationalization of foreign assets—largely of colonial origin—occurred on a broader scale in Africa during this period than in any other region. Assertive African diplomacy played a central role in the ultimately fruitless quest for a new international economic order.[7] A sharp shift in ideological discourse occurred. Populist socialist regimes, such as Tanzania and Algeria, radicalized their projects (the Arusha Declaration of 1967, the agrarian revolution of 1971). Seven states formally adopted Marxism-Leninism as regime ideology.[8]

By the end of the 1970s, a pattern of economic decline became manifest. The 1979 Organization of African Unity summit in Monrovia took note of a report concluding, "Africa . . . is unable to point to any significant growth rate or satisfactory index of general well-being" after two decades of independence. Economic reform returned to the center of preoccupations, within and without Africa. The OAU commissioned a study leading to the 1980 Lagos Plan of Action to counter the economic crisis. By a separate route, the World Bank undertook a diagnosis of economic decline leading to the Berg Report.[9] Political issues faded into the background; a consensus emerged that urgent economic measures were required to restore African well-being. The term that came to dominate the decade—*structural adjustment*—took form, and most African states in one way or another came within its embrace. Its formulation was sharply contested between African states and the international financial institutions and Western donor communities, but over the decade there was a gradual convergence around most of its major themes. For most of the 1980s, accordingly, the pendulum swung far over to the economic side; both the Lagos Plan of Action and the Berg Report prescriptions were profoundly apolitical, in the sense of presuming that reform could be purely economic.

Although within Africa the form of economics now in command—
the structural adjustment package of liberalization measures—evoked
ambivalent responses at best, initially the singular self-confidence of
the economics profession in its capacity to design remedies and a
radiant neoliberal faith in the therapeutic force of freed markets surged
through the international donor community. There seemed a possibility that the leverage of structural adjustment would convince or
compel political autocracies simultaneously to cede authority to tech-
nocracies in partnership with international donor community representatives and to shield them from negative public reaction.

Slowly, over the decade of structural adjustment, the conviction
took root that the origins of the crisis were political as well as economic
and that transcending the crisis required political as well as economic
surgery. When Richard Sklar used his 1982 African Studies Association
(ASA) presidential address to call for democracy in Africa, his views
were quietly dismissed by many as visionary.[10] When Georges Nzongola-Ntalaja returned to this theme in his 1988 ASA presidential address, he was merely one step ahead of his time.[11] Intellectual and
political currents, in and out of Africa, then moved swiftly to place
democratization squarely in the middle of the agenda by 1990. A
remarkably broad consensus among African intellectuals, many of
whom had once accepted the premises of single-party rule, emerged.
In part, this reflected antagonism to structural adjustment policy packages. As Mwesiga Baregu argues in chapter 7, in the Tanzania case,
"traditional opponents of the World Bank and the IMF . . . gradually
realized that they could not dissuade the government from adopting
these policies. . . . Instead, [they] turned their attention to the logical
inconsistency in the government's espousal of economic liberalization
and its rejection of political liberalization."

Although the dramatic collapse of state socialism and Soviet-model
autocracy in Eastern Europe was not in itself a direct cause of African
democratization, it had greater resonance in Africa than in any other
region. At the political summit, a number of African leaders had close
personal ties with some Eastern European rulers; Nicolae Ceauscescu
in particular cultivated the notion that Romania, as a "developing
country," had natural affinities with the Third World, and his summary execution was a profound shock in a number of African presidential palaces. The single-party system as standard model owed
much to the Leninist theory of the state; the now-infamous Article 6
of the Soviet constitution entrenching the "leading role" of the Communist party was echoed in many African states, from Angola to
Zaire, although often shorn of the accompanying commitment to

Marxism-Leninism.[12] The revelation that such a political construction was a hollow shell—beginning with the fall of the Berlin Wall in November 1989 and then amplified by the swift crumbling of such regimes throughout Eastern Europe in the months following—was one more factor emboldening opposition across the continent, particularly among disaffected urban elements (civil servants, teachers, youths, students) most attentive to broad global currents. The contagion psychosis was multiplied by developments in Africa like the national conference in Benin and the release of Nelson Mandela. To be sure, its impact was uneven, contingent upon the particular circumstances in given countries and the degree of the regime delegitimation.

The Western international development technocracy became persuaded that the mixed performance of structural adjustment programs could be explained only by looking beyond purely economic variables. The novel concept of *governance,* first unveiled by an influential academic,[13] provided a more antiseptic substitute than *democratization* for introducing political criteria into the policy discourse of the international financial institutions. By 1989, the term *governance* crept into official texts, defined as "the exercise of political power to manage a nation's affairs," requiring building "a pluralistic institutional structure, a determination to respect the rule of law, and vigorous protection of the freedom of the press and human rights."[14] Key donors (France, the United States, the European Community) spoke more openly of "democratization" as a necessary condition for external financial support for recovery programs.

Within Africa, autocracies everywhere were placed on the defensive by an upsurge of pluralization demands from a newly assertive populace. Some, as in Mali, were driven from power by street actions. Others, as in Benin, were forced to concede their sovereign power to redefine the polity to national conferences, which were assembling the major political forces within the countries. By 1991, more than forty states (by my count, all but Malawi, Libya, Sudan, and Somaliland) had either undertaken political liberalization or pledged implementation of such a program; this number exceeded that of countries formally engaged in structural adjustment. In 1990–91—in a continent where, in the first three decades of independence, even partially democratic systems (for example, Botswana, Gambia, Senegal, and Mauritius) could be counted on the fingers of one hand and where Mauritius was the only unambiguous case of political alternation by electoral process—long-standing regimes were voted out of office in Benin, Cape Verde, São Tomé and Príncipe, and Zambia, with more such changes in prospect. This transformation was stunning.

Superimposed upon this secular pendulum swing between the economic and the political was a profound mood change, from the exhilarating optimism of the 1960s to Afropessimism. The extraordinary economic surge of the 1950s, whose momentum carried through the following decade, combined with the unanticipated speed and (in most instances) ease of achieving independence to create a conviction that these economic and political conquests could be not only sustained but accelerated. Disappointments began to accumulate in the 1970s, with the *crisis* label acquiring common currency by 1980.

Initially, African distress was attributed to economic factors alone and thus believed to be remediable by economic reform. At the second stage, the crisis was viewed as both economic and political. However opinions might have varied as to the specific measures required, consensus was nearly universal that the depth of the crisis commanded changes in both economy and polity. The sheer scale of predatory resource diversion by ruling elites, insulated by autocratic politics from any accountability for their action, catalyzed popular anger, even if the colossal sums reported on *radio trottoir* may have been exaggerated ($5 billion for Mobutu Sese Seko and $1 billion for Moussa Traore, for example). A deep pessimism took hold concerning the severity of the condition, and the obstacles to recovery. The executive secretary of the Economic Commission for Africa, Adebayo Adedeji, lamented: "Africa has moved from being at the periphery to the periphery of the periphery of the global economy—the permanent political and underdog of the world, the world's basket case."[15] Nigerian ruler Olusegan Obasanjo, decrying the decay and dereliction afflicting the continent, warned of a virtual "delinkage" of a "fragmented and drifting" Africa, "disorganized and frustrated, unsure and isolated economically and politically."[16]

To complete our tableau of contemporary dilemmas, one more retrospective excursion is required. One may gain a useful conceptual purchase on the political dynamic by seeking the inner essence of the contemporary African state and its political logic. The particular form of state that emerged in postcolonial Africa combined a heritage of autocracy, an impulse to extend and reinforce the scope of state action and to monopolize resources, and an increasingly venal system of public goods allocation driven by the imperatives of sustaining and reproducing the power of incumbent rulers and regimes. The postcolonial state thus was constructed from the amalgamation of three forms of state (in ideal-typical characterization) and their attendant reasons: the colonial state, whose residues became incorporated in its postindependence successor; the integral state, a vision guiding much of the state class during the 1960s and 1970s; and the prebendal state, a behavioral logic arising from the realities of everyday management of the polity, with preservation of power as the motivating force. Let us examine each of these in turn then consider the implications of the fusion of these three modes of state logic.

As I argue elsewhere, the colonial state in Africa was in important respects distinctive from its counterparts in other regions.[17] Patterns established in its early phase proved enduring and shaped its institutions and behavior. The intensely competitive nature of the "scramble for Africa" in the late nineteenth century and the rules of the game codified at the Berlin Conference requiring "effective occupation" to validate proprietary title made urgent the creation of a skeletal apparatus of hegemony. The absence, in most areas, of established sources of revenue, and the metropolitan requirement that colonial conquest and rule be self-financing, drove the colonial state into the forcible organization of the one extractable resource: African labor. Although this harsh hegemony was mediated through diverse collaborators (chiefs, religious notables, missionaries, merchants), its impact upon society was far more direct and extensive than was colonial rule in most other regions. A stable, self-sustaining, relatively low-cost framework of domination had been achieved by World War II. Although its most coercive features mainly disappeared in the terminal colonial period, its command relationship with society, its quasi-military character, its fiscal base rooted in high taxation of the peasantry, and its highly interventionist, regulatory dispositions were bequeathed to its nationalist successors. One need not doubt the sincerity of intent of the postcolonial successor elite in declaring their determination to construct a new, transformed state at the service of society. Easily underestimated was the inertial force of long-established and deeply entrenched state practice, which inevitably remained embedded in the daily routines and habits of state agents.

Upon this Procrustean bed, however, a new vision of the state— its nature, aims, and ends—took shape. I borrow from Christian Coulon and Jean Copans the notion of the "integral state" to capture the imagined polity constructed by African nationalism. The "integral state," according to Coulon, seeks to act directly upon civil society through its own "hegemonical apparatuses," brushing aside all intermediaries.[18] Copans defines the "integral state" in the following terms: "The objective of the dominant groups in the state apparatus is the control, the maintenance, the augmentation of surplus extraction. . . . The lesson of recent years is the following: the interests of the Senegalese state have won out over local private interests . . . this growing role of the state, rendered concrete through the remodelling and multiplication of institutions for control of the peasantry, leads to a new policy. The Senegalese state aims more and more at a direct administrative, ideological and political control over the dominated masses, be they urban or rural."[19]

The architects of the integral state initially believed themselves driven—as an officially inspired commentary on President Mobutu has it—by "the inflexible will to transform the equatorial forest into terrestrial paradise."[20] Single parties were designated as "the nation politically organized" and were presumed to incorporate the entire population. The vocation of the party-state was the "mobilization of the masses" around its development project; its administrative apparatus was charged with the "encadrement" of these same masses. The associational infrastructure of civil society was to be either brought within the tutelary structure of the party or dissolved. Formally autonomous centers of power were anathema: seedbeds of the mischiefs of faction, fomenters of subversion, artisans of ethnic division. Only the integral state could have the capacity to marshall and organize the resources and forces of society in order to breath into life the "terrestrial paradise" that was promised.

The policy implications of the political logic of the integral state were far-reaching. The regulatory infrastructure of the colonial state was extended and deepened: agricultural marketing monopolies, obligatory state cooperatives, administered prices in key sectors, and the licensing of many economic activities and external trade. The impetus to extended control inherent to the integral state drove the parastatalization of the economy, even in states commonly considered "capitalist" (Côte d'Ivoire, Nigeria). Building upon colonial jurisprudence, the state asserted ultimate proprietorship over land and the allocation of all use entitlements in the first two decades of independence.[21] A similar process operated with respect to natural resource management; "many states assert rights to all natural resources, and often presume to manage resource use through the operation of administrative rules or codes."[22]

The third form of state logic, its prebendal dimension, emerged because neither the hierarchical structure and rational organization inherited from the colonial state, nor the democratic centralist norms, nor the obligations of discipline sufficed to control and motivate the key operatives in the security, political, and bureaucratic apparatuses. Thus the formally Weberian traits presumed in the images of the colonial and integral states—impersonality of office, uniform application of rules, predictability of behavior, and rationality of organizational structure—were interpenetrated by a radically different set of operating mores, characterized as "prebendalism."[23]

In the prebendal state, office is a personal favor of the ruler, from which the occupant is expected to secure a "living." The occupant is assumed to perform the basic functions of the office, above all its control aspects: maximally, to impose effective authority over those subject to its dictates; minimally, to preempt the crystallization of hostile forces within its sphere. In the process, the officeholder may convert some of its public authority into private returns: the "rent-seeking" syndrome (see chaps. 3, 4, and 6, this volume). The official is thus a personal client of the ruler; in turn, the effective management of the domain entrusted to him induces the creation of a subsidiary prebendal network, permitted as long as it does not coalesce into a patrimonial force capable of challenging the authority of the ruler.

Prebendal logic does not entirely obliterate other forms of state logic. Rather, it is a system of power exercise propelled by the ambition of incumbents to ensure the permanence of their rule. However, it goes without saying that it contradicts and undermines colonial and integral state reason. The integral state builds upon and enlarges the vision of the colonial state; the prebendal state subverts both. The relative balance of this dialectical interaction varies substantially. The prebendal element clearly predominates in Zaire and Sierra Leone.[24] Patrimonialism, while present, is far less salient in Botswana and Tunisia. In all cases, the very large scope of state determination of resource allocation, a product of colonial and integral state logic, offers a vast domain for the operation of prebendal logic.

The public policy implications of the prebendal logic are enormous. The contradiction between it and its fellow modes of state reason lie at the heart of the seeming paradox between the hard (overdeveloped) and the soft (underdeveloped) state. The pelf to which it gave rise reached, in extreme cases, extraordinary proportions, diverting—in Zaire and the Second Republic in Nigeria—such a large fraction of the public economy into privatized channels as to discredit, disempower, and bankrupt the state, while simultaneously driving an important part of the private economy underground. In 1989 in Cameroon, long regarded as a relatively well-managed state, the revenue lost to the state through diverse prebendal practices totaled 18–20 percent of GDP (see chap. 6). When corruption pervades the state apparatus, its authority corrodes. Viewed as a simple predator, its legitimacy evaporates; seen as private rental agency for unavoidable public services, its permeability is exploited but detested.

Prebendal logic creates the "rhizome state," whose surface institutions are less critical than its underground root structure, whose "bulbs and tubercules it secretly nourishes, and from which it extracts its vital force."[25] Stretching upward from civil society are tendrils of kinship obligation, extending by survival circumstances over enlarging orbits of affinity and fertilized by the "economy of affection."[26] While the persistence of these modalities of civil society-state connection sustains the tissues of the polity, they contribute to the incapacities for rational management of the public weal. In those instances where the predatory tendencies inherent to this form of state remained within limits and where resources are sufficient, one might argue the viability of the polity (Côte d'Ivoire, Kenya, Zimbabwe, Gabon).[27] But the more flagrant cases of unrestrained predation lead to a

delapidation of public finance, a tumultuous depreciation of the currency, an unprecedented fluctuation of prices, the decay of institutions and decline of political authority. . . . The bulk of national resources became in practice part of the "eminent domain" of an autocrat acting as a mercenary vis-à-vis state funds and the national treasury. . . . A dense network of influences were woven between the merchants, usurers, and brokers involved in contraband and speculative activities, on the one hand, and those holding administrative and political power, on the other. . . . At the same time, the organs charged with administration of violence (police, army, private militias) became increasingly autonomous, leading to a growing criminalization . . . in state interventions against society (rackets, murders, summary executions, violent confiscation of properties by . . . turbulent and miserable soldiers, dishonest tax collectors . . .).[28]

Over time, the synthesis of colonial-integral-prebendal state logics was unsustainable. The state crisis first became visible about 1980, when the bankruptcy of economic policy became apparent. Independence came in relatively favorable circumstances for the public economy, whose expansion during the 1960s to accommodate both integral and prebendal state reason was financed by the substantial flow of new foreign aid. The economy was sustained in the 1970s by external borrowing. By 1980, the outer limits had been reached.

The initial therapy was economic. Although the remedies proposed were of apolitical intent, in reality the formulas associated with structural adjustment struck hard at the existing multiple reasons of state. Government retrenchment, privatization, and the dismantling of parastatal monopolies assaulted the vision of the integral state. External monitoring of economic reform and transparency devices—however limited their effectiveness—attacked the prebendal state. There was, thus, a political subtext implicit in economic reform. Structural adjustment presumed a Weberian state: greatly reduced in its proportions and responsibilities, far more rational in its operation. The epigram of President Abdou Diouf of Senegal captured these implications: "moins d'état, mieux d'état."

The conjunctural consensus by 1990 that liberalization could not be pursued in the economic realm alone partly reflects a conclusion—particularly pronounced in the external community—that for structural adjustment to succeed required a more direct assault upon integral and prebendal state logics. The overlapping but distinct catchwords, *governance* and *democratization*, became seen as necessary vehicles for accountability and transparency. Externally negotiated economic reform packages were insufficient: civil society was required as an ally, activated by a new stress on human rights, the rule of law (an *état de droit* in place of the integral-prebendal state), and participation. One may note in passing the visionary construction of civil society embedded within what is popularly if imprecisely known as the new *political conditionality*. The imagined community will comport itself according to abstract rational choice theory, with its wisely calculated material interests corresponding to the technocratic designs of finance ministries, central banks, and international donor agencies. A newly discovered general will, in its Rousseauvian finery, will naturally choose economic liberalization. As diverse skeptics point out, such a happy outcome is not likely.[29]

Within Africa, *governance* had little resonance, but *democratization* swiftly became a concept of singular force. Here, the thorough delegitimation of rulers and regimes—within a context of sharply declining well-being, especially for urban middle and lower classes—was the catalytic element. Democracy was a lever by which would-be life presidents could be removed, opening vistas of improvement of a now intolerable living condition.

In the present conjuncture, there is no alternative to both economic and political liberalization. Both are imperative to offer the possibility of escape from the impasse, whose political origins have been argued. The excessive concentration—often monopolization—of economic power in the state produced by colonial and integral state logics goes far beyond the capacities of the polity for its effective exercise. The comprehensive parastatalization of the economy yields irrationalities and a bloated apparatus, whose infirmities are now beyond dispute. The configuration of reform that best resolves the growth-versus-equity dilemma poses a host of difficult choices, for which neither international financial institution doctrine nor Economic Commission for Africa analysis supply certain formulas. But the need to embark on a quest for reform is unmistakable. Similarly, in the political realm a remoralization of the state and a relegitimation of the polity are prerequisites for recovery.

Perhaps more important, the coalescence of forces demanding democratization is so powerful, and the residual legitimacy of incumbent autocracies so shallow, that in nearly all cases some form of transition is in prospect. But it would be visionary to imagine that the current trend toward a political opening will enjoy uniform success and bring about a civic polity to sweep away the colonial-integral-prebendal state. The crucial issue now becomes the sustainability of political transitions. One must heed the sober warning of Jeffrey Herbst (chap. 8) that a comparative historical intuition should alert us to the likelihood that "many of the current attempts at political liberalization in Africa will fail." A large chasm separates a national conference and an institutionalized liberal polity. Any number of obstacles stand in the way of a pluralized state capable of managing an expanding economy. Indeed, two transitions of the present generation have already aborted (Sudan in 1989, Algeria in 1992). In Sudan, a military regime of unusually ruthless character, subordinated to elements of the National Islamic Front (NIF), swept away an elected government discredited by its indecisiveness and inability to end the civil war; in Algeria, the military struck preemptively to block an electoral sweep by the Front Islamique de Salut (FIS). As well, one needs to recollect the failed transitions in Ghana (1969 and 1979) and Nigeria (1979), in which high hopes had once been vested.

In some cases, incumbent regimes may succeed in containing democratization forces by seizing the initiative in liberalization and thus controlling it (Côte d'Ivoire, Gabon, Mauritania). To the extent that such reformed autocracies resemble semidemocratic polities such as Senegal or Gambia, with a degree of openness and political space for opposition but without alternation, they may prove viable (or at least an improvement). But politics may also revert to previous patterns with only very circumscribed alterations.

The security apparatus is an especially dangerous element in the posttransition equation. The very nature of personal autocracy led rulers to build armies according to an "ethnic security map."[30] Illustrative of these dangers is the restiveness of the Togo army since Gnassingbe Eyadema ceded the initiative to a national conference–designated prime minister. The inner core of the armed forces is not drawn simply from the small Kabre ethnic group of Eyadema but, on the Saddam Hussein Takriti model, from the more immediate affines of his home community. Neutralizing imbalances often deliberately constructed over two decades or more without triggering the army's intervention will be an extraordinarily delicate task. Transition tensions in Congo, Niger, and Zaire further illustrate this difficulty. Add to this the layer of field officers, in states such as Nigeria, who have closely observed the formidable enrichment of their superiors while in office, and one has a more mundane reason why the military may eagerly await symptoms of failure in democratic regimes (and why democratic regimes may find military cutbacks a way to pursue both economic and political liberalization).

Within civil society, innumerable survival shelters—religious, economic, and social—were constructed, operating largely in a twilight zone outside the formal polity. The evangelical and pentecostal Protestant sects along the west African coast, the integralist and heterodox variants of Islam in the Sahel (Shi'ites in northern Nigeria), indigenous prophetic movements (the Naparamo movement in northern Mozambique), and novel antisocial movements (the turbulent and violent student cults on Nigerian campuses in 1990) represent social forces difficult to incorporate into a civil polity. The economic networks of the parallel economy operate outside the public sphere. The long reign of autocracy has stifled the autonomous associational life in the public realm, which vitalizes a civil society in the institutionalized democratic polity. Decades of monopolization of political and social space by ruling parties and their ancillary organizations has left behind a vacuum that cannot be instantly filled.

In the most seriously deteriorated countries, the unravelling of the institutional fabric—public infrastructure, basic services, the government apparatus—is so far advanced that any alternative leadership that democratization might produce will have few resources or means to reconstruct a functioning state. Civil societies doubtless have far more modest expectations than the terrestrial paradise once promised, but even these limited hopes may be disappointed, with uncertain consequences for the sustainability of democratization. In the worst cases (Zaire, Liberia, Somalia, Ethiopia), where utterly discredited autocrats clung to power through a final paroxysm of destructive violence, the devastation is so far-reaching that successors even with democratic commitments face chaotic circumstances bereft of resources.

Political competition is likely to mobilize populist currents that conflict with economic reform imperatives. Here we come to the heart of the dilemma, which leads some careful analysts to argue the necessity of political formulas that insulate economic decisionmaking from populist passions.[31] But accountability and transparency require that structural adjustment programs be defended before civil society. Multiple parties do not eliminate prebendalism from politics, although they greatly increase the possibility of exposure. India and the Philippines offer sobering evidence of the way patrimonial combines can honeycomb and denature the electoral process. In India, "the desire of those in power to maintain their electoral support was in conflict with their intentions to implement solutions to pressing problems, and the former always won out."[32] The Weberian practitioner of the pure vocation of politics is as much an exaggerated ideal type as the Weberian bureaucrat.

Ethnicity, region, and religion were not exorcised by the autocratic rule that dominated for three decades. Indeed, in Ethiopia, Somalia, and Sudan, authoritarian rule and the brutal violence it engendered catalyzed new forms of consciousness and intensified older ones. But although these forms of cleavage inevitably entangle themselves in pluralist politics, they need not engulf the democratized state; formulas for constitutional engineering are available to contain politicized cultural pluralism within tolerable limits.[33] Competitive elections in Senegal (1978, 1983, 1988) did not foster partisan divisions along ethnic or religious lines, nor did they exacerbate cultural tensions. Communal factors also clearly weigh in—defining alignments in Mauritius, for example—but they interweave with other dimensions of partisanship. The local government and state elections in Nigeria in 1991 revealed complicated distributions of strength among competing parties, which underscore the complexity and indeterminacy of cultural pluralism in the African context and reinforce the argument that such institutional factors as electoral system, representational design, and party system enhance the sustainability of democratic forms of governance.[34]

Finally, not all forces that clamor for democratization are committed to a liberal polity. The more integralist wings of the NIF in Sudan and the FIS in Algeria propose an Islamic state that has no place for those who dispute its moral foundations. As well, aspirant life presidents such as Omar Bongo of Gabon appear converted to multiparty politics only as a new stratagem in an old game.

The very dynamic of transition is itself a source of peril. In many instances, the galvanizing force of the opposition groupings is entirely focused upon the incumbent ruler. The interminable 1991 national conference in Congo-Brazzaville was obsessed by the multiple misdeeds of Denis Sassou Nguesso, even though the euphoria of his disgrace proved ephemeral, as paralyzing disputes threatened to engulf his successors.[35] One may wonder what common goals beyond

an intense animosity toward Mobutu Sese Seko, however well jus-
tified, unite the Union Sacrée in Zaire. The ultimately fatuous nature
of the 1988 electoral slogan of the Senegalese opposition—*sopi,* or
undefined "change"—is a further illustration. The profound cynicism
of the populace toward the state and its agents, above all toward
"politicians," is another major obstacle. The widespread perception
of state as predator will not dissolve with a single election. Indeed,
a disquieting amount of the energies of democratization draw upon
this vast supply of disaffection with the personalized summit of power
and the state apparatus as a whole.

Democratization in reality has multiple trajectories, and these variations in pathway are likely to have an important effect on the sustainability of the transitions. Key variables include (1) the degree to
which political opening is orchestrated by incumbents, whether to
preserve an adapted form of rule (Côte d'Ivoire, Gabon) or to organize
their succession (Nigeria, perhaps Ghana); (2) the role of national
conferences in asserting the sovereign right to draft new covenants
(Benin, Togo, Niger, Mali, Congo-Brazzaville); (3) the degree to which
external brokerage and mediation is involved (Namibia, Liberia); (4)
the success in organizing elections that structure, rather than fragment, the polity (Zambia, Cape Verde, São Tomé and Príncipe); and
(5) the degree to which violent civil strife preceding political opening
defines and constrains the options (Angola, Ethiopia). Some environments for political liberalization (Senegal, Cape Verde) are far more
propitious than others (Zaire, Ethiopia).

If the core premise of this chapter—that some form of democratization is ineluctable in the vast majority of African states—is accurate,
we are then left with the crucial question of what determines the
sustainability of these political experiments. A number of factors may
determine the outcome. The obstacles are so many and economic
deprivation so constraining, that only the most robust optimist can
believe that all or even most will succeed in the simultaneous pursuit
of political and economic reform.

Sub-Saharan Africa is a zone of relatively intense intercommuni-
cation. Whatever the disappointments of pan-Africanism, the reciprocal influence of events within one state upon others is unusually
large. No better validation of this hypothesis can be offered than the
phenomenal contagion of the democratization movement itself or of
certain of its modalities, such as the national conference formula,
especially within the Francophonic sphere. Thus certain critical cases
will have a disproportionate impact; I cite three of pivotal influence:
Nigeria, South Africa, and the post–national conference regimes. Ni-

geria and South Africa stand out in terms of their sheer scale and potent regional impact; and the national conference was such a widely employed device for transition that a swift demise of most of the new regimes designed by this formula would disproportionately deflate hopes vested in democratization.

More broadly, democratic governance has become virtually a requisite for respectability in the international system of states. In this environment, African states that sustain their transitions are likely to enjoy special favor with the donor community and to have higher standing within Africa. Successful democratizers may serve as reference points against which the backsliders are judged, exemplars of the political good that serve as beacons of hope and aspiration for the disaffected in polities that relapse into military dictatorship. Restorationist autocracy may find itself on the defensive in ways that differ sharply from a past, when it was seen as a natural aspect of the African condition.

In states where the decay of institutional infrastructure has been pervasive—Zaire, Mozambique, Angola, Somalia, Ethiopia, Liberia, Sierra Leone—the potential for sustainable liberalization is far less than in Namibia, Senegal, Côte d'Ivoire, or Cameroon. The banalization of violence and the brutalization of not only state-society relationships but also everyday societal interactions has scarred the land and left behind a deeply distrustful citizenry.[36] A new constitution and competitive elections are not instant therapy for these wounds.

Institutional creativity will play a central role, in several ways. The ephemeral independence constitutions mostly failed to survive because they were wooden copies of metropolitan institutions. Liberal institutions, if they are to survive, need to be rooted in an African cultural heritage. In a fundamental sense, the estrangement that prebendal autocracy has created, alienating civil society from the state, lies not just in the economic and political realms but also in the cultural. The text of nationalism fundamentally errs in perceiving "no salvation by any appeal to Africa's own cultures and structures. . . . Africa's past . . . could offer no useable design for political action."[37] Civil society itself will fully flourish when the "baneful dichotomy between western influences and the majority tradition is overcome, building upon a fully indigenized Islam and Christianity, synthesized with precolonial traditions."[38] Interpretations of democracy need comparable moorings, which only the passage of time can make secure.

The concept of democracy was deformed by its appropriation by single-party or Leninist regimes, which failed to meet minimal tests of political openness. However, democracy's core principles and necessary procedures find expression in a variety of constitutional models.[39] At extraordinary historical moments, when foundational structures are being defined—as in South Africa—choices are open for an institutional design that fosters competition that does not rest simply upon ethnic, religious, or racial division. The practice—widespread in, and I believe unique to, Africa—of forbidding political parties directly based upon communal or regional segments is not necessarily antithetical to democracy.

In Nigeria, the visitor cannot fail to be impressed by the energies mobilized in such bodies as the Center for Democratic Studies and the National Electoral Commission to seek a transition built upon the political realities of the polity and to, at each stage, permit the incorporation of learning experiences from prior steps in the move toward the Third Republic. Whatever reservations one may have about the orchestration from the summit of the party, one cannot deny the subtlety and sophistication of the strategems.

Quality of leadership also makes an important difference. This variable is particularly troublesome, as such skills are very difficult to forecast. Ineptitude, however damaging it may be, is not necessarily in evidence during electoral campaigns.

When exclusionary political monopolies are disbanded, civil societies have new opportunities for self-definition. The manner in which this process occurs will play an important part in defining the outcome. One factor making the Ethiopian transition particularly difficult was the ethnicization that occurred under the regime of Mengistu Haile Marriam. The destruction of this regime was brought about by regional armed formations (Tigrean People's Liberation Front, Afar Liberation Front, Oromo Liberation Front, Eritrean Peoples' Liberation Front), whose actions provoked a reconstruction of social identities. With the collapse of the Afro-Marxist regime, a weak center confronts a civil society dominated by armed cultural pluralism. South Africa represents a case at the other end of the spectrum, with a civil society teeming with associational activity. Both economic and political liberalization will push the state out of space it once monopolized. Less certain, at this juncture, is how the vacuum will be filled.

The ideological form in which popular discontent finds expression is another critical question. The liberal market economy has no credible competitor. The implosion of state socialism spattered its debris upon socialist projects of all descriptions. Within Africa, although poor economic performance is not unique to socialist orientation, the generalized perception of the failure of such exemplary models as Ghana, Guinea, Tanzania, Mozambique, and Algeria opens the advocate of socialism to ridicule. African publics no longer expect the terrestrial paradise promised by anticolonial nationalism, but they do aspire to some escape from the dismal present. Under the best of circumstances, improvement will be slow, and more visible in World Bank documents than in *bidonvilles*. New forms of populist ideology, perhaps resurrecting elements of socialism, are likely to appear. How they become incorporated into the political process and coexist with the institutions of the liberalized political economy remain to be seen.

Finally, the role of the external world will have a major effect upon the outcomes. The end of the cold war removes the perversions of geostrategic global reason from external involvement in Africa, but also eliminates an important motivation for any role at all, particularly for the United States (and the former Soviet Union, which rapidly liquidated its African positions). Capital—public and private—will be in short supply in the 1990s, and Africa holds little attraction for the latter category. The resources for recovery cannot come entirely from within; self-reliance, however desirable, is not enough. The terms on which the debt issue is resolved, the capacity to design structural adjustment programs that take enough account of social dimensions to be politically viable in a democratized environment, the ability to support political liberalization in an unobtrusive way without imposition of alien blueprints: so many large uncertainties.

The time is ripe for a shift of focus from explaining transition to understanding the dynamics of sustainability of political liberalization over the longer haul. In contrast to economic reform, whose agenda has been largely dictated by the policy formulas and neoclassical concepts of the international financial institutions and donor community, political change is primarily defined from within. The amorphous discourse of *governance*, which serves as master noun for external reflection on political liberalization, offers only loose parameters (accountability, transparency, rule of law, predictability, constructive reciprocities, and the like).[40] Only empirical observation over time will permit inferences concerning the variables most decisive in shaping outcomes. Particular attention needs to be given to such crucial factors as institutional form and the consolidation of a civil society capable of articulating its preferences and serving as a counterpoise to state power. The ongoing dialectic of economic liberalization and political pluralization merits careful attention; in their reciprocal impact, there are possibilities for both painful tensions and mutual reinforcement. The interplay of the social forces freed by liberalization—cultural pluralism, class, generation, gender, and others—and by the constitutionalized state likewise beckons close observation.

The many forebodings notwithstanding, the political experiment (or gamble) of democratization is as unavoidable as it is indispensable. The pressures from within are too strong to deflect. And the discrediting of rule produced by the marriage of colonial, integral, and prebendal state logics is too thorough for a purely restorationist formula to be viable. The very uneven results from the decade of economic reform demonstrate the difficulty of the task. Integral liberalization, political as well as economic, offers only the possibility of ascent from the abyss. The political forms of the past carry a guarantee of failure. In the face of such stark alternatives, the choice is clear.

Notes

1. Donald Emmerson, "Political Economy of Democratization and the International System: Lessons for Africa," paper prepared for the Workshop on Democracy and Structural Adjustment in Africa in the 1990s, Madison, Wis., 1991.

2. Claude Ake, quoted in *West Africa* (October 14–20, 1991): 1717.

3. Claude Ake, "Rethinking African Democracy," *Journal of Democracy* 2, no. 1 (1991): 32–44, 32.

4. Tony Killick, *Development Economics in Action: A Study of Economic Policies in Ghana* (New York: St. Martin's, 1978).

5. Thomas J. Biersteker, *Multi-Nationals, the State, and Control of the Nigerian Ecomony* (Princeton: Princeton University Press, 1987).

6. See Walter Rodney, *How Europe Underdeveloped Africa*, rev. ed. (Washington, D.C.: Howard University Press, 1981).

7. Richard Rothstein, *The Weak in the World of the Strong* (New York: Columbia University Press, 1977).

8. Crawford Young, *Ideology and Development in Africa* (New Haven: Yale University Press 1982).

9. World Bank, *Sub-Saharan Africa: From Crisis to Sustainable Growth*, a Long Term Perspective Study (Washington, D.C.: World Bank, 1989).

10. Richard Sklar, "Democracy in Africa," in *Political Domination in Africa*, ed. Partick Chabal (Cambridge: Cambridge University Press, 1986).

11. Georges Nzongola-Ntalaja, "The African Crisis: The Way Out," paper prepared for the annual meeting of the African Studies Association, Chicago, 1988.

12. See Mamadou Diouf, "Eastern Europe as a Model of Social State Relationship in Political Thought in Senegal," paper prepared for the Conference on Relationships between State and Society in Africa and Eastern Europe, Bellagio, Italy, 1990.

13. Goran Hyden, *No Short Cuts to Progress: African Development Management in Comparative Perspective* (Berkeley: University of California Press, 1983).

14. World Bank, *Sub-Saharan Africa: From Crisis to Sustainable Growth*, 61.

15. As quoted in the proceedings of the African Leadership Forum, Conference on Security, Stability, Development and Cooperation in Africa, Addis Ababa, November 17–18, 1990.

16. As quoted in ibid.

17. Young, *Ideology and Development in Africa.*

18. Christian Coulon, *Le Marabout et le prince: Islam et pouvoir Senegal* (Paris: Pedone, 1981), 289–90.

19. Jean Copans, *Les Marabouts et l'arachide: la confrerie mouride et les paysans du Senegal* (Paria: Sycamore, 1980).

20. Mugongo, *Le Général Mobutu Sese Seko parle du nationalisme Zairois authentique* (Kinchasa: Okapi, 1972).

21. John Brace, "Land Tenure and Structural Adjustment," paper prepared for the Workshop on Democracy and Structural Adjustment in Africa in the 1990s, Madison, Wis., 1991.

22. Steven Lawry, "Structural Adjustment and Natural Resources," paper prepared for the Workshop on Democracy and Structural Adjustment in Africa in the 1990s, Madison, Wis., 1991.

23. Richard J. Joseph, *Democracy and Prebendal Politics in Nigeria: The Rise and Fall of the Second Republic* (New York: Cambridge University Press, 1987).

24. William Reno, "The Politics of Patrimonial Adaptation to Reform," paper prepared for the Workshop on Democracy and Structural Adjustment in Africa in the 1990s, Madison, Wis., 1991.

25. Jean-François Bayart, *L'Etat en Afrique: la politique du ventre* (Paris: Fayard, 1989).

26. Goran Hyden, *Beyond Ujamaa in Tanzania: Development and Uncaptured Peasantry* (Berkeley: University of Califorina Press, 1980).

27. Richard Sandbrook, *The Politics of Africa's Economic Stagnation* (Cambridge: Cambridge University Press, 1985).

28. Achille Mbembe, "Réformes politiques et logiques autoritaries en Afrique noire," 1991, typescript.

29. Thomas Callaghy, "Political Passions and Economic Interests: Comparative Reflections on Political and Economic Logics in Africa," paper prepared for the annual meeting of the American Political Science Association, San Francisco, 1990; Sandbrook, *The Politics of Africa's Economic Stagnation.*

30. Cynthia Enloe, *Ethnic Soldiers: State Security in Divided Societies* (Athens: University of Georgia Press, 1980).

31. Callaghy, "Political Passions"; Joan M. Nelson, ed., *Fragile Coalitions: The Politics of Economic Adjustment* (New Brunswick, N.J.: Transaction Books, 1990).

32. Atul Kohli, *Democracy and Discontent: India's Growing Crisis of Governability* (Cambridge: Cambridge University Press, 1990), 379.

33. Donald Horowitz, *Ethnic Groups in Conflict* (Berkeley: University of California Press, 1985).

34. Ibid.

35. *Jeune Afrique*, November 12, 1991.

36. Roland Marchal, "On Some Aspects of the Conflicts in Eritrea and the

Sudan," in *Conflict in The Horn of Africa,* ed. Georges Nzongola-Ntalaja (Atlanta: African Studies Association Press, 1991).

37. Basil Davidson, "The Challenge of Comparative Analysis: Anti-Imperialist Nationalism in Africa and Europe," paper prepared for the Conference on Relationships between State and Society in Africa and Eastern Europe, Bellagio, Italy, 1990, 7–8.

38. Jan Vansina, "A Past for the Future?" *Dalhousie Review* 68, nos. 1–2, (1989): 8–23, 21–23.

39. Giovanni Sartori, *The Theory of Democracy Revisited* (Chatham, N.J.: Chatham House, 1987); Giuseppi di Palma, *To Craft Democracies: An Essay on Democratic Transitions* (Berkeley: University of California Press, 1990).

40. Goran Hyden and Michael Bratton, eds., *Governance and Politics in Africa* (Boulder, Colo.: Lynne Rienner, 1992).

PART 4

EPILOGUE

ERNEST J. WILSON III

Creating a Research Agenda for the Study of Political Change in Africa

The purpose of this chapter is to raise and discuss a set of theoretical, conceptual, and methodological issues central to constructing a research agenda on political liberalization in sub-Saharan Africa. Starting in 1990, from the Cape to Cairo, from Mali to Madagascar, Africa has been swept by a tidal wave of political turbulence that rivals the sweep of national independence in the 1960s. A dozen governments have fallen, and ordinary Africans are drawn into the political arena in a variety of new ways, from religion-inspired rebellions in Algeria and Nigeria to explicit demands for liberal democracy throughout Francophone West Africa.

While these dramatic events are exciting and startling, they are also inherently ambiguous in their origins, their likely directions, their sustainability, and their impacts on different social strata and interests. Are we viewing fundamental political changes or merely a flash in the pan? Will the popular classes be empowered or further marginalized? Are the visible political changes prompted more by underlying structural shifts or by intraelite dissensions? This last question is not a trivial one. If the political changes in Africa are rooted in fundamental structural shifts in society and the economy, then we might anticipate that democratization is likely to be sustained, its impacts to be great, and its future direction to be predictable.[1] If on the other hand liberalization flows from dissension among competing elites and the temporarily internalized demonstration effects of similar changes in other countries, then it makes the movements toward democracy more problematic, superficial, and unpredictable. Whatever our personal normative sensibilities may be, these questions can be adequately answered only by further research that is theoretically explicit, conceptually clear, and deliberately comparative.

At the very moment when a sophisticated and widely accepted research agenda[2] on political liberalization would be especially useful as a positive guide to research, or even as a target of scholarly criticism, however, the African studies community in the United States and elsewhere is in a paradigmatic interregnum, when no social science model compellingly dominates our understanding of the continent.[3] The earlier scholarly excitement created by dependency, neo-Marxism, or other structuralist theories has decidedly waned. The appeal of large-scale historical political sociology or world systems approaches has also diminished, and they are attacked with gusto in the journals.[4] Rational choice approaches are on the rise but have as yet relatively few rigorous and theoretically self-conscious adherents in the field.[5] And while Africa is a particular case of this dilemma, our sister fields of Asian and Latin American studies are also experiencing a paradigmatic interregnum as scholars wrestle to understand these very turbulent times.[6]

Given this intersection of perplexing real world events with the absence of a ready and agreed upon research agenda, we are left with rather basic questions: How should we study these complex political changes taking place in Africa? What do we gain and lose when we follow the guidelines of one paradigm or another? In this chapter, I focus on two broad approaches to social science—structuralist and nonstructuralist—and identify their particular ways of setting up the research problem of African political liberalization. After identifying the strengths and weaknesses of each, I suggest an alternative model, which I call a *modified structuralist model*, with its own distinctive research agenda that I believe is superior to the structuralist or nonstructuralist alone.

Four Research Imperatives

Constructing a research agenda on African political liberalization that draws on several different models provides the opportunity to build a cumulative social science discourse that will improve the quality of empirical work and theory building in African studies. As scholars, we can use the models to generate competing research hypotheses, which can be confirmed or disconfirmed in light of different

African countries' experiences with liberalization. As we design such studies, we should remain sensitive to four imperatives.

First, precisely because democratization and liberalization are so very important, so timely, and so hotly contested, there is an understandable urge to rush to judgment. This is especially the case when, normatively, most scholars are probably committed in principle to seeing democracy grow and flourish in Africa after so many years of democratic drought. Our first imperative, therefore, is to avoid reaching premature conclusions based on limited data.[7] One wants to avoid using a few facts from a single case to make generalizations about the continent as a whole. Reform in Nigeria is not the same as reform in "Africa." Reform in Senegal is not the same as reform in Zaire. There is also the danger of relying too heavily on what economists called stylized facts—illustrative stories and examples selectively drawn from several places across the continent but not collected in a systematic and scientific way. Instead, one should conduct research driven by consistent questions and hypotheses derived from theory and tested against evidence from carefully selected research sites. This is especially important in the early stages of studying a phenomenon, when even the most basic information may be lacking and underlying trends have yet to emerge.[8]

Second, one should avoid designing the project solely on the basis of the dependent variable one wants to explore.[9] It is insufficient to study, for example, only examples of democratization. There must be a comparison between cases where liberalization occurred and cases where it did not. But countries can be selected as well according to variation in the independent variable. If one believes that economic dislocation causes political reforms, then one can construct the research project by selecting a sample of countries where economic dislocation ranges from severe to slight and then examine whether democratization varies systematically with dislocation.

Third, scholars should be especially sensitive to the longitudinal aspects of political liberalization. What has been the historical experience of democratization and liberalization through time?[10] Within one African country, what factors have shaped the historical ebb and flow of political openness and repression? For example, many claims are made about the "necessary" relationship among economic liberalization, economic growth, and political democracy. But precisely what has been the relationship between the expansion of the political arena and economic growth in Africa? Political independence and liberalization in the early 1960s came to Africa on the back of rising international commodity markets, and the economy and the polity expanded together. Today, political liberalization comes on the back of falling markets and shrivelling economies; the polity is expanding as the economy shrinks. How can we account for these very different outcomes? How did economic change affect elite and mass attitudes and behavior in the early 1960s, and how does it affect these same groups today? A thorough research agenda should address these questions.

At the broadest level, one could revisit the earlier efforts of scholars affiliated with the Social Science Research Council to find patterned sequences of modernization. They sought sequential and putatively universal challenges of penetration, control, legitimacy, and so forth.[11] Later evidence challenged these theories of political development. Although it produced stimulating work, the history of that scholarly semihistorical enterprise suggests that considerable prudence is necessary before claiming to find strict temporal patterns in contemporary political reforms.

The dominant effort to identify sequences today (but not to explain them) is the three-step sequence of economic reform developed by the World Bank and the International Monetary Fund.[12] They claim that successful reforms proceed from stabilization through structural adjustment to institutional reform, expanded investment, and growth. A parallel approach has been advanced for political reform. Richard Joseph and others have contributed to conceptualizing African liberalization and postulate eight phases through which modern African political reforms typically pass: decay, political mobilization, political decisionmaking, transition, electoral contest, handing over power, legitimation, and consolidation.[13] For both constructs, we want to know whether these stages do in fact occur as described. Are they always in the order described? Are there always identifiable breaks between the phases in each model?

Fourth—less straightforward but with the greatest potential intellectual payoff—is cross-level analysis: examining the origins and dynamics of political reform across levels of social action, from the individual to the macro. The challenge of doing good cross-level analysis is perhaps one of the most central, difficult, and long-standing issues of social science. Phrased somewhat differently, to account for the origins, course, and sustainability of political liberalization in Africa, should one begin at the micro level of social action, the macro level, or somewhere in between? In other words, when starting out to study this phenomenon, where should one pitch one's work to gain the greatest theoretical purchase?

Structuralist versus Nonstructuralist Approaches to the Study of Political Liberalization in Africa

The structuralist approach begins with those relatively enduring features of society that change rarely and usually only over long periods of time, including class, ethnic, and regional divisions. Demographic factors are also key, especially population distribution and size and the sectoral makeup of the political economy. Thus, when comparing political liberalization, structuralists analyze and compare these variables to discover how they determine cross-unit differences in reform.

For example, if in one African country the class structure is dominated by a large, urban business class rooted in trade, regionally divided, and nested within a large ethnically variegated population (e.g., Nigeria), then the institutions and politics generated by this social structure should reflect these broad features. Hence, the politics of reform there should differ substantially from reform politics in a country with a class structure dominated by a civil service elite and where most ethnic groups are relatively small (e.g., Tanzania). Different levels or forms of political liberalization should be associated with and caused by different structural features, such as the degree of urbanization or the nature of class interactions and class power.[14] From such a model one could generate plausible and detailed hypotheses for a structuralist research agenda. For example, the greater the size of the indigenous business class, the greater the likelihood of liberalization; or the greater the urbanization, the greater the likelihood of liberalization; or the higher the GNP per capita, the greater the likelihood of liberalization. There are, of course, many brands of structuralists, from Marxists to dependency theorists to some Weberians. They share an insistence that good comparative analysis should concentrate on the structural features of society.

Let us contrast this approach to scholars rooting their study of liberalization at the micro level. Microanalysts would start with the individual, insisting that differences in individual behaviors, preferences, and beliefs best account for variations in political reform. Working at this level are students of political leadership, behavioralists, and public or rational choice theorists.

Rational choice theorists might formulate their main research question as: Why do rational individuals, who know what they want (preferences), driven mainly by material interests (motivations), and who know what's going on (information), choose greater political democracy? Such analysts would probably devote their scholarly energy to thinking through, deductively, the ways that individual members of various collectivities (large farmers, small farmers, bureaucrats, etc.) calculate their optimal interests and actions and how they act on them. In keeping with the neoclassical origins of the approach, rational choice theorists might articulate the liberalization process in Africa in terms of the demand for and supply of political reform.

Students of political leadership might explore individual leadership styles and the personal histories of heads of states for explanations as to why some countries liberalize more quickly or more thoroughly than others.[15] They might examine the patron-client ties linking the leader to his closest collaborators and how these ties constrain his options for political reform.

Microtheorists in the behavioral tradition, on the other hand, might conduct attitude surveys of many individuals' (especially voters') views of political liberalization and examine how they differ from country to country as a function of the individual's education, age, income, gender, or ethnic group. Such a scholar might then extrapolate from the actually observed sample of individuals to make more general statements about the nature of the reform process for Africa as a whole.

Although there are substantial differences between these subapproaches, all three share an emphasis on individuals and the motives and calculations they make in politics.

The Strengths and Weaknesses of the Two Approaches

Both approaches have their own internal logic and way of framing the research inquiry into political liberalization. Both bring advantages and disadvantages to the study of political liberalization in Africa. For structuralists, there is already a rich theoretical literature on structural determinants of political outcomes in Africa. Concepts like *class* are relatively well spelled out, and some scholars articulate clear if different arguments about class's relationship to political outcomes.[16] Since the reforms are occurring throughout the continent (and indeed the world), then it is likely that very broad and basic phenomena are involved that are structural in nature. In methodological terms, a strict structuralist interpretation can with relative ease identify and specify the independent variable in the cause-effect chain—urbanization, white-collar employment, foreign investment, and so forth. Furthermore, in the African research context it is far easier to obtain genuinely comparable data on these structural features than on individual-level variables, which require more detailed and difficult fieldwork.

There are also distinct limitations to structural approaches to liberalization. Within Africa, broad underlying structures are often surprisingly similar from one country to the next. Most are heavily rural, agricultural, poor, and monocrop, have a tiny elite and a large uneducated peasantry; and are dominated by foreign companies. Yet the politics and economic policies of neighboring similarly structured countries are often quite different, which presents a problem for a strictly structuralist analysis. "If the causal property . . . is . . . a personalization of power at the summit, its very discovery will preclude a very delicate structural explanation. . . . Even the minutest comparative study of their structures will not serve to explain the disparities of their political fortunes."[17]

Furthermore, when we look at structural explanations within countries, in longitudinal terms, we confront another problem. Since the dependent variable one wants to explain—political liberalization or democratization—has explosively appeared only since about 1989, it may be awkwardly accommodated by strict structuralist theories. By definition, structures are aggregates that change rarely and slowly.[18] Precisely because these factors do operate at such a general level, there is a long and sometimes indistinct chain of causality between macro factors and political liberalization. Too often these theories do not spell out in sufficient detail the precise mechanisms that link cause and effect. Too often they assume a kind of functionalism that makes their analyses overly mechanistic. Finally, these theories tend to underestimate the role of individual initiatives and the options for choice that such units possess, whether the units are individual people or individual states.

Not surprisingly, the strengths of the microlevel approaches like rational choice or behavioralism mirror the weaknesses of the structural.[19] They provide far greater appreciation for and analysis of the many small contingencies involved in African political reform movements. Daily press reports out of Africa and personal visits confront one with more apparent chaos than clear pattern. By emphasizing choice, randomness, and strategy, the proactive activities of individuals and their efforts to improve their political position vis-à-vis other actors, these micro models capture much of the contemporary politics of reform. Since contingency and chaos loom so large in the recent reforms, any approach that captures them must appeal to scholars of comparative liberalization. Furthermore, the rational choice approach is often superior in its treatment of cross-level linkages, helping to formalize and render more precise cross-level and intervening ties, especially between individual and institutional levels (rational choice models) and between leaders and coalitions (leadership models). In this period of constitution writing and rule making, where the role of individual political brokers and entrepreneurs is so very important, recent work in this tradition (the new institutionalism) can offer real insights into the strategic calculations of politicians acting under uncertainty as they design new rules of the game.[20] It may also help us understand the more medium-term impact of reforms, in light of the new institutional incentives that are put in place under the reforms.[21]

What are the weaknesses of the strict microlevel approaches? A major problem is their difficulty in accounting for the global and continental nature of the pressures for political reform. Without using structural variables, they cannot easily explain why individual preferences for greater democratization should appear all around the world at nearly the same time. In addition, micro analyses tend to concentrate on the present and to heavily discount the past. They examine the current distribution of assets, resources, and incentives but may ignore the origins and evolution of these distributions. Also, in the rational choice version (but less so in others), there is only a thin notion of the importance of culture when accounting for cross-national political differences.[22] Rational choice accounts of reform may also take a very narrow focus on material motives and overlook or undervalue community, altruism, and autonomy as incentives for individual and collective political action.

Toward a Modified Structuralist Model

In order to advance my arguments for constructing a cross-level research agenda on political liberalization and democracy, I have deliberately drawn the structuralist and nonstructuralist models as dichotomous. Besides its heuristic value, this sharp distinction does reflect, I believe, the way most writers actually organize their research and writing. Scholars tend to operate mainly at only one of these two levels: they theorize at one level; the other becomes residual.[23] They do not necessarily seek explicit links between the levels. Macro and micro remain as very different starting points and preferred fields of analysis.

If descriptions of the relationship between political liberalization and broad social changes appear truncated, thin, and only partially realized when scholars restrict themselves to narrow, nonstructural approaches like rational choice or leadership studies, and if strictly structural models omit too many intervening variables between putatively determinative macro variables and behavioral ones, and if scholars also underexamine individual strategies and choice, then what can they do to overcome the limitations of strict structuralism and strict nonstructuralism? How can we better situate the study of democratization and liberalization within a fuller range of cause and effect than we see offered by these two models?

Some scholars have tried to bridge this theoretical gap in the study of political reform in Eastern Europe, Latin America, Africa, and elsewhere. In an excellent review essay, Ellen Comisso conceptualizes the search for explanations of political and economic reform in exactly these contrasting micro-macro terms.[24] Some of the writers she reviews locate the origins of reform in socialist Eastern Europe within the increasing factionalism and diverging institutional and political interests of the ruling elite. For these authors, the sharp competition for power ruptured intraelite accords and eventually led to the collapse of the communist system. Other writers find the causes of collapse in the very nature of authoritarian, antidemocratic political systems and their accompanying state ownership and control of the economy, structural features that are at the heart of socialism. For structuralists, broader underlying shifts eroded the system, like the change toward more white-collar labor and the fundamental contradiction between nationalist closed systems and an increasingly open world trading system. Barbara Geddes on Latin America and Michael Bratton and Nicolas van de Walle on Africa are other scholars who take structure and agency seriously.[25]

All of these efforts make excellent beginnings. But one wants to go beyond them to bring greater precision to at least three underdeveloped areas, which are also neglected areas in the strict structuralist and strict nonstructuralist approaches described above. One is the need to bring greater specificity to the concepts of *structural* and *nonstructural*. Second, one wants sharper and more sustained analysis of the relationship between the effects of differences at one level on outcomes at another level, especially through the concept of *nesting*, where levels are conceived of as nesting one inside the other, with mixed amounts of autonomy and determination. Third, one needs to conceptualize an intermediate level between the macro social and the micro social. My solution to these and other theoretical and methodological challenges is a modified structural model.

A modified structuralist model concentrates solely on neither the macro level nor the micro level. Instead, it links them by conceptualizing a third, intermediate, level—the meso level, which encompasses institutions and their elites as well as elites in coalition. To account for political reform, the modified structuralist model concentrates directly on the intersection of structure and choice, or what I term the *politics of structure*. By this I mean the conscious and explicit effort by a social actor to rewrite and restructure the rules, regulations, and norms in a sphere of society (such as a market or polity). Social actors try to alter the rules of the game such that outcomes generated tend to favor that social actor (whether individual or aggregate actors).[26] This modified structuralist model looks beyond conventional politics, in which social actors accept the rules of the game and operate within them, and concentrates on the ways actors modify existing structures. It assumes that important cross-national differences in structure are mainly responsible for differences in the patterns of reform. Since genuine liberalization and democratization require substantial rule changes, they are excellent examples of the politics of structure.

A modified structuralist model assumes that strata and groups are differentially placed in a vertical social structure and that they have unique positions, perspectives, interests, and access to resources. Actors struggle to gain both a one-time, short-term advantage and sustained, long-term benefit streams by rewriting the rules of the political economy.[27] The logic of this structuralist position is that strata, groups, and individuals located within a particular structure of opportunities and resources will calculate their positions within that structure and act accordingly. Where these structural regularities hold from one country to another, we can expect that other nonstructural, meso or micro patterns will reflect those continuities.

In this model, structure helps shape and guide coalitions and institutions. Broad societal structures like class provide the raw material from which political entrepreneurs fashion stable coalitions to provide a base for governing or other concerted political action, including rule changing. Coalitions are meso level aggregates, lying between broad structures and individuals. Coalitions are self-consciously constructed aggregates of social elements (elites) who typically share some common, overlapping definitions of self-interest and who act in concert on a particular range of issues—but not all issues. Unlike other aggregates (e.g., tribes or ethnic groups), there is more deliberate volition and choice involved in coalition membership and defection. For their part, institutions are repeatable patterns of human interaction, often site- and function-specific, such as bureaucracies, armies, or chieftancies. Through processes like socialization, they exercise an influence on individuals that is beyond the choice and volition of the individual. They also reflect—in their functions, their organizational forms, and their capacities—the broader structures within which they are embedded.

Where structure does not provide the raw material for a political coalition, it is extremely unlikely that such interests will be powerfully represented within a coalition. They are simply structurally unavailable. A country that lacks an industrial bourgeosie is highly unlikely to have powerful industrial elites within its coalition. Structure does not, however, completely determine all aspects of mesolevel coalitions and institutions. There is substantial evidence in all areas that the national political leadership may act independently to promote certain policies that favor certain economic interests, even in the absence of a strong local constituency. The export-oriented industrialization of the newly industrialized countries of Asia comes to mind, as do the pro-reform policies of President Ibrahim Babangida in Nigeria; in both cases the necessary political constituencies were rudimentary, yet the government pressed ahead. However, these examples are probably the exceptions that prove the rule. More empirical work must be done on the relationships among coalition, leadership, and policy in Africa.

Nested Levels of Social Action: Macro, Meso, and Micro

Scholars in the rational choice tradition have tried to theorize about cross-level interactions. For the most part, however, they restrict their focus to relatively narrow bands of incentive-behavior (or structure-agent) interactions—that is, interactions between the individual and the organization. Concretely, much of the current scholarship focuses on the ways representatives in the U.S. Congress devise legislative rules (often in congressional committees and subcommittees) and the ways those rules in turn shape the behavior of the members.[28] A modified structural model might apply similar logic to the relationships between structural features like sectoral and class structures at one level and between coalitions and institutional rules on the meso level.

How can we understand these cross-level relationships? Although a modified structural approach would privilege structural features, it also assumes that each of the three levels—macro, meso, and micro—retains some degree of autonomy from the other two. This model is thus different from the strict macro and micro models in two ways. First, it puts cross-level links centrally into the analysis, whereas the other, "pure," versions are more monolevel in their focus: modified structuralism both describes and theorizes about more than one level.

Second, the modified model does not assume that one level always determines the others. To the degree that strict structuralists study nonstructural factors, they assume that, in the last instance, the latter mainly determine the former; conversely, microtheorists assume that the individual level determines the macro. The modified structural model assumes that the precise degree of determination and autonomy cannot be perfectly known a priori. Theoretically, it presumes a high degree of structural determination. However, the full answer is partly an empirical one, resolved through careful analysis, within a precise historical context, of all three levels and their interactions.

At least three distinct interpretations are possible of the degree of determination of the nonstructural by the structural. A strict structuralist would argue that structure determines all, with virtually no possibility for autonomous action or initiative at individual or meso levels. Subordinate levels (individuals and institutions or groups) have little room for maneuver. The opposite interpretation of complete level autonomy would define the relationship among the three as random. In the third interpretation, the structural level provides a constraining framework within which the other two levels are bound, or embedded. Actions at the subordinate levels are substantially shaped by determining structures. It is highly improbable that within a given society any outcome at the micro and meso levels would lie outside the range of possibilities shaped by the structural. As I noted earlier, a poor nonindustrialized society with no manufacturing to speak of (and hence no major manufacturing class) is unlikely to produce a political coalition (at the meso level) in which manufacturers are powerful, central actors. To this degree, structure will broadly determine coalition by establishing the probable outer boundaries of likely outcomes. Coalitional and institutional resources, rules, and opportunities will in turn shape individual options and behaviors. However, structure does not necessarily determine the exact composition of the coalition nor the precise public policies that any given coalition may choose to design and pursue.

Within the structurally defined space of society, then, outcomes are contingent, probabilistic, and not inevitable.[29] A modified structuralist model tries to indicate the likely limits of institutional forms, policy outcomes, and coalition politics, including the politics of political liberalization and democracy. It cannot, however, predict the exact content of liberalizing politics and policy. Indeed, a great challenge to studying movements of democratization and liberalization is that, even though they are occurring simultaneously throughout Africa and even though they seem to share certain common features, each retains a number of unique aspects. (One need only consider the differences between "reform" in Russia and "reform" in China.)

Some Hypotheses

How might a modified structuralist model frame research questions capable of teasing out the cross-national or cross-regional similarities and differences in the phenomenon of African political liberalization? First, this model, unlike others, would presume that such broad questions are worth asking, would try to answer them, and would assume that the answers will lead to new information, new interpretations, and a better understanding of why political reform is occurring at once in so many countries. Second, this model would presume that its research propositions be confirmed or disconfirmed. Third, given its trilevel focus, the model would resist any single-factor explanation of reform (i.e., leadership changes or World Bank pressures). Instead, it would search widely in the environment for possible explanations.

Because this model assumes that rule-making power is central and that the interaction of economic, political, and social causation is critically important, the factors originating, sustaining, or blocking liberalization could be political or economic, domestic or international. These are continuities with gradations, not sharp divisions. If this is so, then this insight should be central to the study of reform and not added as an afterthought.

The following hypotheses are compatable with a modified structuralist model of the type I propose here. (I do not argue that these hypotheses can be generated only by this model, only that this model is likely to generate them—that they are compatible with its theoretical and methodological assumptions.) Some of these hypotheses are mainly structural, others more micro. Ultimately, the challenge is to integrate the structural and the nonstructural into a single explanation.

A more structuralist position might hypothesize that the origins of liberalization in Africa lie in the very nature of international capitalism. The spirit and institutional incentives of this world system press all constituent units to conform to capitalist norms and procedures. As the keystone institutions of international capital, the World Bank and the International Monetary Fund impose structural adjustment programs on governments. The argument applies as well to the United States, France, or other capitalist nations that impose political and economic conditionality on governments in Togo, Zaire, or Kenya. These pressures are as political as they are economic, because they often contain explicit political or administrative conditions of transparency, openness, and participation and because their intent is to force African governments to take actions they otherwise would not take in order to transform their economies into capitalist ones. These pressures produce, in turn, demands for political liberalization. This is the *external pressure* hypothesis: those African countries with the strictest structural adjustment programs should experience the greatest political reform.

A second structuralist hypothesis would locate the origins of political liberalization in Africa in the rise of new strata in the local class structure. In this explanation, state-led economic expansion in certain areas of the economy has generated new social forces (elites) that have new political and economic interests and new material and organizational resources. National development, previously promoted almost exclusively by governments, created the conditions for the rise of a domestic commercial class or an incipient bourgeoisie that favors the introduction of wider political participation and greater market forces into areas once the preserve of government bureaucrats.[30] The expansion of bourgeois political rights helps this new class protect its economic interests. This class—professionals, white-collar workers, businessmen—form the constituency for political liberalization in Africa. Therefore, this hypothesis asserts that countries with the fastest growing middle class will experience the greatest political liberalization.

A third hypothesis states that political reform is linked to the international business cycle. During a trough in the business cycle, global market demand declines, dampening domestic economic activity. As a result, export earnings and tax revenues decline. Faced with a shrinking resource base, governments refuse to continue subsidizing certain programs judged nonessential or that impose large financial costs on the state. However, these deflationary measures anger key political constituencies, who rebel against the government and demand more political participation in setting government policies. This hypothesis, as does the first hypothesis, finds the cause not only in direct external political and economic pressures but in more indirect market pressures, which hit especially hard because of domestic economic disequilibria and political tyranny. Both hypotheses work through the actions of domestic political constituencies and elites.[31] Thus, countries with the widest boom and bust cycles will have the most extensive reform programs.

Once the structural analysis is completed and the structural boundaries evaluated, the modified structuralist model turns to nonstructural factors like leadership and sociopolitical learning. Coalition leaders in African countries are keenly aware of new developments in other countries. Anxious to remain in power, they try to follow the example of leaders in other countries who have successfully adapted to political demands in order to remain in power, even in turbulent times. These elites promote their own versions of liberalization before more radical solutions are imposed upon them by local populations or foreign lenders. Diffusion and demonstration effects are especially likely to occur between countries in the same region (i.e., Francophone West Africa) but also across regions (i.e., Eastern Europe and Africa). Individuals and groups in the political opposition also learn from these prodemocracy forces in their region and around the world. Therefore, liberalization in Africa is the result of demonstration effects and cross-border copying. Stated as a hypothesis, political reform is most likely to occur in countries that share borders with reforming neighbors.

These several hypotheses are the kind of answerable questions that a good research agenda should be capable of suggesting to scholars. One would carefully examine the links between broad structural differences between countries, or within one country through time, and the mesolevel or microlevel manifestations of those changes as expressed in the demands for greater democracy and political liberalization. In practice, this requires developing compatable hypotheses that operate at different levels of analysis but that can be fashioned into a single, internally consistent, model. For example, the *external pressure* hypothesis can usefully be melded with both the structuralist *new class* argument and the nonstructuralist *social learning* hypothesis. By doing so, one could construct a more complete and internally consistent explanation of political reform in Africa than could be produced using a single, monolevel hypothesis alone.

Conclusion

In this chapter, I argue that studying processes as complex and contradictory as liberalization and democratization in Africa demand from the scholar a well-defined focus and a broad-ranging review of the empirical and theoretical materials in order to craft the nuanced theories and explanations the subject requires. One approach is to construct a research agenda that identifies the critical questions and then indicates ways one might answer them. The essential ingredients of such an agenda are that the research be genuinely comparative, conceptually clear, and theoretically explicit. The scholarship also should be historically rooted, sensitive to earlier African experiences with the expansion and contraction of the political arena. These core elements provide the starting point for a comparative political economy research agenda, whatever the particular model the scholar uses—Marxist, pluralist, public choice, historical political sociology, and so forth.

Using this modified structuralist model, the researcher avoids reaching premature and perhaps unwarranted conclusions. For example, it is certainly the case that not all political changes we observe today in Africa can be called democratization; and if some are now the genuine article, it is highly unlikely that all will persist over time. If these are not accompanied by underlying structural changes, I am skeptical that liberalization and democratization will persist in Africa. This is not to deny that the process of liberalization will not be advanced through these changes. Rather, we should remember that democratization elsewhere in the world proceded in fits and starts, with alternating failures and successes over many years.[32] The modified structuralist model also suggests extreme caution in extrapolating empirical findings from one national (or even subnational) setting to another. Different structural conditions and the heavy hand of contingency make such extrapolition very risky in Africa today.

I propose a particular way of studying political liberalization in Africa, which provides more analytic leverage than other models. It was constructed as a response to the strengths and weaknesses of two alternative approaches to the study of political reform—structuralist and nonstructuralist—with special emphasis on rational choice, nonstructuralist theories. It is not that these two approaches are wrong; rather, in their strictest form, they are very limited. Given these limitations, I propose that a useful way of studying political reform is to work directly at the intersection of structure and choice, an approach especially well suited to current developments in Africa.

In any essay, one must omit much more than one includes. For example, I fail to consider the more epistemological issue of whether the search for explicit cross-national hypotheses about causation is the best way to enhance our understanding of liberalization. More interpretive approaches—essays, ethnographic literature, even novels—may tell us a great deal about the contradictory ways Africans interpret and respond to current economic and political crises and opportunities. Indeed, a complete understanding of African transitions demands that we take interpretive work seriously. We need to let the participants in this great human drama tell their own story in their own words and using their own indigenous categories. It is one thing for rational choice theorists to tell us why Africans choose to do what they do, or for structuralists to tell us why Africans must do what they do, it is quite another for Africans to tell about these brand new developments in their own voices.

Notes

1. I distinguish between political *liberalization* and *democratization*. These two terms have been confused in the discussions of political changes in Africa. Political *liberalization* refers to steps by the state elite to reduce state control over such political institutions and political activities as interest articulation, interest aggregation, and representation. It means greater liberty, such as fewer restrictions on the press, reduced political surveillance and harassment, less banning of political parties, and so forth. It is essentially the removal of restrictions. *Democratization*, by contrast, typically involves the positive introduction and expansion of political rights, resources, and institutions. The latter might be genuinely competitive elections, new political rights for minorities or women, or an increased number of political parties. While liberalization suggests unilateral state action to reduce state interference, democratization often involves nonstate as well as state actors to build up civil society's capacity for independent action.

2. By *research agenda* I mean an internally coherent set of interlocking questions that identifies and prioritizes issues in terms of their importance and that provides a strategy for answering those questions. Such agendas are especially useful when they focus scholarly attention on a core set of problems and when they spur open and honest debate over the priorities assigned to the topics.

3. Barbara Geddes, "Paradigms and Sand Castles in the Comparative Politics of Developing Countries," in *Political Science: Looking to the Future*, ed. William Crotty, vol. 2 (Evanston: Northwestern University Press, 1991).

4. Edgar Kiser and Michael Hechter, "The Role of General Theory in Comparative Historical Sociology," *American Journal of Sociology* 97, no. 1 (1991): 1–30.

5. Ernest J. Wilson III, and Howard Stein, "The Political Economy of Robert Bates: A Critical Reading of Rational Choice in Africa," *World Development* 21 (1993): 1035–53.

6. Geddes, "Paradigms"; and Richard Doner, "Explaining the Politics of Economic Growth in Southeast Asia," *Journal of Asian Studies* 50, no. 4 (1991): 818–49.

7. Larry Sirowy and Alex Inkeles, "The Effects of Democracy on Economic Growth and Inequality: A Review," *Studies in Comparative International Development* 25, no. 1 (1990): 126–57.

8. Ernest J. Wilson III, "World Politics and International Energy Markets," *International Organization* 41, no. 1 (1987): 125–50.

9. Barbara Geddes, "How the Cases You Choose Affect the Answers You Get: Selection Bias in Comparative Politics," *Political Analysis* 2 (1990): 131–50.

270 ERNEST J. WILSON III

10. Kenneth Bollen, "Political Democracy and the Timing of Development," *American Sociological Review* 44, no. 4 (1979): 572–87, 583.

11. Leonard Binder et al., *Crises and Sequences in Political Development* (Princeton: Princeton University Press, 1971).

12. World Bank, *Adjustment Lending: An Evaluation of Ten Years' Experience* (Washington, D.C.: World Bank, 1988).

13. See Richard Joseph, "Africa: The Rebirth of Political Freedom," *Journal of Democracy* 2, no. 4 (1991): 11–24; Stephen P. Riley, "The Democratic Transition in Africa," *African Demos* 1, no. 3 (1991): 7.

14. Irving L. Markovitz, *Power and Class in Africa* (Englewood Cliffs, N.J.: Prentice-Hall, Inc., 1977).

15. See, for example, Robert H. Jackson and Carl G. Rosberg, "Personal Rule: Theory and Practice in Africa," *Comparative Politics* 16 (1984): 421–42.

16. See Markovitz, *Power and Class*; Issa Shivji, *Class Struggle in Tanzania* (Dar es Salaam: Tanzania Publishing House, 1976); Richard Sklar, "The Nature of Class Domination in Africa," *Journal of Modern African Studies* 17 (1979): 531–52.

17. John Dunn, *West African States, Failure and Promise: A Study in Comparative Politics* (Cambridge: Cambridge University Press, 1980), 216.

18. Robert Jackson, "Cross-National Statistical Research and the Study of Comparative Politics," *American Political Science Review* 29 (1985): 161–82.

19. Dristen Renwick Monroe. *The Economic Approach to Politics: A Critical Reassessment of the Theory of Rational Action* (New York: Harper Collins, 1991).

20. See, for example, William H. Riker, "The Heresthetics of Constitution-Making: The Presidency in 1787, with Comments on Determinism and Rational Choice," *American Political Science Review* 78 (1984): 1–16.

21. Kenneth A. Shepsle and Barry R. Weingast, "When Do Rules of Procedure Matter?" *Journal of Politics* 46 (1984): 207–20.

22. Pauline Peters, "Rational Choice, the Best Choice for Robert Bates: An Anthropological Reading of Bates's Work," *World Development* 21 (1993): 1066–76.

23. See Robert A. Alford and Roger Friedland, *Powers of Theory: Captialism, the State, and Democracy* (Cambridge: Cambridge University Press, 1985).

24. Ellen Comisso, "Crises in Socialism or Crisis of Socialism?" *World Politics* 17, no. 4 (1990): 563–96.

25. Geddes, "Paradigms and Sand Castles"; and Michael Bratton and Nicolas van de Walle, "Toward Governance in Africa: Popular Demands and State Responses," in *Governance and Politics in Africa*, ed. Goran Hyden and Michael Bratton (Boulder, Colo.: Lynne Rienner, 1992).

26. Wilson, "World Politics."

27. Ibid.

28. Shepsle and Weingast, "When Do Rules of Procedure Matter?"

29. Ernest J. Wilson III, "Economic Reform in Socialist and Capitalist Countries," paper prepared for the SSRC Conference on Economic Reform, Hanoi, June 27–30, 1990.

30. Nigel Harris, "New Bourgeoisies?" *Journal of Development Studies* 24

(January 1988): 237–49, and Paul Lubeck, ed., *The African Bourgeoisie: Capitalist Development in Nigeria, Kenya, and the Ivory Coast* (Boulder, Colo.: Lynne Rienner, 1987).

31. Joan M. Nelson, ed., *Fragile Coalitions: The Politics of Economic Adjustment* (New Brunswick, N.J.: Transaction Books, 1990).

32. Samuel P. Huntington, *The Third Wave: Democratization in the Late Twentieth Century* (Norman: University of Oklahoma Press, 1991).

Bibliography

This bibliography has two parts. The first part includes works on political liberalization or democratization in Africa. It is designed to be a fairly comprehensive representation of recent research on democracy in Africa. The second part of the bibliography includes other works cited in the chapters of this book.

Selected Works on Political Liberalization in Africa

Abrams, Elliott. "Pluralism and Democracy." In *Democracy and Pluralism in Africa,* edited by Dov Ronen. Boulder, Colo.: Lynne Rienner, 1986.

Ake, Claude. "The Case for Democracy." In *African Governance in the 1990s: Objectives, Resources, and Constraints,* edited by Richard Joseph. Atlanta: Carter Center, 1990.

———. "Rethinking African Democracy." *Journal of Democracy* 2, no. 1 (1991): 32–44.

Anyang' Nyong'o, Peter. "Democratization Processes in Africa." *CODESRIA Bulletin* (Dakar), no. 2 (1991): 3.

———. "Africa: The Failure of One-Party Rule." *Journal of Democracy* 3, no. 1 (1992): 90–96.

———, ed. *Popular Struggles for Democracy in Africa.* London: Zed, 1987.

Ayoade, John A. A. "The African Search for Democracy." In *Democracy and Pluralism in Africa,* edited by Dov Ronen. Boulder, Colo.: Lynne Rienner, 1986.

Baker, Pauline. "Reflections on the Economic Correlates of African Democracy." In *Democracy and Pluralism in Africa,* edited by Dov Ronen. Boulder, Colo.: Lynne Rienner, 1986.

Baregu, Mwesiga, and S. S. Mushi. "Mobilization, Participation, and System Legitimacy." Typescript.

Barkan, Joel D. "The Electoral Process and Peasant-State Relations in Kenya." In *Elections in Independent Africa,* edited by Fred M. Hayward. Boulder, Colo.: Lynne Rienner, 1992.

Bates, Robert H., and Paul Collier. *The Politics and Economics of Policy Reform in Zambia.* Papers in International Political Economy, Working Paper 153. Durham: Duke University, 1992.

Bayart, Jean-François. *L'Etat en Afrique: la politique du ventre*. Paris: Fayard, 1989.
———. "La Problématique de la démocratie en Afrique noire: 'la Baule et puis aprés?' " *Politique africaine* 43 (October 1991): 5–20.
Beckett, Paul A. "Elections and Democracy in Nigeria." In *Elections in Independent Africa*, edited by Fred M. Hayward. Boulder, Colo.: Westview, 1987.
Beckman, Bjorn. "Whose Democracy? Bourgeois versus Popular Democracy." *Review of African Political Economy* 45 (1989): 84–97.
Bienen, Henry, and Mark Gersovitz. "Consumer Subsidy Cuts, Violence,and Political Stability." *Comparative Politics* 18 (1986): 25–44.
Bratton, Michael. *The Local Politics of Rural Development: Peasant and Party-State in Zambia*. Hanover: University Press of New England, 1980.
———. "Civil Society and Political Transition in Africa: Kenya and Zambia Compared." Paper prepared for the Conference on Civil Society in Africa, Harry S. Truman Institute, Hebrew University, Jerusalem, January 1992.
———. "Zambia Starts Over." *Journal of Democracy* 3, no. 2 (1992): 81–94.
Bratton, Michael, and Nicolas van de Walle. "Toward Governance in Africa: Popular Demands and State Responses." In *Governance and Politics in Africa*, edited by Goran Hyden and Michael Bratton. Boulder, Colo.: Lynne, Rienner, 1992.
Brautigam, Deborah. *Governance and Economy*. Working Paper 815. Washington, D.C.: World Bank, December 1991.
Busia, K. A. *Africa in Search of Democracy*. New York: Praeger, 1967.
Chazan, Naomi. "The Africanization of Political Change: Some Aspects of the Dynamics of Political Cultures in Ghana and Nigeria." *African Studies Review* 21, no. 2 (1978): 15–33.
———. "African Voters at the Polls: A Re-examination of the Role of Elections in African Politics." *Journal of Commonwealth and Comparative Politics* 17, no. 2 (1979): 136–58.
———. "The New Politics of Participation in Tropical Africa." *Comparative Politics* 14 (1982): 169–89.
———. "Planning Democracy in Africa: A Comparative Perspective on Ghana and Nigeria." *Policy Sciences* 22 (1989): 321–57.
Cohen, Herman J. "African Political Changes and Economic Consequences," *Dispatch* 2, no. 36 (1991): 675–76.
Collier, Ruth Berins. *Regimes in Tropical Africa: Changing Forms of Supremacy, 1945–1975*. Berkeley: University of California Press, 1982.
Crook, Richard C. "Les Changements politiques en Côte d'Ivoire: une approche institutionelle." In *Année africaine, 1990–1991*. Paris: Pedone, 1991.
DeCalo, Samuel. "The Process, Prospects, and Constraints of Democratization in Africa." *African Affairs* 91 (1992): 7–35.
Diagne, Pathé. "Pluralism and Plurality in Africa." In *Democracy and Pluralism in Africa*, edited by Dov Ronen. Boulder, Colo.: Lynne Rienner, 1986.
Diamond, Larry, Juan J. Linz, and Seymour Martin Lipset. *Democracy in Developing Countries: Africa*. Boulder, Colo.: Lynne Rienner, 1988.
di Palma, Giuseppi. *To Craft Democracies: An Essay on Democratic Transitions*. Berkeley: University of California Press, 1990.

Eckert, Paul, ed. "Sub-Saharan Africa in the 1990s: Continent in Transition." Special Issue, *Fletcher Forum* 15 (Winter 1991): 1–81.

Emmerson, Donald. "Political Economy of Democratization and the International System: Lessons for Africa." Paper prepared for the Workshop on Democracy and Structural Adjustment in Africa in the 1990s, Madison, Wis., 1991.

Fatton, Robert, Jr. *The Making of a Liberal Democracy: Senegal's Passive Revolution, 1975–1985.* Boulder, Colo.: Lynne Rienner, 1987.

————. "Liberal Democracy in Africa." *Political Science Quarterly* 105 (Fall 1990): 455–73.

————. "Democracy and Civil Society in Africa." *Mediterranean Quarterly* 2 (Fall 1991): 83–95.

Fauré, Yves. "L'Economie politique d'une démocratisation: éléments d'analyse à propos de l'expérience récente de la Côte d'Ivoire." *Politique africaine* 43 (October 1991): 31–49.

Galaydh, Ali Khalif. "Democratic Breakdown in Somalia." In *Democracy and Pluralism in Africa,* edited by Dov Ronen. Boulder, Colo.: Lynne Rienner Publishers, 1986.

Gallagher, Mark. *Rent Seeking and Economic Growth in Africa.* Boulder, Colo.: Westview, 1991.

Gertzel, Cherry, Carolyn Baylies, and Morris Szeftel. *The Dynamics of the One-Party State in Zambia.* Manchester: Manchester University Press, 1984.

Glickman, Harvey. "Frontiers of Liberal and Non-Liberal Democracy in Tropical Africa." *Journal of Asian and African Studies* 23 nos. 3–4 (1988): 234–54.

————, ed., "Challenges to and Transitions from Authoritarianism in Africa." Issue on political liberalization. *Issue: A Journal of Opinion* 20, no. 1 (1991): 5–53.

Goulbourne, Harry. "The State, Development, and the Need for Participatory Democracy in Africa." In *Popular Struggles for Democracy in Africa,* edited by Peter Anyang' Nyong'o. London: Zed, 1987.

Gulhati, Ravi. *Impasse in Zambia: The Economics and Politics of Reform.* Washington, D.C.: World Bank, 1989.

Gyimah-Bouadi, E. "Civil Associations in the PNDC Era: Aspects of the Evolution of Civil Society in Ghana." In *Civil Society and the State in Africa,* edited by Naomi Chazan, John Harbeson, and Donald Rothchild. Boulder, Colo.: Lynne Rienner, forthcoming.

Harbeson, John W. "Constitutions and Constitutionalism in Africa: A Tentative Theoretical Exploration." In *Democracy and Pluralism in Africa,* edited by Dov Ronen. Boulder, Colo.: Lynne Rienner, 1986.

Hayward, Fred. *Elections in Independent Africa.* Boulder, Colo.: Westview, 1987.

Herbst, Jeffrey. "Migration, the Politics of Protest, and State Consolidation in Africa." *African Affairs* 89 (1990): 183–204.

Hill, Stuart, and Donald Rothchild. "The Contagion of Political Conflict in Africa and the World." *Journal of Conflict Resolution* 30, no. 4. (1986): 716–35.

Holm, John D. "Elections in Botswana: Institutionalization of a New System of Legitimacy." In *Elections in Independent Africa,* edited by Fred M. Hayward. Boulder, Colo.: Lynne Rienner, 1992.

Holm, John D., and Patrick P. Molutsi. "Developing Democracy When Civil Society Is Weak: The Case of Botswana," *African Affairs* 89 (1990): 323–40.

———. "State-Society Relations in Botswana: Beginning Liberalization." In *Governance and Politics in Africa,* edited by Goran Hyden and Michael Bratton. Boulder, Colo.: Lynne Rienner, 1992.

———, eds. *Democracy in Botswana.* Gaborone and Athens, Ohio: MacMillan Botswana and Ohio University, 1989.

Huntington, Samuel P. *The Third Wave: Democratization in the Late Twentieth Century.* Normon: University of Oklahoma, 1991.

Hyden, Goran. "Governance and the Study of Politics." In *Governance and Politics in Africa,* edited by Goran Hyden and Michael Bratton. Boulder, Colo.: Lynne Rienner, 1992.

Hyden, Goran, and Michael Bratton, eds. *Governance and Politics in Africa.* Boulder, Colo.: Lynne Rienner, 1992.

Jackson, Robert H., and Carl G. Rosberg. "Democracy in Tropical Africa." *Journal of International Affairs* 38, no. 2 (1985): 293–306.

Joseph, Richard. "Class, State, and Prebendal Politics in Nigeria." *Journal of Commonwealth and Comparative Politics* 21, no. 3 (1983): 21–38.

———. *Democracy and Prebendal Politics in Nigeria: The Rise and Fall of the Second Republic.* New York: Cambridge University Press, 1987.

———. "Africa: The Rebirth of Political Freedom." *Journal of Democracy* 2, no. 4 (1991): 11–24.

———, ed. *Beyond Autocracy in Africa.* Working Papers from the Inaugural Seminar of the African Governance Program, February 17–18, 1989. Atlanta: Carter Center, 1989.

———, ed. *African Governance in the 1990s.* Working Papers from the Second Annual Seminar of the African Governance Program, March 23–25, 1990. Atlanta: Carter Center, 1990.

Kaba, Lansiné. "Power and Democracy in African Tradition: The Case of Songhay." In *Democracy and Pluralism in Africa,* edited by Dov Ronen. Boulder, Colo.: Lynne Rienner, 1986.

Kabongo, Ilunga. "Democracy in Africa." In *Democracy and Pluralism in Africa,* edited by Dov Ronen. Boulder, Colo.: Lynne Rienner, 1986.

Kamau Kuria, Gibson. "Confronting Dictatorship in Kenya." *Journal of Democracy* 2, no. 4 (1991): 115–26.

Karl, Terry Lynn. "Petroleum and Pacts: The Transition to Democracy in Venezuela." In *Transitions from Authoritarian Rule: Latin America,* edited by Guillermo O'Donnell, Philippe C. Schmitter, and Laurence Whitehead. Baltimore: Johns Hopkins University, 1986.

———. "Dilemmas of Democratization in Latin America." *Comparative Politics* 22 (1990): 1–22.

Kasfir, Nelson. "The Tension between Progressive Populism and Democratization in Uganda." Paper prepared for the annual meeting of the American Political Science Association, Atlanta, September 1989.

Kilson, Martin. "Thinking about African Re-Democratization." Paper prepared for the Colloquium on the Economics of Political Liberalization in Africa, Cambridge, March 6–7, 1992.

Kimenyi, Mwangi. "Interest Groups, Transfer Seeking, and Democratization: Competition for the Benefits of Governmental Power May Explain African Political Instability." *American Journal of Economics and Sociology* 48, no. 3 (1989): 339–49.

Kohli, Atul. *Democracy and Discontent: India's Growing Crisis of Governability.* Cambridge: Cambridge University Press, 1990.

Kone, Samba S. 1990: *Une année pas comme les autres.* Abidjan: Presses de la MICI, 1990.

Kpundeh, Sahr John, ed. *Democratization in Africa: African Views, African Voices.* Summary of three workshops organized by the National Academy of Sciences. Washington, D.C.: National Academy Press, 1992.

Lancaster, Carol. "Democracy in Africa." *Foreign Policy* 85 (Winter 1991–92): 148–65.

Legum, Colin. "Democracy in Africa: Hopes and Trends." In *Democracy and Pluralism in Africa,* edited by Dov Ronen. Boulder, Colo.: Lynne Rienner, 1986.

Le Vine, Victor T. "Leadership and Regime Changes in Perspective." In *The Political Economy of Cameroon,* edited by Michael G. Schatzberg and I. William Zartman. New York: Praeger, 1986.

Lewis, Peter M. "Political Transition and the Dilemma of Civil Society in Africa. *Journal of International Affairs* 46, no. 1 (1992): 31–54.

Lijphart, Arend. *Democracy in Plural Societies.* New Haven: Yale University, 1977.

———. *Democracies: Patterns of Majoritarian and Consensus Government in Twenty-one Countries.* New Haven: Yale University Press, 1984.

Lonsdale, John. "Political Accountability in African History." In *Political Domination in Africa,* edited by Patrick Chabal. Cambridge: Cambridge University, 1986.

MacGaffey, Janet. "Initatives from Below: Zaire's Other Path to Social and Economic Restructuring." In *Governance and Politics in Africa,* edited by Goran Hyden and Michael Bratton. Boulder, Colo.: Lynne Rienner, 1992.

Magang, David W. "Democracy and the African Tradition: The Case of Botswana." In *Democracy and Pluralism in Africa,* edited by Dov Ronen. Boulder, Colo.: Lynne Rienner, 1986.

Mamdani, Mahmood. "Contradictory Class Perspectives on the Question of Democracy: The Case of Uganda." In *Popular Struggles for Democracy in Africa,* edited by Peter Anyang' Nyong'o. London: Zed, 1987.

———. "The Social Basis of Constitutionalism in Africa." *Journal of Modern African Studies* 28 (1990): 359–74.

———. "Democratic Theory and Democratic Struggles in Africa." *Dissent* (Summer 1992): 312–18.

Mbikusita-Lewanika, Akashambatwa, and Derrick Chitala, eds. *The Hour Has Come: Proceedings of the National Conference on the Multi-Party Option*. Lusaka: Zambia Research Foundation, 1990.

Médard, Jean-François. "Autoritarismes et démocraties en Afrique noire," *Politique africaine* 43 (October 1991): 92–104.

————. "The Historical Trajectories of the Ivorian and Kenyan States." In *Rethinking Third World Politics*, edited by James Manor. Harrow, England: Longman Group U.K., 1991.

Miles, William. *Elections in Nigeria: A Grassroots Perspective*. Boulder, Colo.: Lynne Rienner, 1988.

Molutsi, Patrick. "Developing Democracy When Civil Society Is Weak: The Case of Botswana." *African Affairs* 89 (1990): 323–40.

Mudenda,Gilbert. "The Process of Class Formation in Contemporary Zambia." In *Beyond Political Independence: Zambia's Development Predicament in the 1980s*, edited by Klaas Woldring. London: Mouton, 1984.

Mugyenyi, Meddi. "Development First, Democracy Second: A Comment on Minimalist Democracy." In *Democratic Theory and Practice in Africa*, edited by Walter O. Oyugi et al. Portsmouth, N.H.: Heinemann, 1988.

Munslow, Barry. "Why Has the Westminster Model Failed in Africa?" *Parliamentary Affairs* 36, no. 2 (1983): 218–28.

Nelson, Joan M. "Political Participation." In *Understanding Political Development*, edited by Myron Weiner and Samuel P. Huntington. Boston: Little, Brown, 1987.

Nicol, Davidson. "African Pluralism and Democracy." In *Democracy and Pluralism in Africa*, edited by Dov Ronen. Boulder, Colo.: Lynne Rienner, 1986.

Nyang'oro, Julius E., and Timothy M. Shaw. *Beyond Structural Adjustment in Africa: The Political Economy of Sustainable and Democratic Development*. New York: Praeger, 1992.

O'Donnell, Guillermo, and Phillipe Schmitter, *Transitions from Authoritarian Rule: Tentative Conclusions about Uncertain Outcomes*. Baltimore: Johns Hopkins University, 1986.

Olorunsola, Victor A. "Questions on Constitutionalism and Democracy: Nigeria and Africa." In *Democracy and Pluralism in Africa*, edited by Dov Ronen. Boulder, Colo.: Lynne Rienner, 1986.

Onyeoziri, Fred. "Consociationalism and the Nigerian Political Practice." In *Federal Character and Federalism in Nigeria*, edited by Peter P. Ekeh and Eghosa E. Osaghae. Ibadan: Heinemann, 1989.

Owusu, Maxwell. "Democracy and Africa—A View from the Village." *Journal of Modern African Studies* 30 (1992): 369–96.

Oyediran, Oydeye, and Adigun Ogbaje. "Two-Partyism and Democratic Transition in Nigeria." *Journal of Modern African Studies* 29 (1991): 213–28.

Oyugi, Walter O., ed. *Democratic Theory and Practice in Africa*. London: James Currey, 1988.

Riley, Stephen P. "The Democratic Transition in Africa." *African Demos* 1, no. 3 (1991).

Ronen, Dov. "The Challenges of Democracy in Africa: Some Introductory

Observations." In *Democracy and Pluralism in Africa*, edited by Dov Ronen. Boulder, Colo.: Lynne Rienner, 1986.

———. "The State and Democracy in Africa." In *Democracy and Pluralism in Africa*, edited by Dov Ronen. Boulder, Colo.: Lynne Rienner, 1986.

———, ed. *Democracy and Pluralism in Africa*. Boulder, Colo.: Lynne Rienner, 1986.

Rothchild, Donald, ed. *Ghana: The Political Economy of Recovery*. Boulder, Colo.: Lynne Rienner, 1991.

Rustow, Dankwart A. "Transitions to Democracy: Towards a Dynamic Model." *Comparative Politics* 2 (1970): 337–64.

Sandbrook, Richard. "Liberal Democracy in Africa: A Socialist-Revisionist Perspective." *Canadian Journal of African Studies* 22, no. 2 (1988): 240–67.

———. "Taming the African Leviathan." *World Policy Journal* 7, no. 4 (1990): 673–701.

Sartori, Giovanni. *The Theory of Democracy Revisited.* Chatham, N.J.: Chatham House, 1987.

Schmitz, Gerald, and Eboe Hutchful. *Democratization and Popular Participation in Africa.* Ottawa: North-South Institute, 1992.

Shivji, Issa G., ed. *State and Constitutionalism: An African Debate on Democracy.* Harare, Zimbabwe: SAPES Trust, 1991.

Sisk, Timothy D. "South Africa Seeks New Ground Rules." *Journal of Democracy* 4, no. 1 (1993): 79–91.

Sklar, Richard L. "Democracy in Africa." In *Political Domination in Africa*, edited by Patrick Chabal. Cambridge: Cambridge University, 1986.

———. "Developmental Democracy." *Comparative Studies in Society and History* 29, no. 4 (1987): 686–714.

Stevens, Christopher, and John Speed. "Multi-partyism in Africa: The Case of Botswana Revisited." *African Affairs* 76 (1977): 381–87.

Szeftel, Morris. "Warlords and Problems of Democracy in Africa." *Review of African Political Economy* 45–46 (1989): 83–84.

Tedga, Paul John Marc. *Ouverture démocratique en Afrique noire?* Paris: L'Harmattan, 1991.

Tripp, Aili Mari. "Local Institutions and Grassroots Party Dynamics in Urban Tanzania." In *Governance and Politics in Africa*, edited by Goran Hyden and Michael Bratton. Boulder, Colo.: Lynne Rienner, 1992.

Uwazurike, P. Chudi. "Confronting Potential Breakdown: The Nigerian Redemocratization Process in Critical Perspective." *Journal of Modern African Studies* 28 (1990): 55–77.

Vittin, Théophile. "Bénin: du 'système Kérékou' au renouveau démocratique." In *Etats d'Afrique noire: formation, méchanismes, et crise*, edited by Jean-François Médard. Paris: Karthala, 1991.

Widner, Jennifer. "The 1990 Elections in Côte d'Ivoire." *Issue: A Journal of Opinion* 21 (1991): 31–40.

———. *The Rise of a Party-State in Kenya: From Harambee! to Nyayo!* Berkeley: University of California, 1992.

Williams, Donald C. "Accommodation in the Midst of a Crisis? Assessing

Governance in Nigeria." In *Governance and Politics in Africa*, edited by Goran Hyden and Michael Bratton. Boulder, Colo.: Lynne Rienner, 1992.

Wiseman, John. "Multi-partyism in Africa: The Case of Botswana." *African Affairs* 76 (1977): 70–79.

Young, M. Crawford. "Elections in Zaire: The Shadows of Democracy." In *Elections in Independent Africa*, edited by Fred M. Hayward. Boulder, Colo.: Westview, 1987.

Young, M. Crawford, and Babacar Kante. "Governance, Democracy, and the 1988 Senegalese Elections." In *Governance and Politics in Africa*, edited by Goran Hyden and Michael Bratton. Boulder, Colo.: Lynne Rienner, 1992.

Other Works Cited in the Text

Abernethy, David. "Bureaucratic Growth and Economic Stagnation in Sub-Saharan Africa." In *Africa's Development Challenges and the World Bank*, edited by Stephen K. Commins. Boulder, Colo.: Lynne Rienner, 1988.

Abrahams, R. G., ed. *Villagers, Villages, and the State in Modern Tanzania.* Cambridge African Monograph 4. Cambridge: Cambridge African Studies Centre, 1985.

Achebe, Chinua. *A Man of the People.* Garden City, N.Y.: Anchor Books, 1967.

Alford, Robert A., and Roger Friedland. *Powers of Theory: Capitalism, the State, and Democracy.* Cambridge: Cambridge University Press, 1985.

Armah, Ayi Kwei. *The Beautiful Ones Are Not Yet Born.* Boston: Houghton Mifflin, 1968.

Austin, Dennis. *Politics in Ghana, 1946–1960.* London: Oxford University Press, 1970.

Ayoade, John A. A. "States without Citizens: An Emerging African Phenomenon." In *The Precarious Balance: State and Society in Africa*, edited by Donald Rothchild and Naomi Chazan. Boulder, Colo.: Westview, 1988.

Bakary, Tessilimi. "Elite Transformation and Political Succession." In *The Political Economy of Ivory Coast*, edited by I. William Zartman and Christopher Delgado. New York: Praeger, 1984.

Barad, Robert A. "Privatization of State-Owned Enterprises: The Togolese Experience." In *State Enterprise in Africa*, edited by Barbara Grosh and Rwekaza Mukandala. Boulder, Colo.: Lynne Rienner, forthcoming.

Baregu, Mwesiga. "The Arusha Declaration Paradox." *African Review* 14, nos. 1–2 (1987): 1–12.

————"The State and Society in Africa." Paper prepared for the annual African Studies Conference, Stanford and Berkeley, April 1991.

————. *The 1964 Army Mutiny in Tanzania.* Dar es Salaam: Dar es Salaam University Press: forthcoming.

Bates, Robert H. *Unions, Parties, and Political Development: A Study of Mineworkers in Zambia.* New Haven: Yale University Press, 1971.

————. *Markets and States in Tropical Africa.* Berkeley: University of California Press, 1981.

————. *Essays on the Political Economy of Rural Africa*. Berkeley: University of California, 1983.

————. "The Reality of Structural Adjustment: A Skeptical Appraisal." In *Structural Adjustment and Agriculture: Theory and Practice in Africa and Latin America*, edited by Simon Commander. Portsmouth, N.H.: Heinemann Educational Books, 1989.

————. *Beyond the Miracle of the Market*. Cambridge: Cambridge University Press, 1990.

Bates, Robert H., and Paul Collier. "The Politics of Economic Reform in Zambia." In *Political and Economic Interactions in Economic Policy Reform*, edited by Robert H. Bates and Anne O. Krueger. Oxford: Basil Blackwell, 1993.

Bauer, P. T. *West African Trade*. London: Routledge and Kegan Paul, 1964.

Bayart, Jean-François. "Un printemps camerounais." *Marchés tropicaux*, September 29, 1983.

————. *L'Etat au Cameroun*. Paris: Presses de la Fondation Nationale de Sciences Politiques, 1985.

————. "La Société politique camerounaise, 1982–1986." *Politique africaine* 22 (June 1986): 5–36.

Benjamin, Nancy C., and Shantayanan Devarajan. "Oil Revenues and the Cameroonian Economy." In *The Political Economy of Cameroon*, edited by Michael G. Schatzberg and I. William Zartman. New York: Praeger, 1986.

Berg, Elliot, and Mary Shirley. *Divestiture in Developing Countries*. Staff Discussion Paper 11. Washington, D.C.: World Bank, 1987.

Bevan, David, Paul Collier, and Jan Willem Gunning. *Peasants and Governments*. Oxford: Clarendon, 1989.

————. *Controlled Open Economies: A Neoclassical Approach to Structuralism*. Oxford: Clarendon, 1990.

Bhat, G. J., and R. S. Patel. "Maternal and Child Health in Zambia." 1987. Typescript.

Bienen, Henry. *Kenya: The Politics of Participation and Control*. Princeton: Princeton University Press, 1974.

————. *Armies and Parties in Africa*. New York: African Publishing Company, 1978.

Bienen, Henry, and Nicolas van de Walle. *Of Time and Power: Leadership Duration in the Modern World*. Stanford: Stanford University Press, 1991.

Biersteker, Thomas J. *Multi-Nationals, the State, and Control of the Nigerian Economy*. Princeton: Princeton University Press, 1987.

Binder, Leonard, et al. *Crises and Sequences in Political Development*. Princeton: Prince University Press, 1971.

Biya, Paul. *Le Message du renouveau: discours et interviews du president Paul Biya*. Yauondé: Sopecam, 1984.

————. *Pour le liberlaisme communautaire*. Paris: Pierre Marcel Favre, 1986.

Biyiti Bi Essam, J. P. *Cameroun: complots et bruits de bottes: quelque données pour ébrouiller l'écheveau*. Paris: l'Harmattan, 1985.

Boahen, Albert Adu. *The Ghanaian Sphinx: Reflections on the Contemporary History of Ghana 1972–1987.* Accra: Ghana Academy of Arts and Sciences, 1989.

Boesen, J., et al. *Ujamaa—Socialism from Above.* Uppsala: Scandinavian Institute of African Studies, 1977.

Bollen, Kenneth. "Political Democracy and the Timing of Development." *American Sociological Review* 44, no. 4 (1979): 572–87.

Bourke, Gerald. "Day of Truth." *West Africa* October 9–15, 1989.

Brace, John. "Land Tenure and Structural Adjustment." Paper prepared for the Workshop on Democracy and Structural Adjustment in Africa in the 1990s, Madison, Wis., 1991.

Bratton, Michael, and Nicolas van de Walle. "Popular Protest and Political Reform in Africa." *Comparative Politics* 24 (1992): 419–42.

Callaghy, Thomas. "Africa's Debt Crisis." *Journal of International Affairs* 38, no. 1 (1984): 61–79.

———. *The State-Society Struggle: Zaire in Comparative Perspective.* New York: Columbia University, 1984.

———. "The State as Lame Leviathan: The Patrimonial Administrative State in Africa." In *The African State in Transition,* edited by Zaki Ergas. New York: St. Martin's, 1987.

———. "Politicial Passions and Economic Interests: Comparative Reflections on Political and Economic Logics in Africa." Paper prepared for the annual meeting of the American Political Science Association, San Francisco, 1990.

———. "Africa and the World Economy: Caught between a Rock and a Hard Place." In *Africa in World Politics,* edited by John W. Harbeson and Donald Rothchild. Boulder, Colo.: Westview, 1991.

Carter, Gwendolyn M. *African One-Party States.* Ithaca: Cornell University, 1962.

Caswell, Nim. "Autopsie de l'ONCAD: la politique arachidière au Sénégal, 1966–1980." *Politique africaine* 14 (June 1984): 39–73.

Chazan, Naomi. *An Anatomy of Ghanaian Politics: Managing Political Recession, 1969–1982.* Boulder, Colo.: Westview, 1983.

———. "The Political Transformation of Ghana under the PNDC." In *Ghana: The Political Economy of Recovery,* edited by Donald Rothchild. Boulder, Colo.: Lynne Rienner, 1991.

Chazan, Naomi, and Donald Rothchild. "Corporatism and Political Transactions: Some Ruminations on the Ghanaian Experience." In *Corporatism in Africa,* edited by Julius E. Nyang'oro and Timothy M. Shaw. Boulder, Colo.: Westview, 1989.

Clapham, Christopher. "Clientelism and the State." In *Private Patronage and Public Power,* edited by Christopher Clapham. London: Frances Pinter, 1982.

———, ed. *Private Patronage and Public Power.* London: Frances Pinter, 1982.

Clark, John, and Caroline Allison. *Zambia: Debt and Poverty.* Oxford: Oxfam, 1989.

Cliffe, Lionel. *One-Party Democracy in Tanzania.* Dar es Salaam: East African Publishing House, 1967.

———. "Nationalism and the Reaction to Forced Agricultural Change in Tanganiyka during the Colonial Period," *Taamuli* 1 (July 1970): 1–15.

Cliffe, Lionel and John Saul, eds. *Socialism in Tanzania: An Interdisciplinary Reader.* Nairobi: East African Publishing House, 1972.

Cohen, Michael. *Urban Policy and Political Conflict in Africa: A Case Study of the Ivory Coast.* Chicago: University of Chicago Press, 1974.

Collier, Paul. "Africa's External Economic Relations, 1960–90." *African Affairs* 90 (1991): 339–56.

Collier, Paul, S. Radwan, and S. Wangwe. *Labor and Poverty in Rural Tanzania.* Oxford: Clarendon, 1986.

Comisso, Ellen. "Crises in Socialism or Crises of Socialism?" *World Politics* 17, no. 4 (1990): 563–96.

Contamin, Bernard, and Yves Fauré. *La Bataille des entreprises publiques en Côte d'Ivoire: l'histoire d'une ajustement interne.* Paris: Karthala, 1990.

Copans, Jean. *Les Marabouts et l'arachide: la confrerie mouride et les paysans du Senegal.* Paris: Sycamore, 1980.

Cornevin, Robert. *La République populaire du Benin.* Paris: Maisonneuve and Larose, 1981.

Coulon, Christian. *Le Marabout et le prince: Islam et pouvoir au Sénégal.* Paris: Pedone, 1981.

Coulson, Andrew. *Tanzania: A Political Economy.* Cambridge: Cambridge University Press, 1982.

Courade, G., I. Grangeret, and P. Janin. "La Liquidation de joyaux du prince: les enjeux de la libéralisation des filières café-cacao au Cameroun." *Politique africaine* 44 (December 1991): 121–28.

Courcelle, Michel. *The Private Sector in Cameroon.* Paris: Organization for Economic Cooperation and Development, 1990.

Cowen, Michael P. "Capital and Household Production: The Case of Wattle in Kenya's Central Province, 1903–1964." Ph.D. diss., University of Cambridge, 1978.

Daddieh, Cyril Kofie. "The Management of Educational Crises in Côte d'Ivoire." *Journal of Modern African Studies* 26 (1988): 639–45.

Dahl, Robert A. *Polyarchy: Participation and Opposition.* New Haven: Yale University Press, 1971.

Davidson, Basil. "The Challenge of Comparative Analysis: Anti-Imperialist Nationalism in Africa and Europe." Paper prepared for the Conference on Relationships between State and Society in Africa and Eastern Europe, Bellagio, Italy, 1990.

Davis, Jeffrey M. "The Economic Effects of Windfall Gains in Export Earnings," *World Development* 11 (1983): 119–39.

Devarajan, Shantayanan, and Jaime de Melo. "Evaluating Participation in African Monetary Unions: A Statistical Analysis of the CFA Zones." *World Development* 15, no. 4 (1987): 483–96.

Diouf, Mamadou. "Eastern Europe as a Model of Social State Relationship in Political Thought in Senegal." Paper prepared for the Conference on Relationships between State and Society in Africa and Eastern Europe, Bellagio, Italy, 1990.

Doner, Richard. "Explaining the Politics of Economic Growth in Southeast Asia." *Journal of Asian Studies* 50, no. 4 (1991): 818–49.

Doriye, Joshua. "Public Office and Private Gain: An Interpretation of the Tanzanian Experience." August 1991. Typescript.

Dunn, John. *West African States, Failure and Promise: A Study in Comparative Politics.* Cambridge: Cambridge University Press, 1980.

Economist Intelligence Unit. *Zambia: Country Profile.* London: Business International Ltd., 1987.

———. *Country Report: Tanzania and Mozambique.* London: Business International Ltd., 1990.

———. *Quarterly Report on Côte d'Ivoire, 1990.* No. 3. London: Business International Ltd., 1990.

———. *Ivory Coast: Country Profile, 1991–92.* London: Business International Ltd., 1992.

———. *Kenya: Country Profile, 1991–92.* London: Business International Ltd., 1992.

Ellis, Randall P., and Bermano M. Mwabu. "The Demand for Outpatient Medical Care in Rural Kenya." 1991. Typescript.

Englebert, Pierre, *Cameroon: Background to a Crisis.* CSIS Africa Notes, 130. Washington, D.C.: Center for Strategic and International Studies, 1991.

Enloe, Cynthia. *Ethnic Soldiers: State Security in Divided Societies.* Athens: University of Georgia Press, 1980.

Epstein, A. L. *Politics in an Urban African Community.* Manchester: Manchester University Press, 1958.

Fauré, Yves, and Jean-François Médard, eds. *L'Etat et bourgeoisie en Côte d'Ivoire.* Paris: Karthala, 1982.

Federal Council of the National Party. *Grondwetlike Regering In 'n Deelnemende Demokrasie.* Pretoria: National Party, September 4, 1991.

Federal Republic of Nigeria. *Report of the Political Bureau.* Lagos: Government Printer, 1987.

Feierman, Steven. *Peasant Intellectuals: Anthropology and History in Tanzania.* Madison: University of Wisconsin Press, 1990.

Feinberg, Richard E., and Valeriana Kallab, eds. *The Adjustment Crisis in the Third World.* New Brunswick, N.J.: Transaction Books, 1984.

Freedom House. *Freedom in the World: Political Rights and Civil Liberties, 1989–1990.* New York: Freedom House, 1990.

Fry, Maxwell. *Money, Interest, and Banking in Economic Development.* Baltimore: Johns Hopkins University Press, 1988.

Gaag, Jacques van der, Merton Stelcner, and Vim Vijverberg. *Public-Private Sector Wage Comparisons and Moonlighting in Developing Countries: Evidence from Côte d'Ivoire and Peru.* Living Standards Measurement Study Working Paper 52. Washington, D.C.: World Bank, 1989.

Geddes, Barbara. "How the Cases You Choose Affect the Answers You Get: Selection Bias in Comparative Politics." *Political Analysis* 2 (1990): 131–50.

———. "Paradigms and Sand Castles in the Comparative Politics of Developing Countries." In *Political Science: Looking to the Future,* edited by William

Crotty. Vol. 2. Evanston: Northwestern University Press, 1991.

Gertzel, Cherry. "Labour and the State: The Case of the Zambia Mineworkers' Union." *Journal of Commonwealth and Comparative Politics* 13, no. 3 (1975): 290–304.

Gershenkron, Alexander. *Economic Backwardness in Historical Perspective.* Cambridge: Cambridge University Press, 1962.

Gombeaud, Jean-Louis, Corinne Moutout, and Stephen Smith. *La Guerre du cacao: histoire secrète d'un embargo.* Paris: Calmann-Lévy, 1990.

Good, Kenneth. "The Reproduction of Weakness in the State and Agriculture: Zambian Experience." *African Affairs* 85 (1986): 239–66.

Gordon, David. "Zambia: The Political Economy of Economic Reform." Memorandum. Nairobi: USAID/REDSO/ESA, January 1991. Typescript.

Gould, David J. *Bureaucratic Corruption and Underdevelopment in the Third World: The Case of Zaire.* New York: Pergamon, 1980.

Gramsci, A. *Selections from the Prison Notebooks.* London: Lawrence and Wishart, 1971.

Gray, Richard, and David Birmingham. *Pre-Colonial African Trade.* London: Oxford University Press, 1970.

Grosh, Barbara. *Public Enterprise in Kenya: What Works, What Doesn't, and Why.* Boulder, Colo.: Lynne Rienner, 1991.

Grosh, Barbara, and Rwe Kaza Mukandala, eds. *State Enterprise in Africa.* Boulder, Colo.: Lynne Rienner, forthcoming.

Guillaumont, Patrick, and Sylviane Guillaumont, eds. *Zone franc et développement africaine.* Paris: Economica, 1984.

Gulhati, Ravi. *Recent Economic Reforms in Africa: A Preliminary Political Economy Perspective.* EDI Policy Seminar Report. Washington, D.C.: World Bank, 1987.

Gyimah-Bouadi, E. "Notes on Ghana's Current Transition to Constitutional Rule." 1991. Typescript.

Haggard, Stephan. "The Politics of Adjustment: Lessons from the IMF's Extended Fund Facility." *International Organization* 39, no. 3 (1985): 505–34.

Hall, Richard. *The High Price of Principles.* New York: Africana Publishing, 1969.

Halpern, Manfred. "Changing Connections to Multiple Worlds." In *Africa: From Mystery to Maze,* edited by Helen Kitchen. Lexington, Mass.: Lexington Books, 1976.

Harris, Nigel. "New Bourgeoisies?" *Journal of Development Studies* 24 (January 1988): 237–49.

Hartmann, Jeanne. "The Rise and Rise of Private Capital." In *Capitalism, Socialism, and the Development Crisis in Tanzania,* edited by Norman O'Neill and Kemal Mustapha. Aldershot: Avebury, 1990.

Hayward, Fred M. "Perceptions of Well-Being in Ghana: 1970 and 1975." *African Studies Review* 22, no. 1 (1979): 110–11.

Helleiner, G. K., ed. *Africa and the International Monetary Fund.* Washington, D.C.: International Monetary Fund, 1986.

Henry, Neil. "Daring to Differ in Tanzania." *Washington Post,* September 10, 1990.

———. "Nyerere Bows out with Tanzania in Deep Decline." *Washington Post,* September 26, 1990.

Herbst, Jeffrey. "The Structural Adjustment of Politics in Africa." *World Development* 18 (1990): 949–58.

———. "Labor in Ghana under Structural Adjustment: The Politics of Acquiescence." In *Ghana: The Political Economy of Recovery,* edited by Donald Rothchild. Boulder, Colo.: Lynne Rienner, 1991.

———. *The Politics of Reform in Ghana, 1982–1991.* Berkeley: University of California Press, 1992.

Hill, Stuart, and Donald Rothchild. "The Impact of Regime on the Diffusion of Political Conflict." In *The Internationalization of Communal Strife,* edited by Manus Midlarsky. London: Routledge, 1992.

Hirschman, Albert. *Exit, Voice, and Loyalty.* Cambridge: Harvard University Press, 1979.

Hodder-Williams, Richard. *An Introduction to the Politics of Tropical Africa.* London: Allen and Unwin, 1984.

Hopkins, A. G. *An Economic History of West Africa.* New York: Columbia University Press, 1973.

Horowitz, Donald L. *Ethnic Groups in Conflict.* Berkeley: University of California Press, 1985.

———. *A Democratic South Africa?* Berkeley: University of California Press, 1991.

Hutchful, Eboe. "The Limits of Corporatism as a Concept and Model." In *Corporatism in Africa,* edited by Julius E. Nyang'oro and Timothy M. Shaw. Boulder, Colo.: Westview, 1989.

Hyden, Goran. *Beyond Ujamaa in Tanzania: Development and the Uncaptured Peasantry.* Berkeley: University of California Press, 1980.

———. *No Shortcuts to Progress: African Development Management in Comparative Perspective.* Berkeley: University of California Press, 1983.

———. "Problems and Prospects of State Coherence." In *State versus Ethnic Claims: African Policy Dilemmas,* edited by Donald Rothchild and Victor A. Oloransola. Boulder, Colo.: Westview, 1983.

———. "The Political Economy of Popular Organizations: The Case of the Sungu Sungu Movement in Tanzania." Stanford: Stanford University, Joint Center for African Studies, April 21, 1989. Typescript.

International Labor Organization. *Zambia: Basic Needs in an Economy under Pressure.* Geneva: ILO, 1981.

———. *Basic Needs in an Economy under Pressure: Findings and Recommendations of an ILO/JASPA Mission.* Addis Ababa: ILO, 1981.

International Monetary Fund. *Government Finance Yearbook.* Washington, D.C.: IMF, various years.

Jackson, Robert. "Cross-National Statistical Research and the Study of Comparative Politics." *American Political Science Review* 29 (1985): 161–82.

Jackson, Robert H., and Rosberg, Carl G. *Personal Rule in Black Africa*. Berkeley: University of California Press, 1982.

———. "Personal Rule: Theory and Practice in Africa." *Comparative Politics* 16 (1984): 421–42.

Javaheri, F. *Soyabean: Combatting Malnutrition in Zambia*. Lusaka: Government of the Republic of Zambia, 1990.

Jeffries, Richard. *Class, Power, and Ideology in Ghana: The Railwaymen of Sekondi*. Cambridge: Cambridge University Press, 1978.

———. "Leadership, Commitment and Political Opposition to Structural Adjustment in Ghana." In *Ghana: The Political Economy of Recovery*, edited by Donald Rothchild. Boulder: Colo.: Lynne Rienner, 1991.

Jenkins, Jerry, ed. *Beyond the Informal Sector*. San Francisco: ICS, 1988.

Jones, William O. "Agricultural Trade within Tropical Africa: Historical Background." In *Agricultural Development in Africa: Issues of Public Policy*, ed. Robert Bates and Michael F. Lofchie. New York: Praeger, 1980.

Jorgensen, Steen, Margaret Grosh, and Mark Schacter. *Bolivia's Answer to Poverty, Economic Crisis, and Adjustment: The Emergency Social Fund*. Regional and Sectoral Studies 9. Washington, D.C.: World Bank, 1992.

Joseph, Richard. *Radical Nationalism in Cameroon: Social Origins of the UPC Rebellion*. Oxford: Oxford University Press, 1997.

Kasfir, Nelson. *The Shrinking Political Order*. Berkeley: University of California Press, 1976.

Katzenstein, Peter J. *Small States in World Markets*. Ithaca: Cornell University Press, 1985.

Killick, Tony. *Development Economics in Action: A Study of Economic Policies in Ghana*. New York: St. Martin's, 1978.

Kiondo, Andrew. "The Nature of Economic Reforms in Tanzania." In *Tanzania and the IMF: The Dynamics of Liberalization*, edited by Horace Campbell and Howard Stein. Boulder, Colo.: Westview, 1992.

Kiser, Edgar, and Michael Hechter. "The Role of General Theory in Comparative Historical Sociology." *American Journal of Sociology* 97, no. 1 (1991): 1–30.

Kitching, Gavin. *Class and Economic Change in Kenya*. New Haven: Yale University Press, 1980.

Klitgaard, Robert. *Adjusting to Reality*. San Francisco: ICS, 1991.

Konings, Piet. "La Liquidation des Plantations Unilever et les conflits intra-élite dans le Cameroun anglophone." *Politique africaine* 35 (October 1989): 132–37.

Kornai, Janos. *Anti-Equilibriums: On Economic Systems Theory and the Tasks of Research*. Amsterdam: North-Holland, 1971.

———. *Rush versus Harmonic Growth*. Amsterdam: New Holland, 1972.

Krueger, Anne O. "The Political Economy of the Rent-Seeking Society." *American Economic Review* 64, no. 3 (1974): 291–303.

Lachaud, Jean-Pierre. *Le Désengagement de l'état et les ajustements sur le marché du travail en Afrique francophone*. International Institute of Social Studies,

Research Series 96. Geneva: International Labor Organization, 1989.

Lancaster, Carol, and John Williamson. *African Debt and Financing*. Special Report 5. Washington, D.C.: Institute for International Economics, 1986.

Landell-Mills, Pierre, and Ismail Serageldin. "Governance and the Development Process." *Finance and Development* (September 1991): 14–17.

Lawry, Steven. "Structural Adjustment and Natural Resources." Paper prepared for the Workshop on Democracy and Structural Adjustment in Africa in the 1990s, Madison, Wis., 1991.

Legum, Colin. "The Postcommunist Third World: Focus on Africa." *Problems of Communism* 41, nos. 1–2 (1992): 195–206.

Lemarchand, René. "The State, the Parallel Economy, and the Changing Structure of Patronage Systems." In *The Precarious Balance: State and Society in Africa*, edited by Donald Rothchild and Naomi Chazan. Boulder, Colo.: Westview, 1988.

Lewis, W. Arthur. *Politics in West Africa*. London: Allen and Unwin, 1965.

Leys, Colin. *Underdevelopment in Kenya*. Berkeley: University of California Press, 1975.

MacDonald, A. *Tanganyika: Young Nation in a Hurry*. New York: Hawthorne Books, 1966.

Liatto-Katunda, Beatrice. "Social Consequences of Structural Adjustment: Effects on Zambian Workers and Workers' Coping Strategies." Lusaka: University of Zambia, Department of African Development Studies, November 1991. Typescript.

Lubeck, Paul, ed. *The African Bourgeoisie: Capitalist Development in Nigeria, Kenya, and the Ivory Coast*. Boulder, Colo.: Lynne Rienner, 1987.

MacDonald, A. *Tanganyika: Young Nation in a Hurry*. New York: Hawthorne Books, 1966.

MacGaffey, Janet. *Entrepreneurs and Parasites: The Struggle for Indigenous Capitalism in Zaire*. Cambridge: Cambridge University Press, 1987.

McKinnon, Ronald I. *Money and Capital in Economic Development*. Washington, D.C.: Brookings Institution, 1973.

———. *The Order of Economic Liberalization: Financial Control in the Transition to a Market Economy*. Baltimore: Johns Hopkins University Press, 1991.

Madison, James. "The Federalist Number 10." In *The Federalist Papers*. London: Penguin Books, 1987.

Maliyamkono, T. L., and M. S. Bagachwa, eds. *The Second Economy in Tanzania*. London: James Currey, 1990.

Mapolu, Henry, ed. *Workers and Management in Tanzania*. Dar es Salaam: Tanzania Publishing House, 1979.

Marchal, Roland. "On Some Aspects of the Conflicts in Eritrea and the Sudan." In *Conflict in the Horn of Africa*, edited by Georges Nzongola-Ntalaja. Atlanta: African Studies Association Press, 1991.

Markovitz, Irving L. *Power and Class in Africa*. Englewood Cliffs, N.J.: Prentice-Hall, 1977.

Pearson, Scott R., Gerald C. Nelson, and J. Dirck Stryker. *Comparative Advantage in Ghanaian Industry and Agriculture,* 1976. Typescript.

Peters, Pauline. "Communal Tenure, the Best Choice for Rural Development?" *World Development.*
76.

Martin, Guy. "Ideology and Praxis in Thomas Sankara's Populist Revolution of August 4, 1983, in Burkina Faso." *Issue: A Journal of Opinion* 15 (1987): 77–90.

Mbembe, Achille. "Réformes politiques et logiques autoritaries en Afriques noire." 1991. Typescript.

Médard, Jean-François. "L'Etat sous-dévelopé au Cameroun." In *L'Année africaine*. Paris: Pedone, 1977.

———. "La Regulation socio-politique." In *L'Etat et bourgeoisie en Côte d'Ivoire*, edited by Yves Fauré and Jean-François Médard. Paris: Karthala, 1982.

———. "The Underdeveloped State in Tropical Africa: Political Clientism or Neo-Patrimonialism." In *Private Patronage and Public Power*, edited by Christopher Clapham. London: Frances Pinter, 1982.

Meillassoux, Claude, ed. *The Development of Indigenous Trade and Marketing in West Africa*. London: Oxford University Press, 1971.

Mihyo, P. "The Struggle for Workers' Control in Tanzania." *Review of African Political Economy* 4 (1975): 62 84.

Mohne, Guy. "Employment and Incomes in Zambia in the Context of Structural Adjustment." Lusaka: ILO/SATEP, 1987. Typescript.

Monga, Celestin. "Bidons d'essence interdits." *Jeune Afrique économie*, no. 129 (March 1990): 93–97.

———. "La recomposition du marché politique au Cameroun, 1991–1992." CERDES, December 1992. Typescript.

Monroe, Dristen Renwick. *The Economic Approach to Politics: A Critical Reassessment of the Theory of Rational Action*. New York: Harper Collins, 1991.

Morna, Collen Lowe. "Ahead of the Opposition." *Africa Report* (July–August 1991): 20 23.

Moutard, Gilbert. "Quelles chances pour la politique de President Biya?" *Afrique contemporaine* 139 (1986): 20–35.

———. "Cameroun: au rythme lent du 'renouveau.' " In *Afrique contemporaine* 143 (1987): 52–57.

Msekwa, Pius. *Towards Party Supremacy*. Dar es Salaam: Tanzania Publishing House, 1978.

Mugongo. *Le Général Mobutu Sese Seko parle du nationalisme zairois authentique*. Kinshasa: Okapi, 1972.

Muntemba, Dorothy. "Impact of the IMF/World Bank on the People of Africa, with Special Reference to Zambia." Lusaka: National Commission for Development Planning. Typescript.

Museveni, Yoweri. *Selected Articles on the Uganda Resistance War*. Kampala: National Resistance Movement, 1986.

Nafziger, Wayne E. *Inequality in Africa: Political Elites, Proletariat, Peasants, and the Poor*. Cambridge: Cambridge University Press, 1988.

Nashashibi, Karim, et al. *The Fiscal Dimensions of Adjustment in Low-Income Countries*. Occasional Paper 95. Washington, D.C.: International Monetary Fund, 1992.

National Democratic Institute for International Affairs. "Cameroon Presidential Elections of October 11, 1992: An NDI Interim Report of the International Observer Mission." Washington, D.C.: NDI, October 28, 1992. Typescript.

National Democratic Institute for International Affairs/Carter Center of Emory University. *The October 31, 1991, National Elections in Zambia.* Washington, D.C.: National Democratic Institute, 1992.

———. *Report of the Carter Center Ghana Election Mission.* Washington, D.C.: National Democratic Institute, 1992.

Nellis, John R. *A Theory of Ideology: The Tanzania Example.* Nairobi: Oxford University Press, 1972.

———. *Public Enterprises in Sub-Saharan Africa.* Staff Discussion Paper 1. Washington, D.C.: World Bank, 1986.

Nelson, Joan M., ed. *Economic Crisis and Policy Choice: The Politics of Economic Adjustment in the Third World.* Princeton: Princeton University Press, 1990.

———. *Fragile Coalitions: The Politics of Economic Adjustment.* New Brunswick, N.J.: Transaction Books, 1990.

Ngu, Joseph. "The Political Economy of Oil in Cameroon." In *Conference on the Political Economy of Cameroon: Historical Perspectives,* edited by Peter Geschiere and Piet Konings. Leiden: African Studies Center, 1989.

Ngugi wa Thiong'o. *Petals of Blood.* New York: Dutton, 1978.

Ninsin, Kwame. "The PNDC and the Problem of Legitimacy." In *Ghana: The Political Economy of Recovery,* edited by Donald Rothchild. Boulder, Colo.: Lynne Rienner, 1991.

Nnoli, O. *Self-Reliance and Foreign Policy in Tanzania.* New York: NOK, 1978.

North, Douglass C. *Institutions, Institutional Change, and Economic Performance.* Cambridge: Cambridge University Press, 1990.

Nugent, Paul. "Educating Rawlings: The Evolution of Government Strategy toward Smuggling." In *Ghana: The Political Economy of Recovery,* edited by Donald Rothchild. Boulder, Colo.: Lynne Rienner, 1991.

Nyerere, Julius. *Freedom and Unity.* London: Oxford University Press, 1967.

———. *Freedom and Development.* London: Oxford University Press, 1973.

———. *The Arusha Declaration: Ten Years After.* Dar es Salaam: Government Printer, 1977.

Nzongola-Ntalaja, Georges. "The African Crisis: The Way Out." Paper prepared for the annual meeting of the African Studies Association, Chicago, 1988.

O'Neill, Norman. "Politics and Development Strategies in Tanzania." In *Capitalism, Socialism, and the Development Crisis in Tanzania,* edited by Norman O'Neill and Kemal Mustapha. Aldershot: Avebury, 1990.

Pearson, Scott R., Gerald C. Nelson, and J. Dirck Stryker. "Incentives and Comparative Advantage in Ghanian Industry and Agriculture." Stanford University, 1976. Typescript.

Peters, Pauline. "Rational Choice, the Best Choice for Robert Bates: An Anthropologist's Reading of Bates's Work." *World Development* 21 (1993): 1066–76.

Pradervand, Pierre. *Listening to Africa: Developing Africa from the Grassroots.* New York: Praeger, 1989.

Pratt, Cranford. *The Critical Phase in Tanzania 1945–1968: Nyerere and the Emergence of a Socialist Strategy.* Cambridge: Cambridge University Press, 1966.

Press, Robert M. "Tanzania Faces Slow Growth and Legacy of Socialist Controls." *Christian Science Monitor,* May 30, 1990.

Proctor, J. E. *Building Ujamaa Villages in Tanzania.* Dar es Salaam: Tanzania Publishing House, 1971.

Ravenhill, John, ed. *Africa in Economic Crisis.* New York: Columbia University Press, 1987.

Reno, William. "The Politics of Patrimonial Adaptation to Reform." Paper prepared for the Workshop on Democracy and Structural Adjustment in Africa in the 1990s, Madison, Wis., 1991.

Republic of Cameroon. "Etude sur la fiscalité." Report of the Technical Commission of the Mission of Rehabilitation of Public Sector and Parapublic Enterprises. Yaoundé: March 1989.

Republic of Ghana. *District Political Authority and Modalities for District-Level Elections.* Accra: Ghana Publishing, 1987.

———. *Report of the Committee of Experts (Constitution) on Proposals for a Draft Constitution of Ghana.* Tema: Ghana Publishing, 1991.

Republic of Zambia. *1990 Census of Population, Housing, and Agriculture: Preliminary Report.* Lusaka: Central Statistical Office, December 1990.

Riker, William H. "The Heresthetics of Constitution-Making: The Presidency in 1787 with Comments on Determinism and Rational Choice. *American Political Science Review* 78 (1984): 1–16.

Robinson, Pearl T. "Niger: Anatomy of a Neotraditional Corporatist State." *Comparative Politics* 23 (1991): 1–20.

———. "The National Conference Phenomenon in Africa." July 17, 1992. Typescript.

Rodney, Walter. *How Europe Underdeveloped Africa.* Rev. ed. Washington, D.C.: Howard University Press, 1981.

Ronen, Dov. *Ethnicity, Ideology, and the Military in the People's Republic of Benin.* Discussion Paper 5. Cambridge, Mass.: African-American Issues Center, 1984.

Rothchild, Donald. "Comparative Public Demand and Expectation Patterns: The Ghana Experience." *African Studies Review* 22, no. 1 (1979): 127–47.

———. *The Rawlings Revolution in Ghana: Pragmatism with Populist Rhetoric.* CSIS Africa Notes, 42. Washington, D.C.: Center for Strategic and International Studies, 1985.

———. "Hegemonial Exchange: An Alternative Model for Managing Conflict in Middle Africa." In *Ethnicity, Politics, and Development,* edited by Dennis L. Thompson and Dov Ronen. Boulder, Colo.: Lynne Rienner, 1986.

Rothchild, Donald, and E. Gyimah-Boundi. "Populism in Ghana and Burkina Faso." *Current History* 88 (1989): 221–44.

Rothchild, Donald, and Letitia Lawson. "The Interactions between State and

Civil Society in Africa: From Deadlock to New Routines." In *Civil Society and the State in Africa*, edited by John Harbeson, Donald Rothchild, and Naomi Chazan. Boulder, Colo.: Lynne Rienner, forthcoming.

Rothchild, Donald, and Victor A. Olorunsula. *State versus Ethnic Claims: African Policy Dilemmas.* Boulder, Colo.: Westview, 1983.

Rothstein, Richard. *The Weak in the World of the Strong.* New York: Columbia University Press, 1977.

Rouquie, Alain. *The Military and the State in Latin America.* Berkeley: University of California Press, 1987.

Sandbrook, Richard. *Proletarians and African Capitalism: The Kenyan Case, 1960–1972.* Cambridge: Cambridge University Press, 1974.

———. *The Politics of Africa's Economic Stagnation.* Cambridge: Cambridge University Press, 1985.

Schaar, J. H. *Legitimacy in the Modern State.* New Brunswick, N.J.: Transaction Books, 1981.

Schatz, Sayre. *Nigerian Capitalism.* Berkeley: University of California Press, 1977.

Schatzberg, Michael. *The Dialectics of Oppression in Zaire.* Bloomington: Indiana University Press, 1988.

Schatzberg, Michael G., and I. William Zartman, eds. *The Political Economy of Cameroon.* New York: Praeger, 1986.

Schmitter, Phillipe C. "Still the Century of Corporatism?" *Review of Politics* 36, no. 1 (1974): 93–94.

Serageldin, Ismael, and Pierre Landell-Mills. "Governance and the External Factor." Paper preapared for World Bank Annual Conference on Development Economics, Washington, D.C., April 25–26, 1991.

Shaidi, L. "The Human Resources Deployment Act, 1983: A Desperate Measure to Contain a Desperate Situation." *Review of African Political Economy* 31 (1984): 82–87.

Shaw, Edward S. *Financial Deepening in Economic Development.* New York: Oxford University Press, 1973.

Shepsle, Kenneth A., and Barry R. Weingast. "When Do Rules of Procedure Matter?" *Journal of Politics* 46 (1984): 207–20.

Shirley, Mary. *The Reform of State-Owned Enterprises: Lessons from World Bank Lending.* Policy and Research Series 4. Washington, D.C.: World Bank, 1989.

Shivji, Issa. *Class Struggle in Tanzania.* Dar es Salaam: Tanzania Publishing House, 1976.

———. *Law, State, and the Working Class in Tanzania.* London: James Currey, 1986.

———, ed. *The State and the Working People in Tanzania.* Dakar: CODESRIA, 1985.

Sirowy, Larry, and Alex Inkeles. "The Effects of Democracy on Economic Growth and Inequality: A Review." *Studies in Comparative International Development* 25, no. 1 (1990): 126–57.

Sklar, Richard L. *Corporate Power in an African State.* Berkeley: University of California Press, 1975.

———. "The Nature of Class Domination in Africa," *Journal of Modern African Studies* 17 (1979): 531–52.

Spenser, John. *The KAU.* London: KPI, 1985.

Steffan, Philip. "The Structural Transformation of OPAM, Cereals Marketing Agency." In *State Enterprise in Africa,* edited by Barbara Grosh and Rwekaza Mukandala. Boulder, Colo.: Lynne Rienner, forthcoming.

Stepan, Alfred. *The State and Society.* Princeton: Princeton University Press, 1978.

Swainson, Nicola. *The Development of Corporate Capitalism in Kenya, 1918–1978.* Berkeley: University of California Press, 1979.

Tanganyike African National Union. *The Arusha Declaration and TANU's Policy on Socialism and Self-Reliance.* Dar es Salaam: Government Printer, 1967.

TANU. *Mwongozo wa TANU.* Dar es Salaam: TANU, 1971.

Tanzania. *Report of the Presidential Commission on the Establishment of a Democratic One-Party State.* Dar es Salaam: Government Printer, 1965.

———. *Report of the Presidential Commission on the National Union of Tanganyika Workers.* Dar es Salaam: Government Printer, 1967.

———. *On the Establishment of Workers Councils.* Dar es Salaam: Government Printer, 1970.

———. *The Agricultural Policy of Tanzania.* Dar es Salaam: Government Printer, 1983.

———. *Budget Speech for 1989–90.* Dar es Salaam: Government Printer, 1989.

———. *Tume ya Rais ya Mfume wa Cham kimoja au Vyama Vingi Vya Siasa Tanzania, 1991, Taarifa na Mapendekezo ya Tume Kuhusu Mfumo wa Siasa Nchini Tanzania.* 3 vols. Dar es Salaam: President's Office, 1992.

Tettah, Ransford, and Vance Azu. "The Presidential Election: Who Wins the Race." *Mirror* (Accra), October 31, 1992.

Tordoff, William. *Administration in Zambia.* Manchester: Manchester University Press, 1980.

Tordoff, William, et al. *Politics in Zambia.* Manchester: Manchester University Press, 1974.

Turner, Thomas. *The Rise and Decline of the Zairian State.* Madison: University of Wisconsin Press, 1985.

Twaddle, Michael. "Museveni's Uganda: Notes towards an Analysis." In *Uganda Now: Between Decay and Development,* edited by Holger Bernt Hansen and Michael Twaddle. London: James Currey, 1988.

United Nations Development Program and World Bank. *African Economic and Financial Data.* Washington, D.C.: World Bank, 1989.

van de Walle, Nicolas. "Rice Politics in Cameroon: State Commitment, Capability, and Urban Bias." *Journal of Modern African Studies* 27 (1989): 579–600.

———. "The Decline of the Franc Zone: Monetary Politics in Francophone Africa." *African Affairs* 90 (1991): 383–405.

————. "The Patron's Problem: Agency and Clientelism [...] spective." Paper prepared for the annual meeting of [...] Association. Washington, D.C., September 1991.

————. "The Politics of [...] Reform in Cameroon." In Her[...] to Africa's Economic [...] edited by Thomas Callaghy [...] New York: Columbia University Press, 1993.

————. "The Politics of Public Enterprise Reform in [...] [...]erprise in Africa, edited by Barbara [...] and Rweka[...] Boulder, Colo., Lynne Rienner, forthcoming.

Vansina, Jan. "A Past for the Future?" Dalhousie Review 68 n[...] 3–23.

Wai, [...] M. "Governance, Economic Development, and [...] External Actors." Paper prepared for the Conference on Gover[...] Economic Development in Sub-Saharan Africa, Oxford, May 2 [...]

————. Managing Development: The Governance Dimension. [...] Washington, D.C.: World Bank, 1991.

Weber, Max. Economy and Society. Edited by Guenther Roth and Claus [...] Berkeley: University of California Press, 1978.

West, Tina. "The Politics of Implementation of Structural Adjustment [...] bia, 1985–198[...]" In USAID/CSIS, The Politics of Economic Reform in Sub-Saharan Africa. Washington, D.C.: Center for Strategic and International Studies, 1992.

Westebbe, Richard. "State Entrepreneurship in the [...] [...] Exploration in Entrepreneurial History 6 (19[...])

Widner, Jennifer. "The Discovery of [...] Smallholder Reactions to th[...] Cocoa Crisis of 1989 [...]" In Hemmed In: Responses to Africa's Economic Decline, edited by Thomas Callaghy and John Ravenhill. New York: Columbia University Press, 1993.

Wilson, Ernest J., III. "Privatization in the Ivory Coast: Three Case Studies." Cambridge: Mass.: Kennedy School of Government, Center for Business and Government. November 1987 [...]script.

————. "World Politics and International Energy Markets." International Organization 41, no. 1 (1987): 125–50.

————. "Economic Reform in Socialist and Capitalist Countries." Paper prepared for the SSRC Conference on Economic Reform, Hanoi, June 27–30, 1990.

————. "Strategies of State Control of the Economy: Nationalization and Indigenization in Africa." Comparative Politics 22 (1990): 401–19.

————. "The Political Economy of Economic Reform in the Côte d'Ivoire: A Micro-Level Study of Three Privatization Transactions." In State Enterprise in Africa, edited by Barbara Grosh and Rwekaza Mukandala. Boulder, Colo.: Lynne Rienner, forthcoming.

Wilson, Ernest J., III, and Howard Stein. "The Political Economy of Robert Bates: A Critical Reading of Rational Choice in Africa." World Development 21 (1993): 1035–53.

Sklar, Richard L. *Corporate Power in an African State.* Berkeley: University of California Press, 1975.

———. "The Nature of Class Domination in Africa," *Journal of Modern African Studies* 17 (1979): 531–52.

Spenser, John. *The KAU.* London: KPI, 1985.

Steffan, Philip. "The Structural Transformation of OPAM, Cereals Marketing Agency." In *State Enterprise in Africa,* edited by Barbara Grosh and Rwekaza Mukandala. Boulder, Colo.: Lynne Rienner, forthcoming.

Stepan, Alfred. *The State and Society.* Princeton: Princeton University Press, 1978.

Swainson, Nicola. *The Development of Corporate Capitalism in Kenya, 1918–1978.* Berkeley: University of California Press, 1979.

Tanganyike African National Union. *The Arusha Declaration and TANU's Policy on Socialism and Self-Reliance.* Dar es Salaam: Government Printer, 1967.

TANU. *Mwongozo wa TANU.* Dar es Salaam: TANU, 1971.

Tanzania. *Report of the Presidential Commission on the Establishment of a Democratic One-Party State.* Dar es Salaam: Government Printer, 1965.

———. *Report of the Presidential Commission on the National Union of Tanganyika Workers.* Dar es Salaam: Government Printer, 1967.

———. *On the Establishment of Workers Councils.* Dar es Salaam: Government Printer, 1970.

———. *The Agricultural Policy of Tanzania.* Dar es Salaam: Government Printer, 1983.

———. *Budget Speech for 1989–90.* Dar es Salaam: Government Printer, 1989.

———. *Tume ya Rais ya Mfume wa Cham kimoja au Vyama Vingi Vya Siasa Tanzania, 1991, Taarifa na Mapendekezo ya Tume Kuhusu Mfumo wa Siasa Nchini Tanzania.* 3 vols. Dar es Salaam: President's Office, 1992.

Tettah, Ranstord, and Vance Azu. "The Presidential Election: Who Wins the Race." *Mirror* (Accra), October 31, 1992.

Tordoff, William. *Administration in Zambia.* Manchester: Manchester University Press, 1980.

Tordoff, William, et al. *Politics in Zambia.* Manchester: Manchester University Press, 1974.

Turner, Thomas. *The Rise and Decline of the Zairian State.* Madison: University of Wisconsin Press, 1985.

Twaddle, Michael. "Museveni's Uganda: Notes towards an Analysis." In *Uganda Now: Between Decay and Development,* edited by Holger Bernt Hansen and Michael Twaddle. London: James Currey, 1988.

United Nations Development Program and World Bank. *African Economic and Financial Data.* Washington, D.C.: World Bank, 1989.

van de Walle, Nicolas. "Rice Politics in Cameroon: State Commitment, Capability, and Urban Bias." *Journal of Modern African Studies* 27 (1989): 579–600.

———. "The Decline of the Franc Zone: Monetary Politics in Francophone Africa." *African Affairs* 90 (1991): 383–405.

———. "The Patron's Problem: Agency and Clientelism in Comparative Perspective." Paper prepared for the annual meeting of the American Political Association. Washington, D.C., September 1991.

———. "The Politics of Non-Reform in Cameroon." In *Hemmed In: Responses to Africa's Economic Decline*, edited by Thomas Callaghy and John Ravenhill. New York: Columbia University Press, 1993.

———. "The Politics of Public Enterprise Reform in Cameroon." In *State Enterprise in Africa*, edited by Barbara Grosh and Rwekaza Mukandala. Boulder, Colo., Lynne Rienner, forthcoming.

Vansina, Jan. "A Past for the Future?" *Dalhousie Review* 68, nos. 1–2 (1989): 8–23.

Wai, Dunstan M. "Governance, Economic Development, and the Role of External Actors." Paper prepared for the Conference on Governance and Economic Development in Sub-Saharan Africa, Oxford, May 2–4, 1991.

———. *Managing Development: The Governance Dimension.* Discussion Paper. Washington, D.C.: World Bank, 1991.

Weber, Max. *Economy and Society.* Edited by Guenther Roth and Claus Wittich. Berkeley: University of California Press, 1978.

West, Tina. "The Politics of Implementation of Structural Adjustment in Zambia, 1985–1987." In USAID/CSIS, *The Politics of Economic Reform in Sub-Saharan Africa.* Washington, D.C.: Center for Strategic and International Studies, 1992.

Westebbe, Richard. "State Entrepreneurship in the United Netherlands, 1815–1830." *Explorations in Entrepreneurial History* 8 (1956).

Widner, Jennifer. "The Discovery of Politics: Smallholder Reactions to the Cocoa Crisis of 1989–90 in Côte d'Ivoire." In *Hemmed In: Responses to Africa's Economic Decline*, edited by Thomas Callaghy and John Ravenhill. New York: Columbia University Press, 1993.

Wilson, Ernest J., III. "Privatization in the Ivory Coast: Three Case Studies." Cambridge, Mass.: Kennedy School of Government, Center for Business and Government. December 1987. Typescript.

———. "World Politics and International Energy Markets." *International Organization* 41, no. 1 (1987): 125–50.

———. "Economic Reform in Socialist and Capitalist Countries." Paper prepared for the SSRC Conference on Economic Reform, Hanoi, June 27–30, 1990.

———. "Strategies of State Control of the Economy: Nationalization and Indigenization in Africa." *Comparative Politics* 22 (1990): 401–19.

———. "The Political Economy of Economic Reform in the Côte d'Ivoire: A Micro-Level Study of Three Privatization Transactions." In *State Enterprise in Africa*, edited by Barbara Grosh and Rwekaza Mukandala. Boulder, Colo.: Lynne Rienner, forthcoming.

Wilson, Ernest J., III, and Howard Stein. "The Political Economy of Robert Bates: A Critical Reading of Rational Choice in Africa." *World Development* 21 (1993): 1035–53.

World Bank. *Adjustment Lending: An Evaluation of Ten Years' Experience*. Washington, D.C.: World Bank, 1988.

———. *Community and Trade Trends*. Washington, D.C.: World Bank, 1988.

———. *Sub-Saharan Africa: From Crisis to Sustainable Growth: A Long-Term Perspective Study*. Washington, D.C.: World Bank, 1989.

———. *World Development Report, 1990*. Washington, D.C.: World Bank, 1990.

———. *Tanzania Economic Report: Towards Sustainable Development*. Washington, D.C.: World Bank, 1991.

———. *World Development Report, 1991*. Washington, D.C.: World Bank, 1991.

Yeboah-Afari, Ajoa. "Post-Election Thoughts." *West Africa*, November 16, 1992.

———. Issues of Governance in Borrowing Countries: The Extent of Their Relevance under the Bank's Articles of Agreement. Washington, D.C.: World Bank, 1991.

Young, Crawford. *Ideology and Development in Africa*. New Haven: Yale University Press, 1982.

———. "The African Colonial State and Its Political Legacy." In *The Precarious Balance: State and Society in Africa*, edited by Donald Rothchild and Naomi Chazan. Boulder, Colo.: Westview, 1988.

Young, Crawford, and Thomas Turner. *The Rise and Decline of the Zairian State*. Madison: University of Wisconsin Press, 1985.

Younger, Stephen D. "Ghana: Economic Recovery Program—A Case Study of Stabilization and Structural Adjustment in Sub-Saharan Africa." In *Successful Development in Africa: Case Studies of Projects, Programs, and Policies*. EDI Development Case Studies 1. Washington, D.C.: World Bank, 1989.

———. "Aid and the Dutch Disease: Macroeconomic Management When Everybody Loves You." *World Development* 20 (1992): 1587–97.

Notes on Contributors

MWESIGA BAREGU is associate professor of political science at the University of Dar es Salaam. He holds a Ph.D. from Stanford, where he wrote a dissertation entitled, "Bitter Sweetener: The Rise and Fall of 'King Cane' in the Capitalist World Economy." He is author of several articles on African politics, including "The Bukoba Rural Constitutency: Voting Along an Intra-Ethnic Cleavage?" (In *National Election Study, Tanzania*, Dar es Salaam: University of Dar es Salaam, forthcoming).

ROBERT H. BATES is professor of political science at Harvard University. He is author of *Markets and States in Tropical Africa, Essays on the Political Economy of Rural Africa*, and *Beyond the Miracle of the Market: The Political Economy of Agrarian Development in Kenya*, as well as numerous books and articles on political economy.

MICHAEL BRATTON is professor of political science at Michigan State University. He is author of *The Local Politics of Rural Development: Peasants and Party State in Zambia* and an editor of *Governance and Politics in Africa* (1991). He has written articles and monographs on civic associations and nongovernmental organization activity.

BARBARA GROSH is assistant professor in the Department of Public Administration at Syracuse University. She holds a Ph.D. in economics from the University of California at Berkeley. She is author of *Public Enterprise in Kenya: What Works, What Doesn't, and Why*. She is editing a book on African parastatals.

JEFFREY HERBST is assistant professor at Princeton University, where he holds an appointment in the Department of Politics and the Woodrow Wilson School. He has written on migration and African politics and the politics of economic reform in Africa. He is author of *State Politics in Zimbabwe* and *The Politics of Reform in Ghana*.

DONALD ROTHCHILD is professor of political science at the University of California at Davis. His books include *Racial Bargaining in Independent Kenya; Scarcity, Choice, and Public Policy in Middle Africa*åd *Politics and Society in Con-*

temporary Africa. Among his recent edited works are *Ghana: The Political Economy of Recovery* and *Africa in World Politics*.

NICOLAS VAN DE WALLE is assistant professor of African studies and political science at Michigan State University. Before receiving his Ph.D. from Princeton University, he worked as a research associate at the World Bank. He is author of articles on the franc zone, privatization, and clientelism in Africa and is finishing a book on the politics of economic reform in Cameroon.

RICHARD WESTEBBE is economic adviser at the World Bank. Previously, he was lead economist in the Africa Division of the bank and senior departmental economist for its West Africa programs.

JENNIFER A. WIDNER is associate professor in the Department of Government at Harvard University. She has analyzed changes in the character of authoritarian rule in *The Rise of a Party-State in Kenya: From Harambee! to Nyayo!* She has also written about civic innovation in rural Africa, drawing on data from Côte d'Ivoire.

ERNEST J. WILSON III has written extensively on the politics of economic reform in *Comparative Politics*, the *American Political Science Review*, and other journals. He served as director of the Center for Research on Economic Development at the University of Michigan where he taught for ten years. He is now on the staff of the National Security Council, on leave from the University of Maryland, College Park.

CRAWFORD YOUNG is Rupert Emerson Professor of Political Science at the University of Wisconsin, Madison, where he has taught since 1963. He has also taught in Uganda, Zaire, and Senegal. His most recent books include *The Rise and Decline of the Zairian State* (co-author, 1985); *Ideology and Development in Africa* (1982); *Cooperatives and Development* (co-author 1981); and *The Politics of Cultural Pluralism* (1976).

Index

accountability, 90, 117, 123, 132–33, 151, 206, 208, 209, 235, 240, 243, 247

Adedeji, Adebayo, 235

administration: autonomy, 203–4, 214, 221–22; capacity, 107, 133, 135, 137, 138, 149, 150, 201, 203, 204–5, 206–7; decentralization, 115. *See also* civil service; institutionalization

agriculture, 15, 34, 57, 84–85, 104, 105–6, 107, 110, 112, 114, 121. *See also* farmers

Ahidjo, Ahmadu, 141, 142, 143, 144, 147, 148, 216

Ake, Claude, 13; quoted, 206, 231

Algeria, 124, 138, 221, 232, 241, 243, 246

Amin, Idi, 163

Anglophone Africa, 6, 51–56, 66, 72–76

Angola, 205, 244, 245

Asia, 83, 149

Banda, Hasting, 13

Bangladesh, 149

banking, 58, 61, 87, 92, 93, 94, 145

Baregu, Mwesiga, 233

la Baule, 8

Bédié, Henri Konan, 70

Benin, 1, 7, 33, 36, 42, 139, 158, 196, 210, 234, 244; agriculture, 84–85; banking, 87, 92, 93, 94; debt, 87; economic growth, 84, 86, 87; economic performance, 84, 86–87; economic policy, 82–83, 85, 87, 88, 89; elections, 96; food imports, 84; form of government, 82, 86, 91, 96; France and, 81; IMF and, 80, 88, 89, 91, 94, 95; interest groups, 81–82, 92, 94, 97; Marxism-Leninism in, 81, 82, 92, 94,

97; military, 81–82, 92, 97, 98; National Commission to Implement the Structural Adjustment Program (CNSAPAS), 91, 92; national conference, 95–96, 98, 140; political crisis of 1989, 93–96; political liberalization, 93–96; press, 98; religious groups, 81, 96; rent seeking and corruption, 80, 87–88, 94, 95, 96, 97; schools and universities, 88, 94, 95, 96, 98; socialism in, 83; structural adjustment, 86, 91–93, 94, 95, 96, 97; trade, 88; World Bank and, 80, 85–86, 87, 88–93, 94, 95, 96, 98. *See also* Dossou, Robert; Kérékou, Mathieu; Soglo, Nicephore

Berg Report, 232

Biafra (Nigerian Civil War), 205

Biwott, Nicholas, 71

Biya, Paul, 141, 143–44, 145, 146, 147, 151, 216–17

Black, Yondo, 145

Boahen, A. Adu, 192

Bokassa, Jean-Bedel, 132

Bolivia, 43

Bongo, Omar, 139, 145, 243

Botswana, 209, 210, 234, 238

Bratton, Michael, 207

Britain, 113, 161, 183

Burkina Faso, 50, 195, 218, 219. *See also* Sankara, Thomas

business and commerce, 167, 193; banking, 42, 58, 61; bourgeoisie, 15, 19, 20, 21, 25, 150; environment for, 19; exporters, 15; foreign companies, 14, 15, 112, 142; import-substituting firms, 15; as interest group, 3, 14, 15,

personalism, 17, 18, 19
Philippines, 35, 243
political community, 202, 205
political conditionality, 80, 95, 188, 240.
    See also donors
political legitimacy. *See* legitimacy
political liberalization. *See* liberalization,
    political
political machines, 17, 18, 55, 132
political parties, 133, 139, 142
political repression, 94, 120, 203, 206,
    207, 231. *See also* internal security;
    one-party rule
populism, 242–43, 247
presidential systems (republican
    constitution), 161, 211
press, the, 1, 50, 56, 69, 76, 96, 98, 103,
    110, 114, 145, 159, 170, 171, 185–86
prices, 16, 35, 40, 44, 133, 141, 237;
    consumer, 15, 34, 103, 105–6, 108, 109,
    130, 142, 193; producer, 32, 53–54, 59,
    60; raw materials, 16; shocks, 4, 106,
    135, 143. *See also* subsidies
private sector. *See* business and
    commerce
privatization, 5; informal, 17; "populist,"
    42, 44; sale of assets, 40–41, 42, 135–
    36, 167–68, 239
professionals, 3, 22, 27, 102, 111–12,
    115, 139, 266. *See also* elites; interest
    groups
protest, 23, 58, 94–95, 103, 108, 112–13,
    115, 117, 122–23, 129–31, 138, 139,
    145, 152, 159; economic development
    and, 90; food riots, 116, 117; insta-
    bility and, 135, 137, 139; intensity of,
    austerity measures and, 4. *See also*
    reform movements
Prussia, 83
public enterprises (parastatals), 31, 38–
    39, 44, 53, 59, 60, 61–63, 64, 85–86,
    105, 112, 121, 133, 136, 138, 143, 167,
    203, 204, 237, 240
public opinion, 191, 204, 212

quasi rents. *See* rents

Rawlings, Jerry, 183, 184–85, 190, 191,
    192, 194, 195–96, 197n. 2, 206, 211–12,
    214

reform movements, 19, 103, 124, 129,
    140; characteristics of, 13–14; economic
    performance and, 15; incidence, 24.
    See also interest groups; liberalization,
    political; protest
religious groups, 21, 22, 66, 81, 94, 149,
    151, 171, 172, 187–88, 242
rent seeking, 4, 5, 18, 19, 44, 51, 52–53,
    60, 63, 67, 80, 86, 87–88, 92, 97, 112,
    131, 133–38, 139, 141–42, 144, 148,
    149, 151, 152–53, 153n. 9, 167, 235,
    238
rents, 3, 5, 35, 36, 37, 38, 52–53, 60, 63,
    72; quasi rents, 20, 32, 153n. 9
Robinson, Pearl, 50, 54
Romania, 233
Rosberg, Carl, 192
Rubia, Charles, 68
Russia (Soviet Union), 82, 83, 184, 233,
    247
Rustow, Dankwart, 149

Sankara, Thomas, 195, 218, 219, 220
São Tomé and Príncipe, 83, 158, 218,
    234, 244
Sassou Nguesso, Denis, 243
Savimbi, Jonas, 205
Schmitter, Philippe, 221
schools and universities, 88, 94, 95, 96,
    98, 110, 130, 145. *See also* students;
    teachers
security apparatus. *See* internal security
Senegal, 42, 132, 137, 209, 210, 234, 237,
    241, 243, 244, 245
Shikuku, Martin, 69
Sierra Leone, 238, 245
Sklar, Richard, 13, 233
social funds, emergency, 42–43, 44, 92,
    98–99
social services, 110, 111, 115, 167, 194,
    205, 246
socialism, African, 83–84
societal disengagement, 202, 204. *See
    also* informal economy; political
    community
Soglo, Nicephore, 96
Somalia, 36, 184, 202, 230, 242, 243, 245
South Africa, 13, 110, 116, 122, 138, 195,
    216, 217, 244–45, 246
South Korea, 83

Library of Congress Cataloging-in-Publication Data

Economic change and political liberalization in Sub-Saharan Africa / edited by
Jennifer A. Widner.
    p.   cm.
Includes bibliographical references and index.
ISBN 0-8018-4758-3 (hard). — ISBN 0-8018-4844-X (pbk.)
1. Africa, Sub-Saharan—Politics and government—1960–   2. Structural adjustment
(Economic policy)—Africa, Sub-Saharan.   I.Widner, Jennifer A.
JQ1875.E265   1994
967.03—dc20   93-21395